THE WHITE ARMIES OF RUSSIA

THE MACMILLAN COMPANY
NEW YORK · BOSTON · CHICAGO · DALLAS
ATLANTA · SAN FRANCISCO

MACMILLAN & CO., Limited
LONDON · BOMBAY · CALCUTTA
MELBOURNE

THE MACMILLAN COMPANY
OF CANADA, Limited
TORONTO

THE WHITE ARMIES
OF RUSSIA

*A Chronicle
of Counter-Revolution and
Allied Intervention*

By

GEORGE STEWART

NEW YORK

THE MACMILLAN COMPANY

1933

TO

MY WIFE

FOREWORD

THIS chronicle has been conceived without bias toward any faction. It is an honest effort to picture a conflict so vast that no one man could view it in its entirety or hope to describe it without loss of proportion in some aspect. I crave the mercy of those who realize the complexity of the Russian scene in this period. My account is, as the title indicates, one-sided. It does not attempt a record of the achievements and sufferings of the Red armies.

The Revolution in its profounder aspects was the judgment day, not only for a dynasty, but for a whole political, social, and economic era in Russian history. The Civil War which followed was a part of the social earthquake which shook Russia in 1917, toppling over every institution of the *ancien régime* and disturbing the remotest nations of the world with its tremors. Sufficient time has elapsed to allow participants to write of events as they saw and lived them. It is now possible to attempt a record of all theaters of conflict. This is the first account in any language that attempts a total picture of all the anti-Bolshevik efforts. What happened in the largest country in the world is of importance to us all.

In this labor I have been assisted by many friends. Soldiers and officers of the White armies have told their stories in restaurants, farmhouses, trains, refugee camps, railway stations, and their homes in a dozen nations of Europe, as have members of the Red armies within and without Russia. The late Colonel Michael Kostenko aided me in drawing the last draft of most of the campaign maps.

vii

Thomas Harris, of Jesus College, Cambridge University, now of the Harvard Faculty, Miss Isabel M. Calder, of the Yale Graduate School, now of the Wells College Faculty, and many others have generously given their assistance at various periods in the preparation of the manuscript.

The struggle in Russia and Siberia was as much a battle of ideas, slogans, social theories, and political shibboleths as an encounter between Red and White soldiers. Politics and strategy were woven into one texture. Inadequacy in the former could not be compensated by heroism upon the field. Talk continued by day and by night. Millions of tongues unfamiliar with the new phrases were set wagging and the loyalties of large sections shifted back and forth as the population accepted or rejected the newest propaganda.

The dates are according to the Western calendar as far as is possible to determine. This calendar is, for the twentieth century, thirteen days ahead of the Old Style or Julian calendar which prevailed in Russia until January, 1918, when the Soviet Government introduced the Western or New Style calendar, decreeing that February 1, 1918, be reckoned as February 14th. The matter of dates in the early years of the Soviet régime is apt to be confused, as the new calendar was not adopted by all writers nor in all official reports. It is, therefore, impossible to determine in every case whether a date is according to Old or New Style reckoning. Putilov's *Khronologicheskiye tablitzy po istorii i S. S. S. R.*, Leningrad, 1929, is helpful as a guide to chronology.

If in word or implication in these pages I have failed to give credit for valor, patriotism, and self-sacrifice amid the welter of lesser passions into which Russia was plunged, such mistakes constitute no willful error. Life was given freely by Red and White alike. Amid hunger, cold, disease, and a miasma of disillusionment and conflicting purposes, a multitude on both sides in the Russian Civil War held to their convictions with singular heroism and devotion. But— let the events speak for themselves!

GEORGE STEWART.

CONTENTS

ix

ILLUSTRATIONS

xi

xii   *ILLUSTRATIONS*

ILLUSTRATIONS

xiii

FACING PAGE

MAPS

THE WHITE ARMIES OF RUSSIA

Chapter I

RUSSIA ON THE BRINK OF CHAOS

RUSSIA was overripe for revolution. Czars, bureaucrats, soldiers, and institutions had sown the wind. Within less than half a decade the people were to reap in body, mind, and estate the whirlwind of retribution. Every atrocity of Red or White in the Civil War had its counterpart in Czarist history. The influence of the French Revolution, a liberalizing factor in Western Europe and even distant America, had little repercussion in the Muscovite world. Russia had stumbled forward with an illiterate, underprivileged population devoid of liberties or an organization of society congruous with modern life. Her thin crust of intellectuals were either identified with the autocracy or found themselves in a discontented minority fomenting unrest among the slowly awakening people.

Political, economic, and social attitudes which emerged in the internecine turmoil were deeply rooted in Russian life. Two series of causes, one remote and the other immediate, made not only the Revolution but the subsequent Civil War inevitable.

The first series were historical, including land hunger among the peasants, desire for a constitutional form of government, and the rapid growth of an industrial proletariat deeply tinctured with the teachings of Nihilists, Anarchists, Socialists, and Communists. Widespread pessimism in Russian letters and the racial and cultural heterogeneity of the population composed of many religions, tongues, and sects were disintegrating forces. The broad gap between the thin crust of intellectuals and the Russian people, the lack of

I

constructive statesmanship in dealing with legitimate aspirations of the masses, the suppression of radical, liberal, or even moderate thought by incarceration in the Fortress of Peter and Paul and other prisons, the practice of answering opposition with exile to Siberia, were creating dark thoughts among the humble. The condition of the peasant since the abolition of serfdom in 1861 was a grave menace to internal peace. A revolutionary movement within the intelligentsia and especially among university students kept pace with unrest among the workers.

The exile system for political offenders was a thorn in the side of Russia. Instead of confining these prisoners in local provincial penitentiaries, the government preferred to send them to Siberia. Among these exiles were men and women of unusual intellectual capacity who clung to the ideal of a more liberal Russian state. In the course of the nineteenth century many thousands accompanied their relatives into Siberia. The uprisings of 1905-06 resulted in a particularly large increase of deportations. Russia was being prepared for chaos!

But more immediate causes were operating upon the minds of the Russian people. The slaughter of one hundred unarmed men and women, Father Gapon's followers, on Red Sunday, January 22, 1905, when they went to the Winter Palace asking redress for their grievances, sealed the fate of the Romanov dynasty. Seven years later, on April 4, 1912, a massacre occurred in the Lena gold fields in which hundreds of unarmed strikers were shot when they came to demand the release of their imprisoned spokesmen. As a result, over two hundred thousand workmen went on strike. From the Lena killings up to the Great War, larger and larger numbers quit work each year in hundreds of strikes.

Incompetence and gross negligence by high officers in the care and command of troops during the Great War, the alleged treason of Sukhoumlinov, Minister of War, and of other officials, and the rapid change of ministers due to the interference of Rasputin created uncertainty in the minds of all men in the public service. Prices were rising to fantastic heights. There was a dearth of food and manufactured goods. The agrarian problem was never settled. The number of men who were laying down their tools was assuming ominous proportions.

Universal suspicion of the government toward every institution, destroying loyalty and paralyzing action, begat an answering distrust. Rights were abrogated and courts of justice stultified. Officials interfered with the Committee on Military Industries, mobilizations were made with no provision for the needs of the farmers. The people were becoming more and more depressed by unparalleled espionage, imprisonments without trial, and defeat of their armies in the field.

Confidence in the government and in the crown was gone. Distrust of the Empress, a German princess whose emotional temperament was dominated by that strange villain, Rasputin, was widespread. She in turn controlled the indecisive and intellectually mediocre monarch.

In addition, all elements which had for decades become dissatisfied, feeling the steel grip of autocracy throttling their mental as well as physical life, were active in spreading discontent and preparing for revolution. In peasant taverns, Vankas and Mikhails exchanged wild tales about officials and murmured drunkenly over their miseries; in factory board meetings directors conferred regarding restless workers, and in officers' messes along the unstable front that zigzagged its way through Poland and Galicia and Rumania, men looked into each other's faces and asked, How long?

The Revolution, although threatened from the early months of war and planned for during many years, took even the avowed revolutionists by surprise. None of the Bolshevik leaders was in Russia at the moment. Lenin did not arrive in Petrograd until April 4th, and Trotsky some four weeks later. The Revolution was neither the result of propaganda, German or otherwise, nor the culmination of the efforts of any one group, but a local Petrograd affair. It flared up spontaneously after a strike of some seventy thousand metal workers, followed by the desertion of the Volhynsky Foot Guards. Nevertheless, it had roots running deep into Russian history. Neither Prince Golitsin, the head of the Cabinet, nor Protopopov, Minister of the Interior, nor General Khabalov, Military Governor of Petrograd, had the clarity of mind and the iron will necessary to crush it at the beginning.

The Revolution of March, 1917, was welcomed by nearly every section of the population. General Denikin, the most prominent leader in the subsequent warfare against the Bolshevik régime, remarked of the feeling at that moment:

Owing to the unrestrained orgy of power in which the successive rulers, appointed at Rasputin's suggestion, had indulged during their short terms of office, there was in 1917 no political party, no class upon which the Czarist Government could rely. Everybody considered that government as the enemy of the people. Extreme Monarchists and Socialists alike, the united nobility, labor groups, grand dukes, and half-educated soldiers —all were of the same opinion. . . . All the institutions of the state and of society—the Council of the Empire, the Duma, the nobility, the Zemstvos, the municipalities—were under suspicion of disloyalty, and the government was in open opposition to them, and paralyzed all their activities in matters of statesmanship and social welfare. . . . Lawlessness and espionage had reached unheard-of proportions.

If such a picture could be drawn by a general noted for loyalty and patriotism, it is small wonder that determined revolutionists could inflame the mind of Russia by reference to contemporary conditions as well as to former incompetency of the Czarist Government. The first Revolution came as the inevitable consequence of the irresponsibility and ill repute of the ruling classes.

By the middle of March, 1917, affairs were rapidly approaching a crisis in Petrograd. The time had passed when a change of Cabinet could stay the rising feeling against the Czar and his entourage. Relations were fast becoming strained between him and the Stavka at Mogilev. General Alexeyev reported black news telephoned from Petrograd by Grand Duke Michael Alexandrovich, the Czar's brother. The Grand Duke urged that the Council of Ministers be dissolved, that a new government responsible to the Duma be created, and that the formation of the new Cabinet should be in the hands of the President of the All-Russian Association of Zemstvos, Prince Lvov, or the President of the Duma, M. Rodzianko. The Czar was stubborn in his resistance to such advice and responded in a telegram refusing concessions, ordering strong measures against mutineers at the capital, and conceding dictatorial rights to the President of the Council of Ministers throughout the Empire save in those territories immediately under the supreme commander-in-chief. Prince Golitsin was at the time acquainted with the fact that Aid-de-Camp General Ivanov was being dispatched to Petrograd as military dictator to suppress the revolt. Alexeyev as chief-of-staff begged the Emperor to change his mind, but to no avail. The Emperor, against the advice of Alexeyev, who had been persuaded by General Lukomsky to see him again, set out for Tsarskoe Selo, anxious for the safety of his family. The train was stopped at Dno and he finally went to Pskov on March 14th. Ivanov's train was halted at Tsarskoe Selo and surrounded by soldiers. Disorder in the capital was growing daily more ominous. All realistic observers knew the last hour of the Romanov dynasty had arrived. Could leaders now direct the new enthusiasm, save the army, and escape the horror of civil war?

M. Guchkov and M. Shoulgine met the Emperor in Pskov and informed him that only his abdication in favor of his son, with his brother, Grand Duke Michael as Regent, could end the Revolution, which was daily growing in power in Petrograd. Before the Emperor arrived at Pskov, General Rusky, commander-in-chief of the Northern Front, with headquarters at Pskov, had asked Alexeyev, who by virtue of army regulations as chief-of-staff was the supreme commander-in-chief, now that the Emperor had severed his connections with the Stavka, to sound out commanders-in-chief on various fronts in order that he might better advise the Czar.

General Lukomsky drafted a wire which was dispatched to all front headquarters, giving them information of the situation. General Rusky, General Evert, commander-in-chief of the Western Front, Grand Duke Nicholas in the Caucasus, and General Sakharov of the Rumanian Front, were agreed that only abdication in favor of the Heir Apparent could save Russia.

General Rusky informed the Czar on the afternoon of March 15th of the opinion of his high officers. On the same day the Emperor agreed to abdicate. When he was about to affix his signature, he was told by Guchkov that he must leave Russia but that the Czarevitch must remain. Whereupon the Emperor refused to sign the document. Later, finding himself unable to separate himself from his invalid son, who was an hæmophiliac, he abdicated in favor of his brother, Grand Duke Michael Alexandrovich. Somewhat earlier he had issued a ukase dismissing all his ministers and ordering Prince Lvov to form a new Cabinet. In an Order of the Day to the army and navy, and a ukase to the Senate, he appointed Grand Duke Nicholas to the supreme command of the army.

As many of the Stavka had anticipated, Michael refused to assume power. Rodzianko requested Alexeyev to send General Kornilov, commander of the Twenty-fifth Army Corps, as chief of the military district of Petrograd. For several days the Emperor remained at the Stavka in Mogilev conferring with the Dowager Empress Marie Fedorovna, but on March 21st indicated his willingness to go to Tsarskoe Selo. With great dignity he bade his officers farewell, urging them to be loyal to the Provisional Government and to bring the war to a victorious conclusion. The scene was one of tense emotion; a few broke into hysterical fits of weeping, others fainted. Nicholas II saluted the assemblage

Czar Nicholas II reviews his troops

Kerensky as head of the Provisional Government

Lenin speaks on the Red Square

The result in the army

and withdrew. Before leaving for Tsarskoe Selo, where he was to be a prisoner of the Provisional Government until his fatal journey to Ekaterinburg, he issued an address to the soldiers:

I appeal to you for the last time, my beloved troops. After the abdication of myself and my son, all the authority has passed into the hands of the Provisional Government, formed by the initiative of the State Duma. So may God help them to lead Russia on the way to prosperity and glory!

And you, my valiant troops, God help you to defend our country against the cruel foe! For two and a half years you have daily and hourly borne on your shoulders the heavy burden of war. Much blood has been shed; many efforts have been made, and the day is near when Russia, closely united to her gallant Allies in their common aspiration to victory, will break the resistance of the enemy. This war, unprecedented in history, must be continued and brought to a victorious end. Any one who dreams of peace at the present moment is a traitor to his country. I know that every honest soldier thinks so. Go on fulfilling your duty; stand to guard your glorious Fatherland; obey the Provisional Government, and your chiefs. Do not forget that all disorder, all weakening of discipline, are so many assets for the foe.

I firmly believe that the love of your great country is, and ever will be, alive in your hearts. God will give you his blessing and St. George the Victorious will help you to triumph over the foe!

NICHOLAS.

21st of March, 1917. The Stavka.

While the Provisional Government debated in the weeks that followed, the army and navy rapidly disintegrated. Soldiers' committees, with wild ideas of an immediate Utopia, destroyed discipline. The will to fight disappeared. A measure of fitness existed only in a few divisions, and there due to the moral force of the commanders.

The Provisional Government possessed the flower of Russian liberalism but was wholly unable to command the situation. Prince Lvov, Professor Paul Miliukov, A. J. Guchkov, A. J. Shingarev, and A. F. Kerensky constituted a group which even the most sanguine reformer could scarcely hope would ever come to power. Yet they were not enough! The murmurings and complaints of soldiers, sailors, workers, and peasants had now become a full-throated roar. While liberals bandied parliamentary concepts, the Reds, psychologically more acute, spoke directly to the primary human desires of Russia's people.

The officer and the soldier no longer trusted each other. Events had severed the tie which binds man to his leader in an army. Kerensky's tragic order Number One had abolished the salute, and the overdose of liberty given to a soldier who had never had it destroyed obedience and thus he lost respect for himself. When discipline in the army broke up, personal restraint went with it. The officer, no longer able to insist upon military punctilio, eyed the common soldier with suspicion. Something fatal to battle had happened to the man in the ranks. He had lost respect for authority. The muzhik unbuttoned his overcoat, thrust his hands into his pockets, and admired his muddy boots—he had ceased to be a man-at-arms. The villages of Volhynia, Tambov, Orel, the settlements along the Volga, and the great rivers of Siberia beckoned to him. He wanted to go home!

Shifts in the high command were constant. In June Brusilov was named supreme commander-in-chief in place of Alexeyev. Denikin was shifted from chief-of-staff at the Stavka to commander-in-chief of the Western Front, and General Lukomsky named in his stead. On leaving Mogilev, Denikin, who on occasion had great power as a speaker, addressed the assembly of officers:

Gentlemen Officers:
   The supreme commander-in-chief, who is resigning his post, sends you his greetings, and bids me tell you that his heart—the heart of an old soldier—beats in unison with your hearts; that he suffers the same agony, and clings to the same hope of seeing the tortured, yet great, Russian Army once more regenerated and strong!
   Let me say a few words on my own account. You have come here from the far-off borders of a land soaked with the blood of

our sons, bringing with you the boundless distress and anguish of your souls. And the tragical picture of the officer's life and work in the midst of the troubled ocean of the Russian Army has unrolled itself before your eyes in all its vivid truth!

You who have repeatedly looked into the face of death; you, who have marched fearlessly, at the head of your men, against the thick rows of the enemy's barbed wire, hampered in your advance by inadequate artillery, inadequate because of the shortage of ammunition; you, who have thrown a handful of earth over the grave of a fallen son, a brother or a friend, and though full of sorrow are still undaunted, will you now waver?

No!

Let whoever are weak lift their heads boldly. And you who are strong instil your energy and resolution, your impulse, your ardent desire to work for the happiness and welfare of your country, into the thinned ranks of your comrades at the front. You are not alone. All who are honest and have not lost the capacity to think and reason; all who have stopped on the outskirts of common sense—now vanishing and discarded—are with you.

Your men will follow you. . . . They will understand that you are not leading them back to slavery and spiritual poverty, but onwards to liberty and light!

A heavy blow will then be dealt to the enemy, which will break his resistance, and bring the war to an end.

I have lived with you through three years of the war, sharing your life and your thoughts, the joy of victory and the bitterness of retreat. And I have the right to throw the words "You lie!" into the face of those who have cast their dark shadow over our souls, who, from the very first days of the revolution, have done their Cain's deed in regard to the officers' corps!

You lie! . . . The Russian officer has never been a mercenary or an "Opritchnik." Miserable and downtrodden though he was by the conditions of the former régime, our army officer yet retained, through all his life of hardships and thankless labor, the thirst for heroic deeds, carrying it high, like a lighted torch, and bringing it undimmed to the threshold of the war for his Fatherland, for his country's happiness and welfare.

Let these walls echo my appeal, and let it reach the builders of the new Russian life!

Help and protect the officer! For he has ever stood, and ever will stand, on the watch, guarding the Russian State. Death alone can relieve him!

General Denikin's speech had a marked effect upon the officers at the Stavka, strengthening their morale and encouraging them for future efforts. No one class in Russia suffered more than the officer. Having been kept apart from politics, he was compelled to bear the blame for the mistakes of the crown and the government, for in the common mind he was identified with the standing order. The Russian officer was defenseless against the jibes of every class. Here at last a clear, determined voice was speaking to men who were fast becoming overwhelmed in the confusion of retreating soldiers and the chaos of new ideas.

Every political party in Russia was contending for power. Profound changes had taken place, giving opportunity for all shades of opinion to find expression. Monarchists, Left and Right Wing Socialist-Revolutionaries, Constitutional-Democrats, Mensheviks, and Bolsheviks vied with one another for supremacy. Only Lenin and his adherents possessed a highly centralized and coherent idea. Both the League of Officers, with headquarters in Petrograd, and the so-called Union of Public Men in Moscow, where business men and officials of the army and navy rubbed elbows with intellectuals of every type, showed the fatal mixture of reactionary elements battling with liberal thought.

The Bolsheviks intellectually and in will power gradually dominated the Petrograd Soviet. They saw in the proletariat, in the poorer workingmen's quarters of the city a seedbed for their ideas. Poverty-stricken workers, under their guidance, were to be the creators of a new order. All other classes in society had proved their incompetency. Lenin saw no hope in any policy of reform. Class war to the death should determine the issue, after which all things should be made new. Holy Russia possessed a Messiah and no social Messianism. The Bolsheviks would furnish a Messianism without a Messiah—such had been their dreams as they froze in Siberia or crowded together in noisome prisons. Now in the smoky atmosphere of the Smolny Institute and other public buildings where endless speeches were being made, they saw the opportunity to test their teaching.

The Provisional Government alternated between parliamentarianism and dictatorship. The bourgeoisie knew not how to defend themselves. The army, breaking up on all fronts, had no one leader, universally acknowledged, who was ready and able to command. As week after week passed, the Bolsheviks grew in strength and were preparing for a desperate thrust for power.

The government was really under the dual control of the Soviets and the Provisional Government and the latter lacked courage to drive out its competitor. The hodgepodge of officials made up of various political complexions possessed no Spartan discipline or common ideas to direct them through situations for which they had no precedents. Meanwhile the Petrograd Soviet gradually changed from an informal meeting place where any one could come to lounge, to speak, or even to smoke and sleep, into a militant organization more and more under the control of Lenin and his associates who were preparing to test their strength.

The Bolsheviks, frankly throwing over all ideas of morality and mercy in the interest of the dictatorship of the proletariat, behind which was to stand a directing group of professional revolutionists, were steel where the Provisional Government was putty. Lenin had written:

We repudiate all morality that proceeds from supernatural ideas or ideas that are outside class conceptions. In our opinion, morality is entirely subordinate to the interests of the class war; everything is moral that is necessary for the annihilation of the old exploiting social order and for the union of the proletariat. Our morality thus consists solely in close discipline and in conscious war against the exploiters. We do not believe in eternal principles of morality, and we will expose this deception. Communist morality is identical with the fight for the consolidation of the dictatorship of the proletariat.

Important changes were continually made in the Provisional Government. No one of its members proved adequate for the turbulent situation. In July, Prince Lvov resigned as head of the government and Kerensky took his place.

Kerensky and his government shrank from blood baths in the streets and countrysides. The Bolsheviks did not. They had expected and planned and hoped for a bloody Revolution, for they considered it inevitable. When the Revolution came in March it was not in reality their Revolution, but a general and more moderate uprising. With enormous energy, Lenin and his lieutenants, in the summer days of 1917, labored to seize this softer thing and weld it into the steel Revolution they had so long cherished.

Kerensky, imperfectly sensing the danger, attempted to strengthen the army. He again shifted the high command, appointing General Lavr Kornilov to succeed Brusilov at the end of July.

Kornilov was chosen because of his popularity and his proven ability as a commander in the field. He had held at bay the redoubtable Mackensen, who had behind him some of the crack troops of the German Army. When captured by the Austrians during the Great War, Kornilov escaped, returning to the Russian lines amid wild scenes of affection and excitement. Ludendorff unleashed against him the full onslaught of German strength, snatching away Tarnopol and Stanislaw on July 24, 1917, while the German fleet and army took Riga on September 3d of that year. In this bitter fighting, Kornilov rose steadily in the estimation of the Stavka, the troops, and the foreign observers. The query upon many lips now was, how long could the hard-hitting general work with Kerensky, with his penchant for speeches and inability to use the power which for a few short weeks was within his hands.

Kornilov's Mongolian blood showed in his small, sinewy figure, his black goatee and mustache, and his slanting eyes. A sun-bitten face, darkened by exposure in Siberia, his thin body, supported by legs bowed by years in the saddle, and his exploits as a soldier made him a romantic figure in a country steeped in military tradition. A Cossack, and the son of a Cossack, Kornilov as a young captain stationed at Tashkent had become a hero by a reconnaissance of Afghanistan disguised as a merchant. While in Tashkent he had married the daughter of a minor official. In society he was regarded as crude and abrupt. Although the high offices he held would have admitted him to the drawing-rooms of Petrograd, Moscow, and provincial cities, he had remained aloof from the world of fashion. He was known in the army for his directness of speech, his simple manners, and his unimpeachable patriotism. From his lowly origin Kornilov had acquired a more liberal outlook upon social and political problems than was generally held by high officials. But he was more distinguished for his iron will, forthright speaking, and valor than for his ability in dealing with those of different views. Alexeyev and Denikin, two other leading counter-revolutionary figures, were also men of humble birth and democratic tendencies.

Before taking command, Kornilov laid down his terms to Kerensky and they had been accepted. They were: Full powers for the commander-in-chief; no governmental interference in his military orders; and the restoration of military discipline.

At the National Political Conference, which met on August 27th, it became obvious that a break between Kornilov and Kerensky was inevitable. Both received ovations from their friends. Political power in Russia was now split three ways—between the Bolsheviks, Kerensky's group, and the growing strength of the army in other than purely military affairs. The half-Kalmuck chief of the fighting forces was intent upon continuing the war against the Central Powers and would have been pleased to rid the military of the Provisional Government. From the beginning, Kornilov had the support of reactionaries, Monarchists, all Right Wing groups, and many of democratic views. The presence of so many officers representing the old order serving under him fed the suspicions of the Provisional Government and of the Communists, who were rapidly gathering strength, that the reactionary groups would profit should Kornilov succeed. At the front the new ideas of democracy and freedom were overcoming his best efforts to strengthen the army. He attempted to restore discipline on September 8th through reinstating the death penalty for military offenses. His plans for the rehabilitation of the troops brought him into open opposition to Kerensky, who asked for his resignation on September 9th.

Kornilov refused to resign, and on the following day issued a proclamation which was dispatched by wire to all parts of Russia, asking for support against the Provisional Government:

I, General Kornilov, Supreme Commander-In-Chief of the Russian Army, declare, before the whole of the nation, that my duty as a soldier, my feelings as a self-denying citizen of Free Russia, and my boundless love for my country, oblige me, at this critical moment of its existence, to disobey the orders of the Provisional Government, and to retain the Supreme Command over the Army and Fleet. Supported in this decision by all the Commanders-In-Chief of the Front, I declare to the whole of the Russian people that I prefer to die rather than give up my post as Supreme Commander-In-Chief. A true son of Russia remains at his post to the end, and is always ready to make the greatest of all sacrifices for his country . . . that of his life.

In these truly terrible moments of our country's existence, when the approaches to both of the capitals are almost open to the victorious advance of the foe—the Provisional Government, forgetting the great and essential question of the very independence of Russia, frighten the Russian people with the phantom of counter-revolution, which they themselves call forth by their inability to direct the affairs of the country, by the weakness of their authority and their hesitation in action.

It is not for me—a son of the people—who have given myself up, heart and soul, to the service of that people, to go against the great liberties and the great future of Russia. But up to the present moment this future is in weak and impotent hands. The arrogant foe uses bribery, corruption and treachery, as though he were the master here, and not only threatens the liberties, but the very existence, of the Russian Nation. Come back to your senses, O sons of Russia, recover from your madness, and see the abyss into which our country is rushing blindfold!

Trying to forget all strife, forestall all shedding of Russian blood and civil war, forgetting all affronts and offenses, I appeal to the Provisional Government, and I say to them: "Come to the Stavka, where your liberty and safety are guaranteed on my word of honour, and, conjointly with me, work out and create an organ of popular defense, which will secure the liberties of the people, and lead Russia to a great future, worthy of a free and mighty nation."

Kornilov followed this proclamation by ordering General Krymov to move on Petrograd. Krymov's efforts ended in futility, and, despairing of a solution of Russia's troubles, he committed suicide. The triumph of Kerensky over Kornilov, who was immediately arrested, lost the former many of the most resolute spirits in Russia. Large sections of the people, weary of the feeble policies of the Provisional Government, turned to the clear and unequivocal program of the Bolsheviks.

Kerensky now replaced many generals with Socialist officers, a fact which measurably aided the Bolsheviks, and had himself appointed as supreme commander-in-chief.

General Alexeyev was recalled as chief-of-staff after Kornilov's abortive effort in opposing the Provisional Government. Alexeyev assumed his duties at Great Headquarters, the Stavka, at Mogilev, on September 14th, having accepted on the express understanding that the demands of General Kornilov regarding regeneration of the army should be complied with immediately, to which Kerensky had acceded. On the evening of the same day that Alexeyev took command, he discovered to his chagrin that Kerensky was either unable or unwilling to keep his word. Under orders from Kerensky, Alexeyev, who still had hope that obedience to the Provisional Government might stave off a general catastrophe, was compelled to arrest Generals Kornilov, Romanovsky, and Lukomsky, with a number of other officers, including Kissliakov, Assistant Minister of Communications, Pliushtchik Pliushtchevsky, Second Quartermaster

General, General Tikhmenev, Chief of Military Communications, and many other staff officers, including the entire executive committee of the Union of Officers in Mogilev.

Military Prosecutor Shablovsky was appointed chief of the military tribunal to examine the prisoners and the questioning proceeded in leisurely fashion. Agitation in the press against trial by court-martial of former high officers by colleagues who were suspected of being sympathetic to the prisoners, together with the presence of two regiments loyal to Kornilov, so disturbed the Workers' and Soldiers' Delegates in the Mogilev and Petrograd councils that the prisoners were sent to Bykhov.

During this time, General Denikin, General Markov, General Erdeli, Lieutenant General Varnovsky, Commander of the First Army, Lieutenant General Selivatchev, Commander of the Seventh Army, Lieutenant General Elsner, Chief of Supplies to the Southwestern Front, General Elsner's assistants, General Parsky and General Sergievsky, Major General Orlov, Captain Prince Kropotkin and Lieutenant Klecanda of the Czech Legionnaires, and others had been confined at Berdichev, where there was serious danger that unruly soldiers might lynch them at any hour. Through the good offices of Shablovsky, most of the Berdichev prisoners were brought to Bykhov, thus uniting in captivity several commanders who were to play leading rôles in the bloody conflicts of the months ahead.

Kerensky, unable to give Alexeyev support in carrying out Kornilov's policies with the army, allowed him to resign, placing General Dukhonin in his post. From prison General Lukomsky wrote to General Dukhonin and to General Dieterichs, Quartermaster General at headquarters, urging them to station several trustworthy regiments at Mogilev against the day when the Bolsheviks should inevitably sweep into power, in order that headquarters could be removed to Kiev and thus save the Southwestern and Rumanian fronts. But Kerensky would hear of none of it and refused his consent to these measures.

The time was now ripe for the Bolsheviks to strike. With a supineness which even now amazes both Red and White, the bourgeois and former governing classes permitted the Bolsheviks to gain control. Again and again in these days, resolute action by the Provisional Government could have changed the course of Russian history, but such resolution was lacking. The army chiefs trusting too long in Kerensky, hampered by the punctilio of military law, many of their ablest men refusing to mix in politics, let pass the hour when by a concerted effort officers and loyal regiments might have marched to Petrograd and seized the government. That moment, unseized, was lost forever.

General confusion consequent upon the rapid break-up of discipline in the army and the lack of unity among all parties save the Bolsheviks, hastened the latter's rise to power. In October, 1917, the Bolsheviks gained control of the Petrograd Soviet and its Military Committee, which proceeded immediately to initiate rebellion against Kerensky, though he failed to recognize this fact.

The scene in Petrograd in November of 1917 was a crowded canvas. Lenin, Trotsky, Zinoviev, Dzerzhinsky, Kamenev, Stalin, Rykov, Chicherin, Lunacharsky, and scores of Communists who had labored for a Red revolution saw that their day had arrived. The Military Committee of the Soviet, controlled by the Bolshevik group, issued its first command to the troops within the city on the night of November 4th, directing them henceforth to take orders from the Reds only. Although this meant war with the Provisional Government, Kerensky and other representatives of Moderate parties continued to talk rather than take ruthless action, the only course possible if they were to keep power in their hands.

Red soldiers occupied the principal government buildings on the night of November 7th and placarded the city with the program of the Bolshevik party: Immediate peace; the partition of large estates; the control of factories by workers; and the creation of a government by Soviets.

Leaving the government under the direction of his ministers, with no reliable troops to back up their decrees,
Kerensky left the city in order to arouse soldiers near the
front to the dangers of the capital. Red troops attacked the
Winter Palace, where the Cabinet was in session, and met
only the feeble resistance of a handful of cadets and a battalion of women. The Cabinet was imprisoned and the whole
apparatus of government at Petrograd was in the hands of
Lenin and his followers!

The watchword, the Dictatorship of the Proletariat, was
upon the tongues of thousands of workers in the great factory centers and was beginning to penetrate the thinking
of the peasant. Along with it was that other slogan, All
Power to the Soviets, a welcome sound to Lenin, Trotsky,
and all orthodox Bolsheviks who labored for the establishment of a new social order, for they knew the inability of
the workers, peasants, and soldiers to do much for themselves. The workers needed intelligent and determined
leadership, and Lenin and his group saw in themselves those
who were prepared to direct the rising tide. When at last
the Reds seized power it was to the shouts of All Power to
the Soviets! roared by soldiers, sailors, and workers rioting
in the streets of Petrograd.

Over the protests of the Mensheviks and Socialist-
Revolutionaries, Red leaders convened the second Congress
of Soviets on the following day, November 8th. The Congress approved the program of the Bolsheviks, and formed
a council of People's Commissars under Lenin, with Trotsky in the Foreign Office, Rykov, Commissar of Internal
Affairs, Stalin, Commissar of Nationalities, Lunacharsky,
Commissar of Education, and immediately began issuing
decrees.

The Decree of Peace was sent by wireless to all warring
states, asking for immediate *pourparlers* looking forward to
a democratic peace without annexations or indemnities.
Western nations paid no attention to this message sent "To
all, to all, to all." The next order, the Decree of Land,

abolished private ownership in land, declaring it should be apportioned equally to the tillers of the soil. Such were the stupendous changes which occurred on the night of November 8th!

Lenin, with a sure sense for the sorest spot in Russia, appealed straight to the peasant. The Emancipation Act of 1861 had fallen short of making the peasant a self-sustaining person. Redemption payments, allotments of land, the uneconomic aspects of overdivision of land in the communes, legal disabilities and uncertainty about titles, coupled with overpopulation of the country districts, low earning power, squalid living conditions, poverty and hunger made the peasant susceptible to Red ideas. The peasant felt that the sure remedy for all his miseries was to march upon his rich neighbor's property and claim a few acres for himself. Kerensky and the liberals in the Provisional Government dreaded an agrarian revolution and upheld the sacredness of private property. Lenin welcomed rebellion in the thousands of villages, with all that it entailed of murder, rapine, and pillage, as the only way to handle Russia at the moment, and flung to the winds the idea of private property. While the Provisional Government sought to uphold their rule by promises of a Constituent Assembly and by appeals to national honor to finish the war, the peasant wanted to go home. He coveted neither the defeat of Germany, nor the Dardanelles, nor the prestige of Russia, as much as he desired his wife, his child, his land.

Kerensky in Pskov was refused aid by General Chermisov and was received coldly by nearly all officers. Even the railway authorities indicated they would not assist in an attack on the Bolsheviks. He besought General Krasnov, who commanded the Third Cavalry Corps, to move to his assistance and overthrow the Red power in Petrograd. Krasnov, a monarchist of the old school, despising the very odor of republicanism, was opposed to Kerensky. Nevertheless, he consented to move a small detachment of his widely scattered horse, which reached Tsarskoe Selo, near Petrograd, where they were met by sailors and armed workers. After some fighting with no decisive result, one Dybenko, a Red leader, offered to hand over Lenin to Krasnov's Cossacks in exchange for Kerensky!

An uprising against the Bolsheviks occurred in Petrograd on November 12th by cadets, most of whom were shot. Kerensky, seeing that Red forces were consolidating their power at the capital and fearing that Krasnov's Cossacks might seize him and hand him over to the Bolsheviks, fled the scene of action and was no longer a moving force in the drama of revolution and civil war.

Two points of view emerged sharply when the iron flail of Bolshevism swept away the speechmaking régime of Kerensky—the Red and the White.

Who were these Reds reported in the Western world to be the scum of humanity which rises to the surface in the cauldron of any revolution? Were they jailbirds and *apaches* of Russian cities who came from back streets and exile to seize opportunity for plunder, or were they something else? Criminals many of them undoubtedly were, opponents of the existing order. And resolute they were, for whom the half-hearted Provisional Government was no adequate adversary. In glacial winters in Siberia they had warmed their souls with the promise of a Red to-morrow, which had now arrived.

The Red leaders were men and women diverse in culture. Thousands of them were of ordinary intellectual caliber, incapable of political dialectic, but hundreds were of exceptional mentality and qualities of leadership, who would have risen high in society, art, letters, industry, and politics, had there been room for persons of pronounced democratic views. With them were allied numbers of the industrial proletariat, small in comparison to the mass of Russian population, determined, class conscious, and faithful to their leaders, willing servants of the controlling minds.

Czardom for convinced revolutionists had come to mean an irresponsible nobility, a bureaucracy riddled with graft which laid heavy hands upon a defenseless population, an expensive army, the Okhrana or Secret Police, floggings, rotting in medieval jails, the long march to Siberia, and the subjugation of free thought. They hated the Czarist régime as well as the Church, and the military and judicial establishments which were subservient to it, dedicating themselves to its destruction and the erection of a Marxist State. All the more radical elements, those who had accounts to settle with the old order, those whose minds had been filled with hatred by exile and prison and surveillance, those whom the yoke of monarchy galled deepest, sided with the Bolsheviks.

The Bolshevik program came from many sources welded together by fervid debates and hot words in meetings of Russian radicals. In 1898 the First Congress of the Russian Social Democratic Labor Party met clandestinely in Minsk. The Bolsheviks broke with the programs of Terrorists and Anarchists as hopeless romanticism, seeing salvation for the masses only in a thoroughgoing political and economic revolution with seasoned revolutionists in actual control of the whole machinery of society. They relied upon proven strong men with iron will and the brains to conduct the state according to Marxist ideas. In the toiling masses they saw the possibility of a military party free from any inhibitions of bourgeois ethics and ideology. Only through a party disciplined by strong-minded and ruthless leadership did they hope for victory.

Underground branches of the Social Democratic Party had sprung up in industrial sections. Workers had been dispatched hither and yon organizing strikes and demonstrations and indoctrinating the minds of the workers. Lenin, abroad, was editing *Iskra*, the *Spark*, which was smuggled in to give direction to the revolutionary leaders. In 1903 the Second Congress of the Russian Social Democratic Labor Party met in London. Here Lenin opposed Plekhanov and Martov and developed the doctrines which finally divided the Social Democrats into Mensheviks and Bol-

sheviks, the former favoring reformation, the latter un-
alterably for a revolution which should smash to bits every
institution in the existing state. A Bolshevik conference had
been held in Tammerfors, Finland, in 1905 for the Russian
group, and a meeting of Bolsheviks and Mensheviks in
Stockholm in 1906, followed by another in London in 1907.

After the 1905 upheaval due to widespread discontent
following Russia's defeat by Japan, the Czar had quickly
rescinded the liberties he had given the people. Stolypin in-
augurated many measures which, although hailed by the
government as liberal, were in reality reactionary. For half
a decade the revolutionary spirit had burned low. Many
quit the movement entirely. Efforts were made to achieve
union between the Mensheviks and Bolsheviks. Lenin and
his group had fanned the embers of revolutionary ideas,
sending emissaries and correspondence far and wide by
underground channels. The Central Committee of the Social Democratic Party had met again in Paris in January
of 1910. Two years later, in Prague, a Bolshevik Central
Committee had been organized in defiance of the party.

The Reds had steeped themselves in the doctrines and
terminology of the revolutionary thinkers for the last century and a half and had modified Western conceptions of
class warfare into a program distinctly Russian. Marx,
Bebel, Bakhunin, Lasalle, Babeuf, Blanqui, and Wilhelm
Weitling had each contributed to the Social-Democratic
revolutionary idea. The members of that party had taken
what they wanted from Saint-Simon, Fourier, and English
social thinkers. They had read Alexander Herzen and Cher-
nishevsky and had debated the statements of Zaichnevsky,
Tkachev, and Nechayev, determining that when the day
arrived nothing should stand in the way of their program—
neither family, former political alliances, nor personal interest. They saw realistically what this involved: those who
opposed should be shot!

During the war, when the Socialist Internationale was
split into as many fragments as there were warring states,

two conferences were held in Switzerland, at Zimmerwald and at Kiental, where the members, listening to the slowing pulse beat of the Czarist régime, plotted the defeat of Russia and a social revolution. From month to month revolutionists had waited and planned in Russia and Siberia and in a dozen foreign lands. Then came the Russian Ides of March!

Who were these Whites who were to oppose the Bolsheviks during three and a half years of civil war? The anti-Bolshevik point of view was represented by the nobility, officers of the army and the navy, the professional classes, the Church, the landowner and manufacturer, Cossack communities whose large liberties and soldierly training made them antipathetic to town-made radicalism, and large masses of loyal, pious, illiterate peasantry who had not yet been aroused to their economic and social degradation. Mensheviks, Constitutional-Democrats, Socialist-Revolutionaries, republicans of various hues, and many thousands of a liberal turn of mind who found themselves in active or passive opposition to the old government stood out against Lenin and his party. For them, Czarism represented the assurance of their status in society, their livelihood, honors, Holy Russia, a social order built upon privilege and force, pleasant in its rewards to the fortunate, comfortable to parasitic groups which found their life in serving it, an ancient system which had its sanction in long centuries when Russia was building. For the most favored, the old order meant glittering distinction, luxury, all that power, titles, decorations, ancestral names, and estates could bring.

Admixtures of theory and savage disputes occurred in the counsels of every party in Russia, but throughout the course of the Civil War the contest was basically between two groups—the privileged and the underprivileged.

The Allies wished to believe that Russia would fight the Germans. They hoped for it and asserted, both in their press and from their chancelleries, that this would come to pass. But representatives of the press and state departments were out of touch with the actual power in Russia, which was in the Soviets. In vain did editors, correspondents, and statesmen repeat that Bolshevik Russia would not last. Many times Red Moscow was represented as overthrown or about to fall, yet Bolshevism persisted and eventually defeated all who sought to destroy it.

Chapter II

KORNILOV AND THE RISE OF THE VOLUNTEER ARMY: FROM THE FALL OF 1917 TO THE TREATY OF BREST-LITOVSK

EVERYWHERE except in Southeastern Russia, Red forces were winning. In Petrograd the Bolsheviks easily put down a small uprising of cadets. Only in Moscow did a sizable force combat Lenin's new units. Students, shopkeepers, and soldiers, representative of the bourgeoisie, made a stubborn resistance for several days as they fought from square to square in the city. Bullet-scarred walls and doorways still bear mute evidence of the direction of the strife. After a week of wolfish pursuits and hand-to-hand conflicts in boulevards, alleyways, and houses directed by a Lettish officer, Vatsetis, destined to be a prominent Bolshevik general, the Reds triumphed, and the dead were buried or thrown beneath the ice of the Moskva River. The citizens of Moscow came out of hiding to see the strange drama of a new order succeeding to the power of Ivan and Peter, of Catherine, of Alexander, and of Nicholas II.

The Soviet Government had appointed Ensign Krylenko supreme commander-in-chief on November 28th to succeed Dukhonin, who was dismissed for refusing on the previous day to open negotiations for an armistice with Germany. Krylenko immediately sent an expedition against Great Headquarters at Mogilev, which he knew to be counter-revolutionary.

When the Bolsheviks were advancing on Mogilev, Dukhonin, who knew he was suspected and probably condemned to die, decided to leave by motor for Kiev on December 1st but was halted by the local Council of Workmen's and Soldiers' Delegates. About noon on the same day he telegraphed the prisoners at Bykhov to make use of a train he was sending them in the evening to depart for the Don with the Tekintzy Cavalry who were loyal to Kornilov. Later, he countermanded the order for the train, whereupon the Bykhov prisoners took matters into their own hands, Kornilov ordering all the horses of the Tekintzy regiment to be shod and the squadron which had been left at Mogilev brought up for departure.

General Dukhonin's failure to leave Mogilev cost him his life. On December 3d the vanguard échelon of Krylenko arrived. A detail immediately arrested Dukhonin, taking him to the train of the new supreme commander-in-chief where, amid great excitement, unruly soldiers haled him forth and shot him. After rough treatment and narrow escapes, Denikin, Romanovsky, Markov, and Lukomsky started for the Don separately, employing disguises, while the redoubtable Kornilov saluted the Tekintzy, swung into the saddle, and set out on a fifteen hundred verst journey to the Don.

But the road to the Don was a long road across the frozen steppe. The Bolsheviks soon raised the cry, sending an armored train to intercept Kornilov and the Tekintzy, which suffered heavily from machine-gun fire. Escaping this tragedy, they encountered an ambuscade in a wood on the following day, whence machine guns again made havoc with horse and rider. Disentangling itself, the regiment crossed the River Seim into a country covered with frozen swamps in which many mounts were lost. Frost bit into the thinly clad cavalrymen, the horses' shoes were becoming dull, and, added to these perils, the population in some places was so hostile that it was difficult to obtain provisions. After many hardships and dangers, Kornilov decided to permit the Tekintzy to disband and work their way eastward as best they might, while he journeyed alone disguised as a peasant to

Novocherkassk, in the Don region, where he arrived on December 19th.

By dangerous paths, all high officers who had been imprisoned at Bykhov reached Novocherkassk, the capital of the Don, where they reunited to plan with others for the future. General Alexeyev had arrived early in November, and, with the permission of Kaledin, Ataman of the Don Cossacks, had begun to form a Volunteer Army on Cossack soil. Recruiting was aided by the Officers' Union and by secret groups in Petrograd and Moscow, which gave information to former cadets and officers. At the same time an anti-Bolshevik organization composed largely of officers was being formed on the Rumanian Front.

The Don offered a favorable base for the formation of a Volunteer Army. The Don Cossacks were well-to-do farmers and fighters who cherished their independence, one of a series of Cossack groups with large liberties who had been settled by different Czars in a broad arc reaching from Siberia to the Crimea, acting as a *cordon militaire* against the barbaric hordes of Turkestan and bordering tribes. Their communities were a mixed group of fugitives from serfdom and high-spirited pioneers priding themselves on their fighting qualities. The Cossacks of Little Russia had located themselves in the Ukraine with the Zaporojtzy along the Dnieper River. The Don, Terek, Kuban, Orenburg, and Ural Cossacks were in the southern and eastern provinces, while farther east were the Cossacks of Siberia, Semirechinsk, Semipalatinsk, Orenburg, Transbaikal, Ussuri, Nerchinsk, and several smaller groups. These liberty-loving settlements were in a constant state of preparation, furnishing cavalry regiments for the Czar's army. The military chief or Ataman of the Don Cossacks had formerly been elected by the *Krug* or legislative assembly, but since the time of Peter the Great, who had deprived them of some of their liberties, the Ataman had been appointed by the Czar. After the 1917 Revolution the Cossacks claimed again their ancient right to elect their Ataman, asserting that the *Krug* had the supreme power within the confines of the Don Cossacks.

In Novocherkassk the *Krug,* composed of some four hundred members, had elected in June of 1917 their new Ataman, General Alexey Maximovich Kaledin, who had formerly commanded the Eighth Army on the Southwestern Front. Associated with him was the famous cavalry leader, General Piotr Nikolayevich Krasnov.

Before these seasoned officers lay no easy task. The *Krug* had only two dependable Cossack divisions which had been stationed on the Don in anticipation of being dispatched to the Caucasus to coöperate with the English Mesopotamian army. General Kaledin proclaimed the independence of the Don and attacked the troops of the Donetz Socialist Republic which had been organized on November 16, 1917.

Kaledin also faced a grave problem on his own territory and from the south. In the Don region were large numbers of non-Cossack peasants who had settled in the region under many disabilities regarding land and civil rights, and a smaller group of workingmen and miners inclined to a Soviet orientation. Together these categories formed fifty-nine per cent of the population. Danger also threatened from masses of troops, drunk with the watchwords of the Revolution, who were retreating north through the Caucasus after the break-up of the Russo-Turkish Front, making their way across Cossack territory to their homes.

The Don Cossacks not only held back Red forces but also offered hospitality to White generals who had arrived on the Don to rally an anti-Bolshevik army. Both Kaledin and the non-Cossack officers approached the authorities in the Terek and the Kuban with a view of coöperating in the war against the Reds.

General Mikhail Alexeyev, around whom officers and men of the old Imperial Army were gathering, was born in 1857, and had served in the General Staff College and become a general in 1904. He had fought in the Turkish War of 1877-78 and in the Russo-Japanese War as director of operations

Civil War begins

General Kornilov (small man in center), General Denikin at his right, and other officers imprisoned at Berdichev

General Lukomsky   General Kornilov

Kornilov receives ovation   General Alexeyev

of the Second Army. In 1912 he commanded the Thirteenth Army Corps and during the war distinguished himself as chief-of-staff of the Southwestern Front in Galicia. Later he commanded armies on the Northwestern Front. In August of 1915, when the Czar took supreme command, Alexeyev was called as his chief-of-staff, where he served until compelled to leave because of heart trouble. Western military critics have ranked him with Foch and Ludendorff as a strategist. Kerensky had called him to the colors again as commander-in-chief in March of 1917 and dismissed him two months later, only to send for him again in September as chief-of-staff. Alexeyev was a man of the people, with democratic tendencies, rather professorial in his speech and appearance. He was slightly less than average height, wore glasses, and a pair of white mustaches with no beard. His capacity for detail had made him invaluable as a staff officer in the Czar's army.

Lukomsky urged Alexeyev, who was very popular, to send out an appeal for recruits, but Alexeyev refused, saying he was unable adequately to feed and clothe the five hundred officers who had already rallied to his standard. On December 8, 1917, Denikin and Lukomsky approached Kaledin, who gave them good hopes concerning the formation of a Volunteer Army. At the same time Kaledin warned Kornilov, Markov, Lukomsky, and Denikin that because they were so well known for their anti-Bolshevik tendencies it would prove advantageous for them to leave the Don during the period of organization. Thereupon Denikin and Markov went to Ekaterinodar, capital of the Kuban, and Lukomsky set out for Vladikavkaz, the capital of Tersky Province.

General Lukomsky had a long and distinguished record as a Russian soldier. He was a stocky, handsome man with a grizzled goatee, bright brown eyes which bespoke high intelligence, and bristling hair. When the war broke out he was made Secretary to the War Office, and later Assistant War Minister, dealing with supplies. In the spring of 1916 he found himself at the front commanding the Thirty-second Infantry Division and with it breached the Austrian line in July with the Ninth Army before the Carpathians. As chief-of-staff of the Tenth Army and later as Director of Military Operations at the Stavka, he performed notable services. In April of 1917 he had commanded the First Army Corps and from June 16, 1917, he had been chief-of-staff of Brusilov and Kornilov when they were supreme commanders-in-chief. General Lukomsky was to have prominent rôles in the White armies of South Russia, with Kornilov, Denikin, and later with General Wrangel. He was chief-of-staff of the Volunteer Army until Kornilov's death, and by Denikin was made Chief of the Military Administration, tantamount to the post of Minister of War, and assistant commander-in-chief. From July, 1918, up to January, 1919, he was to be President of the Special Council of Denikin's government, an office comparable to that of Premier.

The ferment of the Red Revolution pervaded the Don, arousing the sleeping minds of peasants and disturbing the loyalty of men and officers. On December 10th a Red rising occurred in Rostov, lasting for several days, finally crushed with the aid of the first company of the embryonic Volunteer Army which was coming into being at Novocherkassk. New ideas were seething in every village. Muzhiks and workmen dropped tools and talked endlessly at pothouse and road corner about land and new rights and the rise of the people. An epidemic of discussion broke out in every village, but another and more serious epidemic was soon to overtake them.

Until November of 1918 the Volunteer Army and the Army of the Don were fairly free from typhus, which had been the scourge of all Eastern armies during the winters of the Great War. When the Revolution had broken out, a section of the former Imperial Army was stranded in Armenia for many months. This army, under a Russian officer named Sorokin, attempted to make its way to South Russia. Inasmuch as the Kuban was embroiled in guerrilla warfare it attempted a short cut along the west shore of the Caspian, across a lean and savage steppe to Astrakhan and the Volga. Most of Sorokin's men were without any decided political views—they only wanted to regain their villages.

Sorokin's army of approximately two hundred thousand men was stricken with the wings of death and only a few thousand finally made the Volga. The rest perished from typhus and exposure in the steppe. Thousands of them lay in the snow like starved cattle. The local population from far and near moved out into the steppe to retrieve the arms of the soldiers, to pick their pockets, and to strip them of their clothing, thus contaminating an ever-widening area with the plague. As a result, in January of 1919 a tremendous epidemic of typhus broke out among the White troops. The shortage of doctors, nurses, medicines, and hospitals made adequate care of the soldiers impossible.

At the town of Naltchik a young Russian officer in the midst of a snowstorm opened the huge iron door of a railway shed and found every inch of the floor covered with the half-frozen dead bodies of soldiers who had perished from typhus. Trains of forty and forty-five common railway vans moved in to Taganrog, on the Sea of Azov, with only one male nurse in attendance, who ran along the train pounding on the doors and shouting, "Everybody who is alive, get out!" Slowly the doors would open and haggard ghosts which once were men stumbled forth into the light, supporting themselves upon swords and rifles. The vans often contained as many as twenty to thirty dead apiece, soldiers and officers who had died together upon the floor while in transit.

Troops from the Caucasian Front disturbed the Tersky Province, menacing the small Volunteer Army, diminishing food for man and beast, while Red agitators filled the peasants' minds with ideas of Utopia. Their zest for fighting was gone, their only desire being to settle in their *stanitzas* (villages) and enjoy the freedom they had been promised. Grave clashes took place in many localities between these

well-armed soldiers and Kaledin's loyal troops. Ataman
Karaulov of the Tersky Cossacks did all in his power to
assuage the unrest, but was finally killed by rioting peasants.

Matters were further complicated by the fact that Kornilov and Alexeyev were not able to agree about the command
of the Volunteer Army. The former held that there should
be one supreme chief, while Alexeyev was of the opinion
that he should deal with political and financial problems
while Kornilov should organize and train the troops. Kornilov, who was familiar with Siberia, wished to go there to
organize opposition to the Bolshevik. Representatives of
the National Center, a secret organization for rallying
counter-revolutionary forces, came from Moscow to Novocherkassk and insisted upon his remaining in the South with
Kaledin and Alexeyev. Kornilov gave his reluctant consent,
and on January 7, 1918, assumed the military command.
Finally the whole military organization was handed over to
him, while all questions of a political or financial character
remained entirely in the hands of Alexeyev.

To aid him in the difficult operations in hand, Kornilov
immediately secured Lukomsky as chief-of-staff. There lay
before the staff the task of organizing a Volunteer Army
with a divided headship in Cossack territory, where a growing section of the population was becoming indifferent to
White hopes.

Political dissension was so severe among the Don Cossacks that it was plain no official conscription could be
decreed by Ataman Kaledin. The Ataman, to strengthen his
forces, permitted the formation of partisan bands, with the
result that several adventurers took the field, disgracing the
name of Kaledin and Kornilov by plundering Red and
White alike. Although some of these chiefs were brave and
loyal soldiers, others were brigands who robbed and massacred without mercy.

The Volunteer Army was launched upon a sea of troubles.
Kornilov's fears were justified about the unwisdom of the
dual command, for friction sprang up where functions of

the two generals overlapped in the organization and administration of the growing forces. Further to augment the difficulties, rifles, guns, horses, and munitions were very scarce. Some equipment was obtained in the sparse military stores of the Don; arms were taken at Rostov and Novocherkassk from regiments on their way home from the Russo-Turkish Front. Some were obtained by raids into Stavropol Province, where decided Red tendencies prevailed.

Finance never ceased to be a pressing problem. In the beginning the sole support of the Whites consisted of contributions received by Alexeyev and Kornilov from the Moscow Right Center, in all some five million rubles. By an agreement with Kaledin and officials of banks and the state treasury at Rostov, sums were taken from these institutions which, according to Lukomsky, amounted to some thirty million rubles. Later, in order to purchase equipment and food and to pay the soldiers, paper money was issued which soon suffered from depreciation.

Kornilov and Alexeyev received some comfort from the fact that the Red Government also faced a crisis not only in a military sense but in matters of food, industry, and finance. By denunciation of Western nations as slaves of bandit capitalists the Bolsheviks had cut themselves off from the sympathy of the outside world. With phenomenal energy they held the apparatus of government together and maintained the various fronts. Russia was prostrate when they seized power. Reaction to defeats on the front, revolution, uncertainty, dissolution of old loyalties, lawlessness consequent upon revolution, decreased production in the mills and on the farms. The peasants, dreading requisition of grain and other farm products, hid their food and decreased their plantings. Heavy industries had fallen off a third before the Bolsheviks came into power, transportation became disorganized especially in the matter of repairs, thousands of trucks and locomotives rusted on side tracks, while demands for increased pay and threats of strikes occurred in every section of the country. The finance problem was solved temporarily in the orthodox manner then employed by nearly all European nations—the printing press! Paper rubles by the million were soon inflating the currency, while government income rapidly decreased. Rostov-on-Don printed Volunteer Army rubles on paper with the colors of St. George and a picture of Moscow's bell tower upon them. The people called these one thousand ruble notes "Little Bells." Novocherkassk printed money for the Don Army. The Bolsheviks moved small printing presses to the front and flooded villages and towns with Kerensky rubles which for some reason were still accepted. Each type of money was quoted at a different rate of exchange, adding confusion to an already tangled fiscal problem.

News reached the Don that the long expected Constituent Assembly planned during Kerensky's régime had met in Moscow on January 18, 1918. A working agreement had been made between the Bolsheviks and the Left Socialist-Revolutionaries, but the Right Socialist-Revolutionaries, with a small group of cadets or Constitutional-Democrats, had been in the majority. Chernov, a Right Socialist-Revolutionary, was elected President, defeating Marie Spiridinova of the Left Wing of that party, whereupon the Bolsheviks closed the Assembly the day after its opening with a battalion of Red guards. Maintaining that they were still the legitimate representatives of the Russian people, the members later worked for the organization of governments in Siberia and upon the Volga.

Kornilov's forces by this time consisted of about five thousand men, comprising a company of ex-officers, the Kornilov Regiment which had been brought from the Southwestern Front by its commander, Captain Nezhintzev, a battalion of cadets, a newly organized battalion of St. George, a company of engineers, an officers' squadron of horse, and other incomplete small units. Recruits were mostly officers, cadets, and students, giving the Volunteer Army a class rather than a national flavor. The men on the Don cast anxious eyes toward Moscow, where the Red power was becoming more securely entrenched day by day.

In the early months of the Volunteer Army patriotism ran high among the men, who had cut away their insignia of rank, employed disguises, and shaved off their beards, on the long road to the Don to fight the new order of Russia. Some seventy-five to one hundred arrived daily, having traveled hundreds of miles of perilous country. Although many were monarchists, numbers were sincere, if moderate, republicans. Nevertheless the White Army achieved and kept a reputation for monarchist sympathies, a fact which hindered it throughout. There were meetings, reunions, old friendships renewed, old vows retaken. But the *esprit de corps* of the Whites was marred from the first by jealousies and indifference to the suffering of the civil population.

During the period when the Don Cossacks and Kornilov's Volunteer Army were organizing the Bolsheviks were not idle. They had consolidated their position in the interior and had formed military units of respectable proportions. Lenin and his aids had labored ceaselessly, organizing transport, securing supplies and munitions, indoctrinating the troops with Red principles, and deploying them against the opponents of the Communist state.

The Red Army had been formed by a decree of the Council of People's Commissars on February 3, 1918. At the start the soldiers, mostly workers and former troops in the Czar's forces, received high pay as compared to factory laborers and peasants. At first the distinction between officers and men was slight, with consequent insubordination. A spirit of lawlessness had prevailed, as the Red Army in the beginning was employed chiefly against unarmed civilians and farmers. When, however, it was confronted with the exigencies of combat against a determined adversary, discipline was strengthened, the death penalty restored, and the line between officers and men widened. Lenin and Trotsky allowed no revolutionary shibboleths regarding equality to hinder them in the formation of an effective fighting force. From the beginning the Red Army had the advantages of a unique command, fighting on inner lines, and an enthusiasm for a new social order.

Chiefs of the Volunteer Army wished to recruit the White forces up to ten thousand men before aggressively moving against the Reds. A decision was made to remove their base to Rostov, where they hoped conditions would be more favorable. Kaledin agreed to guard the Don toward the north, and at his request the Officers' Battalion and one battery of field artillery of the Volunteer Army were left with him.

The situation now became extremely hazardous. All rail lines leading to the Don were in the hands of Soviet soldiers; only men taking desperate chances could win through to join their comrades. Tsaritsin, Stavropol, and large sections of the Terek were held by the Reds. Volunteer forces were not as yet large enough to justify a sally in force, while to remain on the defensive would risk annihilation by being caught in the pincers composed of retreating forces from the Caucasian Front and Red troops from the old Northern, Western, and Southwestern fronts which were moving south against them.

By February Red troops occupied Taganrog and Bataisk, which was opposite Rostov on the left bank of the Don, and were exerting pressure along the rail line from Voronezh toward Novocherkassk, while cavalry units continually harassed territory in the hands of the Don Cossack and Volunteer troops. The Cossacks were becoming more restless and disorganized and the area held by these two armies was daily growing smaller.

In the opinion of Kornilov, nothing could be gained by remaining at Rostov. He favored moving at once to Ekaterinodar, where he hoped to join with Kuban Cossacks who had not yet become Red. General Kaledin, realizing that he would be unable to defend the Don without the help of the Volunteer Army, wished to concentrate the combined forces at Novocherkassk, but this proposal met with scant favor from Kornilov. On February 8th the Ataman telegraphed Alexeyev and Kornilov to come to Novocherkassk to attend a conference of the *Krug*. In answer to Kaledin's request, Lukomsky was sent as the personal spokesman of these generals. Representatives from the secret organizations in Moscow were also invited.

The conference quickly revealed the state of disorganization among the Don Cossacks. There were only a few loyal *stanitzas.* Lukomsky informed the assembly that Kornilov could send no troops to Novocherkassk, but, on the other hand, earnestly requested that the Officers' Battalion from the Volunteer Army be returned immediately to Rostov. The majority urged upon Ataman Kaledin that he leave at once with the Parliament to apprize Cossacks in loyal regions of the true state of affairs. But Kaledin replied that he would die before he left the capital of the province, whereupon the conference ended in a draw. On February 11th the gallant Cossack leader, hopeless of the future of his cause, put an end to his life.

The death of their Ataman shocked the Don Cossacks into a temporary rally. Several thousand came to Novocherkassk to be formed into new fighting units, but the staff and quartermaster departments were unable to care for the influx of recruits, and most of them, becoming discouraged, made their way back to their *stanitzas* to augment disaffected elements in the population.

A combined effort of Volunteers and Cossacks was essential if the Bolsheviks were to be overcome. On February 15th Lukomsky went to Novocherkassk as the representative of Kornilov, to insist that the new Field Ataman, General Nazarov, form fresh regiments and continue the struggle. Two days later all were encouraged by the arrival of the Sixth Don Regiment from Ekaterinoslav, with a full complement of officers, demanding to be dispatched at once against the Reds. A mass was sung in the cathedral square and the Ataman and the President of the Don Government welcomed the troops. On February 19th they were sent to the front and two days later, conquered by Bolshevik propaganda, they refused to fire a shot! Such rapid changes of attitude made

it impossible for military commanders to foretell the out-
come of any engagement.

Affairs had taken such a turn that Kornilov and his advisers believed it futile to attempt a defense of the Don.
Accordingly, on the night of February 21st, the Volunteer
Army evacuated Rostov and began the march famous in the
annals of the White armies as "The Ice Campaign."

"It is customary," writes Miliukov, "to speak of this campaign in epic terms. Indeed, never did the idealistic, self-
sacrificing spirit of the White movement reach greater
heights than in this enterprise; never was the moral discipline
stronger; never did love for our suffering country burn more
brightly. But admiration of the heroism of the participants
does not exclude a realistic estimate of the events. The small
Volunteer Army moved among a population either frightened
or sympathetic to the Bolsheviks, and had to make its way by
fighting endless engagements with detachments of the Red
Army numerically superior, if incomparably less fit for
battle. March winds, bitter cold, the fording of ice-cold
rivers, and forced marches in snowdrifts and slush worked
extreme hardships on the ill-clad, underfed men." Here
burned the pure flame of patriotic devotion in the hearts of
young and old. The suffering of the troops was abysmal. The
decoration chosen by the commander to commemorate their
exploits was a crown of thorns pierced by a dagger!

General Lukomsky regained the Volunteer Army by
sledge, leaving Novocherkassk after a vain attempt to persuade Ataman Nazarov to join Kornilov, saying that to remain in Novocherkassk would mean death. But Nazarov,
believing that the Bolsheviks would not interfere with the
elected Ataman and the Cossack *Krug,* refused to move. In
this he was mistaken, for Red soldiers occupied the city on
February 25th, arrested him, and, after a few days' imprisonment, executed him as a traitor to the new order.

The day of the Bolshevik occupation, a council of war was
held at Olginskaya, attended by Alexeyev, Kornilov, Romanovsky, Denikin, Markov, Nezhintzev, Popov, Field Ataman

of the Don Cossacks, and others. Kornilov desired to proceed to Astrakhan, where he could retreat into the fastnesses of Siberia, if necessary. The majority of the staff favored waiting at the *zimovniki* or steppe farms, while Alexeyev favored marching to Ekaterinodar in the Kuban territory, where it was hoped counter-revolutionary troops might be recruited. After prolonged discussion, it was finally decided to follow this latter plan.

At this time the Volunteer Army numbered 3,500 men with eight guns and six hundred shells. The first third of the long journey of three hundred versts to Ekaterinodar lay through Don territory, where elements in the population sympathized with the Bolsheviks. At every *stanitza* Kornilov called together the landowners, explained the aims and purposes of the Volunteer Army, and tried to obtain recruits, but few men enlisted. On the 9th of March, the army entered Kuban territory, but support expected there did not materialize, the Kuban Cossacks remaining passive. The Bolsheviks engaged the army in daily skirmishes and the number of wounded who had to be carried rose from one hundred at the beginning of the long march to a thousand or more as the army neared Ekaterinodar. The groans of their wounded and dying friends in the carts and wagons further depressed the weary campaigners.

Kornilov had hoped to obtain both shelter and supplies, but when the army was about seventy versts from the town news came that the Bolsheviks were in occupation and that the Kuban Government had withdrawn to the hills. Once more the staff must settle the question of destination. Alexeyev would have proceeded to Ekaterinodar, but Kornilov, taking into account the condition of the troops, advised a period of rest in the foothills of the Caucasus.

Korenevskaya was taken on March 17th at the point of the bayonet. From there the army moved toward the Ust-Labinskaya *stanitza* and three days later the weary troops crossed the Kuban. Six days of continuous fighting followed as the column moved slowly toward mountain villages where it was out of danger and could relax and care for the wounded. During the period of rest, friendly Circassians gave what assistance they could.

After recuperating, a junction was made on March 27th with Kuban soldiers and with General Erdeli, who had been imprisoned at Bykhov with Denikin and Lukomsky. The combined forces were placed under the command of Kornilov, and the decision made to march on Ekaterinodar immediately and take it by storm. Before making this desperate step, Kornilov said to Denikin: "If we do not take Ekaterinodar I shall have to blow out my brains."

Between March 29th and April 6th the advancing army fought six battles. The engagement on March 30th at Novo-Dmitriyevskaya is characteristic of the others. After marching in rain, snow, and hail across swampy ground, knee-deep in water, General Markov and his detachment plunged into the icy waters of a river. Half frozen, they were lifted off their horses on the farther bank. Few Bolsheviks escaped alive from the unexpected attack which followed. At Smolenskaya a twelve-hour engagement was fought and won. In Elizabetinskaya, the last *stanitza* before Ekaterinodar, Alexeyev and Kornilov were enthusiastically received and eight hundred volunteers were added to their army.

In Ekaterinodar 17,000 Bolsheviks with thirty guns and unlimited ammunition awaited Kornilov, whose forces now numbered 3,000 infantry, 4,000 swords, with eight three-inch guns and seven hundred shells. In spite of this meager force, Kornilov would undoubtedly have taken Ekaterinodar on April 8th had the newly formed Kuban soldiers not retreated before the enemy's fire.

For five days the storming of the town continued. During the siege, Colonel Nezhintzev, the commander of the Kornilov Regiment, was killed, a grievous loss soon followed by one even more disastrous. The staff of the Volunteer Army lived in a small wooden house in a copse upon a hillside constantly swept by artillery fire. On April 13th a shell burst near Kornilov, killing him almost instantaneously. Black depression settled upon the attackers as news spread of their commander's death, and the siege was raised.

Kornilov was characterized by Miliukov as "first of all a soldier, a brave fighter capable of inspiring an army in time of battle by his personal example, fearless in his plans, resolute and persistent in executing them. But his intellect was not on a level with his will." A rival general declared that he had "a lion's heart, a sheep's head." Kornilov was the very stuff of which Slavic military legends are made, a son of Russia to the core. Even his mixed blood made him beloved of a people deeply tinctured by infiltration of many racial strains. For guerrilla warfare, which was to be the lot of the White forces, no single chief possessed greater qualities as a combat leader. In the days that followed, White troops were to miss the flash of his black eyes, his wrinkled face with its tawny Cossack mustaches, and his lean figure at the head of their column.

The defense of Ekaterinodar had cost the Reds fifteen thousand lives. So remarkable had been the *élan* of the White forces that hundreds joined their colors upon their withdrawal from the attack.

General Anton Denikin immediately took command, a hard-fighting, honest soldier, forty-five years old, of humble birth and democratic sympathies. He was a handsome man of medium height, with regular features, a grizzled beard and mustache. During the World War he had risen rapidly to the rank of lieutenant general and had led a division creditably upon what was known as the Danube Front. In comparison with the shibboleths of the Revolution his more moderate ideas seemed weak to radicals clamoring for a new social order. It was not difficult for Red advocates to create a caricature of Denikin in the mind of the average peasant, making him appear as a representative of reaction surrounded as he was by many associates of the old ruling classes. His success had been won by sheer hard work and devotion to duty.

Although the defeat of the Volunteer Army before Ekaterinodar was not as complete as Soviet papers described it at the time, it was a serious blow. As the army left Ekaterinodar on April 14th they carried with them the bodies of Kornilov and Nezhintzev, interring them in a lonely spot on the steppe, leveling their graves with the surface of the ground to prevent discovery by the Bolsheviks. Medical officers and Sisters of Mercy, left behind to care for the severely wounded, were massacred by the Red Army. The next day a stubborn battle was fought at Nemetskaya Kolonka, and after another sharp attack the railway at Medvedinskaya was reached and successfully crossed.

Both Red and White were in desperate need of all supplies. Although the Red Army had immense military resources in the interior, amid the wreckage of the Imperial stores, its troops in the Caucasus were poorly munitioned and compelled to forage off the countryside. The White armies had very scanty munitions; every shell and gun was carefully husbanded against extreme need.

Social and political upheaval loosed dark forces within the troops. Requisitions broke down respect for property and soon developed into robbery. In spite of any compunctions the high command might have had, cold and hungry troopers took what they wanted and sold the remainder. So bitter was the enmity between Red and White that few prisoners were taken. Russia was launched upon a period of utter lawlessness. The hardships of the army were severe; the sufferings of the civil population were extreme.

The Kuban Government and Rada traveled with the army and en route enlisted its people by conscription. Bolshevik prisoners asked to be taken into the ranks and the army grew steadily during its journey.

Proceeding through Zhuravskaya, the troops rested at Ilyinskaya on April 23d, and on April 25th occupied Uspenskaya. There the first news reached them of happenings in the Don territory, where Novocherkassk had been cleared of Bolsheviks and a White government established.

The Volunteer Army decided to retrace its steps to the

Don, beginning the journey on April 28, 1918, while the Kuban Government remained in its own territory. When the Don was entered, Egorlitskaya, Metchetinskaya, and other *stanitzas* after sharp fights were snatched on May 3d. The Volunteer Army had fought forty engagements in fifty days. In no single campaign was their *esprit de corps* higher. At Metchetinskaya newspapers were found which told the news of Brest-Litovsk!

Denikin's officers and men asked one another why any Russian group had signed so severe a treaty. The explanation was simple. The new Red power had soon felt the mailed hand of Germany at its throat. One object occupied the attention of Lenin and his advisers—peace with Germany as soon as possible. There would be time to crush their White opponents later!

Thereupon Lenin, on November 20, 1917, had ordered the Soviet high command to "propose to the enemy authorities immediately to cease hostilities and enter into negotiations for peace," followed with a note by Trotsky to the Allied ambassadors in Petrograd proposing an "immediate armistice on all fronts and immediate opening of peace negotiations," to which no reply was made. Brushing Dukhonin aside, inasmuch as he had refused to deal with Germany, the Bolshevik War Office had ordered fraternization with German soldiers.

No Russian army in a proper sense had remained between Germany and the rich food-producing region of the Ukraine. Germany could have taken what she would by force, but chose to cloak an iron hand with at least a semblance of diplomacy. Knowing the defeatist policy of Lenin and the Bolsheviks, Berlin had been unwilling to force them too far lest they fall into the arms of the Allies and the Eastern Front be reëstablished. The Central Powers had notified Petrograd on November 28th that they were willing to consider an armistice, and on December 2d guns had ceased firing upon a front where Russian valor during the attack on Verdun and in the Italian crisis saved the Allied nations from grave losses. Then had begun three months of tortuous negotiations, in which Trotsky had clung to his baffling formula of "No peace and no war," finally issuing in the Treaty of Brest-Litovsk on March 3, 1918, which the Germans forced by the thinly veiled threat of a wholesale advance.

Western Europe, America, and the whole non-Russian world during the last months of 1917 and the year 1918 had little accurate information regarding events in the former empire. News was more optimistic than facts supported. From the beginning of the Bolshevik revolution there was a serious misappraisal of Red strength. Neither ordinary citizens nor the governments of the West had before them a realistic statement of the situation. Representatives of the press, diplomats, and military missions often colored the news in accordance with their hopes, a process which added confusion to Western opinion throughout the Civil War. From the November Revolution of 1917 to the Peace of Brest-Litovsk, the Allies, hard pressed by the Germans, hoping for help from any quarter, were uncritically pro-Bolshevik, due to the hope that the Reds would continue the war against Germany. But after February 12, 1918, when Red Moscow declared it would not continue the war, the Allies gradually turned to White commanders.

By the date when the peace of Brest-Litovsk was signed the Bolsheviks were menaced by bayonet and saber in every direction. White and Allied troops had landed at Archangel. The Ukraine was in turmoil. A campaign to seize Petrograd was in preparation on the Baltic. Kolchak was preparing a drive toward Moscow from the east. The Red Commissariat of War worked feverishly to secure troops, munitions, clothing, wheat, guns. Inexperienced men who had never shot a rifle were placed, because of their status in the party, in positions of power as commissars alongside experienced Czarist generals. Against them were arrayed able officers commanding the White armies but lacking coördination of movement to time and place their blows.

Chapter III

SOUTH RUSSIA: THE UKRAINE, THE DON, THE
KUBAN, AND THE TEREK; FROM BREST-LITOVSK
TO THE ARMISTICE

THE Volunteer Army and the Cossacks who were fighting in
the White cause were appalled at the conditions Germany
had demanded at Brest-Litovsk to which Soviet delegates
were compelled to accede. More than a half-dozen new nations were to be carved out of Russia! By this dismember-
ment Russia lost one-fourth of her population, a fourth of
her farm land, a third of her average crops, a fourth of her
railway system, a third of her factories, three-fourths of her
iron industry, three-fourths of her coal fields, and agreed to
pay a sizable war indemnity. Denikin with all the more
tenacity held to the slogan of Russia, One and Indivisible!
But the new states were to be tenacious of their freedom.

According to the treaty, Finland, Esthonia, Latvia, Lithuania, Poland, the Ukraine, Bessarabia, and various provinces
in the Caucasus were permitted to secede from the former
territories of the empire. These lands, especially the Baltic
provinces, Poland, and the Ukraine, having hated Czarism,
hated the Red power no less, and immediately after the
Bolshevik Revolution had set about establishing governments. One after another they declared their independence.
On April 9, 1918, Bessarabia united with Rumania by an
understanding which left her a doubtful autonomy. In the
same month the Transcaucasian Council declared its freedom without recourse to the Treaty of Brest-Litovsk. During
the next month the Transcaucasian Federal Government
broke up into Georgia, Armenia, and Azerbaijan. All these

territories hailed Brest-Litovsk as a vindication to their claims to independence.

After the signing of the Treaty of Brest-Litovsk on March 3, 1918, the Soviet power, no longer concerned with foreign conflict, was able to concentrate on the Civil War. Though Brest-Litovsk was a crushing blow to White hopes, it did not in itself spell defeat for their cause.

All of South Russia was embroiled in civil war. The Ukraine, the Don, the Kuban, and the Terek suffered from cross-political currents, war requisitions of food, horses and men, the capture and recapture of towns, and the economic and moral disintegration inevitable on a terrain which is the scene of guerrilla warfare. Events is one locality directly affected the status of all contiguous regions.

Denikin and the Volunteers had little to hope from the Ukraine because of the nascent nationalism in that territory. Since 1859, the Russian Government had taken measures to put down cultural and political separatism among the Ukrainians. Suppression had fallen heaviest upon the intelligentsia. Poets, dramatists, novelists, journalists, and professors saw their work interdicted and all publications in the Ukrainian tongue finally banned. Small groups nurtured a resentment against St. Petersburg, but the rank and file of artisans and peasants took comparatively little interest in the matter until the breakdown of Russia in the World War.

The Ukrainian situation had been further aggravated for the Czarist Government by the influence of German and Magyar statesmen. The Dual Monarchy, which included large groups of Slavs in Bukovina, Galicia, Bohemia, Slovakia, and Ruthenia, although unwilling to allow cultural or political advances among its own Slav minorities, nevertheless welcomed the rise of Ukrainian nationalism as a vulnerable spot in the armor of Russian Pan-Slavism. For Austria-Hungary, friends in the Ukraine meant help against an ancient enemy, Imperial Russia, whose interest in the Western Slavs was a constant source of worry to the chancelleries of Vienna, Budapesth, and Berlin. Austrian hopes for assistance in Ukrainian separatism were not, however, fulfilled in the war, as the movement was too narrowly confined to the intellectuals.

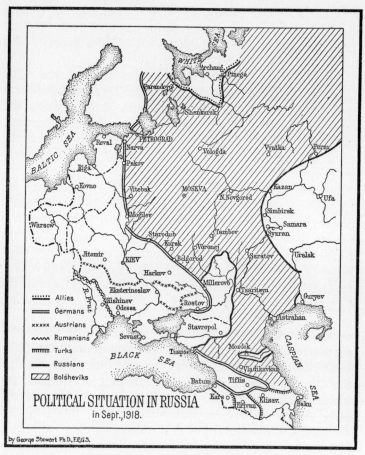

German-Austrian invasion of Russia in 1918.

When the Great War broke upon Europe, Ukrainian exiles had immediately organized a league for the liberation of the Ukraine which threw in its lot with the Central Powers. A Ukrainian Legion had been organized in much the same manner as Pilsudski formed the Polish Legion, to strike at Soviet Russia. Following the March Revolution of 1917 the Ukraine had demanded autonomy of the Provisional Government. Notables from all parties had assembled at Kiev on March 21st under the leadership of Professor Michael Hrushevsky, organizing the Ukrainian Central Rada which assumed the functions of a Revolutionary Citizen's Committee for the administration of the region.

Professor Hrushevsky, then in his late fifties, was born of a rich family and had studied in Kiev. Shortly before 1900 he had been called to Austrian Galicia to take the chair of Ukrainian history at the University of Lemberg, a post which he had held until the outbreak of the war. While in Lemberg he wrote a monumental history of the Ukraine. Inasmuch as he was a Russian subject, he returned to Kiev upon the outbreak of hostilities. There the government arrested him and interned him on the Volga until the Revolution, when he immediately made his way home to Kiev and became President of the Central Rada. Although in his younger years he had been a Conservative, he had turned to the Left. He was a man of dignity, high intelligence, and courage, but too theoretical for the times.

Taking matters into their own hands, on March 23d the Central Rada proclaimed the Ukraine autonomous but federated with Russia. All efforts of Kerensky's régime to suppress the Rada failed because it had won support from Ukrainian regiments in the old army. An agreement was drawn up on June 16, 1917, between Kerensky and the Rada whereby the Provisional Government recognized the Rada as the National Assembly of the Ukraine. Immediately the Rada proceeded to organize a Cabinet of Ministers under the leadership of Vladimir Vinnichenko. Vinnichenko was a man in his early fifties, born of a peasant family in the province of Kiev. He had been expelled from the university at Kiev because of membership in the Ukrainian Revolutionary Party. In 1901 he had escaped from prison in Galicia and had journeyed to Paris. Before the war he had returned illegally to Russia, where he became a leader among the Social Democrats and achieved fame as a novelist and playwright.

When the Bolsheviks came into power the Rada declared the Ukraine a sovereign republic on November 21, 1917. The Red Government immediately declared war and at the same time a Bolshevik revolution took place, with many uprisings throughout Ukrainian territory. The Reds began negotiating with the Rada for the cessation of help to Kornilov and Kaledin. Throughout the remaining months of 1917 the Ukraine was in an unsettled state. During the whole Civil War this unfortunate section was plagued with guerrilla bands who robbed, plundered, and raped where they could.

On January 28, 1918, the Rada, which had been recognized not only by Germany but by France and England as well, again declared the Ukraine a sovereign republic and severed all connection with Red Russia. As the result of recognition by Paris and Berlin and a half-hearted acquiescence by Moscow, the Ukraine was allowed to send a separate peace delegation to the conference at Brest-Litovsk. There, on February 9th, the Central Powers, Turkey, and Bulgaria signed a treaty recognizing the Ukraine as a sovereign and independent nation. The new state set about immediately to organize an army. General Simon Petlura was appointed Minister of War. General Petlura was the son of a Cossack family in the province of Chernikov. He had graduated from the Gymnasium and had become a member of the Ukrainian Revolutionary Party about 1900. The university had expelled him and he became a statistical official of the Zemstvo organization in Poltava. Later he had served as an editor on the *Ukrainskaya Zhyzn,* a periodical published in Moscow. At the beginning of the war he had been deported, but after the Revolution broke he appeared again in Kiev as one of the leaders of the Right Wing of the Ukrainian Social Democratic Party. Among his friends and associates he was known as a modest, kindly, and loyal man. His wife, a comparatively young woman, accompanied him on his various campaigns. The family usually lived in a railway van. Petlura had a high reputation for valor in battle, often leading his troops, rifle in hand. During his campaigns and afterward, his name was associated with bloody pogroms which were perpetrated in several sections of the Ukraine. His enemies claimed that he was responsible, while his friends maintained that he was the object of slander. In the end the Jewish killings were to cost Petlura his life.

Moscow, fearing the power of the new state and acting in the name of the Rada's rival, the new Ukrainian Soviet Republic which had been proclaimed on December 17, 1917, at Kharkov, unleashed the Red Army which wrested Kiev from Petlura on February 8, 1918. Petlura rallied and with the help of German bayonets recaptured Kiev on February 28th.

Rada representatives had invited the Central Powers to help them drive out the Bolsheviks. To this end they had concluded a treaty with both Germany and Austria by the terms of which material resources were handed over in return for recognition of Ukrainian independence.

After Brest-Litovsk, Germany immediately started several divisions marching eastward across the Ukrainian steppes. Rich grain lands were occupied with alacrity, her forces penetrating to Kharkov, which they entered on Palm Sunday, 1918, amid the rejoicing of many sections of the population. The townspeople rubbed their eyes as they beheld the lean and hardened soldiers. Neither the men nor their horses had had sufficient food, but they were clean, silent, and disciplined. Soldiers obeyed orders without comment. German organization was at its best. Regiments, companies, and platoons led by scouts with maps marched away to their billets on side streets as if they were going to familiar barracks in a garrison town. Upon people accustomed to the slackness of revolutionary soldiers the furbished accouterments and businesslike demeanor of the field-gray companies made a sharp and pleasant impression.

Underwood & Underwood

Professor Hrushevsky, "Father of the Ukraine," addressing Ukrainian troops

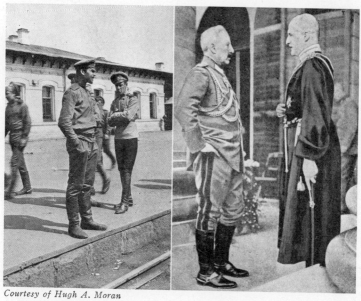

Courtesy of Hugh A. Moran

Soldiers leaving the front

Hetman Skoropadsky talking with the Kaiser

Action front!

Homeless

Germany had every reason to wish for a dismembered Russia and for an independent Ukraine under German hegemony. Outposts were extended to Belgorod and Chuguyev and the Crimea were placed under German control. Odessa was occupied on March 13, 1918, Nikolayev on the 17th, Kherson and the Crimea in April. The Bolsheviks offered no resistance but shifted their forces eastward, reinforcing the front opposed to the Don Cossacks and the Volunteer Army. In the Ukraine proper the Central Rada remained for a time under German protection.

Food was a major objective for the German Army of Occupation. They had entered the Ukraine upon the invitation of a Socialist Government, but they were determined to prevent it from carrying out radical land reforms, for to do so would break up large estates and, at least temporarily, diminish the grain supply and increase the difficulty of securing foodstuffs. Although the Germans controlled only large towns and the principal railroad lines, they exported enormous quantities of food to Germany. A parcel-post system was organized, each soldier being obliged to send half a pood (eighteen pounds, avoirdupois) of food, which included flour, salt, sausages, sugar, and different grains, for in these months millions of hungry mouths in the Fatherland were crying for sustenance. Requisitioning began immediately of every kind of war material.

Count von Eichhorn, in command of the German Army of Occupation, had large landed interests in the Ukraine, having married the Countess Durnovo, one of the richest landholders of the province. His wife's sister was married to Paul Skoropadsky, a Russian general of Ukrainian origin and sympathies, who was the largest proprietor in the occupied territory. Throughout the period of German occupation the large landholders were favored.

Each day the tension between the Rada Government and the German Army of Occupation increased. Finally the Germans overthrew the government, and on April 28th established a military dictatorship under Hetman Skoropadsky.

Skoropadsky was a descendant of Ukrainian Hetmans. He had been trained in the Czar's page corps and had served in the old army during the Russo-Japanese War in the same division with General Baron Wrangel, who later was to take so prominent a part in the fortunes of the White forces in South Russia. When the Great War came, Skoropadsky was a colonel of horse guards, rising rapidly to the rank of major general, with Wrangel as his chief-of-staff.

By May 1st, the Germans had taken possession of Sebastopol and a portion of the Black Sea Fleet, and by May 8th they had penetrated as far eastward as Rostov-on-Don. So strange are the fortunes of armed conflict that the Ukrainians, who, a few months previously, had been in a death grapple with the Germans, now welcomed them as deliverers from the Red power at Moscow!

The new government under Skoropadsky was built by capitalizing discontent among large landed proprietors and smaller peasant farmers, the *kliboroby*. To both factions the proposed agrarian reforms meant impoverishment and confiscation of ancestral acres. The Germans agreed that these landholding groups should call together a grand assembly of *kliboroby* who should elect a Hetman to replace the Socialist Government. Over nine thousand of the *kliboroby* came together, and, on April 28, 1918, elected General Skoropadsky as Hetman of the Ukraine. A group at the conference protested against the election and broke away, forming the Spilka, or separate assembly. The Germans carried forward their plans by immediately recognizing the dictator, proclaiming that they would not only support him but would suppress any measures calculated to overthrow his government. Thereupon they dispersed the Spilka and arrested some of its members. As a consequence of these events, the Socialist Government, headed by Hrushevsky, Vinnichenko, and Petlura, fled for refuge to the provinces or across the frontier into Galicia and Rumania.

After the overthrow of the Central Rada, all Ukrainian parties, even the moderate National Democrats, turned against the Germans and Skoropadsky. General Petlura, who worked for the downfall of Skoropadsky's régime, was imprisoned but was later released. At first the Hetman approached Ukrainian liberals for support, offering them posts in his Cabinet. Upon their refusal he was compelled to organize a Cabinet of wealthy Russians, Poles, Jews, and conservative Ukrainians. Some of these men were sincerely interested in organizing a Ukrainian state, others had Russian sympathies.

Hetman Skoropadsky many times gave public assurance that he had no desire to join Red Russia, and began promoting Ukrainian learning and culture. He was well meaning, but lacked political intelligence to foresee the impossibility of building an autonomous Ukraine with the help of Russian aristocrats. Dreaming of an hereditary Hetmanate while the powder smoke of the Russian Revolution was still in the nostrils of agitated peasants awakening them to visions of a new day, Skoropadsky tried to restore the estates of the big landowners. Punitive detachments terrorized the countryside, shooting peasants and overcrowding the jails.

Finally Skoropadsky succeeded in persuading a few Ukrainians into his Cabinet, until, by September, 1918, the entire body was composed of Ukrainians of National Democratic and conservative sympathies. Gradually moderate Ukrainians became reconciled with the Hetman, but radicals remained aloof.

Let us now shift our gaze to events which occurred on the Don and in the adjacent regions, the Kuban and the Terek; and to momentous happenings in Red Russia which affected the White forces in the South. East of the Ukraine, the Germans had found a sympathizer in General Krasnov, elected Ataman by the *Krug* of the Don Cossacks, as successor to Kaledin, on May 16, 1918. The Cossacks preferred the Germans to the Bolsheviks. Krasnov wheedled a large amount of supplies from the German command, who were pleased to have an ally in the field against the Reds. The Volunteer Army under General Denikin, on the contrary, persisted in its loyalty to the Allies and its antagonism to Germany. True, it received part of the munitions obtained by Krasnov from the Germans, yet the temper of the Volunteers remained pro-Ally. Alexeyev and Denikin, in spite of the fact that no substantial aid had come from England and France, refused for patriotic reasons to coöperate with the Germans, deciding not to proceed to the Don, where they would embarrass Krasnov, but to return once more to the Kuban.

The Volunteer Army, after the Peace of Brest-Litovsk, was regrouped and reinforced. Denikin and his staff remained at Metchetinskaya while Alexeyev proceeded to Novocherkassk to form new regiments and accumulate supplies necessary for a second campaign in the Kuban.

Not only did the Germans aid General Krasnov in the summer and fall of 1919; they also created the Astrakhan Volunteer Army. Planes were sent to equip four escadrilles and money to care for 7,000 men and officers. This small force was a thoroughgoing monarchist organization. They flew the Romanov flag, printed millions of the old Czarist rubles, and wore on their left sleeves the Romanov black, orange, and white, while the Volunteers wore the red, blue, and white chevron. This army operated more or less independently as a Partisan force until finally absorbed in January of 1919 by the Don Cossack forces.

One of the most daring exploits of the Civil War occurred in June when Colonel Drozdovsky, with 2,000 officers and men, eight guns, ammunition, and two armored cars, marched straight across South Russia from the Rumanian front and arrived at Metchetinskaya. At any moment during his journey he might have encountered hostile Ukrainian troops, Red commands, or brigands.

Events affecting the Soviets were occurring as important at the time to the White forces in South Russia under General Krasnov and General Denikin as victories upon the battlefield—the Socialist-Revolutionary uprisings in the summer of 1918. These distractions to the Red Government

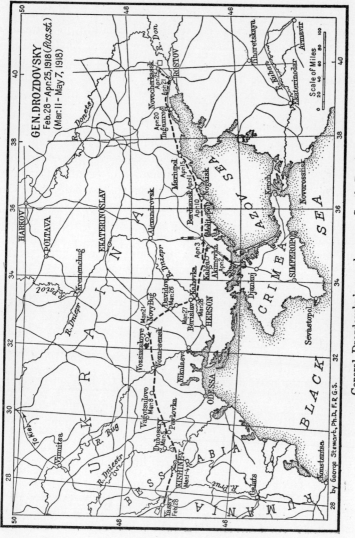

General Drozdovsky's march across South Russia.

afforded substantial aid to Admiral Kolchak, Denikin, anti-Bolshevik leaders throughout Siberia, and the Czechoslovak Legionnaires. Powerful elements which had suffered and planned for the Revolution had seen the new Red power disregarding their wishes, whereupon they became active in opposition. The most important group opposed to the Bolsheviks were the Socialist-Revolutionaries, largely composed of members from the villages who resented the claim of the Bolsheviks that the land belonged now to the state. Two principal tenets distinguished their party—an agrarian policy placing land in possession of the peasant, and terrorism. It was one of their number, Kalyayev, who assassinated Grand Duke Sergius in Moscow in 1905.

Although the left Socialist-Revolutionaries had continued to work with the Bolsheviks for some time they were suspected and soon broke away altogether, due to their wrath at the conclusion of the Treaty of Brest-Litovsk. After various episodes in which they attempted to blow up depots of munitions and supplies, railway bridges and trains, one of their number, Blumkin, assassinated Count Mirbach, the German ambassador to Red Russia, on July 6, 1918, with the idea of disrupting the precarious peace established at Brest-Litovsk. Immediately Left Wing Socialist-Revolutionaries started a rising and seized control of the telegraph agencies. Red leaders rallied and, with the aid of Vatsetis, a Czarist officer in command of a Lettish regiment, quickly put down the insurrection on July 7th. As a result, two hundred Socialist-Revolutionaries were executed, among whom were such seasoned revolutionaries as Alexandrovich, Katz-Kamkov, and Marie Spiridinova, one of the most famous women among the opponents of Czardom. Germany was desperately involved on the Western Front and made no reprisals for the murder of Count Mirbach. Dr. Karl Hefferich, a former Vice Chancellor, was sent immediately as ambassador.

The Socialist-Revolutionaries now attempted to arouse the population to rebellion. The Left Wing group had many sympathizers in the provinces and many high officers at the front.

A small revolt took place in the Bolshevik ranks when Muraviev, chief of the Red Army against the Czechs, dispatched a telegram on July 11, 1918, directly to the German Government, declaring war, and ordered an advance on Moscow. This rebellion was ended by the shooting of Muraviev by a Red agent sent to watch his movements. Vatsetis, who had won glory in the Moscow affair, was immediately appointed to take his place.

Savinkov, with a small but resolute group of Right Wing Socialist-Revolutionaries, took Yaroslavl, located one hundred and eighty miles north of Moscow on the railway leading to Vologda and Archangel, on July 5th. However, a company of German prisoners aided the Reds and on July 21st the Socialist-Revolutionaries surrendered to the Germans, who, in spite of their pledged word, handed them over to the Reds. Savinkov escaped and worked under cover, making a trip abroad.

Boris Victorovitch Savinkov was typical of many revolutionists. He was born in Warsaw in 1879, the son of a judge, a man of high intelligence and great will power. For nearly two decades he had been an influential member of the Socialist-Revolutionaries and had risen until he was one of the five members of their "Militant Organization" which carried out numerous terrorist plots. He aided in the murder of Von Plehve, the Minister of the Interior, and of Grand Duke Sergius. His *Memoirs of a Terrorist* give a clear picture of the desperate group of men and women whose assassinations struck fear into the hearts of all the higher nobility of Russia for many years. With Savinkov were associated nearly all the prominent terrorists of modern times: Kalyayev, Sazonov, Gershuni, Karpovitch, Suliatitsky, and Schweizer, many of whom died for the cause they had espoused. For years he worked hand in hand with the famous Azev, a man of iron nerves and phenomenal daring. Azev sold terrorist secrets to the police and sold police secrets to

the terrorists. Savinkov helped in finally revealing the true
character of the man, a twentieth-century Judas of appalling
proportions. Becoming discouraged at the slow process of
social betterment in Russia he had withdrawn from participation in the party's activities and published a novel, *The
White Horse,* which gave evidence of his despair over the
position of the intelligentsia in Russia. When the war broke
out in 1914 he threw in his influence on the side of those
carrying on the conflict. For a time he served as a private in
the French Army. When the Revolution broke out he returned to Russia and aided Kerensky, becoming Vice Minister for War in the second Coalition Government of 1917.
Later he was involved in Kornilov's short-lived rebellion.
When the Bolsheviks swung into power he quickly alienated
himself from the Red Government.

Following the incidents at Yaroslavl and Moscow in July
of 1918, Savinkov went abroad and wrote *The Black Horse.*
Upon his return to Russia he was arrested by the Cheka and
sentenced to ten years' imprisonment. He made an announcement that he had repented of his opposition to the Soviets,
but as this failed to secure his release he committed suicide
in 1925.

Denikin's forces rejoiced at the news of any disorders
within the Soviet frontiers, as any preoccupation within
Red circles relieved the pressure upon their fronts.

The White soldiers on the Don were also aided by the embarrassment which came to the Reds through the murder in
Kiev on July 30th of Field Marshal von Eichhorn, commanding officer of the German forces in the Ukraine, and
his adjutant, Captain von Dressler, by Boris Danskoi, a
youthful Left Socialist-Revolutionary. General Count Kirch-
bach was immediately sent to take charge as Eichhorn's
successor. Socialist-Revolutionaries are also alleged to have
caused a great explosion in Kiev in which seven hundred
German soldiers were killed. The Socialist-Revolutionaries
hoped to embroil the Reds with Germany.

Taking advantage of Ukrainian separatism, strikes were

fomented in the Ukraine throughout July, two hundred thousand men participating in an action directed against Hetman Skoropadsky and the Germans. Strikers clamored for the restoration of constitutional rights, convocation of a Constituent Assembly, and cessation of food shipments to Germany. They scored in bitterest terms the German punitive expeditions which were sent against the rebelling peasantry. One of their placards read:

The enemy is despoiling us and stealing our bread in order to continue fighting. All this delays the revolution in the west. Comrades, we have put up with the Kaiser's dogs long enough. Cease railway traffic and thereby help thousands of armed peasants to overrun the towns at a given moment.

An attempt was made on the life of the Railway Minister, and M. Stelshenko, former Minister of Education, was murdered at Poltava.

That Germany was despoiling the Ukraine was obvious. Special days were set aside for gathering iron, lead, copper, and other metals which the hungry maw of war devoured without ceasing.

Following the Socialist-Revolutionary uprisings the Bolsheviks instituted the Red Terror in earnest, employing the Cheka, which had been instituted by Lenin on December 20, 1917, as a special arm of the government against counter-revolution. Its chief, Felix Dzerzhinsky, a tall, sinister-looking man with an extraordinary capacity for work, set about "liquidating" all enemies of the Bolshevik régime. Although some hundreds had been executed during the winter of 1917-18, after August 3d, when Fanny Kaplan, a Socialist-Revolutionary, attempted the assassination of Lenin, the numbers began running into the thousands. A mass Red Terror was officially instituted by the All-Russian Central Executive Committee on September 2d. The total killed, while exaggerated by many writers, nevertheless ran in the neighborhood of seventy thousand souls officially executed during the years 1918-19, while local units of the Cheka on their own authority put to death thousands of others. Denikin's commission of investigation reported that one million seven hundred thousand had been killed by the Cheka in South Russia alone, a number probably greatly exaggerated. It may be said in palliation of the White Terror instituted by the counter-revolutionaries that their atrocities and killings were mainly of individuals or units acting on their own authority. The numbers thus killed by the Whites in South Russia were small in comparison to the slaughters of the Cheka. Factional feeling ran deeply. The smell of blood was in the nostrils of the Russian people, and shooting, hanging, stabbing, garroting, and even flaying became daily occurrences. In these mad months victims were horribly mutilated and many reports indicate that some were buried alive.

The Red Government was also hindered from releasing its full strength against the Don because of trouble on the agricultural front. During these summer weeks of 1918, had there been unity among the peasants, a general uprising might have occurred against the Soviet Government, due to discontent over the distribution of land. The Soviet Government had made no distinction whatever between estates seized from the landlords, the farms belonging to some six million small owners who had acquired their acres after the reforms of Stolypin, and the lands owned by the village communes. The lands within each county were reallotted on a numerical basis, and as the density of population differed from county to county great inequalities resulted. In order to prevent an uprising the Soviet Government by a clever device instigated social divisions and warfare within the peasant villages by the organization of Committees of the Poor. Thus the *kulaki* and the *seredniaki,* the rich and the less well-to-do peasants, were set over against the *bedniaki* or very poor peasants who had only land, with little or no cattle, implements, seed grain, and other means of production. Authority in the villages was delegated to these committees, who kept watch over the well-to-do groups and prevented them from hiding grain from the government, having been empowered by Moscow to seize surplus grain or cattle. Although the Committees of the Poor gave the Bolsheviks a hold on every village, their abuse of power slowed up and disorganized the agricultural life of the country.

The majority of the people, although hostile to a return of Czarism, were not in favor of the Red régime, as was indicated in the election of delegates to the Constituent Assembly. Only the city proletariat can be said to have espoused the cause with enthusiasm. Lenin and his group were faced with constant crises.

Food was an all important matter in those days. Various schemes were put in force for feeding the town population which were in reality requisitioning and recognized as such by the peasantry. Plantings fell off and the farmers hid their food until the resistance became so strong that expeditions in the nature of foraging parties were necessary to feed the hungry townspeople.

Industry declined in spite of all efforts to keep up production. The workers were slack, thousands did not report at factories and mines. Incessant demands for more pay and benefits compelled Lenin to conscript workers as he conscripted soldiers. The rapid depreciation of the ruble, the demands for more wages, necessitating more printing of paper money, became a vicious economic circle which further inflated Soviet exchange. The central administration was fighting a war on two fronts, the economic and the military, and, on the whole, showing more energy and intelligence than the disunited White leadership.

Dissensions among Red leaders threatened to break the unity of their command through the summer of 1918, a fact which was of no little aid to the armed forces of South Russia. It was at this period that the opposition of Stalin and Trotsky became acute, a difference of opinion which, after some years, ended in the exile of the latter. Stalin had been dispatched to the Volga as Controller of Food Supplies, and while there turned his energies to the organization of Tsaritsin and the surrounding territory which was threatened by the Cossack forces. His activities soon in-volved military matters. He built up a circle of officers under his influence who acted independently of Trotsky, the com-mander-in-chief. This inevitably led to conflict between Stalin and Trotsky, with Lenin in Moscow as arbiter. Voro-shilov and Minin associated themselves with Stalin in his opposition to Trotsky. Stalin, during this period, rendered invaluable aid in securing grain for Moscow and the cities of the north, and with the use of the Cheka shot without mercy all opponents of the Red régime.

The matter in dispute between Trotsky and Stalin was Trotsky's employment of Czarist officers as "experts," to which Stalin objected as opposed to the spirit of a proletarian Revolution. Trotsky insisted they were necessary and would brook no interference with his high command. In the end he won his point. The issue was so sharp that, on October 4th, Trotsky telegraphed Lenin:

I insist categorically on Stalin's recall. The Tsaritsin front is in a bad way, despite the abundance of troops. Voroshilov can command a regiment but not an army of fifty thousand soldiers. Nevertheless, I leave him in command of the Tenth Tsaritsin Army on condition that he submit to the commander of the south-ern front, Sytin. Until now the men in Tsaritsin have not even sent reports of operations to Kozlov (general headquarters). I made them undertake to send in reports of operations and recon-noitering twice a day. If this is not done by to-morrow, I will com-mit Voroshilov and Minin to trial and announce it in an order to the army. So long as Stalin and Minin remain in Tsaritsin, they are endowed, in accord with the constitution of the revolutionary war council, only with the rights of members of the war council of the Tenth Army. There is only a short time left for an offensive before the roads become impassable for infantry or cavalry. Without coördinating operations with Tsaritsin no serious action is possible. There is no time for diplomatic negotiations. "Tsarit-sin" must either submit or get out of the way. We have a colossal superiority of forces but complete anarchy at the top. With this one can cope in twenty-four hours on condition that you lend your firm and decisive support. In any event, this is the only way out that I can see.

Lenin temporized in this quarrel in order to save the services of both his valuable lieutenants and perhaps to let each checkmate the dangerous and rising power of the other. Stalin and his collaborators were sent to the Ukrainian front at Kharkov, where they pursued the same policy of interference with Trotsky's command.

Difference of opinion between Trotsky and Stalin flared up throughout the Civil War, aggravated by a growing personal dislike. Trotsky was brilliant, impulsive, and not averse to expressing himself. Stalin was methodical and kept in the background biding his time, which came years later in 1929, when, after a year's banishment to Siberia, Trotsky was exiled to Turkey, the only Western nation which would receive him at the time. The White commanders knew of these terrific tensions among the Bolsheviks, but so adroit was Lenin in smoothing out difficulties that at no time did they prove of such importance as to substantially aid the counter-revolution.

While the Red Government was dealing with revolts, the Germans, the peasants, and the quarrels between various officials, Denikin steadily groomed his growing army.

In October the Volunteer Army began to move southward, following the railway lines. It now numbered twelve thousand men, and as it marched its ranks were augmented by captured Bolsheviks, who begged to be enlisted. Some doubtless joined from a sincere change of heart, but many joined the Whites through fear or in order to secure food and clothing.

General Alexeyev was worried regarding the relations between Krasnov and Denikin, who had spoken sharp words regarding supplies the Cossack leader was receiving from the Germans. Alexeyev no more than Denikin approved of the "Germanophile" policy pursued by Krasnov, but realized the expediency of the measure under the circumstances. To General Alexeyev the Don was a more favorable base of operations than the Kuban, an opinion which he strongly urged upon Denikin, who favored a campaign into that region. In a letter to Denikin, Alexeyev set forth his views:

The relations between the command of the Volunteer Army and General Krasnov have reached the highest point of exasperation, owing less to the essence of the question than to the tone and character of the telegrams and notes exchanged, and, indeed, of the whole intercourse. I must frankly say that this renders all work impossible, for we depend, as yet, in many respects on the Don. . . .

If I do not receive any money (from the Allies), the only course left us will be to return to the Don, for you know well enough that there is no hope of obtaining anything on the Kuban. Owing to our relations with General Krasnov, however, I do not know how I shall manage to ensure the existence of the Army for this month (I want five million rubles) and in this month we shall be able *to reach the Volga*. This I consider *indispensable*, for it is only there that I can hope to obtain further means for maintaining the Army. If we remain in that rotten hole—the Kuban—we shall be obliged, irrevocably, to raise the question of liquidating the Army in two or three weeks. . . .

My personal conclusion is that our further advance on the Kuban may be the cause of our ruin. Circumstances clearly indicate that we ought to march on the Volga, where the Bolsheviks, acting on the orders and with the coöperation of the Germans, will evidently concentrate all their efforts in defeating the Czechoslovaks and thus preventing the formation of an Eastern front. Information has reached us that the Germans will insist on the Czechoslovaks being delivered into their hands if they are defeated. The center of events which are decisive for the fate of Russia will now be in the East. We must not be late in leaving the Kuban and appearing at the principal theatre of the war.

But Alexeyev's observations left General Denikin unconvinced.

Torgovaya, Kavkazskaya, Tikhoretskaya, and Stavropol were taken by the Whites, and on August 15th, after a three-day battle, Ekaterinodar. On the following day, General Denikin, with Filiminov, Ataman of the Kuban Cossacks, and the members of the Kuban Government followed by the Volunteer Army, entered the town in a victorious parade amid the demonstrations of the populace. Two days later

General Alexeyev reviewed the troops in Ekaterinodar and thanked them for their work.

General Lukomsky was named by Denikin, on August 15th, assistant commander-in-chief of the Volunteer Army, thereby associating closely with headquarters an officer of wide experience who was taken from the post of chief-of-staff.

Notwithstanding his recent victories, Denikin was faced again with the recurrent problem of separatism on the part of the Ataman and Government of the Kuban. They looked forward to a federation of liberated autonomous provinces embracing the Terek, the Kuban, the Don, and certain sections of the Caucasus. Their minds were turned toward peace. As soon as Ekaterinodar was taken by the Volunteer Army the Kuban Cossacks began to assert their claims for full jurisdiction over all affairs in their territory and an entirely independent fighting force, much to the embarrassment of the commander of the Volunteer Army, who held that only a united force could bring victory. Denikin, from the beginning, looked upon the Cossacks with suspicion. He feared their loyalty to the cause of uniting Russia within frontiers previous to Brest-Litovsk.

To add to its complications, the Volunteer Army was dependent upon the Cossacks for food. Although Denikin was opposed to Krasnov's relationship with the German forces of occupation, he was compelled to maintain cordial relations with the Don Cossack leader.

The coming meeting of the *Krug* of the Don, composed of representatives from all the *stanitzas,* was regarded with mingled hope and fear by Alexeyev and Denikin. If this assembly should form a government subordinate to General Alexeyev, thus giving him complete command over the troops of the Don and the Volunteer Army, great things might result. If they set up an independent organization, the Kuban might follow in their footsteps. General Lukomsky was sent to Novocherkassk to be present when the *Krug* convened and to exercise his powers of persuasion.

The *Krug* was opened on August 31st by General Krasnov, who explained his conciliatory policy toward the Germans in the Ukraine. "I am obliged to accept shells and cartridges from the Germans," he admitted, "but I wash them in the clear waters of the silent Don."

General Afrikan Petrovich Bogayevsky was the only formidable rival of General Krasnov for the post of Ataman. At a closed session of the *Krug,* Bogayevsky read a telegram which he had received from German headquarters in Rostov, declaring that the German command would withhold all support in the way of shells and ammunition should any other than Krasnov be chosen. Krasnov was elected, no other course being possible under the circumstances.

General Alexeyev was active on the Kuban steppe at the time, and nearly all officers expected him to take supreme command of all counter-revolutionary forces during a projected trip to Siberia, but illness overtook him and he died on October 8, 1918. Upon his death, General Denikin assumed the complete leadership in the South for the non-Cossack contingents, with the title of commander-in-chief of the Volunteer Army, taking charge of financial and political affairs as well as the conduct of the army in the field. With Alexeyev dead and Denikin forced by the necessity for constant and immediate decisions due to pressure by the Red Army without, and reactionary influences among many of his officers overbalancing his own liberal views, there quickly came into being a simple dictatorship of the sword.

Month after month the barbarity of the Civil War increased. The psychology of revolution was at work. All standards of decency and fair play, all rules of civilized warfare were abandoned. Drunkenness and debauchery flourished among officers and men of both armies, and endless bickering about authority, promotions, and rewards.

Lack of ammunition and the extreme fatigue of the troops lessened what, under more favorable circumstances, could have been sweeping victories. The men were indifferently fed and clothed and desertions were frequent.

The Red Army now had a single commander, Trotsky. He was a tyro as far as military experience went, but when he had been made chief of the Military Revolutionary Committee in June of 1918, he drew to the Red Army some 30,000 officers of the old Imperial forces, who joined from fear of reprisals, as a means of finding bread, to protect their families, or from a sincere desire to serve the new order. A common practice was to hold families of former Czarist officers as hostages to insure their adherence to the Red cause. The Red high command was composed almost exclusively of such officers, which included Colonel S. S. Kamenev, who had served on the Czar's general staff. New chiefs of marked ability developed, among them Tukhachevsky and Budenny, the latter a cavalry commander of unusual skill. Although conscription had been disappointing to the Kremlin and had raised only half of the number demanded, nevertheless in the fall of 1918 the Red Army was to number 400,000 men. Trotsky organized a train, which was his headquarters for over three years, in which he carried technicians, staff officers, and teachers of Communist theory from front to front with amazing mobility.

The Red Army with one directing mind, ruthless in the use of the death penalty, had an advantage over Denikin, who was compelled to persuade and pacify his loquacious and often inefficient and insolent lieutenants. Both the Red and the White armies were showing signs of the burden of eight months of continual fighting. Although the revolutionary troops had achieved a formidable measure of discipline, were well armed and munitioned, and numbered one hundred thousand in this region, they nevertheless had suffered severely in the ranks, and the high command was rife with accusations of graft, favoritism, and treachery.

Substantial aid was being rendered Denikin by Krasnov's Cossacks, who were pressing against Tsaritsin in the summer and fall of 1918. Because of separatist tendencies and rapid changes in public opinion, Denikin was never wholly certain as to the extent upon which he could depend upon the Cossacks. But then and later the Don Cossacks rendered him invaluable support.

The liberation of Northern Caucasia was an immediate necessity for Denikin. At this time the Volunteer Army was composed of some thirty-five thousand men and about eighty guns. With the exception of two infantry regiments and the cavalry, made up of Kuban Cossacks and Circassians, nearly all the troops were former officers who served in the ranks.

General Wrangel was chosen by Denikin as one of the leaders to carry out· this operation. Wrangel was tall, thin, with sparse hair and cold, gray-blue eyes; an aristocrat by birth, he carried the haughtiness of his class with him. He had graduated as a mining engineer before he entered the army. For twenty years he had been an officer in Cossack regiments whose uniform set off to advantage his commanding figure. His career before he became a White Army leader was a colorful one. In 1916 he had commanded the Czarevitch's own regiment of Nerchinsk Cossacks in a division of Ussurian Cossacks from Eastern Siberia, winning high praise repeatedly for himself and his men in Galicia. At this time Semyonov and Baron Ungern-Sternberg, both of whom distinguished themselves later in the White cause by their ferocity in Siberia, were squadron commanders in his regiment. After having served for a time under Kerensky's régime, Wrangel had become disgusted and retired with his family to the Crimea where he lived during the German occupation. When he presented himself to General Denikin and his chief-of-staff, General Romanovsky, they gave him the rank of lieutenant general, placing him in command of a division in contact with the Reds in the Maikop district.

The Terek through which the Northern Caucasian campaign was waged was a rich farming district suffering heavily from Red reprisals and general lawlessness. General Wrangel, with General Pokrovsky's cavalry division on his left, was to drive the Reds eastward across the Urup, a branch of the Kuban River. Wrangel was a gifted cavalry leader and among the most resourceful and daring commanders in any

White Army. After sanguinary fighting in September, in which no quarter was given on either side and few prisoners taken, White troops entered Mikhailovskaya on October 2, 1918, where they were jubilantly greeted by the populace. When General Wrangel came out of church after mass he was greeted by a delegation of Circassian fathers flying a green Mohammedan flag, offering their sons for service against the Bolsheviks and complaining of atrocities in their villages. Wrangel handed over to them a number of prisoners to take home for trial, whom the Circassians promptly slaughtered as soon as the general was out of sight.

Pillaging became the order of the day. Some commanders favored and joined in the practice. After futile attempts to discourage such robbery by hangings and shootings, Wrangel was compelled to acquiesce, requiring equal division of the spoils among the soldiers. The baggage trains of captured troops of both sides in this grisly warfare yielded not only cash, but tobacco, rugs, pianos, silverware, jewelry, books, clothing, and every article which was movable and thought to have value. The troops were destitute, and in the confused state of the commissariat forced requisitions afforded the easiest and in most cases the only available reëquipment and forage supplies. Many White officers saw the disastrous results of this policy of license but were powerless to stop it.

Maneuvering eastward against the Reds, the Whites crossed the River Urup on October 19, 1918, and in a hot fight took three thousand prisoners and a quantity of machine guns, resulting in the evacuation by the Bolsheviks of the whole of the left bank of the Kuban.

Wrangel's troops were so depleted that he decided, on reaching the village of Uspenskaya, to reinforce them with prisoners, whereupon he lined up three hundred and seventy officers and noncommissioned officers among the Red prisoners and ordered them shot. Telling the remaining prisoners that they also deserved death, he gave them a chance to rehabilitate themselves by fighting under his pennon. The battalion thus formed became one of the best in General Denikin's army.

An advance, with bitter fighting all the way, was now pushed toward Stavropol, which was entered on November 2d amid the hysterical joy of the populace, who embraced the troops and loaded them with wine, cigarettes, and even money. The town had gone through an inferno. The Reds had shot their own commander and pillaged, murdered, and raped as they pleased. Such stories inflamed the White troops, whose Circassian soldiers the next day broke into a hospital and massacred seventy of the Bolshevik wounded! The governor of the prison also executed many prisoners before the commander heard of the atrocity and arrested him.

Denikin was anxious regarding the forthcoming meeting of the Kuban Rada. The Kuban Cossacks constituted a special problem to Alexeyev, Kornilov, Denikin, and later to Wrangel. The Kuban region is a country between the Sea of Azov, the Black Sea, and the Caucasus. Formerly it was a Tartar pasture land. In 1775 the stronghold of the Ukrainian Cossacks on the lower Dnieper, Zaproghian Sitch, was destroyed by Catherine the Great and some twenty thousand Zaproghians had the alternative of disbanding or migrating to the Kuban region. They chose the latter and, dispossessing the Tartars, settled on the shores of the Kuban River. Through the years large numbers of Ukrainians joined their fellow countrymen. At the time of the Revolution nearly three million Kuban Cossacks lived in this area, constituting about forty per cent of the population as rich or middle landowners. After the Revolution they followed the example of the Ukraine and organized the Kuban Republic to which they joined the adjacent provinces which contained population of Ukrainian stock—Stavropol and the Black Sea Maritime Province. In the spring of 1918 they proclaimed their full independence of Russia and a movement under the leadership of Nicholas Ryabovil was organized to unite the Kuban and the Ukraine. However, conditions in the Ukraine became so turbulent that the Kuban Rada decided to remain aloof, giving a qualified allegiance to the White establishment in the south.

The Rada of the land of Kuban convened on November 14, 1918, at which time General Denikin addressed it in stirring language, appealing for unity in the name of Russia's salvation. His speech laid down the principles which governed his action as chief of the armed forces of South Russia:

In February, realizing the impossibility of further remaining and carrying on the struggle on the Don, the Volunteer Army, under the command of General Kornilov, moved on toward the Kuban. From that time on, the fate of the Army has been closely linked to that of the Kuban Cossacks by comradeship in battle, by the hardships and sufferings they had to undergo in common, by the graves of thousands of our brothers-in-arms, and by the triumph of our military victories.

The Volunteers marched on, in frost and heat, enduring the most terrible privations, perishing by thousands . . . moved by no selfish motives or impulses; a wooden cross or the life of a cripple was the lot that awaited most of them.

One sacred innermost thought, one vivid hope and desire inspired them all—that of saving Russia. . . .

Is it, then, possible for the Kuban Cossacks to be at rest and settle down to their home affairs? No!

It is time to cease all quarrelling, intrigue and conflict about precedency! Everything for the struggle with Bolshevism. It must be annihilated. Russia must be free—or your happiness and welfare will be but a toy in the hands of her enemies at home and abroad.

The Volunteer Army, in whose ranks many Cossacks of the Kuban gallantly fight, has not come here for conquest, but as a deliverer. . . .

The rancour and wrath of our enemies grow in proportion to the power and military successes of the Volunteer Army, and the number of our friends increase. To my great satisfaction, I must state that all over the Kuban the Army has met, and meets, amidst the brave, kind and courteous Cossacks—kindred to us in blood and spirit—with the most cordial and heartfelt welcome and hospitality. Lately, however, a wide agitation is being carried on, partly by traitors in foreign pay, and partly by people who are greedy of power, and not over-fastidious as to the ways and means of attaining it. They are trying to bring discord into the ranks of the Army—between the Kuban Cossacks and the

Volunteers especially. They wish to disorganize the Army and bring it back to the pitiful state in which it was in 1917. Those are the people who bowed humbly before the Bolsheviks, who hid underground or took shelter behind the bayonets of the Volunteer Army. . . . We must keep together in the cruel and bloody struggle, to which there is as yet no end. . . .

There must be no Volunteer, Don, Kuban, Siberian Army. There must be one Russian Army, one front and one Command, invested with full authority, and only responsible before the Russian Nation and its future Supreme and Lawful Authority. . . .

I believe and profess that the great Russian nation, when it recovers and throws off the evil charm of Bolshevism, will once more become a terrible force, and will never forget either those who disinterestedly and lovingly upheld it in its hour of need, or those who cruelly and selfishly sapped its very foundations and drove it into the abyss of anarchy. . . .

. . . The union of all the new State formations in Russia, and of all Russians who understand and care for the interests of the State, is all the more possible because the Volunteer Army has no reactionary aims in view, and does not decide beforehand what the future form of the state in Russia shall be, nor even in what way the Russian nation shall declare its will.

We are told that we must hoist the banner of the party to which we belong. But is not the Tricolor Flag of Great Russia above all party banners or flags? . . . Union is possible, for the Volunteer Army considers it indispensable, at present as well as in the future, to grant the widest autonomy to all the integral parts of Russia, and to respect the rights and privileges, and the order of life of the Cossacks. . . .

. . . Pursuing its Way of the Cross, looking upon itself as the successor of the Russian Army, the Volunteer Army has always, in the darkest and seemingly most hopeless hours of its existence, remained faithful to our Allies, and has never for a moment stained its honour by treachery. . . .

. . . I firmly believe that the "Kraievaia Rada" will have sufficient sense, courage and strength to heal the deep wounds caused to the Cossack people by the fanaticism of the rabble, that it will create a strong authority, in close contact with the Volunteer Army, and will not sever the filial ties which unite it to Great Russia, whole and undivided. I am certain that the "Rada" will not break the fundamental laws of the country, which will be radically revised by the future Legislative Assembly of All Russia, and will not repeat the social experiments which have brought the nation to mutual savage hatred and destitution. . . .

But reason and passion were equally powerless to move the Kuban Cossacks. When the vote came a majority were in favor of independence. Denikin addressed himself to a task which had grown immeasurably more difficult with the possibility of only a qualified assistance from the West.

In addition, the commander-in-chief was tormented with anxiety as to the possible course England would take regarding Caucasian and Cossack separatism. England was anxious to secure a foothold in the Caucasus. The ostensible reason for intervention by the British was the maintenance of order. In reality Britain desired to employ the new Caucasian republics formed after Brest-Litovsk as a barrier against the spread of Communist propaganda in her possessions in Central Asia. The petroleum of Baku was also an enticing prospect.

The Transcaucasian Diet, which had been formed after the first Revolution in 1917, had for a long time been loyal to the idea of "Russia, One and Indivisible." As late as February, 1918, the convention of the Transcaucasian members of the Constituent Assembly had declared its allegiance to the "United Russian Federated Democratic Republic." The Diet had refused to recognize the Treaty of Brest-Litovsk, inasmuch as that convention ceded the province of Kars and the district around Batum to Turkey, deciding to act independently of Russia.

A delegation, headed by one Chkhenkeli, had been sent to Trebizond on March 2, 1918, to treat for a separate peace with the Turks, still flushed with their prowess at Gallipoli and the success of their German Allies in the East and West. The *pourparlers* had lasted many days, until Turkish delegates grew impatient and threw down the gauntlet in the shape of an ultimatum which demanded that the Diet either recognize the Treaty of Brest-Litovsk or declare Transcaucasia separate and independent of Russia. Chkhenkeli had at first recognized the Treaty of Brest-Litovsk, but this created such a furore that the decision was reversed and an independent Federated Transcaucasian Republic was proclaimed on

April 22, 1918. This declaration of independence had released Turkey from any obligation to abide by the terms of the Treaty of Brest-Litovsk and she immediately moved troops farther into the Caucasus and declared the annexation of half of Erivan Province and parts of the provinces of Tiflis and Kutais, her aim being the formation of an independent Moslem republic in Azerbaijan.

Georgians had been discontented with these arrangements and had turned to Germany for help against Turkish aggression. With the advice and consent of Germany they had disposed their military forces at strategic localities on their frontiers, declaring their independence on May 26, 1918, in the presence of German troops. At the demand of the Georgian Government, the Diet had been dissolved and Transcaucasia had been divided between three independent republics—Azerbaijan, Georgia, and Armenia. The Georgians not only claimed and confiscated all the war material on the Caucasian front, but avenged themselves on all Imperial Army officers and White Army sympathizers that fell across their path. At the instigation of the German command, the Georgians had occupied Abkhasia and the district about Sochi in the Black Sea Province, from which region food had been sent in large quantities to Germany and to Batum.

Azerbaijan was composed of Elisavetpol Province and the districts of Zakatalsk and Baku. The population was predominantly Mohammedan, and the new government, headed by Khan Khoisky, was composed of a National Mussulman Council distinctly favorable to Turkish interests. When the Turks occupied Elisavetpol they had assumed nearly all the functions of government for Azerbaijan. Armenia by the end of 1918 was prostrate, the Turks having occupied her entire territory. The British had made efforts to establish themselves at Baku in July, 1918, under the pretext of defending it against the Turks. They were assisted in this enterprise by Colonel Bicherakhov, a soldier of fortune who gathered about him a force of irregulars. But they had soon evacuated the city, under strong Turkish pressure, and retired to Enzeli, farther south on the Caspian, within Persian territory. In November the English reappeared at Baku and this time they stayed a number of months. After some hesitation, the British command took a clear stand in favor of the new republics and against Denikin's dogma of "Russia, One and Indivisible." Then military and political operations so close to the base of the White armies were a constant source of anxiety to Denikin.

The Volunteer Army grew steadily throughout the fall of 1918, but in no such numbers as would counterbalance the mounting strength of the Bolsheviks. Officers and men continued to make their way through Red Russia to the Don. Denikin, following the lead of the Reds, was forced to employ conscription, making use of prisoners to fill his shattered regiments, depleted by constant and bloody fighting. The Volunteer forces were further augmented in November of 1918 by five thousand Terek Cossacks who had refused to remain in their *stanitzas* when it became evident that the Reds would occupy that territory, a feat which was accomplished in January of 1919 when a Red government was set up at Vladikavkaz.

The Armistice on the Western Front was hailed in the Volunteer Army as a turning point in their destinies. Indeed, the cessation of hostilities in the West did profoundly affect affairs in Russia, but not to the extent which the hard-pressed White leaders on the Don had hoped.

In the Ukraine, immediate changes occurred upon the collapse of the Central Powers. German regiments there became imbued with the principles of Bolshevism and mutinied. Skoropadsky dismissed his Ukrainian Cabinet and formed a new one headed by S. N. Gerbel, all the members of which were of the aristocratic class.

Skoropadsky was in touch with the French, who had landed at Odessa shortly after the armistice with Turkey. Paris promised support if the Hetman would engage to federate the Ukraine to a restored Russia. France, who had

absorbed many millions of Russian loans, looked with disfavor upon any move that would dismember Russia. But
any promises Skoropadsky could make were without value,
as he was soon to fall from power. The Hetman's manifesto
regarding federation, which was published on November
18th, brought about an uprising of the Ukrainian small farmers, the *samostiyniky*, headed by General Simon Petlura,
Vladimir Vinnichenko, and several other leaders of Left
Wing parties represented in the Ukrainian Central Rada.
Most of these men had fled when the German-inspired election had made Skoropadsky the Hetman of the Ukraine. They
formed the Ukrainian Directory and were hastening to overthrow Skoropadsky and set up a Socialist People's Republic
of the Ukraine before Allied forces should arrive.

All the disaffected rallied to the new leaders. Small farmers
and tradesmen were dissatisfied with Skoropadsky because
he allowed the large landowners their old rights. The watchword of the uprising, "For land and liberty," appealed to
many who looked forward to a division of the large estates.

German forces immediately began retreating through the
Ukraine and Poland to their homeland. Skoropadsky accompanied them, disguised as a German soldier, and ceased to
exercise any influence in Russian affairs. The German soldiers no longer marched in iron battalions. The discipline
which they had brought with them when they were hailed
as saviors by many on the sidewalks of Kiev and Kharkov
had disappeared. They had lost the war. Their Kaiser had
fled. They now had the same vacuum in their souls which
the Russian soldier felt when his Czar abdicated. In addition,
the seeds of revolution were sprouting in their ranks. No
longer did they march silently, with dreadful precision. Officers knew not when an order would be flung back with an
insolent jest. The German soldier, too, now that his capital
was in revolution, unbuttoned his overcoat, thrust his hands
into his pockets, admired his muddy boots, and determined
to go home.

On December 16th the troops of the Ukrainian Directory

entered Kiev and took possession of the apparatus of administration. Vladimir Vinnichenko was finally made President, and Petlura commander-in-chief of the army. Thus, at the end of 1918, the Hetmanate was replaced by two rival governments: The Ukrainian People's Republic, under the Directory, with headquarters at Kiev, and the Ukrainian Soviet Government at Kharkov. Petlura immediately set about raising an army and in a few weeks had a force of some two hundred thousand poorly equipped men. Vinnichenko and Petlura disagreed sharply on policy; the former advocated *rapprochement* with the Soviets, which the latter as stoutly opposed.

Farther west in Galicia and Ruthenia lived some four million people of Ukrainian stock. Under the Dual Monarchy, those living under Austrian rule enjoyed large liberties, with their own schools, gymnasia, university chairs, press, and theater. They had the privilege of sending their deputies to the Parliament and Diets, with their language in official use. But a half million who lived under Hungary in Ruthenia endured no little oppression and curtailment of their cultural life. During the war the Galicians were on the whole loyal to Austria-Hungary, hoping that if the Central Powers won the Great War they would be given permission, with a section of the Russian Ukraine, to organize a Ukrainian state.

When it had become evident in the fall of 1918 that the Germans and Austrians were losing the war, Emperor Karl sought to satisfy all Austrian national minorities by reorganizing the empire into a federation of racial states in place of racially mixed provinces. On October 8, 1918, Emperor Karl had issued a manifesto empowering Nationalists to organize their own Councils.

On October 18th the Ukrainian peers, deputies, and delegates of parties in Galicia assembled in Lemberg and proclaimed themselves as the Ukrainian National Rada of Galicia, claiming for their territory the whole of the region occupied by Ukrainian-speaking peoples in Austria-Hungary. At the same time they denied the right to any Austrian or Hungarian Minister of Affairs to speak for the Ukrainians at any peace conference.

During the last days of October the Bulgarian and the Austrian armies collapsed, revolution broke out, and Hungary and Bohemia were declared republics. On November 1st the Galician Ukrainian National Rada in Lemberg, with the help of Ukrainian regiments and the population, took over the government of Eastern Galicia and Northern Bukovina and proclaimed the full independence of the West Ukrainian Republic. Dr. Eugen Petruchevich, who had been for many years a member of the Austrian Parliament, was elected President. A civil administration was set up throughout the country which maintained good order and an army was organized which numbered over 150,000 men. At the beginning they had refused to join the Ukraine proper, as they lacked confidence in Hetman Skoropadsky. But when the Directory was formed they immediately entered into negotiations looking toward military coöperation and eventual union.

The whole of South Russia was ranged against the Bolsheviks. But Petlura and Denikin, who could have helped each other, were hostile and soon to be at war. Denikin's forces by hard fighting in the fall of 1918 had driven the Bolsheviks from Novorosiisk and had liberated the Chernomorsky, the Kuban, and the Stavropol provinces, inflicting and receiving heavy losses. The Reds dreaded a retreat into the Astrakhan steppes, which meant starvation. Both sides were fighting for life and neither showed mercy to prisoners.

It was now possible for the Allies to intervene in South Russia. Germany and Turkey no longer barred them from this arena. The eyes of Denikin and his staff turned wistfully toward the West. Had not the Allies stated that they proposed to aid any group in Russia which was antagonistic to Germany? True, the German armies were no more, but might not the Allies aid old comrades-in-arms who were struggling against the new Red power which threatened world revolution and death to the bourgeois nations?

Military missions arrived and negotiations began for assistance, checkmated at every turn by the rival policies of France and England and often rendered impotent by the indecisiveness and preoccupation of Paris and Westminster. The West was weary of bloodshed and such help as did arrive was as much due to the difficulty of slowing down vast war organizations which were in full motion at the time of the Armistice as to any settled policy for the succor of the White armies.

Chapter IV

NORTH RUSSIA: CIVIL WAR AND INTERVENTION; FROM THE TREATY OF BREST-LITOVSK TO THE ARMISTICE

THE effect of the March Revolution of 1917 was the same in North Russia as in other sections of the country. Citizens were at first stunned and then looked hopefully toward the new day. However, when the Bolsheviks seized the Petrograd Soviet and began to establish their control, the same division of opinion took place in Archangel, Murmansk, and outlying regions as occurred throughout Russia.

The region had never been highly industrialized and was therefore measurably free from the radical proletariat which existed in large numbers in Moscow and Petrograd. The population was chiefly interested in lumber, fishing, trapping, and farming, with a small amount of manufacturing at Archangel and the larger towns. A slow-moving type of civilization had developed, off the main current of Russian life. Nevertheless, there were numbers of Socialist-Revolutionaries and men and women of more moderate Socialistic views who had grown discontented with the Kerensky régime. The bourgeoisie, land-owning, professional, and official classes were almost solidly against the Bolsheviks, while the workers, the poorer peasants, and the underprivileged orders of society welcomed the November Revolution.

There was an absence of several psychological factors which strengthened the White movement in the Ukraine, on the Don, and in Siberia. North Russia cherished no nascent nationalism based upon ancient cultural and linguistic differences as in the Ukraine, no long history of semi-independent

military organizations as among the Cossacks, and no incipient notion of autonomy as existed in Siberia. There were,
however, all the elements of class animosity which existed in
the interior of Russia and the same cleavage between landlord and peasant and between rich and poor.

In itself the North Russian region did not offer a sufficient
food supply nor a sufficient area of maneuver to engender
great hope as a rallying ground for a White Army. Neither
were White elements in the population of such number or
quality as to assure the development of a force of fighting
strength capable of dealing with the Red armies Moscow was
creating from the wreckage of the Czar's divisions.

North Russia had one great asset open alike to Germany
and the Allies: a few ice-free harbors on the White Sea.
White officers knew they could count upon the Allies for
some assistance as long as Russian forces remained hostile
to the Central Powers, for the Supreme War Council on
December 22, 1917, had recommended support to all national
troops of Russia who purposed to continue the struggle
against Germany. Large numbers of the North Russian
population were thought to be loyal to the Allied cause and
thus deserving of support.

Neither officers nor ranks in the White contingents raised
in the North were equal in quality to large numbers of those
who fought under Denikin and Kolchak. The cream of the
White forces were fighting on the Don.

Neither did the command of the Russian troops in the
North achieve the freedom of action attained by both Kolchak and Denikin, notwithstanding their dependence in
many respects upon the Allies. The White struggle in the
Russian Far North was really an Allied intervention with
auxiliary Russian White troops, while Kolchak and Denikin
conducted a Russian campaign with Allied assistance. No
serious military leader could expect a conclusive victory in
the North.

The character of the Russian Far North made all military
operations hazardous, especially in the long winter. Lying in

wait for every soldier was the glacial cold. A wounded man, unless quickly rescued, would be slain by the frost. North Russia is a vast, gloomy tundra, covered with forest, penetrated by rivers navigable in summer, and by roads far better known to the natives than to the cartographer. The Murmansk-Petrograd and the Archangel-Vologda railways are separated their entire length. Communication by sea is limited during the winter to a few unfrozen harbors. Penetration inland was compelled to follow either the two railroads or the rivers.

From the Allied point of view, the Russian Revolution which had been hailed in the West as the overthrow of a pro-German court was soon recognized as a prelude to the withdrawal of 12,000,000 troops from the Allied cause, the release of over seventy German divisions from the East, and the appropriation by Germany of the wheat, coal, and iron of the Ukraine and Donetz territories. Kerensky had failed to lead the Russian Army to victory and thus secure its confidence.

The Bolsheviks had from the first proclaimed their intention to seek a general peace. Negotiations with the Central Powers were opened four weeks after the Petrograd Soviet seized power. After a short postponement to afford an opportunity for the Allies to join in their efforts, the Bolsheviks declared that they would seek to achieve a separate peace. The Treaty of Brest-Litovsk threatened the Allies with the breakdown of the blockade of Germany, aside from depriving them of the assistance of the once powerful Russian Army.

Vast quantities of munitions from English, French, and American factories stored in Russia, timber from Russian forests, as well as grain and coal, lay open to German seizure. There was also the danger of German war prisoners in Siberia reorganizing under arms, which added to the anxiety of the situation. The German submarine menace gained further terrors from the prospect of new bases at Murmansk and Archangel. The Allies had also committed themselves regarding the safety of the Czechoslovak legions whose hatred of the Central Powers made them a source of potential assistance whatever course events took in Russia.

More than 600,000 tons of munitions and military equipment, with a like tonnage in coal, had been landed at Archangel and Murmansk from the United States, Great Britain, and France. The Red Government had repudiated all debt for these and other supplies furnished to Russia, which in the Allies' opinion gave them the right to recover it. Would this material fall into German hands? Would Germany utilize some port on the White Sea as a submarine base? Or would the Bolsheviks employ these munitions against such sections of their people as were still loyal to the Allies? Such were the questions forced upon Western statesmen and military experts when the Communists came into power, even before they had made peace with Germany at Brest-Litovsk.

Allied policy was based upon the military situation in the late winter and spring of 1918. With Germany transporting hundreds of thousands of men and three thousand guns from the Russian to the Western Front and the Austrians utilizing troops thus liberated against Italy, in the view of Allied statesmen it behooved them to save what they could of the mountainous stores on the White Sea and prevent Germany occupying any of the North Russian harbors. That they would drift into a *de facto* war with Red Russia was perhaps not contemplated, although a strong body of opinion existed in the West that some military force should be provided to prevent the spread of Bolshevism. As far as North Russia was concerned, the Allies advocated both war and peace. As a result, there was fighting without a war. They conceived no comprehensive policy toward Finland, the Baltic States, and Poland, all of whom might have coöperated in any military operations in the north of Russia. The anti-German policy of the Allies went hand in hand with an anti-Soviet attitude, as soon as it became apparent that Red Russia would not continue the war.

The view that the Bolsheviks were German agents prevailed, not only among the populace in Allied countries, but among statesmen who should have known better. A few Red leaders at the beginning were undoubtedly in touch with Germany, but the vast majority were acting solely upon their own motion and in adherence to Bolshevik ideas of creating a new Russia. Red repudiation of the Russian debt on February 8, 1918, augmented the antipathy of the Western world to the new Bolshevik Government, causing much feeling among Allied bondholders, especially in France.

Foreign diplomats at Petrograd were hopelessly befogged by events. Accustomed to court intrigue and circuitous diplomatic negotiation, they were scandalized by the brusque realism of the Bolsheviks and shocked by a revolution directed not against persons but against a whole social and economic system. Accustomed to deal in the comprehensible terms of capitalistic nationalism, they were confronted with an amazing galaxy of new ideas couched in terms of international communism. Even the old name, Russia, was gone. True, there were among them a group of men including a Britisher, R. H. Bruce Lockhart, who asserted that "a policy of Allied intervention, with the coöperation and consent of the Bolshevik Government," was "feasible and possible," and a number of others, including Raymond Robins, who saw something new had occurred in history. But this school of realistic opinion did not triumph.

Diplomacy might have won the allegiance of the Bolsheviks who, at the beginning, were willing to assist the Allies in securing the Russian heavy artillery scattered along the Eastern Front. But diplomats, because of their failure to see the historical inevitability of the Russian Revolution and its sources of strength in a land-hungry and resentful population, were too confused to give substantial aid. Military intervention was accepted as a simple means of dealing with the exasperating Bolsheviks. Having failed to see that the Reds were the *de facto* power in Russia and seize the opportunity to possess themselves of the big guns of the old Imperial

A Poilu and a Doughboy dig a grave

Red troops on the White Sea

Doughboys feed the hungry population

Transport of the wounded in the Far North

A railroad patrol

Army, the Allies suffered from this same artillery in the spring drives of 1918 when the Germans moved Muscovite cannon to the Western Front.

The Allies saw in the North, on the Murmansk coast and at Archangel, an opportunity not only to retrieve millions of dollars in supplies but also to organize and support friendly governments which might prevent this region from falling into the hands of Germany, who was then aiding White Finns in their struggle for independence. Thereupon, one hundred and fifty British marines were landed in April of 1918, followed by three hundred and seventy more in May. As the Allies became committed to the local population and more extended in their operations, they were compelled to send more soldiers, until the British contingent alone numbered 18,400 of all ranks. Coincident with the landing of Allied troops efforts were put forward to arouse anti-Bolshevik elements of the population and to form a White Government.

In the Murmansk region, neighboring Finland, the Allies at first worked hand in hand with the Bolsheviks, each for his own reason. The Reds had a score to pay with White Finland and the Allies were at war with Germany, the only nation that substantially aided Finland in her struggle for independence. Thus war makes strange bedfellows!

Throughout the war Finland had prayed for Russia's defeat. Her citizens who were imbued with the spirit of nationalism looked on the empire as a foreign master, while her radicals hated it as an autocracy. After the Revolution the Finns had turned their eyes toward Germany as the savior of their country from Russian domination, while Socialists and those of redder hue hailed Soviet Russia as the champion of the workers against exploitation by capitalists.

Recognition had been given Finland by Red Russia on January 4, 1918, but the Bolsheviks had nevertheless invaded that country on January 28th. All the brutality and barbarism released by war and revolution flooded over the land in a tide of Red terrorism.

Finland, having suffered under Red rule, was soon to feel the wrath of the Whites. During the Finnish Civil War Germany sent General von der Goltz with a division of troops which defeated the Red contingents. White Finns gained the upper hand under General Baron Mannerheim, an ex-guard of the Russian Imperial Army, who vindicated his title to the sobriquet "Butcher" Mannerheim by executing hundreds of Communists in cold blood. Helsingfors was reoccupied by von der Goltz and Mannerheim on April 13th. The White Terror was no less crimson than the Red!

It was an invasion of the Murmansk region by this Finno-German Army that was feared by Allied statesmen and soldiers early in 1918. Neither the local population nor the central authorities were in a position to defend the territory, particularly the Murmansk Railway, which stretches over more than twelve hundred versts. This line had been completed by prisoners of war who had endured terrific hardships, many hundreds dying of cold, undernourishment, and neglect. As the result of the threat of a Finno-German onslaught the Red Government was forced to authorize the local Murmansk Soviet, headed by an ex-fireman, to secure Allied help for the protection of the region.

Notwithstanding the protests of some local organization, an agreement was reached between the regional Soviet and the Anglo-French representatives on March 2, 1918. Small detachments of Allied troops were then landed and an Allied military council formed. The immediate objectives avowed by the Allies were to repel the threatened Finno-German invasion, to protect war supplies, to prevent the establishment of a submarine base on the White Sea, and to pin down as many German troops in Finland as possible.

For months Allied soldiers worked in perfect accord with the Red Guards. In the meantime, the Finno-German attack failed to materialize, and the Bolsheviks, no longer at war with Germany, having concluded the Brest-Litovsk Treaty, were beginning to be alarmed at the number of Allied troops stationed in that remote northern section of the country.

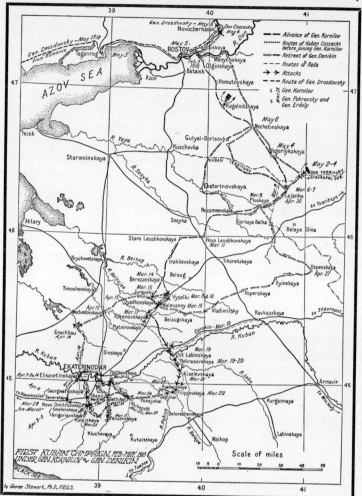

First Kuban campaign, spring of 1918, under General Kornilov.

On June 30th, the regional Soviet received an order from their government to oust the Allies from the territory. The Soviet met and refused to obey the order, preferring to lean upon military assistance from the Allies. The government retaliated by outlawing the head of the Murmansk Soviet, but for the time being was unable to take any other steps against the rebels.

A treaty was concluded on July 6th between the Murmansk Soviet and representatives of Great Britain, France, and the United States, which remained in force until the end of the Allied occupation. Article One of this treaty stated the purpose of the agreement to be the securing of "coördinated action on the part of those who have signed this agreement for the defense of the Murmansk region against the Powers of the German coalition." Article Two described the territory involved. Article Three stated that a Russian army under Russian command is to be recruited. Article Four stated that such troops are to be supplied with munitions and equipment by the Allies. Internal administration, by Articles Five and Six, was left entirely in the hands of the Murmansk Regional Soviet, except actually at the front. Article Seven embodied the promise of the representatives of Great Britain, the United States of America, and France "to secure food for the whole population of the region, including all immigrant workmen with their families, with rations to equal in food value the rations which the privates of the Allied armed forces in Murmansk are receiving." This distribution of food, according to Article Eight, was to be carried out by trustworthy Russian troops. Articles Nine and Ten declared that manufactured goods, of which all Russia stood in need, were to be imported as freely as possible, and Articles Eleven and Twelve stated that all expenses were to be set down to the Allies, while some financial assistance would be given the Murmansk Soviet. The Allies disclaimed all intention of conquest and declared, in Article Fourteen, that the only object of this agreement was to guard the integrity of the Murmansk region for a Great United Russia. The breach between the Allies and the Soviet of Moscow was now complete!

The North Russian Government was composed of Right Socialist-Revolutionaries under the domination of the foreign Powers whose soldiers were in occupation. The government never had a completely free hand and was always subservient to the military.

By the middle of July, Allied forces in the Murmansk region comprised about ten thousand men—English, French, Americans, Serbs—in possession of all necessary military supplies. By then the Allies had extended their occupation as far as Sorokskaya. Some Soviet troops encountered were disarmed and imprisoned; others escaped southward toward Petrograd.

Meanwhile the Soviet Government was not inactive in its diplomatic arm. On July 13th, Chicherin issued a protest to Great Britain and an appeal to America, in which he observed:

In spite of repeated assurances by the British Government that the landing of the British troops in Murmansk is not a hostile act against the Russian Soviet Republic, the British Government has not fulfilled our elementary demand for the removal of troops from Soviet territory. . . . Soviet officials are being arrested and sometimes even shot. Railroad guards are being disarmed. . . . After occupying Kem and Sorokskaya, the British troops moved further east and occupied Sumski-Posad, on the road to Onega. . . . Such actions of the British troops can be considered only as an occupation of the territory of the Russian Soviet Republic. We have stated, and we are stating once more, that Soviet troops will do everything possible in order to protect Russian territory, and will offer the most determined resistance to the foreign armed invasion. . . .

The same tone is heard in Chicherin's note to the Consul General of the United States, printed in *Izvestia* of July 13, 1918.

The achievements of the Murmansk force of Russian and Allied troops up to the Armistice are soon told. General Maynard, who had arrived on June 4th, heading a small expeditionary force, had as his first objective the establishment of a hold on the railway, an end which he attained by disarming all centers known to be disaffected. He then turned his atten-

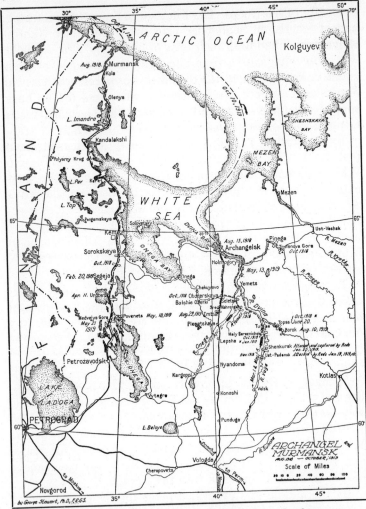

Allied intervention on the White Sea, August, 1918–October, 1919.

tion to clearing Karelia of Finnish White Guards who, under
German leadership, had penetrated far into that section,
terrorizing the inhabitants and attempting to raid various
points on the railway. This task Maynard entrusted mainly

to locally raised troops. The Finns were repeatedly defeated, and at length, on September 11th, were routed at Ukhtin-skaya, which had been their base of operation. But, while he was employing native troops to fight the invaders of their country, he was using Allied soldiers to march southeast of Sorokskaya against the Bolsheviks, who were driven back some forty miles. Maynard thus kept the Germans under General von der Goltz in a state of acute anxiety.

By November 11, 1918, the troops in Murmansk could look back with satisfaction on their record. The Finnish White Guards had been expelled from Pechenga and the German scheme of establishing a submarine base on the White Sea had been frustrated; moreover, Maynard's vigorous action had detained German regiments in Finland that were badly needed on the Western Front; thus Allied troops at Murmansk had contributed some share toward the dramatic victory of their comrades in France and Belgium.

Turning now to the Archangel expedition, it must be recalled that rumors of an intended Allied landing at Archangel had been current since March. Throughout June and July intrigue had been busily at work, Archangel taking on the air of some medieval Italian duchy, so thick were plots and counterplots. Long before the first Allied troops arrived at Archangel, members of the Russian White organization, helped by the British Secret Service at Petrograd, made their way north to Archangel. A Russian naval captain acting as a British officer was at the head of the movement, while the White Sea Cavalry Regiment was another organization whose aim was to start a revolt against the Reds, the commander of this force being in touch with the French.

By the middle of July, Allied plans for the occupation of Archangel were ready to be hatched. The ambassadors left Vologda for Archangel on July 25th. A week later General Poole began his occupation of that region. The advance party of American troops landed in Archangel on August 3, 1918.

Modyugski Island held by the Reds surrendered to General Poole's expedition after a short but spirited resistance.

Simultaneously a force of Serbs and Russians under Colonel Thornhill of the British Secret Service proceeded to Onega and thence to Obozerskaya in order to cut the Archangel-Vologda line and attack the Bolsheviks from the rear, at the same time preventing the evacuation of stores and rolling stock. However, this force met with such determined resistance that it was compelled to withdraw to Onega, and the Bolsheviks were able to retreat along the railroad without serious hindrance.

The long prepared anti-Bolshevik uprising broke out in Archangel on August 2d, forcing Soviet troops to retire by rail and river. The coup was accomplished by Russian officers, leaning upon the assistance of the Allies.

These preliminary actions were so much theatrical property for the proper setting of the drama of Allied intervention. The government that was set up by the victorious rebels against Moscow—the Supreme Administration of the Northern Region—though formed with the support of the Allies, was made up of Socialist-Revolutionaries and headed by the venerable populist, Nikolai Vasilyevich Chaikovsky.

On August 22, 1918, the government published a statement at Archangel to the effect that:

The Allies, then, were called to Russia by the only legitimate and representative authority, for the purpose of military action in common aiming at the expulsion of the Germans and the complete suppression by force of arms of the Brest-Litovsk treaty, traitorously signed by the Bolsheviki.

America became more involved as the summer passed, her Expeditionary Forces to North Russia being enlarged by some five thousand, five hundred men which were landed at Archangel on September 5, 1918. The campaign was popular with neither officers nor men and grew less so as the winter deepened.

The military element that had engineered the coup soon grew dissatisfied with the government as too Red. Accordingly, on the night of the 5th of September, President Chaikovsky and all but two of his Cabinet were kidnapped and imprisoned in the Solovetsky Monastery on the island of that name. The instigator was a certain Chaplin, a Russian naval officer attached to General Poole's staff, who was one of the ringleaders in the *coup d'état*. He admitted the kidnapping and excused himself by saying that "The ministers were in General Poole's way, and were hampering Colonel Donop. . . . I see no use for any government here anyway." This frank statement shocked diplomatic decency and respect for convention; still more, it annoyed the townspeople, who may not have loved the Bolsheviks of whom as yet they knew little, but certainly did not love the Czarist régime of which they had known too much.

Two of the kidnapped members of the government issued an appeal to the people, declaring that the officers intended to restore the monarchy. The workmen struck, and disturbed peasants called upon the American ambassador who, they believed, would not tolerate a return to despotism or to the police methods of Czarism. Trains were left idle and traffic tied up, except in so far as service was maintained by Detroit motormen and conductors in the American forces recently landed.

General Poole sided with the officers who had staged the coup, while the diplomatic corps favored Chaikovsky, to the chagrin of the military, and insisted upon the return of the kidnapped Cabinet. Shortly thereafter, General Ironside, a British war hero, came to replace the high-handed General Poole.

The ministers returned on September 8th, but with the understanding that Chaikovsky should form a more moderate Cabinet. Finding themselves in an intolerable position, they resigned and a Governor General was appointed. Thereafter the North Russian Government fell into oblivion, the region being virtually under a military dictatorship.

Russian officers, busy with intrigue, neglected their troops who were supposedly consumed with eagerness to free their country from Bolshevik oppression. At this time Russian forces consisted of one infantry regiment, a battery, and a motor-car division, but no one troubled to provide them with food or lodging, nor to maintain discipline. Many Russian officers entered Franco-British-Slav units as privates. This was precisely what Allied military authorities desired, for the sake of efficiency, though it might have been more politic to have made a parade of a National Russian Army.

In order to fix responsibility and have a leader for the scattered Russian forces, General Miller was put in command of the White troops, backed by the Allies. He was a man of a rather German type and appearance, who had a distinguished career as staff officer in the Imperial Army.

The Allied and White Russian troops were spread out like fingers of a hand whose wrist was Archangel, extending to Pinega, occupied in October, Seletskoe and Tulgas on the River Dvina, Ust-Padensk and Shenkursk on the Vaga; Kodish, the scene of heavy fighting and bitter disappointment, just outside Emptsa on the railroad, and Chekuyevo on the River Onega. The importance of Onega was that it kept open the difficult lateral line of communication between Archangel and Murmansk by the Onega-Sorokskaya road. The Vologda force, which captured Obozerskaya, hoped ultimately to take Vologda, but the offensive halted a few versts north of Emptsa owing to ill-laid plans, the determination of the Bolsheviks, and to some degree the weariness of the French troops.

The Dvina force, with its base at Bereznichek, had as its ultimate objective Kotlas, but after varied fighting in which Seletskoe was taken and lost, the line settled down at Nizhnitoimi and an offensive at Tulgas in late October and early November failed to dislodge it.

The Vaga force was of crucial importance, for any serious reverses there would imperil the Allies. The capture of Shenkursk on September 17th without a shot being fired enabled the Allies to occupy Ust-Padensk by the early winter.

Lieutenant Colonel Gavin captured Kodish, Shred Mahrenga, and Tarasova in October. Plesetskaya might have been taken, but orders were given to dig in. Red troops had time to pluck up courage, and in November made a determined effort at a counter-attack.

The loyalty of the Pinega force was dubious. The soldiers had been recruited from local villages which were politically of a delicate pink, but this key position on the left flank was not seriously threatened until December of 1918.

Sketchy communications, marshes, the melancholy of the woods and the weird arctic night compelling troops to work almost all day by flares and artificial light, combined to depress the spirit of the non-Russian troops. The Murmansk and Archangel operations were distinct and could only with difficulty support each other, thus isolating the two sections of a perilously small expeditionary force.

The Armistice found the North Russian Expedition hotly engaged on the River Dvina at Tulgas, and at Kodish, with every sign that the Bolsheviks were preparing to take the advantage they were given by winter, which rendered communications with their home base more difficult for foreign troops and shipments of food for the local population uncertain.

Official explanations were made as to why this expedition, started as an anti-German measure, was not terminated with the end of the war. The Allies were not sure of being able to remove the whole force from Archangel before the port was closed by ice; moreover, they had involved themselves with friendly Russian elements they could not easily desert. Having induced these pro-Ally groups in the North to take the field against the Reds, they could not precipitately abandon them to the swift vengeance which would surely follow if Allied contingents should be evacuated. Thus, little by little, the Allies were entangled in the Russian morass, one commitment following another.

Chapter V

THE CZECHOSLOVAK ANABASIS TO THE ARMISTICE

To understand the part played by Czechs and Slovaks in the Russian Civil War it is necessary to scrutinize their status within the empire in 1914. Without discrimination between Czechs and Slovaks, they shall all be spoken of as Czechs or Czechoslovaks.

Colonies of business men, merchants, and artisans resided in the larger cities, while in Volhynia and the Caucasus were large agricultural settlements which possessed their own schools. The government had suppressed their educational institutions with the exception of the Comenius School at Kiev where their paper, the *Čzechoslovan,* was published.

The war profoundly stirred these scattered colonies which, though Slav by race, were largely Austro-Hungarian by education and citizenship. The Czar's manifesto proclaiming war between Germanism and Slavism aroused enthusiasm among those who had looked forward for an opportunity to strike at the Dual Monarchy. The political romanticism of the '60's awoke once more. Young enthusiasts who were Austrian subjects attempted to renounce their nationality and to enter the Imperial armies. At the end of August a suggestion was adopted by the War Council for the formation of a Czech volunteer detachment, and the Česká Družina was formed at Kiev, the center of Czech life in Russia.

By the beginning of September there were enough volunteers enrolled to form three divisions under Russian officers, and a little later a fourth was added. Czech leadership was

in the hands of young business men and instructors from
their athletic clubs, the Sokols, who introduced a camaraderie quite different from the stiff formality of the Russian
Army. It is not surprising that Russian officers suspected
the democratic spirit of Czech contingents and questioned
the loyalty of foreigners who were technically traitors to
their own government. Great rallies were held in Volhynia,
in Kiev, and in the Caucasus, with the purpose of convincing
the Russians of the strong Slav feeling among the Czechs
and Slovaks.

At the end of October, 1914, seven hundred volunteers,
with three hundred Russian subalterns and instructors, left
Kiev for the army of General Ivanov on the Southwestern
Front, where they first met General Dieterichs, one-time
Quartermaster General at the Stavka, the Russian general
staff headquarters at Mogilev, who was to prove one of the
most influential of their Russian friends. They were chiefly
employed as spies and agitators among Czech regiments in
the Austrian Army. The success of the Družina encouraged
political workers to expand by enrolling those of their fellows who were serving in Russian regiments and to secure
permission to add Czech prisoners of war. Delegates were
sent to far-off prison camps in Turkestan and Siberia and
to industrial districts where interned Czechs were working in factories.

Czechoslovak prisoners of war found themselves in a
variety of places and occupations. Being Slavophiles they
were generally given larger liberties than Germans, Austrians, or Hungarians. Many were skilled workers and as
such were in demand for munition factories where they
received a wage one-third that of Russian mechanics, each
contributing a tenth part to the funds raised to promote their
national independence. The munition works at Taganrog
employed seventeen hundred Czech prisoners who were allowed the liberty of the city. Others did not fare as well.
Hundreds of Czechs, Germans, and Magyars perished miserably in building the Murmansk Railway. On the windy

steppe of Turkestan they were compelled to make huts
from material carried upon their backs for many miles.
Sandstorms, malaria, typhus, exposure, and sheer home-
sickness decimated their number. They were also impressed
into service in the construction of the railway from Bokhara
to the Afghan border. The formation of the Družina offered
a way out of intolerable hardships or tedium to thousands of
Czechs who were more fortunate than all other prisoners of
war of any nation then held in Russia or Siberia.

The Družina gradually won favor, but internal disputes
and suspicion of Russian military authorities prevented any
marked increase until October, 1915, when Czechs and
Slovaks of Volhynia who owed military service to Russia
were added. This concession was in part due to the fine conduct of their military units during the disastrous retreat
from the Carpathians in 1915.

At the moment when better relations were being established with the Russian Government new discords arose
among themselves. The *Comité Tchèque à l'Etranger,* which
had been formed in the fall of 1915, had proclaimed a revolution against Austria on November 4th of that year, and with
the help of Thomas A. Masaryk, a brilliant professor who
became one of the great politicians and statesmen of the
period, and Dr. Edourd Beneš, had attempted to secure the
coöperation of the Allies. The first congress of the Czech
League (Svas) held at Kiev in the spring of 1916 revealed
two definite factions. Differences appear to have been due in
the main to local and personal jealousies. In spite of these
cross-currents, the Družina grew from a regiment to a brigade, while other Czechoslovak officers and men joined Serbian units on the Dobrudja front. By the summer of 1916,
some twenty-five thousand Czech prisoners had enlisted in
their regiments.

P. Dürich, a former member of the Austrian Parliament,
came in July, 1916, as head of the entire Czechoslovak
movement in Russia, with the special mission of bringing as
many of the Czechs as he could to the French front. His

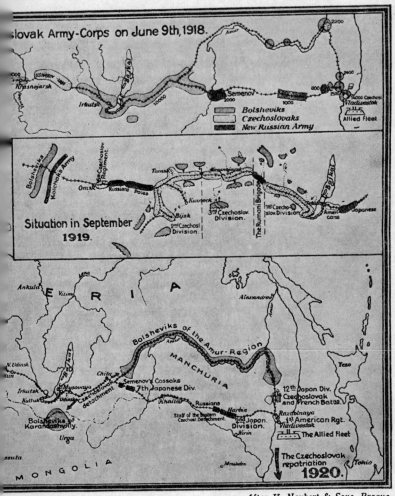

...slovak Army-Corps on June 9th, 1918.

Bolsheviks
Czechoslovaks
New Russian Army

Situation in September 1919.

Bolsheviks

Kolchak's Army

1st Czechoslov. Regiment.

Omsk   Russians   Poles

Tomsk

Krasnojarsk

Kuznieck

Bijsk

2nd Czechosl. Division.

3rd Czechoslav. Division.

The Ruman Brigade

1st Czechoslov. Division.

Americans

Japanese

Baj Kal

Ankula

ERIA

Vilem

Lena

Alexandrov

Amur

N. Udinsk

Bolsheviks of the Amur-Region

MANCHURIA

Yezo

Irkutsk

Mysovaya

Chita

Semenov's Cossaks
7th Japanese Div.

12th Japan. Div.
Czechoslovak
and French Bats.

Kultuk

Uslanje   Czechoslov.
detachment

Khailar   Russians

Harbin

Razdolnaya
1st American Rgt.
Vladivostok

Bolsheviks of
Karandashvilly.

Staff of the Eastern
Czechosl. Detachment.

2nd Japan.
Division.

Kirin

The Allied fleet

Urga

MONGOLIA

Moukden

The Czechoslovak
repatriation
1920.

Tokio

After V. Neubert & Sons, Prague

N SIBERIA.

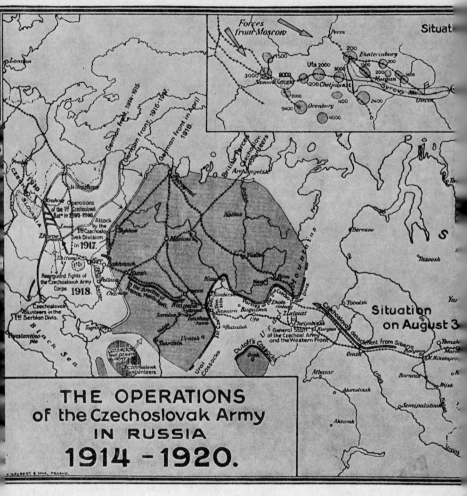

THE OPERATIONS
of the Czechoslovak Army
IN RUSSIA
1914 - 1920.

DISTRIBUTION OF CZEC

arrival precipitated a crisis, for he was won over by the reactionary party in the Imperial Government of Stürmer and Protopopov, both of whom were suspected of pro-German tendencies. The Czechs for the most part were inclined to favor such liberals as Paul Miliukov, head of the progressive party in the Duma.

The Czechs welcomed the Revolution of March, 1917, as a victory of Russian democracy. As a result, Dürich was soon superse'ed by M. R. Stefánik. At once all obstructions to the formation of a strong and independent Czech army were removed. Two months after the Kerensky Revolution the second Czech Congress met at Kiev in May of 1917. It approved the statement of policy proclaimed by Stefánik and the appointment of Masaryk as head of the Czechoslovak movement, settling the quarrel between the two factions. Efforts were initiated at once to enlist Czech recruits in all prison camps of Russia and Siberia, and a loan for 20,000,000 francs was successfully negotiated. Dr. Girsa, who proved himself to be a capable diplomat as representative of the colonists, was even invited to the State Conference at Moscow in the summer of 1917. A Czech army corps was established composed of two divisions, and, by an order of September 26, 1917, placed under General Dukhonin, then commanding officer of the Kerensky Government.

The break-up of the Imperial Army made the position of the Czechs very difficult. However, being more accustomed than Russians to democratic organization, they were better able to sustain discipline and absorb the new idea of liberty which was strong wine to the muzhik. When the utter collapse of the Russian Army was patent, the old project—of which much more was to be heard—of diverting a part of the Czech Army to France was revived. The French Government agreed to the transport of thirty thousand to the Western Front, but owing to disturbed conditions only one thousand were sent, some by way of Archangel.

After prolonged negotiation, Masaryk succeeded on October 9, 1917, in securing permission to form an entirely independent Czech army corps. All commands henceforth were issued in their own tongue, and the system of discipline was adapted from that of other Continental armies. As the organization of the Russian Army decayed, that of the Czech battalions grew.

A new difficulty occurred when the Ukraine, where the greater part of the Czech Army was located, declared itself an independent state. This situation Masaryk attempted to meet by ordering absolute neutrality toward the internal affairs of Russia, as it was of the utmost importance not to make commitments to such insecure governments.

When the Bolsheviks seized power in November, 1917, the Czechs entered upon a hazardous period. Armies of the Central Powers who were deadly enemies of the Czechs, and considered them traitors to Austria, were advancing speedily into the heart of the Ukraine. All Russia seemed on the point of breaking up into autonomous states of dubious political color and of a highly uncertain orientation with regard to their former enemy, Germany. Anxious not to compromise themselves with any party, the Czechs watched the policy of the Allies and found in the French their most willing advisors, as France welcomed any resolute group which could fight Germany.

Two days after the Bolsheviks took command in Petrograd, retreating Czech troops arrived at Kiev. Although their forces had adopted the regimental committees instituted by the revolutionary Russian army, they considered themselves entirely separate from the Russian military. They had by this time abandoned Russian uniforms and organized independent auxiliary units—sanitary corps, flying squads, and heavy artillery—which previously had been provided by the Russians. The commander-in-chief and the minister of war of the Soviet Government of the Ukraine recognized their strict armed neutrality—and therefore, by inference, their independence from Moscow.

Although the Czechs were neutral in name, it was obviously difficult for them to be so in fact, in an atmosphere

charged with conflicting political ideas. The Ukraine was unstable from a political standpoint. Strong Bolshevik sentiment flared up, following which the Soviets were rejected
for pro-Germanism, since the Germans offered protection to
property. Finally, in February, 1918, the region was recon-
quered by the Red Army. In this period the contagion of
Communist ideas had begun to infect the Czech Army.

In order to restore confidence in the West, both among
their leaders and among the Allies, the Czech League met
again in Kiev on January 30, 1918, and made a solemn
promise of fidelity to Masaryk, restating its determination
to continue fighting Austria-Hungary till that empire should
be destroyed and the lands which were to compose Czechoslovakia, freed. This declaration created a division between
the radicals and the moderates. The *Svoboda,* a new pro-
Bolshevik paper, advocated the establishment of a confederation of Slavic republics under the leadership of Bolshevik
Russia. Moreover, it began an energetic campaign among
Czech prisoners, calling upon them to enlist in the Red Army,
accusing Masaryk and the League of counter-revolutionary
sympathies. At the same time some Czechs abandoned their
units to join up with General Kornilov who was forming a
White center in the neighborhood of Rostov-on-Don and
Taganrog. The Communists attracted more men than
Kornilov, due to superior propaganda and the material advantages of the Red Army, but the vast majority remained
in the Czech legions under the leadership of Masaryk.

Neutrality was a difficult achievement in a land fermenting
with internecine strife. With the political ideas of the old
régime in Russia the Czechs had little sympathy, but the
foreign policy of the Bolsheviks, unfortunate brushes with
their troops and representatives, and the advice of Allied
missions, especially the French, created a feeling of hostility
among the Legionnaires toward the new government at
Moscow.

The Ukraine had become exceedingly dangerous for the
Czechs on account of the rapid advance of German and Aus-

trian armies. They were in no position to withstand an attack in force. President Masaryk, on February 7, 1918, declared the Czechoslovak Army everywhere in Russia to be an integral part of the autonomous Czech Army in France, and on February 10, 1918, a proclamation was published to this effect.

Necessity compelled the immediate retreat from Kiev before the Germans and Austrians, who had been invited into the Ukraine by the Ukrainian National Government, should arrive. The Czechs, by defeating the vanguard of the Central Powers near Korostyshev, insured their evacuation to the eastern bank of the Dnieper. They then retreated to Poltava Province and centered around the railway triangle, Bachmach-Ichna-Kruty, where they fought a successful battle with the Germans, securing their line of retreat eastward. By arrangement with the commander of the Soviet forces, they handed over their superfluous military equipment, and in return received promises that their evacuation would be facilitated.

The Treaty of Brest-Litovsk drove the Czechs into the arms of the counter-revolutionaries. After this event they considered themselves under the protection and in a sense under the orders of the Allies in any manner in which they might seek to prosecute the war against Germany. Their *esprit de corps* was strong and they asked to be sent to the Western Front. The Allies in their turn saw in the Legionnaires a possible means of counterbalancing the disastrous effect of the Russo-German Treaty which released not only seventy divisions to fight against them in Belgium and France but also opened to Germany the food resources of Russia.

An agreement was drawn up between the Bolshevik commander-in-chief and the Czechs on March 26, 1918, whereby they were to be evacuated via the Trans-Siberian Railway on the route to Kursk, Penza, Chelyabinsk, and the east. Starting with forty-two thousand, five hundred troops, their numbers increased until at times they mustered between sixty

General Stefánik   General Syrový

Czech armoured train

General Janin arrives

Decorated freight van

Embattled freight cars

and seventy thousand men. Naturally the German high command and the German ambassador, Count Mirbach, used every means to defeat the purpose of this resolute group.

The Czechs were divided into transport detachments or echelons of about the same size as were used in European armies to move an infantry battalion, making a total of sixty-five trains. In practice it became necessary to vary the composition of the echelons. The larger part of the Czech prisoners of war were located between the Volga and the Caspian in a region too remote from the route of the echelons to make contact. Their military was organized into an army corps composed of two divisions, each division consisting of four regiments, and each regiment made up of three battalions, with four companies in each battalion. In addition there were two artillery brigades of six batteries each, two companies of engineers, two field hospitals, an aviation group, field kitchens, signal corps, and courier units. As the legions grew they finally employed over one hundred and ninety trains which were to be their home and their fortress until they sailed for Europe in 1920.

The Russian officer, General Dieterichs, accompanied the first echelons of some twelve thousand men from Penza through to Vladivostok with little difficulty, where they arrived in May of 1918. The succeeding echelons encountered what was tantamount to a separate government in every large town.

Once out of the Ukraine and in Soviet territory, negotiations began afresh with the government in Moscow. At first there seemed to be no difficulty about arranging the evacuation of the Czechs with military equipment carried as baggage via Vladivostok, but at Penza the situation suddenly became strained, as the Soviet commissar, influenced by local Czech Communists, wished to prevent their evacuation with war equipment. The Czechs were obliged to accept the severe terms of the Penza Soviet. Beyond Penza new obstacles were encountered and harsher terms exacted. Samara, Ufa, Zlatoust, Omsk, Chita all made fresh demands.

The Legionnaires were facing trouble in many directions. Czech Communists attempted to persuade their comrades to enter the Red Army, by delaying evacuation under the pretext of bad conditions at Chita, and by hinting—as was indeed becoming true—that the Czech Army was the tool of Western capitalistic nations seeking to overthrow Bolshevism. Mutual suspicions were kindled. The landing of the Japanese contingent at Vladivostok with the promise of American units in the near future, as well as antagonistic Allied missions in European Russia who were friendly to the Czechs, alarmed the Bolsheviks.

Chicherin, on behalf of the Red Government, wired the representative of the Czechs that all detachments must be sent out of the country via Archangel and Murmansk and ordered them to make disposition accordingly. The Czechs refused and ordered their echelons to continue their journey toward Vladivostok.

A general meeting of Czech delegates, both officers and men, was called at the important junction of Chelyabinsk on May 14th. The aged revolutionary, Katherine Breskovskaya, attended the meeting, a tragic figure. She had worked for a lifetime for the Revolution only to see it slip out of the hands of her weak associates into the iron grip of Lenin. A decision was made to fight the Bolsheviks, if necessary, to secure their freedom of action. The legions were divided into two divisions with General Ček in command of the first and General Gajda of the second, with General Syrový as chief of the entire force.

General Syrový was a stocky man of distinctly Slavic type. He wore his hair close-shaven, had a strong, round face and a quiet mien. Before the war he had been an architect, practicing for some years in Warsaw. He had begun his military service as a lieutenant in the Družina, losing an eye at the Battle of Zoborov. His poise and deliberation contrasted sharply with General Gajda, who was one of the most colorful and dashing leaders of the Czechs. Gajda had been a junior medical officer who had served in the Austrian Army until captured by the Russians, when he entered one of the Czechoslovak legions formed in the Ukraine. He was a tall man, with flashing blue eyes, an abundance of straight brown hair, and regular features. He was endowed with outstanding qualities of personal leadership and was to become one of the stormy petrels of the warfare in Siberia. By the time the Czechs began their evacuation by way of Siberia Gajda commanded a brigade. Making common cause with the Socialist-Revolutionaries, he lent his support to the Siberian Regional Duma, playing an important part in the seizure of the Trans-Siberian Railway by the Czechs, and assisting the Western Commissariat of the Siberian Government in establishing its power. Promotion came rapidly through various grades until he held the rank of general and was put in command of the Ekaterinburg district.

In the station yard at Chelyabinsk, alongside the Czech coaches, stood several trains of German-Austrian prisoners, who, under the terms of Brest-Litovsk, were returning to fight once more in the German armies. As one of these trains was drawing out of the station, a Magyar prisoner threw a piece of iron from a window, killing a Czech soldier, and in return was immediately slain. Soviet authorities held an investigation and imprisoned ten Czech soldiers who were promptly rescued by their comrades, who seized the station. There were then at Chelyabinsk some eight thousand, four hundred Czechs, of whom one thousand, six hundred were armed with rifles, with an additional equipment of six machine guns.

After the fight at Chelyabinsk the Czechs were in the vanguard of anti-Bolshevik forces for many months. Their exploits, their loyalty, their *esprit de corps* in a day of slackened morale, astonished Allied and Russian officers, both Red and White, and showed what a small, determined force might accomplish if thoroughly imbued with a fixed purpose.

Trotsky wired to prevent the evacuation of the Czechs on the Trans-Siberian, to disarm their echelons, to send them to prison camps, and in case of refusal to shoot all who offered opposition. From then on a state of open warfare existed between Red Russia and the Czechs.

In order to facilitate their movements the congress elected a Military Executive Committee, composed of twelve men, half soldiers and half officers, charged with the evacuation of the Legionnaires from Siberia and their transport to France. Commissars were elected to deal with local and regional Soviets to the disgust of foreign officers. Nevertheless, the mental flexibility of the Czech leaders in these confused times preserved the loyalty and purpose of the men.

Czech delegates at Moscow had been arrested on May 21st, while secret telegrams were dispatched to Soviets along the railway, ordering them to halt and disarm the echelons. This was followed by instructions from Moscow to intern them as prisoners of war, whereupon the Congress, or Legionnaires' Parliament at Chelyabinsk, determined to ignore orders from Moscow and to oppose any attempt to evacuate their units via Archangel, as they feared a plan to divide their forces and to hand them over to Germany. The Siberian Soviets pathetically inquired of Moscow: "When will you answer our statement about the impossibility of sending the Czechoslovaks to Vladivostok? We categorically demand that they be sent over to Archangel." The Red commissars were beginning to lose temper with one another.

A series of Bolshevik attacks now played into Czech hands, giving them an excuse to seize control of the Trans-Siberian, a circumstance devoutly hoped for by the Allies. The Sixth Czechoslovak Regiment was set upon at Marianovka on the night of May 25th-26th, losing ten killed and ten severely wounded. The staff of the First Regiment was fired upon at Zlatoust and lost six killed. This regiment was compelled to make its way across the Urals on foot.

A fight near Irkutsk completely disillusioned the Czechs regarding any permanent understanding with the Bolsheviks. When the first Czech echelon reached the railroad station they were by agreement disarmed, save for thirty carbines and a few hand grenades. When the train halted a demand was made, backed by a vastly superior force of Red soldiers, to surrender their arms within a quarter of an hour. During the discussion which followed among the astonished Czechs a machine gun opened fire upon their train. They immediately retaliated and with captured weapons defeated local Red troops several days later. The Second Artillery Brigade was attacked at Inokentievskaya, near Irkutsk, and another attack was made at Serdobsk, south of Penza. These forays convinced the Legionnaires that safety lay in the strength of their arms.

The Reds were eager to be rid of the Legionnaires and demanded of Major Slaughter and Colonel Emerson, two American railway engineers who tendered their good offices as mediators during the fighting west of Lake Baikal around Mariinsk in late May, that the Czechs give up their arms before they would allow their transit east. They laid down four other conditions: that the Russians would expedite the Czechs eastward as soon as possible; that the Legionnaires should not interfere in Russian affairs; that a joint commission be appointed to investigate the trouble at Mariinsk, and that the Russians would deliver to the Czechs all foreign arms and ammunition they had surrendered when they arrived at Vladivostok. The Czechs, fearing attack, refused to disarm. They admitted that there was a concerted action on their part to capture the towns along the Trans-Siberian on May 28th, and suggested that Colonel Emerson go to Novonikolayevsk to consult General Gajda. Colonel Emerson, however, returned to Soviet headquarters, where a Red official exclaimed: "France, through concerted action with the Czech troops, has taken Siberia in twenty-four hours!" At Mariinsk the Czechs re-equipped themselves from captured supplies.

Further fighting occurred near Irkutsk, after which the American consul, General Harris, and the French consul saw that the echelons in that vicinity were practically disarmed and sent east with thirty rifles for each train. Gajda, west of Lake Baikal, was infuriated and threatened punishment to the Czechs for their actions in going east under these circumstances. As the Czech echelons moved toward Vladivostok, White Guard governments of a sketchy sort sprang up in the towns they protected. Having for the time broken all effective Red opposition, the possibility of the Czechs establishing themselves along the line of the Urals was now certain.

Distances which separated their echelons along the vast expanse of Siberia, while apparently a dangerous weakness, were in reality a military advantage, inasmuch as they now controlled the railway, a single artery reaching for hundreds of miles to the east.

They immediately began taking over the stations and apparatus to maintain an aggressive self-defense. At times an echelon, cut off from its neighbor and unable to move forward on the railway, would abandon its train and by a detour achieve liaison with the next group. Many were the heroic deeds accomplished in these adventures. Foreign observers looked upon the Czech efforts with approval and admiration. While they became unpopular with the Reds and the very White groups, the common people were friendly to them save in localities where they were compelled to make heavy requisitions.

Arrayed against them on the Volga and in the Urals was a Red Army rapidly being whipped into shape by Muraviev, a former colonel in the Imperial Army. He had taken an active part in the early days of the Red struggle in Petrograd and had commanded Red soldiers during the short advance made by Krasnov and Kerensky against that city. Later, in February of 1918, he had successfully led revolutionary troops against the army of the Ukrainian Rada and had seized Kiev, only to be turned out by the Germans.

By June 9, 1918, the Legionnaires were spread from Samara to Vladivostok with intervening bodies of Red troops or sympathizers breaking them into large groups upon the Trans-Siberian. Many towns were captured by small echelons of Czechs against vastly superior forces. Nizhneudinsk was taken by a force only two companies of which had rifles, the remainder being armed with clubs or other improvised weapons. Looking eastward from Samara where there were 8,000 Legionnaires under Čeček was Ufa, a Red center, dividing Čeček's forces from the Chelyabinsk group under Syrový, whose 8,800 soldiers extended beyond Omsk where they made contact with General Gajda's forces of 3,000, which, in turn, extended from Novonikolayevsk to halfway between Tomsk and Krasnoyarsk, another Red center. The next anti-Bolshevik group was beyond Krasnoyarsk, consisting of 1,000 White Russians under the popular Russian officer Usakov, on the line about halfway between Krasnoyarsk and Irkutsk. The railway was then solidly Red west of Lake Baikal through the Transbaikal territory until Semyonov's small force was encountered at the Manchurian frontier. Twenty-two hundred Czechs were at Khabarovsk on the Amur Railway and some 12,000 under General Dieterichs at Vladivostok. This alignment was, of course, rapidly changing due to the varying fortunes of the White armies which were being formed in Western Siberia and to changing conditions along the railway.

General Gajda's echelon had experienced difficulty in May, inasmuch as it was divided into three separate parts facing the strongest Bolshevik forces. Novonikolayevsk and Chulimsk had been taken on May 26th, and two days later, on May 28th, nearly all Siberian towns west of Irkutsk had been seized by a united action of the Czechs with the knowledge and encouragement of England, France, and Japan. On June 1st Gajda made contact with the Mariinsk group. In the same period, Taiga and Tomsk had been occupied, and the united forces commenced operations against Omsk, which fell on June 7th. Thus by June 9th the Trans-Siberian all the way from Chelyabinsk to Mariinsk, some 1,700 versts, was in Czech hands.

It was still necessary to push eastward. On June 20th, Gajda with 1,500 Legionnaires and Colonel Boris Usakov with 1,000 White Russians attacked and captured Krasnoyarsk. At that city the legions, which were short of food, clothing, ammunition, and arms, equipped themselves for a blow at Irkutsk.

After the fall of Krasnoyarsk Gajda moved rapidly eastward. He captured Irkutsk with 3,500 Czechs and the White sections of the Russian Barnaul Regiment ranged against 8,000 Reds. Gajda discovered that the retreating Bolsheviks had carried away with them several carloads of dynamite. They had wrecked the line behind them and had stopped near the station of Baikal, beyond which were a series of tunnels. Neither the Czechs nor the Reds wished the tunnels destroyed; for the former it meant annihilation and for the latter the division of Siberia into two parts. A force of five hundred men from the Seventh Regiment and a storm battalion under Major Hásek made a détour of three days through the mountains and by a surprise sortie blew up the enormous quantity of dynamite, thus saving themselves from being trapped in the heart of Siberia. The explosion was heard nearly forty miles away in Irkutsk.

In the hot fighting around the end of Lake Baikal the Legionnaires were compelled to battle for every one of the numerous tunnels. Tunnel Number Thirty-nine was blown up by Bolshevik soldiers, requiring an operation of two weeks to clear. Mysovaya was the next town of consequence in Red hands and beyond that Verkhneudinsk. An expedition of 500 men was sent against Troitskavask on the Selenga River which succeeded in driving off a Bolshevik force of some 3,000 men who sought refuge in the Mongolian steppes. Mysovaya was then taken against superior numbers.

In preparing to storm Verkhneudinsk the Czechs lost one of their best Russian friends, Colonel Boris Usakov, who in employing a ruse took the port of Raskolskaya on Lake Baikal and was shot by a Red commissar who recognized him. Verkhneudinsk fell a few days later. The Soviet garrison fled to Mongolia from whence they issued as guerrilla bands. The way to Chita and Vladivostok now lay open.

The Ural group in May had been compelled to fight desperately in order to join up with the next echelon to the east. On May 27th it had seized Chelyabinsk; by June 2d it had reached Zlatoust and Kurgan on the west, and a few days later Petropavlovsk on the east. At Petropavlovsk, Colonel Zák, who had been a law student before the war, learned of a contemplated attack against him by a force of 2,000 Bolsheviks whose numbers included many Letts, Esthonians, and some German and Magyar prisoners of war. He assaulted them where they had fortified themselves in a tinned fruit factory. Those who escaped were confronted with Kirghiz peasants whose methods were far from gentle. Immediately afterward the Ural groups secured Marianovka, where it had effected a junction on June 7th with the Novonikolayevsk group under Gajda.

The whole Volga group was safe on the left bank of that river by June 4th, but there remained the yet more formidable task of capturing Samara, a stronghold of Bolshevism —an effort which was crowned with success after a sharp battle. A battalion of 500 rifles captured Kazan, a city of 200,000 inhabitants, but were forced to evacuate it after twenty-four hours. By June 6th their echelons held the section from Omsk to Krasnoyarsk, while farther west they controlled the line from Penza to Nizhneudinsk.

The Czechs at Samara during June assisted in the formation of a government which in turn lent them valuable assistance. This new government, composed of Socialist-Revolutionary members of the former Constituent Assembly, although weak, nevertheless raised a People's Army of sorts. With its aid the Czechs on July 14th occupied Stavropol, and on July 22d captured Simbirsk. Buzuluk on the Orenburg Railway was then seized. The Legionnaires continued their advance to Buguruslan and eventually, in the first week of July, to Ufa and Orenburg, the headquarters of General Dutov, the anti-Bolshevik Ataman of the Orenburg Cossacks. On July 6th the Volga echelon had established contact with the Czechs in the Urals at the station of Berdansk.

Three thousand miles to the east were General Dieterichs and his echelons at Vladivostok. Dieterichs had encamped his men on the outskirts of the city. Vladivostok at the time had a sizable Red garrison with whom the Czechs were having more and more friction. An agreement was drawn up on June 20th whereby the Bolsheviks were to cease sending arms inland without a Czech indorsement and were to retain the Red troops within the confines of their barracks and the fort. This agreement the Bolsheviks violated. The Czechs attacked and, aided by a demonstration from the Japanese cruiser *Asachi,* captured and formally occupied the city on June 28th. Agarev, the former Russian mayor, was reinstalled and the life of the city moved on with a fair degree of order and security.

In the Far East the Czechs immediately set about re-equipping themselves, caring for their wounded, and clearing the district of Bolsheviks. The line to the Suchan coal mines was freed of Red forces and after a bloody battle on July 5th the junction of the Amur and Chinese Eastern Railway at Nikolsk-Ussuriski was secured. Thereafter in the sections under their control the Czechs policed the railway, leaving a squad or two at small stations along the line. They were in no particular peril at this time and could have been evacuated had the Allies wished it.

The Czechs were now occupying territory up to the Manchurian frontier, where they made contact with General Horvath, a Czarist in charge of the Chinese Eastern Railway with his own constabulary and almost dictatorial powers.

The Vladivostok group of the Czech Army pushed northward along the Amur Railway toward Khabarovsk in the vicinity of which had gathered a force of some 10,000 poorly equipped Soviet troops. Continuous fighting occurred along the railway until the first of August. In their occupation of the line the Czechs were aided by the railway men, many of whom at the time dreaded Soviet rule and had not yet experienced the doubtful pleasures of the White Government of Admiral Kolchak and his associates.

News was abroad that the legions were not to sail home but were to assist the Allies in Siberia by holding the railway and preventing German and Hungarian prisoners from returning to their homes. This was a bitter disappointment to the Czechs, but they willingly obeyed the wish of their influential friends and by early fall the eastward echelons were moving back along the Trans-Siberian. At this time a general mobilization of Czechoslovaks in Siberia was ordered. Many prisoners of war came forward along with numbers of Lithuanians and Russians. General Dieterichs was placed as Syrový's chief-of-staff over all these forces which came to number nearly 100,000 men.

During this period, secret organizations of Czech officers associated in Siberia with the Socialist-Revolutionaries. The policies of White officers were creating unrest among the Ural Cossacks and the liberty-loving peasantry, who resented the requisitioning of grain, food, and other supplies. Local managers and helpers in the Peasants' Coöperatives were in most instances Socialist-Revolutionaries. To these groups, the Legionnaires, most of whom were Socialists, were sympathetic.

At the risk of a slight repetition in Chapter VI it is well here to review in short compass Allied and American action which encouraged the Czechs to remain in Siberia. As a matter of fact, the Legionnaires were compelled by circumstances to do what their powerful patrons advised. Representatives of France, England, and the American State Department on the ground had evidently determined not to rush the Czechs out of Siberia. The legions might be of assistance in forming an Eastern Front, to help overthrow the Reds, or to prevent the return of hundreds of thousands of German, Austrian, and Magyar prisoners of war.

That the French were planning to use the Czechs for their own interests is evident in a message from Major Guinet to the American officer, Colonel Emerson, who was in Western Siberia on June 23d. Major Guinet wired from Omsk: "The French Ambassador makes known to Commander Guinet that he can thank the Czechoslovaks for their actions, this in the name of all the Allies. They, the Allies, have decided to intervene the last of June and the Army Czechoslovaks and the French Mission form the advance guard of the Allied Army." This statement was without authority as far as America was concerned, and misled the Czechs into believing that an Allied intervention in force would extend into Western Siberia.

The Czech cause was now thrusting itself upon the attention of Allied statesmen. On July 2, 1918, the Supreme War Council at Versailles made a new appeal to President Wilson to aid the Czech legions, who responded with a proposal for a joint international contingent composed of Americans, Japanese, and British with the purpose of maintaining contact with the Czechs. Three days later Washington announced that it had decided upon a limited intervention to protect the Czechs against the Germans and "to assist in the efforts at self-government or self-defense in which the Russians themselves may be ready to accept assistance."

President Wilson was interested in the Czech fight for freedom. The *Aide Memoir,* dated July 17th and signed by the American State Department, which was handed General Graves to guide his actions in Siberia, stated that one of the reasons for intervention was "to help the Czechoslovaks consolidate their forces and to get into successful coöperation with their Slavic kinsmen." However, the Czechs had been in possession of important points on the Trans-Siberian two months before the United States took action for their safety!

United States Consul Gray at Omsk received a cipher message dated July 22, 1918, forwarded from the United States Consulate in Samara, directing him to inform the Czechs "confidentially" that "pending further notice the Allies will be glad, from a political point of view, to have them hold their present position. On the other hand, they should not be hampered in meeting the military exigency of the situation. It is desirable, first of all, that they should secure the control of the Trans-Siberian Railway, and second, if this is assured, at the same time possibly retain control over the territory which they now dominate. Inform the French representative that the French Consul General joins in these instructions."

Enormous indirect aid accrued to the Czechs as well as various White governments coming into being in Siberia in the summer of 1918 through the uprisings of the Socialist-Revolutionaries in Yaroslavl, Moscow, and in the Ukraine.

Eager to win favor with France, England, and America, the legions willingly remained, a provocation to the Reds and an irritation to many Whites. Their presence was the cause of much suffering on their own part and no little bloodshed during the winter of 1918-19.

Meanwhile, far to the west, the Czechs were active. Before the Volga front could be established safely, it was necessary to possess the important railway junction of Ekaterinburg, a feat which was accomplished on July 25th. Many armored trains and abundant supplies and munitions were taken as booty. During the battle for the city, Colonel Zák in storming an armored car was shot through the leg but continued to direct his troops from a hired droshky.

When the Czechs and White Russians entered Ekaterinburg they corroborated the gruesome news of the execution of the Czar's family, Dr. Eugène Sergevich Botkin, physician to the royal family, and three servants, eleven persons in all, on July 17th. An investigation was begun on July 30th under Judge Nametkin and later given over to Judge Nicholas Sokolov of the Omsk Tribunal, who carried through a painstaking research which revealed their murder at the instigation of Jacob Sverdlov in Moscow, employing Beloborodov, Goloshchekin, and Yurovsky as the executioners. Although the bodies were burned and seemingly every evidence removed and thrown in an abandoned mine shaft near the village of Koptiaki, hundreds of clues remained to tell the bloody story. The box containing the relics was finally smuggled out of Russia and placed in the family vault of General Janin in Paris. Judge Sokolov's compilation of evidence was published in 1925, a volume containing one hundred and twenty thousand words.

Kazan fell next, early in August, which gave the Czechs rich military stores and the gold reserve of the State Bank of Russia. The moral effect on the Bolsheviks was, for the time, decisive.

The Czechs were disappointed in the lack of enthusiasm and poor fighting quality of the White troops in this area. General Gajda reported that when the Czechs and Russians took Kazan he found four thousand Czarist officers were in the city who could have assembled at least fifteen thousand effectives. Only three hundred of the officers joined up, others fled, found safer occupations, or gave themselves over to debauchery. More intimate acquaintance with Russian officers in White armies in Siberia did not improve Gajda's opinion either of their resolution or their fighting qualities.

The Czechs were soon to meet with serious attacks. The Red Army along the Volga had been reinforced. Trotsky, chagrined at the loss of Kazan and Simbirsk, concentrated four Red armies under his personal leadership upon the two cities. The attack began on August 12th. A bloody battle was fought near Simbirsk on August 17th in which General Kappel with White troops and the Czechs defeated Trotsky's regiments. Among the conscripted men in the White ranks were many boys who had no heart for fighting. A more severe attack upon Kazan was launched on September 5th, Trotsky promising his soldiers a chance to loot the town and a cash prize to the first regiment to enter. Kazan was hard pressed. Regiments of citizens, some in cutaways and patent leather shoes and others barefoot and clad in peasants' tunics, could offer little help to Kappel and the Czechs, who saw that the evacuation of the town was inevitable. Kazan was lost on September 10th and Simbirsk three days later. Red occupation of Kazan meant the loss, eventually, of the whole Volga front. The Czechs were outspoken regarding numbers of Russian officers who were taking their ease in the city during the heavy fighting preceding the loss of Kazan. In order not to separate the westward echelons from larger groups east, Samara also was evacuated under pressure from the Red Army on October 8th. At Samara some twenty-five thousand Bolsheviks were deployed against nine thousand Legionnaires.

A tragedy occurred in this series of battles which stiffened the morale of the Czechs in the west. They were becoming confused and were asking why they should be fighting in the Russian turmoil and where were the soldiers the Allies had sent to aid them! Colonel Švec, having ordered his men from their trains, met with a refusal and promptly shot himself. On the table in his car he left a note, giving reasons why they should continue the struggle. The next day, under a young officer, Lieutenant Špála, Colonel Švec's regiment marched to the front and fought for the next month in some of the most savage battles they were to experience in the Civil War. Colonel Švec's impressive funeral was held on October 28th, the day Czechoslovak independence was declared in Prague.

Everything combined to dishearten the Legionnaires; they were not receiving the expected help from the Allies, they were irritated by Allied attempts to do away with their soldiers' committees, and they were being driven back by the Bolsheviks. At the end of October the front ran from Verchoturje, over Kinovsky Zavod to Buguruslan and Buzuluk in the south, where contact was made with a Cossack Army under Dutov. The entire anti-Bolshevist forces numbered only fifty-five thousand men against an army twice as strong, under experienced ex-Czarist officers who were trying to recapture Ekaterinburg in the north and in the south to force their way to Turkestan.

The Czechs had neatly picked the French chestnuts from the fire and had found too late that such operations are painful. Friction between them and the Allies reached such a pass that they were quite ready to listen to Chicherin, when on November 1st another offer was made by him to transfer them to their own homes. Moreover, they had democratic leanings and as such were out of sympathy with the reactionary forces that were now winning their way to power.

The principal task of the Czechs from September until the Armistice was to protect themselves and guard the railway. The very fact that they were in control of the one essential artery of communication made their presence of enormous importance to Red and White alike, both of whom would have been happy if the Legionnaires had been out of Siberia, although they rendered much useful service to the White movement throughout 1918 and much of 1919. Plans were under way which would effect them. They knew that Japan was already in the Russian Far East in force, as well as British, French, and Italian missions which were arriving with many officers, but few soldiers. The Americans had landed the Twenty-seventh Infantry at Vladivostok on August 16th, Admiral Knight having been there for some six months previously. The British were represented by General Knox with a large mission of officers and a few hundred Canadian troops who were later sent home because of their liberal views. The Czechs received orders from President Masaryk to stay where they were for the present.

In the Urals and farther west there were frequent small battles with Red troops, while eastward on the railway constant vigilance was demanded to prevent surprise by Red and Partisan bands. Not only were they required to defend their bodies but also their minds from the cynicism and barbarity which had spread over Siberia like a miasma.

Small bodies of their soldiers patrolled the railway and occupied the stations. Several armored trains were constructed, one of which, the "Orlik" or "Little Eagle," thrust its beak into many a hornet's nest. On occasions they commandeered factories for the making of supplies and machine shops to repair locomotives, guns, and rolling stock. In the ranks were many who were tool-makers, machinists, and munition workers whose knowledge now had a special timeliness. The Legionnaires were often compelled to seize shops to manufacture medicines and clothing.

The Czechs impressed all foreign observers with the sincerity of their purpose and their discipline, in spite of a democratic camaraderie among officers and men unfamiliar to Western commanders. Having fallen out with the Soviets, they soon began to be less friendly with White commanders whose harsh methods reminded them of the manners of the Dual Monarchy.

The echelons patrolling the Trans-Siberian contained all types. Among their number were accomplished musicians, artists, and professional men. The songs of the Legionnaires are among the finest soldiers' music produced by the war. Scenes in Bohemia, Moravia, and Slovakia were painted in bright colors upon scores of railroad vans inhabited by their troops. The Hradcany palace in Prague, symbolizing the national hopes of these young men, was a favorite subject for their artists. Often the soldiers in a car painted upon it names of villages from which they came, thus facilitating reunion with comrades and relatives as men from different echelons passed each other in the shuttling back and forth along the Trans-Siberian. A readable account of their exploits in English occurs in Baerlein's *The March of the Seventy Thousand.*

During 1918 the Czechs formed a Legionnaire's Bank which carried on extensive financial operations necessary for provisioning and equipping the troops. Many foreigners made use of this institution which in the spring of 1919 was transferred to Czechoslovakia. A Revolution Loan in Russia to which colonists and soldiers alike contributed gave the bank a sizable working capital. Each legionnaire had a share in the bank, their average savings amounting to two hundred and eighteen French francs. Their pay was small but their monetary needs were few; an officer received about the same pay for a month as a British lieutenant received for a day.

Their peripatetic military newspaper, the *Československý Deník*, which appeared first in Kiev in 1918, was printed on board their trains in a hundred different places. Special Magyar and German editions were published in order that prisoners of war whose homes were in the confines of the new state of Czechoslovakia might be acquainted with conditions. These prisoners were allowed to attach themselves to the legions as labor battalions, cooks, tailors, cleaners, and in various noncombatant capacities, while some entered actively into the fighting. The Czech press also printed paper money for Admiral Kolchak's government. The Kolchak administration dumped bundles of old Kerensky rubles over the Red lines with a statement printed across their face, "You can have these for nothing!" The Reds did likewise, turning out bushels of forged notes which they sold by the pound!

Men stood out in the adventures of the Legionnaires, many of whom were destined to hold high offices in the new state of Czechoslovakia. General Šyrový saw from the outset the hopelessness of the White effort in Siberia. Syrový was respected by Allied and Russian officers and beloved by his men. Upon his return to Czechoslovakia he was to become commander-in-chief of the army. Professor Maxa, who had organized Czech prisoners in Turkestan, arranged voluntary contributions among the munition factory workers, recruited for the Družina, and did much important diplomatic service. Medek, a poet, Colonel Eisenberger, a doctor, and Husák, who rose to the rank of general and was in charge of a contingent which sailed via Archangel to France, made outstanding contributions to the spirit of the Legionnaires. Švec, the hard-hitting officer who committed suicide when his troops refused to obey an order, was cherished as a hero along with many other courageous men, who, dreaming of the meadows of Bohemia and Slovakia, had met death in the fastnesses of Siberia. Dr. Langer served equally well as surgeon, poet, playwright, and soldier. George Klecanda, who drew up the special memorandum presented to the Imperial

Government regarding the formation of the Družina, had been imprisoned by the Reds at Berdichev with high Czarist officers and later escaped to the Czech forces. Dr. Vaclav Girsa, as a representative of the National Council, rendered valuable service as a diplomat in Russia and Siberia.

A Russian leader much esteemed by the Czechs was Colonel Usakov, the commander of a small force of anti-Bolshevik Russians, who fought beside the Legionnaires in many desperate encounters at Krasnoyarsk, Irkutsk, and Baikal, his tall form in the front of every *mêlée*. General Dieterichs, who had conceived the Brusilov offensive of 1916, became Syrový's chief-of-staff. He was a faithful friend of the Legionnaires and was in turn adored by them.

Vladislav Klecanda, quartermaster general to General Dieterichs, finally resigned his command in the tortuous days when the Legionnaires were embroiled along the whole length of the Trans-Siberian, because he either wanted to attack the Bolsheviks or go home.

General Čeček, who had lived in Russia as a representative of a motor-car firm before the war, distinguished himself with the Družina when it was fighting as part of the Russian Army, later commanding the First Division of the Czechs. Colonel Zák, the law student turned soldier with the Legionnaires, became an officer in the Army Staff College at Prague. Major Hásek, whose battalion of storm troops had distinguished itself in many a fracas, achieved added fame among the Legionnaires in blowing up the trainload of dynamite near the Baikal tunnels.

Kadlec was another Czech who possessed some of Gajda's *elan*. He had worked for the Belgians in the Congo. Later he had served in the Austrian Army, was captured and sent to Turkestan, where he was liberated in 1916 and found a place in the Cabinet of the President of the Czechoslovak Union. He had been wounded at Bakhmach and rose rapidly in rank. Kadlec disliked the term "brother" and the familiar "thou" employed by the Legionnaires. Resentment was aroused among his troops at his severe measures as a disciplinarian. Finally he was placed in command of Rumanian troops in Siberia in the summer of 1918, succeeding a Rumanian major, Dambov, who had been assassinated by his men at Chelyabinsk.

Among the many women who performed extraordinary service for the Legions was Božena Seidlova, who later became the wife of Major Holeček. Her father and brother had been sent via Archangel to fight with the Czechs in France. She with her mother and younger sisters stayed behind in Kishinev in the Ukraine. When the Czechs became involved with the Reds she made a journey from Kiev to the Volga, disguised as a peasant. At one stage of the journey she was compelled to walk two hundred miles on foot, and in the course of three secret journeys in which she carried important messages she traversed over nine thousand miles back and forth through the Bolshevik lines.

Stefánik, a Slovak astronomer, who became a French general with the Czech forces fighting in France, with Professor Thomas Masaryk and Dr. Edouard Beneš, formed the triumvirate which brought into being the new state. They formulated principles to which the legions gave enthusiastic assent. In 1916 Stefánik had been received in a kindly manner by the Czar and had succeeded in winning a favorable hearing for the Czech cause as well as gaining the friendship of Bazali who was chief of the Political Department at Russian headquarters. He was conscious of anti-Czech influence at the Russian capital in the persons of Stürmer and Priklonski, both high in the councils of the Imperial Government. Toward the end of 1918 Masaryk and Beneš felt that Stefánik's presence among the legions was necessary to acquaint them with events in Western Europe and to keep up their enthusiasm with news of their new homeland.

Stefánik arrived at Vladivostok in the special capacity of Minister of State with General Janin, who laid claim to the title of commander-in-chief of all Allied forces in Siberia, a title emphatically denied by the commanding officers of the American and Allied contingents. Stefánik sedulously avoided meeting Kolchak and set about establishing discipline according to the approved methods of the West. He announced that the Czechs in Siberia were a part of the Czechoslovak Army and as such should not have a Parliament. Many of the Legionnaires resented this intrusion of discipline into the camaraderie which had prevailed between both officers and the ranks. One of his least popular actions was the dismissal of General Dieterichs, who had been a devoted friend and helper of the Czechs.

No Czech chief aroused more admiration and criticism than did Gajda. His career in Siberia revealed a man of extraordinary courage and strength of will. He was impatient of delay and the wishes of others, working well alone but often blind to the needs of his superior. His weakness was an imperious disposition and a somewhat erratic nature. He was still to feature prominently in the régime of Admiral Kolchak.

Siberia was a witch's cauldron of blood, politics, pillaging, and intrigue. With a standard of culture never high, lawlessness was to be expected after war and revolution. Partisan bands worked their will upon villages and towns. A blood lust, Asiatic in its ferocity, led to killings and mutilation of innocent victims by the thousand. The Red Terror in Russia was met by a White Terror of equal brutality in Siberia. The deeds of the two White chieftains, Atamans Semyonov and Kalmykov, would have done credit to Genghis Khan. The example of such excesses was enough to deter the Czech legions from allowing discipline to perish as it had in the Russian armies. Ruthlessness by Reds, Whites, and Partisans bred a dislike for the Russian scene. Never did the hills around Prague and Gratz and Pilsen seem greener than in the impoverished, typhus-ridden towns of Siberia, whose populace lived in terror of friend and foe alike.

Czech soldiers were not expert in the politics of Red and White Siberia; few representatives of any nation were, much less the Russians. For the most part they were men of integrity whose settled purpose was to bring the downfall of the Dual Monarchy, and once that had been accomplished, to disentangle themselves from the Russian *mêlée* and return home.

The immediate effect of the Armistice of November 11th was to raise the morale of the Czechs. The situation was psychologically changed for them. They were now citizens of a free state and no longer compelled to bear the opprobrious term, deserter. Bohemia, Moravia, Slovakia, Silesia, and Ruthenia had thrown off Hapsburg rule. The stimulation of victory and hope for the future buoyed them up amid the frustration in which the Siberian population found itself.

For the Reds and Whites in Siberia the Armistice made little difference. Admiral Kolchak, lately come to power as War Minister of the All-Russian Directory of Omsk and soon to be Dictator, surrounded by reactionary officers, was impatient of the Czechs' liberal attitude. He was eager to have them out of his way and yet knew they were among the most reliable troops fighting on his anti-Bolshevik fronts and the only troops capable of guarding the railway from Baikal west to the front. The Reds would have rejoiced at their departure. The American commander at Vladivostok maintained a strict neutrality in Russian affairs but stood ready to help the Czechs in case of need.

The Czechs now possessed a homeland. They were beginning to suspect that the Allies were more afraid of Bolshevism than they were interested in aiding them. The Great War was over and they were eager to set foot on the soil of their new nation. But the Civil War in Siberia had not spent its force and they were yet to see much bloodshed in the months that followed.

No body of troops in the Russian Civil War had shown such resolution and unity as the legionnaires. A hunger for independence which had been frustrated since the Battle of Bílá Hora in 1620 buoyed them up many times when events threatened to drown them in the morass of politics and bloodshed. The knowledge that they were creating a sentiment which would determine the attitude of powerful nations toward their new state laid upon them a sense of responsibility unshared by many thousands in other armies. When they took strong measures in insuring their own safety they were doing only what every other armed force in Siberia was compelled to do. They had proved their ability to care for themselves—there were still tribulation and hazard to prove their endurance in the troublous days before them.

Chapter VI

SIBERIA: WHITE GOVERNMENT AND INTERVENTION; TO THE ARMISTICE

RUSSIANS of every shade of anti-Red opinion were active throughout Siberia in early 1918, planning governments and armies to stem the tide of Bolshevism and to seize power from each other. Each group looked to the Allies and to the United States for aid. At the same moment Western statesmen turned toward any quarter which promised to relieve pressure upon the Western Front. Every German division detained in the East was of vital importance.

The Siberian situation was complicated not only by the long, vulnerable line of the Trans-Siberian Railway along which all cities and towns of importance were located, by the character of the country and the mentality of its citizens, but also by the conflicting interests of various military and political factions which were operating. The lack of a definite policy upon the part of the Allies, the dream of Siberian autonomy, Red uprisings, the presence of the Czechs, the rise of Socialist-Revolutionary and other anti-Bolshevik governments, all contributed to swamp Siberia in bloodshed and disillusionment.

The Allies had debated their course of action throughout the year 1917. As early as December 14, 1917, the *Journal des Débats* had advocated the control of the Trans-Siberian Railway by a joint force of Americans and Japanese.

As far as the West was concerned, confidence in the Soviet Government disappeared on February 12, 1918, when Moscow declared that the Great War was over. The Allies had hailed Lvov, Miliukov, Kerensky, Kornilov, and Trotsky, in turn, as friends of the Allied cause against Germany. Red Russia had been treated as friendly as long as there was a possibility of her fighting Germany. All news was biased by hope, until Russia was definitely out of the Great War. Russia's weaknesses were minimized and the slightest shred of favorable news was magnified.

Intervention received one of its initial impulses from a famous interview given by Foch to Grasty, published on February 26, 1918:

If America will look ahead I am sure she will see another field in which she can render immense service without relaxing her efforts on the Western Front. She should give her attention to the Orient.

Germany is walking through Russia. America and Japan, who are in a position to do so, should go to meet her in Siberia. Both for the war and after, America and Japan must furnish military and economic resistance to German penetration. There should be immediate steps in this important matter. Don't wake up after it is too late. Don't wait until the enemy has too much of a start. . . .

Thus intervention before the Armistice was advocated and begun as a part of the grand strategy of the European war against Germany.

From the Peace of Brest-Litovsk to the decision of the Allies to intervene in the summer of 1918 news from Russia had changed radically. Organized propaganda for intervention was at work through the West. Indignation rose high against the Soviet régime for having failed to reëstablish the Eastern Front. The March offensive of the Germans on the Western Front was in full swing, the most formidable thrust of the Central Powers throughout the war. Danger to the Allied cause made them especially sensitive to what they felt to be the defalcation of Russia.

Western and Central Russia were solidly Bolshevik in the early months of 1918. The chance of Denikin conquering the Reds from the South was doubtful. But Siberia offered the possibility of organizing a formidable anti-Bolshevik and anti-German army and could be reached from Vladivostok, while only a comparatively unimportant territory could be held from Archangel and Murmansk and the Black Sea ports were still inaccessible to Allied shipping. Also, in Siberia there existed a nascent nationalism which might be capitalized to Allied and anti-Bolshevik advantage.

Siberian autonomy was by no means a new idea. It had been agitated intermittently throughout the last half of the nineteenth century and in the years before the Revolution. Vast distances, coupled with a pioneer type of mind, a thinly settled region far away from central authority, nourished the idea of independence not only among the intelligentsia but also among large numbers of artisans, woodsmen, and adventurous settlers. The Cossacks of the region possessed larger liberties than the ordinary citizen of Russia. Under the circumstances of war and revolution it was natural that Siberians should think of autonomy. The more extreme conceived of it in terms of permanent separation, the creation of a new and independent state, while the more moderate discussed a provisional and temporary measure until the Soviet régime could be destroyed and a free Russia established.

The mentality of Siberia was the product of the streams of emigration which had settled the land. The landlord-peasant quarrel which had proved nettlesome in Russia was comparatively non-existent in Siberia, as there were few landlords, although there did exist the social and political tension between the privileged and the underprivileged. The country had the characteristics of a frontier in any section of the earth. Resolute and independent citizens inhabited the narrow zone of the Trans-Siberian Railway and small towns dotting banks of rivers flowing north to the Arctic Sea. The population consisted of troopers, lumbermen, fishermen, trappers, and miners, as well as many thousands connected with the railway, the civil administrations, and the army—a hardy people, with a frontier culture. Illiteracy was high, and schools, hospitals, and other public-service institutions generally of a lower grade than in European Russia, although many distinguished and professional men had been compelled to spend much of their lives amid Siberia's melancholy forests and steppes.

The idea of autonomy was strengthened also by the presence of large groups of Cossacks settled by the Czars along the frontiers, receiving grants in money and arms, with large political liberties. When Count Muraviev conquered the Amur country in 1851 he immediately changed the status of the Nerchinsk population to that of Cossacks.

The government made a policy of establishing garrisons of Cossacks and Imperial regiments in remote regions and settlements of Yamschiks who provided remount and relay stations along post routes. The non-military classes turned to hunting, fishing, and mining more than to agriculture. Many settled to the east and north, where furs were to be had as a means of livelihood. In the country south of the railway were peasant farmers who were firmly wedded to the soil.

As early as 1648 exiles were employed as a means of colonization. Thousands were sent to Siberia for ordinary civil and criminal offenses as well as for political causes. The fate of these men and women and of their families, who often voluntarily accompanied them, has formed the theme of many artists and writers of both drama and novel. Their sufferings in the long trek, often for many hundreds of versts in the snow, were pitiable, arousing widespread indignation at times.

Other colonizing elements were the descendants of Raskolniki (Schismatics) who objected to the reform of Nikon, who, in 1625, revised the rites and books of the national church and two years later, with the aid of the Patriarchs of Alexandria and of Antioch, excommunicated large groups who had formed a schism or Raskol. Still other elements were the descendants of *stryeltsy* or rebels against Peter the Great, the "Decembrists" who opposed Nicholas I, the Poles of the uprising of 1863, those who were arrested after the 1905 Revolution, and those who for various causes were sent to the Asiatic territory of the Czars. Exile as a punishment for political crimes was abolished in 1900 but restored in 1904.

Many of the most learned and influential men and women of Old Russia had at times been in exile and made their contribution to the cultural, economic, and political life in Siberia. The brother of Prince Kropotkin gave much time and labor to the archeological museum at Minusinsk. The "Decembrists" built the town of Chita. From the national point of view the Raskolniki and the Skoptsi sect, a pious and industrious group, were the best colonizers, as they settled on small farms, building up the agricultural resources of the land. Throughout its history Siberia has been troubled by escaped convicts who, because of the scanty population, the lack of roads, and the immense forests could easily avoid capture.

In addition there have always been numbers of free settlers, the most important group in Siberia. Many came first as fugitives from serfdom, military conscription, or ecclesiastical persecution. Along with all elements of Russians in Siberia they intermarried freely with the Buriats, Yakuts, Kirgis, and other mongoloid peoples.

The close of the Russo-Japanese War was a signal for large-scale emigration from Russia. Some 350,000 families settled in Siberia between 1909 and 1913. In the latter year the number of settlers reached 234,877.

Distance from administrative headquarters, the peculiar conditions of the country, the primitive scale of life, all contributed to lessen the discipline of both the civil bureaucracy and the military, producing a slow-moving, simple state of culture with a jealous regard for all rights and privileges which had been granted by the Czars and something of the frontiersman's disdain for what they were wont to consider the softer populations of the West.

Such a social *milieu* with strong leanings toward independence was a fertile seedbed for uprisings not only against Czarist encroachments and the harsh rule of the Soviets, but also against the equally heavy hand of White leaders.

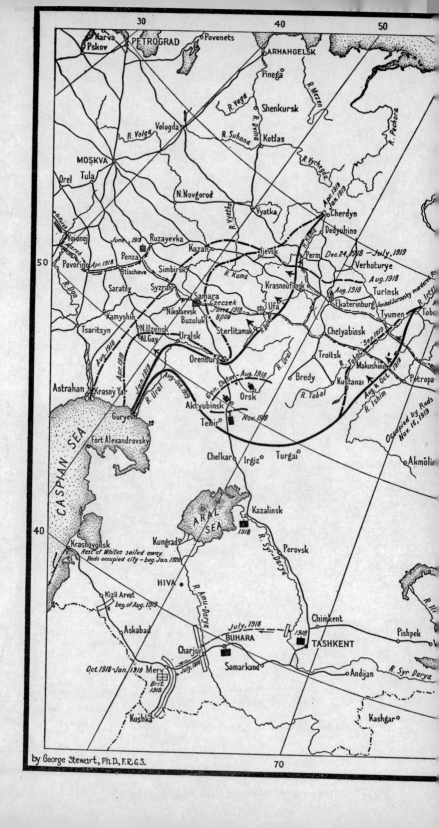

by George Stewart, Ph.D., F.R.G.S.

Before any White movement was established, Red uprisings from the frontier of Europe to Vladivostok followed the Soviet's ascent to power in Petrograd and Moscow. In almost every city and town a Bolshevik reign of terror was set up, during which hundreds of the old ruling class were murdered, many in the most atrocious manner.

The politicals in Siberia had been ceaseless in preparation for the creation of a Siberian Regional Government before the Bolshevik coup of November, 1917. A conference of revolutionary democratic organizations was held at Tomsk in August. In October of 1917, when delegates from these public bodies assembled as an All-Siberian Congress, they convoked an Extraordinary Siberian Regional Congress to meet in December for the purpose of setting up an autonomous Siberian Government. This Congress met and elected an executive organ, the Provisional Regional Council, which it entrusted with authority to summon the Siberian Regional Duma. This body was radical in character and planned to exclude the bourgeoisie from representation, but this did not save it from the enmity of the Bolsheviks, who despised such halfway measures. It was strongly Siberian-Nationalist and looked forward to free and complete autonomy from Russia.

The Siberian Regional Duma was to be convened in Tomsk on February 1, 1918. But Tomsk went Red, and the Bolsheviks arrested several members of both the Regional Council and the Duma. Thereupon the most active member of the Council, a Socialist-Revolutionary by the name of Derber, called a secret session of the Duma in a private apartment. This session, which was attended by some twenty of the one hundred and fifty delegates, elected the Provisional Siberian Government of sixteen regular ministers and four ministers without portfolio, mostly Socialist-Revolutionaries. A manifesto was drawn up in the spirit of Chernov and the decisions of the Constituent Assembly of January, 1918, which the Bolsheviks had closed. The members of the Council and of the Duma decided to leave the city secretly, making their way singly to Harbin on Chinese territory. Later, several members of this group, headed by the Socialist-Revolutionary Vologodsky, returned in June of 1918 to Omsk, when that city was in the hands of the Czechs.

In Harbin, Derber's government found a competitor in General Horvath, Director of the Chinese Eastern Railway, who was regarded by leaders of the so-called Far Eastern Committee as a likely candidate for the post of premier of the future All-Russian Government. Negotiations for that purpose were being conducted in Pekin with the Allies, but the formation of the government was delayed until an army could be organized, whereupon an invitation was extended to Admiral Kolchak, then residing in Japan, to assist in raising an army. The Derber Siberian Government was radical but not Red, while Horvath and his group represented the more conservative elements of manufacturers, bankers, and traders.

The Allies meanwhile were casting apprehensive glances toward the Russian Far East. As early as December 23, 1917, military representatives of the Supreme War Council had recommended that all possible support should be given to Russians who were resolved to continue the war against Germany. Hundreds of thousands of prisoners of war, Germans, Austrians, and Magyars, might return west to their homelands should Russia conclude an immediate peace with Germany and in addition there were mountainous war stores shipped by Allied countries to Russia in Vladivostok. Equally fearsome was the new Communist idea which was sweeping Russia and threatening the morale of Europe. Such was the shortage of man power on the Western Front that some Allied statesmen advocated the dispatch of a strong Japanese force through Siberia to the Eastern Front in Poland or Rumania, but this the United States viewed with disfavor, not wishing her rival on the Pacific to secure so strong a foothold in Siberia.

Japan was closest to, and most interested in, Siberia, but was nevertheless a dangerous ally to employ, as all Russians viewed her with suspicion and might rejoin by making common cause with Germany. On the other hand, Japan was eager to move troops into Siberia but was unwilling for the United States to participate. Downing Street had raised the question with President Wilson on December 31, 1917, who replied that the United States opposed intervention either by Japan alone or by both acting in concert. In March of 1918 Japan requested that she alone take control of the Chinese Eastern and Amur railways, but this proposal was not viewed by Washington with favor. After months of tortuous diplomatic negotiations conducted by England and France, desperately pressed by German armies and reaching out for help in any quarter, a joint Allied intervention with limited objects was agreed to by the United States on July 2, 1918, and forces were dispatched.

A proclamation addressed to the population of Vladivostok was placarded throughout the streets on July 6th, placing the city and its environs "under the provisional protection of the Allied Powers," stating that the activity of "Austro-German agents" justified a move that was "taken in a spirit of friendship and sympathy for the Russian people" and not in support of "any political faction or party." This proclamation was signed by Admiral Knight, of the United States Navy, Vice Admiral Kato, of the Japanese Navy, Captain Paine, of the Royal British Navy, Colonel Pons, Chief of the French military mission with the Czechoslovaks, the commandant of the Chinese cruiser, *Hai-Yun,* and the commandant of the city, Captain Badiura, of the Czechoslovak Army.

On the same day, July 6, 1918, that this important declaration was issued at Vladivostok, marking the beginning of open Allied intervention in the Russian Far East, a Czech committee, influenced by Allied representatives, decided to form a Volga front and to aid the Allies on the soil of Russia instead of on the battlefields of France, a decision they were later to regret. The Czechs at the time would far rather have gone home to Europe!

Japan's action in Siberia was prompted by both fear and

self-interest. She was haunted by the grim specter of Communism. Although the Japanese people, the press, the government, and, in fact, the War Office were divided regarding intervention in force, they united to prevent the Soviet régime from extending to the Pacific, an attitude which threw power into the hands of the military party and was tantamount to giving the War Office a free hand. Japan also had in view certain objectives which many of her leaders felt necessary for her security as a great Pacific power, the securing of that portion of the Island of Sakhalin which the Treaty of Portsmouth denied her, the extension of her territory about Korea, and greater railroad facilities in Manchuria. The project of reviving an Eastern Front along the Urals met with little response from Japan, who instructed her military not to advance beyond Lake Baikal. But because of her own anxieties a Japanese warship had steamed into Vladivostok as early as December of 1917. At the time, Britain was expected to coöperate, but orders issued for British troops to proceed to Vladivostok at the moment were canceled. The French favored the Japanese as an Allied force in the Russian Far East, who further strengthened their position by landing a naval force in early April of 1918.

Gradually President Wilson had been won over and America became committed in the Siberian imbroglio. Washington on July 17th notified the Allies that though opposed to a policy of armed intervention, the United States had decided to join the Japanese in landing armed contingents at Vladivostok. America stated that she was coöperating with the French and British at Murmansk and Archangel and proposed to the Japanese Government to coöperate in sending a force of a few thousand men to Siberia. She insisted that no interference with the political sovereignty of Russia was contemplated, but that at the earliest possible opportunity she hoped to send to Siberia a commission of merchants and agricultural experts to restore Russia's damaged trade. The significant points of difference between the declarations of the American and the Japanese governments were that

Tokyo expressed no doubts about military intervention and made no mention either of the project of reconstituting the Eastern Front, or of economic aid, as did Washington. One of President Wilson's chief reasons for intervention was the safety of the Czechs who from late May, 1918, were in a position to defend themselves. The Czechoslovak National Council made an announcement from Washington on July 27, 1918:

The Czechoslovak Army in Russia was created in order to fight the Germans and Austrians, and when Russia deserted the cause of the Allies, arrangements were made by Professor T. G. Masaryk, president of the Czechoslovak National Council, and Commander-In-Chief of the Czechoslovak forces with the Allied representatives in Russia, and also with the Bolsheviks, to march the Czechoslovaks out of Russia and take them to the Western Front. It should be kept clearly in mind that the occupation of Russian territory or the restoration of an Eastern Front was not thought of when these arrangements were made, in February, 1918. It was due to one of those German blunders, like the one that brought America into the War, that the Czechoslovaks, instead of withdrawing from Russia, are now in control of Siberia and a considerable territory west of the Urals. . . . A week ago (July 20th), Professor Masaryk received a lengthy cable report from the leader of the Czechoslovak forces in which the following words are found, indicative of the present desires of the men: "In my opinion, it is most desirable and also possible to reconstruct a Russia-Germany front in the East. We ask for instructions as to whether we should leave for France or whether we should stay here to fight in Russia by the side of the Allies, and of Russia." Professor Masaryk has since then instructed the forces in Siberia to remain there for the present.

The Czechs whose future national existence depended upon an Allied victory were willing to perform any service for the Allies even to risking their lives in the Siberian *mêlée*.

America and Japan both made statements regarding their policies on August 3, 1918. Japan announced:

In adopting this course (intervention) the Japanese Government remains constant in their desire to promote relations of enduring friendship, and they affirm their avowed policy of respect-

ing the territorial integrity of Russia, and of abstaining from all
interferences in her national politics.

The United States' announcement recited:

As the Government of the United States sees the present circumstances, therefore, military action is admissible in Russia
now, only to render such protection and help, as is possible to
the Czechoslovaks, against the armed Austrian and German
prisoners who are attacking them, and to steady any efforts at
self-government or self-defense in which the Russians themselves
may be willing to accept assistance. Whether from Vladivostok
or from Murmansk and Archangel, the only present object for
which American troops will be employed, will be to guard Military stores which may be subsequently needed by Russian forces.

Great Britain stated on August 8th:

We are coming as friends to help you to save yourself from dis-
memberment and destruction at the hands of Germany, which
is trying to enslave your people and use the great resources of
your country to its own ends. We wish to solemnly assure you
that we shall not retain one foot of your territory. The destinies
of Russia are in the hands of the Russian people. It is for them,
and them alone, to decide their forms of Government, and to find
a solution for their social problems.

The British on August 3d had landed the Twenty-fifth
Battalion of the Middlesex Regiment at Vladivostok. On the
12th of August the Japanese landed their Twelfth Division,
and on August 16th the Twenty-seventh United States Infantry arrived from Manila with fifty-three officers and one
thousand, five hundred and thirty-seven men under Colonel
Henry D. Styer. France sent five hundred troops from Pekin,
and eight hundred men were dispatched from Canada. General William S. Graves, in command of the American Expeditionary Forces, arrived on September 4th from San Francisco. The American contingent was augmented until it
reached the number of seven thousand, seven hundred men
and officers. Admiral Knight had been on duty in the harbor
for six months previously. The United States Government
wished to keep its contingent at a minimum and tried in vain
to persuade Japan to do likewise.

The *Aide Memoir* handed to General William S. Graves by Newton D. Baker, Secretary of War, was signed by the Department of State. Usually such missions were given the commanding officer of an expeditionary force through regular channels by the chief-of-staff. Had critics of American action in Siberia, including many Allied officers and not a few Americans, especially those connected with the Department of State, been cognizant of the strict terms of General Graves' instructions their strictures might have been less severe. The *Aide Memoir* recited in part:

. . . It is the clear and fixed judgment of the Government of the United States, arrived at after repeated and very searching reconsiderations of the whole situation in Russia, that military intervention there would add to the present sad confusion in Russia rather than cure it, injure rather than help her, and it would be of no advantage in the prosecution of our main desire to win the war against Germany. It cannot, therefore, take part in such intervention or sanction it in principle. Military intervention would, in its judgment, even supposing it to be efficacious in its immediate avowed object of delivering an attack upon Germany from the east, be merely a method of making use of Russia, not a method of serving her. Her people could not profit by it, if they profited by it at all, in time to save them from their present distresses, and their substance would be used to maintain foreign armies, not to reconstitute their own. Military action is admissible in Russia, as the Government of the United States sees the circumstances, only to help the Czechoslovaks consolidate their forces and get into successful coöperation with their Slavic kinsmen and to steady any efforts at self-government or self-defense in which the Russians themselves may be willing to accept assistance. Whether from Vladivostok or from Murmansk and Archangel, the only legitimate object for which American or Allied troops can be employed, it submits, is to guard military stores which may subsequently be needed by Russian forces to render such aid as may be acceptable to the Russians in the organization of their own self-defense. For helping the Czechoslovaks there is immediate necessity and sufficient justification. Recent developments have made it evident that it is in the interest of what the Russian people themselves desire, and the Government of the United States is glad to contribute the small force at its disposal for that purpose. It yields, also, to the judgment of the Supreme Command in the matter of establishing a small force at Murmansk, to guard the military stores at Kola and to make it safe for Russian forces to come together in organized bodies in the north. But it owes it to frank counsel to say that it can go no further than these modest and experimental plans. It is not in a position, and has no expectation of being in a position, to take part in organized intervention in adequate force from either Vladivostok or Murmansk and Archangel. It feels that it ought to add, also, that it will feel at liberty to use the few troops it can spare only for the purposes here stated and shall feel obliged to withdraw these forces, in order to add them to the forces at the Western Front, if the plans in whose execution it is now intended that they should develop into others inconsistent with the policy to which the Government of the United States feels constrained to restrict itself. . . .

It hopes to carry out the plans for safeguarding the rear of the Czechoslovaks operating from Vladivostok in a way that will place it and keep it in close coöperation with a small military force like its own from Japan, and if necessary from the other Allies, and that will assure it of the cordial accord of all the Allied powers; and it proposes to ask all associated in this course of action to unite in assuring the people of Russia in the most public and solemn manner that none of the governments uniting in action either in Siberia or in northern Russia contemplates any interference of any kind with the political sovereignty of Russia, any intervention in her internal affairs, or any impairment of her territorial integrity either now or hereafter, but that each of the associated Powers has the single object of affording such aid as shall be acceptable, and only such aid as shall be acceptable, to the Russian people in their endeavor to regain control of their own affairs, their own territory, and their own destiny. . . .

No other foreign representatives in Siberia were held to such definite instructions as were the American forces. From the standpoint of active intervention in Russian affairs in which the mood and enthusiasm of the moment carried the French, the British, and the Japanese a long way, General Graves' instructions were a handicap and won for him and the American military no little unpopularity. On the other hand, upon the basis of events as they transpired, even though no one can claim credit in Washington for having foreseen them, General Graves and the American forces did as much good and far less harm than any other foreign group.

Since June 28, 1918, the Czechs were policing Vladivostok. No organization, Czech, Allied, or Russian, was actually in full control, leaving many ordinary functions of the government in abeyance. Posts, telegraph, and railway facilities were subordinated to the needs of the military.

Another power on the scene in the Russian Far East was China. Early in January of 1918 the Chinese had occupied Harbin on the invitation of General Horvath, who was forming a nucleus of anti-Bolsheviks from among soldiers that Russia was allowed by treaty to station along that line. They refused to meddle in Russian affairs and won the approval of at least the commander of the American contingent in Siberia.

When General Graves landed, he found a campaign in the Ussuri Valley in progress. He was informed that it was against Bolsheviks and German prisoners of war who had been armed by the Reds. These troops were alleged to be threatening the Czechs. Some of the American infantry was engaged in this operation, the only case aside from a few local clashes in which American troops were ranged against armed Red forces in Siberia. The Japanese occupied Khabarovsk on August 16th and Blagoveshchensk on September 18th. A mixed Allied force had been dispatched on the 18th of August to drive out the Red forces on the Ussuri River. After some reverses, with reinforcements from General Oi's recently landed Twelfth Division and Kalmykov's Cossacks, the Red troops were routed. Although the operations were minor from the standpoint of numbers engaged and casualties suffered, they were decisive, halting Bolshevik uprisings for several months.

Up to the date of these engagements the Czechs were retreating eastward, but with the annihilation of the Bolshevik forces east of Lake Baikal they turned westward and displayed little anxiety about their evacuation, which was one of the alleged reasons for the presence of Allied troops in Russia.

On September 8th, General Graves was notified that the English, French, Japanese, and Czechs desired to move west to the Volga before the winter and wished to know the attitude of America. On September 19th, General Graves cabled Washington:

French and English are, undoubtedly, trying to get the Allied forces committed to some act which will result in the establishment of an Eastern Front.

The War Department on September 27th notified the American commander that the United States military were not to proceed farther west than Lake Baikal and that if the Czechs withdrew farther to the west, American responsibility would consist only of guarding the railroad line. The English and the French were equally concerned regarding any aid possible in prosecuting the war against Germany and destroying Bolshevism, while Japan was preoccupied with her position as an Eastern power in Siberia, as well as in combating Red Moscow.

General Gajda came to Vladivostok in September of 1918 accompanied by General Paris, the ranking French officer in the Far East, and several other French officers, seeking Allied aid for operations in Western Siberia. General Graves informed him explicitly at the time that he must not depend upon American troops to go west of Baikal.

The Amur Railway was soon under anti-Bolshevik domination. The Fourteenth Japanese Division was assigned to the Amur district and was soon in effective occupation. Ataman Kalmykov was strengthened in his position at Khabarovsk by the presence of Japanese troops and immediately began a series of extortions, tortures, imprisonments, and murders.

Ivan Pavlovich Kalmykov, Ataman of the Ussuri Cossacks, nominally a subordinate of Ataman Semyonov, was ensconced on the Amur Railway under the protection of the

Japanese. Throughout his period of power, this *franc-tireur* was guilty of murders and plunderings which would have disgraced any medieval footpad. When fifteen Austro-Hungarian prisoners of war formed a musical organization at Khabarovsk to earn food and clothing they were reported as spies, and, without the least pretense of trial, were brutally massacred. At another time, Kalmykov, after twice robbing two members of the Swedish Red Cross, had them hanged. The Swedish Government, when Kalmykov was a prisoner in Chinese hands, did not cease to press for his punishment. At a moderate estimate, one thousand, five hundred persons were executed without trial by this monster. Bolshevism held no terrors for the inhabitants of Khabarovsk! Kalmykov not only ordered the sacking of villages and wholesale robberies, but beat and killed with his own hands. Not only did he oppose the civil population, but treated his troops with such cruelty that many fled his brutality and sought refuge where they could find it. His reign of terror, extortion, and bloodshed encouraged many moderate men, despairing of the White cause, to throw in their lot with the Bolsheviks. He recognized no leader among the Russians save Semyonov, but necessity compelled him to be obedient to the Japanese who armed and supported him. General Graves remarks of him:

He was the worst scoundrel I ever saw or heard of and I seriously doubt, if one should go entirely through the Standard Dictionary, looking for words descriptive of crime, if a crime could be found that Kalmykov had not committed. He was armed and financed by Japan in their efforts "to help the Russian people." I say this advisedly, because I have evidence that would satisfy any open-minded person. Kalmykov murdered with his own hands where Semyonov ordered others to kill.

The Whites throughout the Civil War suffered from a political shortsightedness which made no provision for a middle view, considering all who were not avowedly White as Bolsheviks and as such deserving of death.

Ataman Grigori Mikhailovich Semyonov, the protégé of

Japan, was operating in Manchuria and Transbaikalia. Semyonov was born at Trans-Baykoe, Siberia, in 1890, with not a little Mongolian blood in his veins. He had been an officer in the Russian Army since 1908. When the Revolution broke out he was made a commissioner in the Transbaikal country and in the province of Irkutsk, gathering volunteers for the new army. He worked at this for about five months and sent several companies to the then German Front.

Semyonov took the field against the Reds early in the year 1918, moving out from Manchuria into the Transbaikal. His officers were, on the whole, the dregs of the old Russian officer class, although many of the better grade served with him at various times because his army offered a livelihood and a chance to lift a sword against the Soviets. His battalions were filled with Buriats, Yakuts, Cossacks, and many soldiers from semi-barbarous Mongol tribes.

For three and a half years he was to control an irregular army, raising it from a handful until at its peak he mustered over sixty thousand men. Semyonov was responsible to no one save the Japanese and lived off the country. Although he did recognize Kolchak, he never obeyed him. In April of 1918 Kolchak was compelled to move forces eastward with a view of attacking Semyonov at Chita. Semyonov pulled up the railroad and massed his forces to fight Kolchak's army, but through the efforts of the Japanese a conflict was avoided.

Semyonov had led the anti-Soviet revolt which broke out at Verkhneudinsk on November 19, 1917, one of the first armed efforts against the Soviets. Later he was badly beaten at Blagoveshchensk in March of 1918, when some Japanese troops sent to his rescue were killed. Such government as he possessed had been founded upon Chinese soil. An agreement had been made between the Chinese and the Soviets that Semyonov should not be allowed to leave Chinese territory until April 5, 1918, but by the end of the period he had acquired large sums of money with which to pay his nine hundred officers and Hunhuzas and fourteen pieces of artil-

The Imperial train in Siberia

Japanese transporting light artillery on the Amur

Russian cavalry

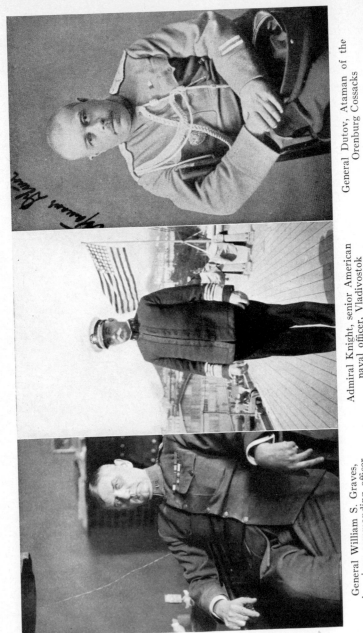

General William S. Graves,
American commanding officer

Admiral Knight, senior American
naval officer, Vladivostok

General Dutov, Ataman of the
Orenburg Cossacks

lery. He quickly gained control of the railway from Chita, the junction point of the Amur and the Chinese Eastern railways, north and east to Khabarovsk and westward as far as Lake Baikal.

Semyonov was stocky, dark, with a pair of tawny Cossack mustaches, a heavy face, and piercing black eyes. He had quick mentality, was fearless in battle, and had a good military record behind him. An inordinate love of conspiracy and intrigue marked his career. He had received no education, save a desultory sort in the army, and was utterly without culture and the amenities of civilization. Nevertheless he was held in esteem among his Cossacks and fellow officers in the old army and was the type equipped to lead a command of semi-brigands in the loose warfare of movement and sudden raid which came into vogue in Siberia. His headquarters at Chita were notorious for debauchery, his forays marked by slaughter and pillage.

When Semyonov was threatened by a fresh Bolshevik advance, he persuaded General Foudziy of the Japanese Expeditionary Force to go beyond his formal instructions and send aid which forced the local Reds to retreat. This was technically a breach of existing Allied arrangements and the Japanese Foreign Office feared the consequences; however, the Allies, with the exception of the American Government, which maintained a disapproving silence, were quite content.

More and more it became evident that the evacuation of Czechs and danger from Austro-German prisoners were either pretexts employed by the Allies to justify the pursuits of their own interests or mistaken reasons for their presence. President Wilson had never been an ardent advocate of armed intervention. It cannot, therefore, have come as a great surprise when on September 27th he declared that any attempted military activities west of the Urals would be impossible for America, and suggested the retirement of Czech troops to the eastern side.

During 1918, while the Allies were conducting deliberations

which eventuated in their intervention via Vladivostok, conditions in Siberia were growing constantly more disturbed. Those who had money or salable property fled to Vladivostok, China, and Japan. The ordinary citizen suffered dumbly, hoping for a better day. Prisoners of war by the hundreds of thousands looked on and wondered when the madness would cease, allowing them to gain their homes in mid-Europe.

The formation of competing White governments had been stimulated by the prospect of Allied help. The troubles of the Bolsheviks in organizing their new states and supplying their armies, the serious Socialist-Revolutionary uprisings in Moscow, at Yaroslavl, and in the Ukraine deflected the attention of Moscow from counter-Revolutionary movements in Siberia. The presence of the Czechs and the independent nature of the Siberian population were additional factors in favor of the Whites.

A government was set up at Samara, formed of a group of seventy Socialist-Revolutionary members of the Constituent Assembly after the Czechs had occupied that city on June 8, 1918. The delegates elected a temporary committee of the Constituent Assembly and declared it to be the supreme authority in the land, claiming the shadowy power of the Constituent Assembly which had been so unceremoniously disbanded by the Bolsheviks on January 29, 1918. This improvised government, headed by Viktor Chernov, President of the Constituent Assembly, adopted the program of the left Socialist-Revolutionaries and proceeded to build up an army of volunteers and drafted men. This People's Army, numbering some forty thousand by August 1st, had coöperated with the Czechs in taking Kazan and in other operations. Inasmuch as the land policy of this government was not radically different from that of Moscow, the peasants did not give it their support.

The Samara Government was popularly known as the Komuch, a Russian name in telescoped form. Acting as a parliamentary body, the committee placed the executive power in the Council of Heads of Departments. For military support it depended on the Czechs and on the People's Army. In theory, this military organization united all anti-Soviet forces, but in practice the Czechoslovaks were virtually independent. The People's Army, headed by General Galkin, who was afterward appointed chief of the War Department, included some six thousand volunteers and twenty-five thousand recruits officered by Socialist-Revolutionaries, a force which materially increased in the following weeks. The Komuch soon came to control the middle Volga region, which was declared "the territory of the Constituent Assembly." Zemstvos and municipal dumas were restored, free commerce allowed, banks denationalized, and trade unions practically forbidden. This régime failed to win the sympathies of any class of the population. The propertied group demanded military dictatorship and even the peasants were dissatisfied, although ownership of land by large proprietors was not restored.

At Omsk, a right wing Socialist-Revolutionary group, encouraged by victories over the Bolsheviks, formed a government with power lodged in a group of five under the presidency of P. V. Vologodsky. This government was moderate and enjoyed the support of the Peasants' Coöperatives. General Grishin-Almazov, a man of talent and energy, was in charge of the military forces, which grew from a few hundred to two hundred thousand men and continued as the main anti-Bolshevik army in Siberia after the defeat of the People's Army of the Samara Government in the fall of 1918. The leaders of the Omsk Government looked forward to a temporary autonomy for Siberia until a new Russia should come into being free from Communism. Many men of democratic views, although not technically Socialist-Revolutionary, associated themselves with the Tomsk, Omsk, and Samara governments as the best practical means of achieving results at the time.

Following Czech advances, still another government was established at Novonikolayevsk on the River Ob in July,

1918, composed of members of the Tomsk Government, with a program including the liberation of Siberia from Bolshevism, the avoidance of foreign intervention, the restoration of order, the convocation of the Constituent Assembly on the basis of universal suffrage, distribution of land among the landless, state control of economic activities, the creation of a provincial organ of self-government, and a labor bureau. These Socialist-Revolutionaries were more moderate than the Derber group of the Provisional Siberian Government which had fled to Harbin. The strength of the Novonikolayevsk government lay in the support it had from a Siberian Volunteer Army formed of various units.

General Horvath, striking for supreme power, declared himself temporary governor on July 9, 1918. He had for years given a good account of himself in commanding the Chinese Eastern Railway under a treaty arrangement between China and the old Imperial Government. He possessed his own *gendarmerie* and had maintained an orderly régime, seizing more power in the confused days following the revolution. But his power as dictator lasted scarcely an hour, for he was confronted with the combined protest of the diplomatic representatives of Great Britain, France, and Japan on the grounds that such an assumption of authority would hinder the evacuation of the Czechoslovak Legionnaires. He did, however, continue to operate the Chinese Eastern, the only Russian officer of high rank to hold his position following the Revolution.

In addition, several other regional governments formed; an ephemeral government was set up at Nizhneudinsk, the Ural Government at Ekaterinburg, the Kirghiz Government in Turkestan, the Bashkir Government, a Turco-Tartaric Government, and other small regional groups on the outskirts of the former empire. Unable to seize and hold the territories of Old Russia at once, the Red leaders temporized and gave their blessing to the organization of national groups, thus making a bid for the interest of many sections suffering from occupation by various White armies.

Both the Allies and the Czechs were anxious to bring about a fusion between the Omsk and the Samara governments. On July 15th representatives of the two centers met at Chelyabinsk. The Samara group laid claim to the supreme authority, but Omsk was not in a mood for concessions. Before the conference adjourned it was decided to meet again and to invite delegates from regional governments and from the central committees of the political parties.

The Samara Government was incensed by a series of measures enacted by the Omsk Government which abolished Soviet organizations, dissolved the Land Committees, restored private land ownership, and removed the troops from the control of local self-government to that of the provincial governors. The majority of the Siberian Regional Duma, which the Bolsheviks had prevented from meeting in January of 1918, and which was largely Socialist-Revolutionary in sentiment, demanded that the proposed government should be elected by the members of the original Constituent Assembly, delegates representing political parties and minor nationalities.

Another conference met at Chelyabinsk on August 23, 1918, to achieve an understanding with regard to the composition of the government. No sooner did the sessions open than it was decided, because of the approaching Red offensive, to shift the conference to Ufa. A serious Red attack had been gaining headway against the Czechs and Russians along the Volga in September. Kazan fell on the 10th, Simbirsk on the 13th, and Samara, October 8th. Ufa now occupied the center of the line.

In the Ufa State Conference, which had opened on September 8, 1918, the points of view of the Samara and of the Omsk governments came into head-on conflict. The Omsk delegates, acting in conjunction with representatives of the Cossacks and of the Cadets (the Constitutional-Democratic Party), took the attitude that the Directory to be elected should owe no allegiance to any parliamentary body until the election of a new Constituent Assembly, while the

Samara group, acting under instructions from the Socialist-Revolutionaries, as well as the delegates to the Siberian Regional Duma of Tomsk, demanded that the government should be responsible to the conference of the members of the old Constituent Assembly. The arguments were endless.

A compromise was reached whereby the new government was to recognize the existing Constituent Assembly and surrender its authority thereto, provided that a quorum of the members of the Constituent Assembly would meet before January 1, 1919. This could hardly have represented good faith, for it would have been extremely difficult to gather a quorum by that date. A moderate program for the government was adopted, largely in accordance with secret plans made in Moscow, but instead of three members of the Directory, of whom one was to be Socialist, five members were elected, including three Socialist-Revolutionaries.

The plenitude of All-Russian authority was entrusted to Avksentyev and the Directory of Five on September 23, 1918. Vologodsky at the same time succeeded, by means of private negotiations conducted in Vladivostok, in persuading Derber's Provisional Siberian Government (which had been formed when the Reds seized Tomsk on February 1, 1918, and arrested several members of the Siberian Regional Duma) to give up the claim to authority. He also effected a fusion between Horvath's Government and the new Siberian Government. General Horvath received the title of "Vice Regent of the Siberian Government." The new government made its base at Omsk, claiming authority throughout the territory of the former empire. Overtures were made to General Alexeyev in the South to command forces of this new government, but he died before he could set out for Siberia.

The Ufa Government stated that its National Convention was composed of:

1. The present members of the Constituent Assembly and representatives of the committee of the same assembly.
2. Representatives of the Temporary Government of Siberia,

the Regional Government of the Urals, the Temporary Government of Esthonia.

3. Representatives of the Cossacks of Orenburg, Ural, Siberia, Irkutsk, Semirechinsk, Enisseni, and Astrakhan.

4. Representatives of the Government of the Bashkirs, the Kirghiz, the Turkestan, and the Turko-Tartars of interior Russia and Siberia.

5. Representatives of the Convention of Municipalities and Zemstvos of Siberia, the Urals, and the Volga.

6. Representatives of the following parties and organizations: Socialist-Revolutionaries, Social-Democrats of the Social Democratic organization "Iedinstvo," and of the association of the "Rebirth of Russia."

In a unanimous effort to save the Fatherland, to reëstablish its unity and its independence, the Convention has decreed to transmit the supreme power over the whole territory of Russia to the Provisional Government, composed of five persons:

Nicholas D. Avksentyev, Nicholas I. Astrov, Lieutenant General Vassili B. Boldyrev, Peter V. Vologodsky, Nikolai V. Chaikovsky.

The program of the new Provisional Government is formulated in its constitutive act:

1. Until the moment of the convocation of the Constituent Assembly, the Russian Provisional Government is the sole possessor of supreme power over the whole territory of Russia.

2. On the order of the Russian Provisional Government all functions of supreme power temporarily exercised by Regional Governments are transmitted to the Provisional Government.

3. Definition of the limits of the power of the Regional Governments, which are to be founded on the principles of broad regional autonomy and in accord with the program stated below, is confided to the judgment of the Russian Provisional Government.

The manifesto further stated that:

The Provisional Government will aid the Convention Members of the Constituent Assembly, which is acting as a State institution, in its work, aiming to secure the attendance of members of the Constituent Assembly and to prepare for the opening of the session of the assembly as elected in November, 1917, at the earliest possible date.

The All-Russian Directory, thus composed of the Samara, Omsk, and Siberian leaders with a strong Socialist-Revolutionary flavor, entered upon its labors in a land whose terrain and historical background were different from the theater of war in European Russia.

One of the first problems the Directory faced was conflict betwen the Tomsk Regional Duma, which was controlled largely by Socialist-Revolutionaries, and the Siberian Government located at Omsk. The Duma, dissatisfied with the Siberian Government, dispatched several radical Cabinet ministers to that city. Reactionary military circles at Omsk decided to anticipate any move of the Socialist-Revolutionaries, and illegally arrested three radical ministers. The Directory immediately ordered their release, but meanwhile one of them had been killed by the convoy.

This action aroused the anger of the Czechs, among whom there were many Socialists. From the time of this incident they began to have grave doubts about the White cause.

The Tomsk Regional Duma demanded two members of the Siberian Government whom they held responsible for the arrest and murder. The Siberian Government retorted by imprisoning several members of the Duma. The two warring factions were ready to resort to arms when the Directory moved to Omsk on October 9th, and that provincial town, from the White point of view, became the capital of all the Russias. The new government persuaded the Regional Duma to declare its own dissolution and abolished the Siberian Government. But in doing so it incorporated nine members of that body into its Cabinet of fourteen ministers. The portfolio of Minister of War was entrusted to Admiral Kolchak.

The Directory found itself between the anvil and the hammer. On the one hand, the Socialist-Revolutionaries, particularly of the more radical persuasion, were dissatisfied with the Directory, its policy, the membership of its Cabinet, the selection of Omsk as its residence. In the middle of November the Central Committee of the Socialist-Revolutionaries issued a proclamation calling upon members to arm and hold themselves ready to repel the onslaught of counter-revolution. On the other hand, conservative and reactionary elements, particularly the military, lacked confidence in the government. They believed that it was run by the hated Socialist-Revolutionaries, notably Chernov. In these circles, the idea of placing absolute authority in the hands of a military dictator was rapidly gaining ground.

A banquet was given at Omsk on November 6, 1918, to celebrate the conclusion of negotiations between the Directory and the Siberian Government. Soldiers, diplomats, government officials with their ladies, made a gay setting. Among the guests were members of the Directory: Vologodsky, a rather self-effacing individual; Avksentyev, a gifted speaker; General Boldyrev, commander-in-chief of the new government's army, a big, brave, bemedaled Russian officer; and General Knox, who throughout befriended Kolchak; and many representatives of the Allies.

Anxious to consolidate its authority in the Far East, General Ivanov-Rinov was dispatched by the Omsk Directory as Kolchak's representative in late October of 1918 to command all Russian troops in that area. One of his first acts was to declare Amur, Primorskaya, Sakhalin, and Kamchatka provinces under martial law, assuming unto himself almost dictatorial powers. All who were not of his political opinion were considered Bolsheviks and worthy of death. Ivanov-Rinov was a Czarist officer with little or no understanding of the profound changes occurring in the minds of the Russian masses.

When the Armistice was signed, the governments of Siberia were achieving a union of dubious strength, while in other sections of the former empire White governments were organized with the intention of combating the Soviets. A nucleus had been formed in the northwestern provinces which had been under German occupation during the Great War. The inhabitants of Pskov looked with anxiety to the day when German troops would return to their own country, for they were the only force which had held the threatening Red Army in check. Upon the German withdrawal the population decided upon the formation of a corps to defend the region. Local merchants and landholders found money for this undertaking, obtaining supplies from the German stores. The strength of this Northern Corps, which originated in September, 1918, was at first not in excess of two thousand men, mostly former officers of the Russian Army. This was the beginning of the Northwestern campaign which Yudenich commanded. The Northern outlets, Archangel and Murmansk, were in the hands of the Allies and the regional government created at their dictation. The South was held by several military groups, including the Volunteer Army, the Cossacks, and the Ukrainian Army under General Petlura directed by the Ukrainian Directory. Western Siberia was in the hands of the Czechoslovaks and the Directory, while Russia's Far East was under Allied occupation or controlled by White commanders who were their protégés.

Newspaper staffs in Western nations colored reports from Russia by the intrusion of editorial opinion. Such misplaced enthusiasm deceived public opinion throughout the world until confronted by the stark facts that Red Russia was in power and that no White forces could throw it out. Contrary to many assertions in the West, the Germans neither controlled Lenin nor Trotsky nor their delegation at Brest-Litovsk, nor their decisions in the months that followed. An American correspondent, Carl Ackerman, cabled from Siberia on October 20, 1918:

> In Khabarovsk the Russians believe that the Bolshevik life is measured by the ability of Germany's military to hold out. With the splendid advance in the West, every foot gained is also a gain in Russia, because Germany is being weakened here, too. Once her prestige is destroyed, the power of the Bolsheviki will crumble.

Such miscalculations made by an experienced man on the field revealed the unreality of many of the judgments of observers of the Russian scene. The Russian Information Bureau in America issued a statement on November 5th:

The Bolsheviki, who rule in part of Central Russia by means of mass terror, are able to stay in power only through German support. As soon as this support is withdrawn the population will overthrow them.

Allied expeditionary forces in Siberia, in addition to guarding bridges, organizing transport, aiding the Czechs, and engaging in guerrilla warfare with Red bands which sprang up along the Trans-Siberian Railway, found themselves not unfrequently at loggerheads with one another. Especially did the Americans disapprove of Japan's substantial aid to such a brigand as Semyonov.

By the time of the Armistice, Japan realized that since Germany had lost, their presence in Siberia depended upon the Allies and America. The Czechs saw that they were the pawns of Allied diplomacy and that they were engaged in supporting a reactionary government of which they disapproved; the Americans were concerned solely with watching the Japanese and guarding the railway; the British were eager to set up a strong government under Kolchak; and the French, now that the Great War was won, were content to support Kolchak.

Once initiated, the process of intervention involved larger commitments. On September 15, 1918, there were in the Russian Far East sixty thousand Japanese troops, as against eight hundred and twenty-nine British, one thousand, four hundred Italians, one thousand, seventy-six French, and some seven thousand Americans.

When fighting ceased in the Great War, anti-Bolshevik forces were apparently winning with only the central portion of European Russia under the Soviets, a territory whose boundaries roughly coincided with those of sixteenth-century Moscovy.

Chapter VII

SOUTH RUSSIA: FROM THE ARMISTICE TO THE
POINT OF DENIKIN'S FARTHEST ADVANCE,
OCTOBER, 1919

DENIKIN and his officers looked at each other hopefully.
The Great War was over. Now, perhaps, the nations who had
fought beside Imperial Russia would remember old comrades
and send adequate help.

The Allies had increased their efforts to establish contact
with the opponents of Red Russia in the fall of 1918.
Clémenceau had instructed General Franchet d'Esperey, on
October 27, 1918, to make plans for the formation at Odessa
of a military base for operations of Allied forces in South
Russia. Shortly before the Armistice, representatives of several political groups with White tendencies had been invited
to Jassy, in Rumania, where French and English diplomats
were stationed, reaching the city in late November. Members
of this delegation, though pro-Ally, were divided in political
sympathies. Conservatives stood for a military dictatorship,
liberals advocated some form of constitutional régime. The
former supported the candidature of Grand Duke Nikolai
Nikolayevich as generalissimo of White troops, the latter that
of General Denikin. All agreed on the necessity of military
assistance from the Allies. Accordingly spokesmen were dispatched to General Berthelot, commander-in-chief of Allied
armies in Rumania, Transylvania, and the south of Russia,
and to General Franchet d'Esperey, commander of Allied
armies in the Balkans.

The Armistice of November 11th was fraught with important consequences to all parties in Russia. The Red All-Rus-

sian Central Executive Committee, no longer occupied with Germany, canceled the Treaty of Brest-Litovsk two days after the cessation of hostilities in the West. White leaders hoped for substantial assistance from the Allies. Lenin, knowing Western resentment against the Communist régime for not fighting out the war against Germany beside the Allies, expected England, France, and perhaps America to send sizable forces against the Red order. But the Whites overestimated the possible help they might receive, and Lenin had little to fear from governments whose weary populations were clamoring for the liquidation of the Great War. Only Winston Churchill among Allied leaders conceived of intervention in large enough terms to spell a decisive victory and he could not command support in England or elsewhere to launch an attack in force against the Red Army.

But Western statesmen were compelled to find a reason for continued intervention. The danger from Austro-German prisoners of war was gone. The Czechoslovaks were able to care for themselves. Such intervention as did take place after the Armistice was due to the momentum of the Western war machines whose complicated nature it seemed impossible to slow down quickly, to commitments already made to White commanders, and to the chagrin of the West which had hoped vainly that Red Russia would take the field against the Germans. Now that Germany had collapsed, intervention was urged because of the menace of Bolshevism itself. The Red Peril had been proclaimed for a short time after Brest-Litovsk, but the feeling died down only to flare up again in sudden and continued intensity after the Armistice. Until the last White Army had ended in disaster, the Red Peril, though often unconfessed, was the chief *raison d'être* of intervention as far as European states were concerned after the Armistice.

The Germans retreated hastily, following the Armistice, eager to be out of Russia. Not a little infected with the ideas of the new Red state, they relaxed their discipline, selling arms, ammunition, and supplies as their trains crawled across the Ukraine and Poland.

A radiogram to Denikin's headquarters on November 22d stated that an Allied fleet was sailing for Novorosiisk, and the following day the ships anchored in that port. Four days later, representatives of France and England arrived at Ekaterinodar and informed Denikin in behalf of their governments that war supplies, including airplanes, would be forthcoming in a short time, via Novorosiisk. In the course of the months of November and December Allied troops were landed at Odessa, Sebastopol, Batum, and Baku. With the coming of help from the West, the pro-German orientation of a section of the counter-revolutionary troops completely disappeared.

Denikin received a communication in November regarding results of preliminary negotiations with General Berthelot. Twelve Allied divisions were to be rushed into Southern Russia to seize Sebastopol and Odessa, where headquarters were to be established with General d'Anselme as commander-in-chief. Kiev and Kharkov were then to be occupied, as well as the regions of Krivoi Rog, the Don, and the Kuban. Under the protecting wing of the Allies, Russian troops were then to be formed for the purpose of marching on Moscow. To that end supplies from former fronts in Russia, Bessarabia, and the Ukraine were to be turned over to the White armies, as well as additional stocks of arms, tanks, planes, and rolling stock. On his part, General Denikin prepared a detailed report on the situation in South Russia, the needs of the Volunteer Army, and a plan of campaign against Moscow, transmitting it to General Berthelot and General Franchet d'Esperey. The leaders of the Volunteer Army hoped that Allied forces would occupy the larger cities in South Russia, assuring a quiet *place d'armes* in the rear, and also that war material would be furnished in sufficient quantities to make possible a general offensive in the spring of 1919.

The proposals made did not, however, receive the approval of Paris. Anxious to receive definite commitment from the Allies, the Jassy delegation in December, 1918, dispatched several of its members, including Paul Miliukov, to obtain

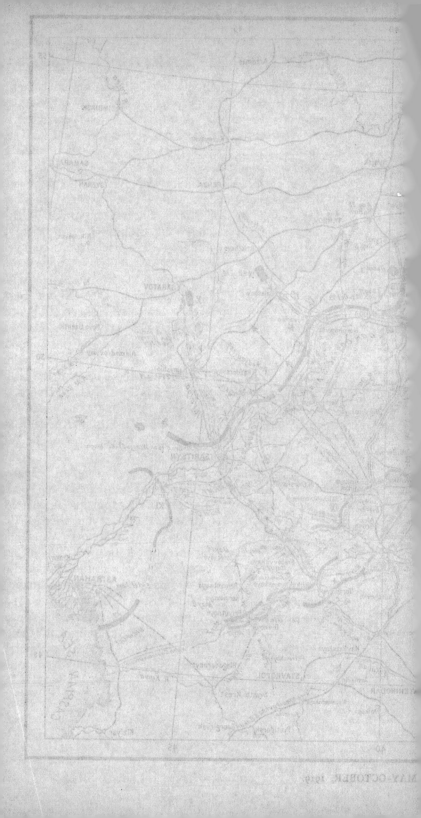

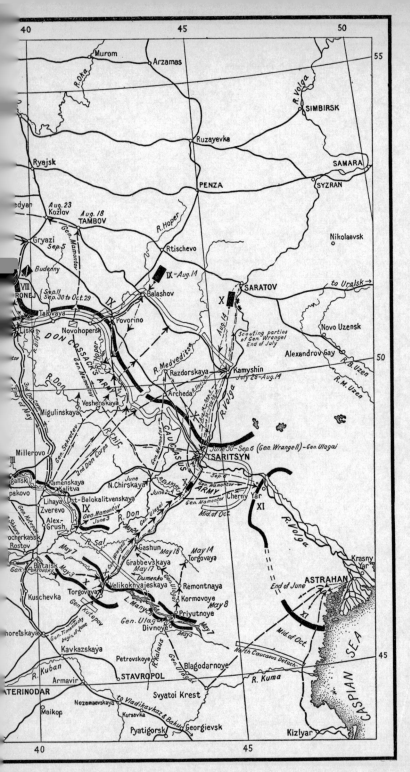

MAY–OCTOBER, 1919.

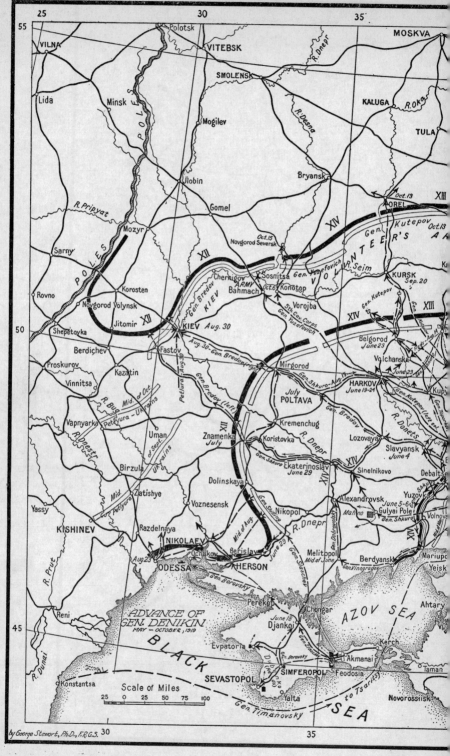

ADVANCE OF GENERAL DENI

immediate help in the shape of the 150,000 Allied troops remaining in the Balkans.

At this juncture occurred an unexpected event. Clémenceau had previously given public expression to his belief that a *cordon sanitaire* should be effected by an Allied army which would permit "the elements of order" in Russia to assert themselves. Now, with a sudden change of attitude, he not only refused to see the emissaries but actually had them deported from Paris. Neither did the plan of intervention elaborated by French generals in accord with Denikin find favor in the eyes of Great Britain and the United States.

The action of the Allies gave reason to White leaders to suspect that Western interest in Russia was not altogether altruistic. England and France entered into a special agreement in December of 1918, whereby they divided Russian territories subject to occupation into two zones of influence: The French zone comprised the southwestern region, the Ukraine, the Crimea, Poland, and territory west of the Don River. The English zone was composed of Northern Russia, the Baltic provinces, the Caucasus, Kuban territory, and the eastern part of the Don region. This agreement was not made known to the command of the Volunteer Army. The Allies and the White forces in South Russia were working at cross-purposes, with inevitable friction.

The Western Powers looked with favor upon the independence of the new nations—Poland, the former Baltic province, Finland, and the Caucasian states. Pressure was brought to bear upon Denikin to break down his opposition to the independence of the secessionist states which had been granted independence at Brest-Litovsk. Meanwhile the French occupied Odessa on December 18th. On December 28, 1918, *de facto* recognition had been extended by Great Britain to Azerbaijan and two days later to Georgia. But Denikin held to his principle of an undivided Russia which lost him possible support from the seceded border states.

At the same time, a detachment of Allied troops from Baku entered Tiflis, the capital of Georgia, for the purpose of policing the city, with the understanding that there would be no interference with the affairs of the Georgian people. Nevertheless, as long as the possibility of defeat of the Soviet Government by the Whites was not excluded, Allied Powers were prudent enough not to give a full *de jure* recognition to the Caucasian republics.

The policy of England in the Caucasus was a source of worry to Denikin throughout the entire period of his service as head of the armies in South Russia. The British authorities actually drew a line of demarcation between the territory under Denikin's control and that of the Transcaucasian republics, forcing Denikin to respect it, with the result that he had no access to Caucasian oil. The line extended from Kizil-Burun, between Derbent and Baku, to Zakataly, and along the crest of the Caucasian range as far as Tuapse on the Black Sea.

Throughout the entire Caucasian and Transcaspian region changes of government were taking place, due to the ebb and flow of victory between Reds and Whites. Simultaneously with the appearance of the English troops at Baku, an English flotilla entered the Black Sea and landed a detachment of approximately 800 English and 1,200 Indian troops at Batum. The civil government was subordinated to the English commander, who was named Governor-General. England also occupied certain strategic points in the Transcaspian region.

In Eastern Turkestan the Soviet power had established itself immediately after its triumph in Central Russia. But in July, 1918, a successful anti-Bolshevik uprising, led by Mensheviks and Socialist-Revolutionaries, had resulted in the establishment of the Transcaspian Executive Committee. This government turned to the English in Persia for military assistance, who agreed to help in return for economic privileges in the export of cotton and particularly of petroleum, via Krasnovodsk on the Caspian.

According to an agreement concluded by the Committee with General Malisson, the British Government engaged "to defend to the last moment the city of Baku by all means in its power and to export petroleum from there to Krasnovodsk, also . . . to protect Krasnovodsk with infantry and artillery against all attempts of the enemy to effect a landing." This agreement rendered the Transcaspian Government totally dependent on the British command. The export of cotton from Turkestan was prohibited, except by special permission.

With the help of English troops—their number at first amounted to eight hundred, with a half battery of artillery— the counter-revolutionists took the offensive, occupying the Merv-Kushka Railway line and menacing Tashkent, a Bolshevik stronghold. They also seized Charjui and Bokhara, forcing Soviet troops to evacuate these cities. The English gradually occupied the most important points on the Transcaspian Railway, using as their base the northern unit of the English Army in Persia, which was encamped at Enzeli, Kavzin, and Khamadan. In addition to monopolizing the export of natural resources, the English interfered with civil administration. Thus, on January 3, 1919, British troops occupied government buildings at Askhabad, as a result of a coup effected by an agent of their command. Little by little Great Britain became embroiled in the Caucasian tangle.

As Denikin anxiously surveyed the political and military movements south and east of his armies he was energetic in clearing the Northern Caucasus of Red soldiers and in strengthening his forces. Upon the successful liberation of the Kuban in the latter part of 1918, Denikin had made Wrangel commander-in-chief of the Volunteer Army, with General Yuzefovitch, an able soldier, as chief-of-staff. Shortly afterward, White troops in the Donetz coal region were grouped as the Volunteer Army, and Wrangel's units were renamed the Volunteer Caucasian Army.

By the close of the year 1918, Denikin, unsuccessful in achieving any marked diplomatic victories on the political front with Russia's former Allies, had cleared the Northern Caucasus of Bolsheviks, although troublesome bands threatened to assume proportions at any moment, and had for a few months secured a fairly peaceful base for his growing armies.

The Cossack question was always disturbing the high command of Denikin. "Volunteerism" became distasteful to the Cossacks and associated with Denikin's stubborn adherence to the idea of Russia, One and Indivisible, while Cossack "Separatism" seemed to Denikin and his group as downright disloyalty. Under pressure from General Poole, chief of the British Mission at Denikin's headquarters, something in the nature of a unique command in South Russia was achieved by long negotiations. On December 26, 1918, a convention was signed between Denikin and the Don Cossacks' government, whereby the Don kept its autonomy and Denikin became commander not only of the Volunteers but of the armed forces of South Russia, including the Don Cossacks.

The Caucasian campaign of Denikin was a serious blow to the Red forces. Their units were split up and unable to achieve liaison, some were completely destroyed, and others fled southeast in the direction of Vladikavkaz, only to be confronted there by Tersky Cossacks working their way up to join the Volunteer Army. At the same time a small English force had been landed at Petrovsk on the Caspian, proceeding inland on the railway that led to Groznyi, which had been evacuated by the Reds. Both Vladikavkaz and Groznyi were occupied by Volunteers on February 8th, which for a period of several months put an end to Bolshevik domination of the Northern Caucasus.

In this period the high command of General Denikin hoped to move headquarters to Sebastopol and consolidate their forces with any White units in the Crimean area, but the French intervened.

Early in 1919 Denikin called a council of war at which General Dragomirov, his adjutant for civil affairs, Romanovsky, chief-of-staff, General Liakhov, General Yuzefovitch, and General Wrangel were present. He proposed that their troops should first free the rear of all Bolshevik bands and then concentrate operations from the Donetz coal fields, which were in possession of General Mai-Maievsky, commander of the Volunteer Army, on the direct route to Moscow. Only troops sufficient to guard the line of the Manych River should be left behind. Wrangel urged a union on the right flank with Kolchak's left flank, but Denikin's plan prevailed, a strategical blunder which was to cost the commander-in-chief dearly.

In accordance with Denikin's plan, Terek in the rear of the Cossack and Volunteer troops was the next region which was liberated. In a brilliant campaign during the early weeks of 1919, commanded by Wrangel, in which General Pokrovsky's cavalry played a leading part, the Red Army was driven out of the region. In bloody battles in the vicinity of Mozdok a force formerly numbering 150,000 troops was destroyed, leaving 31,000 prisoners, 8 armored cars, 200 guns, and 300 machine guns in the hands of the White troops. The advance guard had pushed as far east as Kizlar and White patrols were on the shores of the Caspian Sea. The cavalry had covered three hundred and fifty kilometers in twelve days of continuous fighting.

Desolation and anguish gripped the countryside. Typhus had broken out, trains were full of decaying bodies, while dead horses, wagons, guns, and equipment blocked the roads. Medical service, anesthesia, and disinfectants were almost non-existent. Thousands of wounded died untended, prisoners in piteous condition struggled along highways, guarded by a handful of soldiers. The railroad from Kizlar to Kargalinskaya was crowded with trains containing ammunition, weapons, and booty from the Red Army. All Red troops who escaped fled either to the mountains or, as in the case of the cavalry, made for the Astrakhan steppes. The whole of the Northern Caucasus was now in Denikin's hands.

With a rich base abounding in foodstuffs, Denikin was now in a position to plan his campaign for the capture of Moscow. Wrangel was ill and took leave to regain his health. Yuzefovitch, in command of his troops which had been transferred to the Donetz, made his base at Rostov-on-Don. General Ulagay was left behind with a cavalry corps to control the Sviatoi-Krest district and General Shatilov with a small force remained in Daghestan to clear out Red bands.

But Denikin was to receive no rest. Far to the west General Borovsky's troops were driven back into the Crimea. At the same time large guerrilla bands of Greens, the deserters of both armies, were conniving with the Georgian Government which had grown hostile to Denikin, whose victories threatened its independence.

The Caucasus and Russian territory to the south of it had been stewing with new political ideas of every description. No one knew when their improvised governments would turn Red and give Denikin a lance thrust in the back.

Burdened with the provisioning of his troops, harassed by tantalizing political problems with the Cossacks and Transcaucasia, Denikin sent repeated requests for aid to the representatives of England and France. But the statesmen gathered at Paris were absorbed with their own problems and were slow to give heed to prostrate Russia writhing in the agonies of civil war and ravaged by epidemics of typhus and smallpox. It was not until January of 1919 that they decided to deal with the Russian question. Many countries represented at Paris had troops in Russia and Siberia. Disturbing voices from their constituencies further confused the babel of tongues at the peace table. Congressmen and members of Parliament were asking embarrassing questions no one could answer. Journalists were demanding reasons why Englishmen and Americans should be fighting a government against which they had never declared war. Clamor for the recall of troops increased. Only a few influential voices insisted upon a unique command and adequate military and naval support in force until a full victory was won for the White cause. But these voices were drowned by those eager to achieve peace in the more familiar world of the West, then dangerously fermenting in sullen post-war moods of discontent.

Russia remained an enigma to Western minds. It was dis-

tant, Asiatic, and incomprehensible. That a handful of proletarians and street speakers should win control of the vast
domain of the Czars was unthinkable. Immediate problems
demanded the attention of the statesmen at Paris: the Rhine
frontier, the Saar, Upper Silesia, Greater Greece, the
Dobrudja, the Polish Corridor, war debts and reparations,
6,000 miles of new frontiers, and consequent minority problems! Nervous statesmen who saw the fruits of victory slipping from their hands because of disagreements and mistakes
could neither know nor care much about the travail of 140,-
000,000 human beings entering the largest political, social,
and economic experiment ever made.

The French were more interested in South Russia and
Poland. But intervention in other theaters of conflict was
favored both by the Foreign Office and the financiers. Russian bonds, largely held in France, had been repudiated by
the Soviets and the French *rentier* class wanted assurance
that they would be paid.

President Wilson had already repented of giving even a
qualified consent to intervention and was eager to withdraw
his country from an awkward entanglement in a new war,
knowing that public opinion in the United States was against
the enterprise. Meanwhile, far to the north on the White Sea,
American, British, and Canadian soldiers at Archangel
found themselves in a precarious position. Winter was upon
them and there was imminent danger that they might be
wiped out any day.

The situation at the Peace Conference in January, 1919,
as far as Russia was concerned, was one of futile indecision.
Three possible courses lay open: to intervene in force, to
form a *cordon sanitaire* around Russia to hedge in Bolshevism, or to achieve an immediate peace. In England opinion
was divided, both in the general populace and the Cabinet.
Lloyd George was quite undeceived by the apparent success
of Kolchak and of Denikin, who, he said, was "occupying a
little back yard near the Black Sea." He refused to entertain
a thoroughgoing project either of intervention or isolation.

His views were that armed intervention on a scale large enough to be successful was an impossibility. The policy of a *cordon sanitaire,* involving the starvation of innocent women and children, he considered both inhuman and impracticable. He argued that fully 400,000 men were needed to make it effective. As the Allied governments did not see their way to furnishing even a fraction of this contingent, discussion of such a plan was obviously academic.

The third course, immediate peace negotiations, was favored by President Wilson. The idea was put forward at Paris of a conference between Red and White leaders, to be held on Prinkipo Island in the Sea of Marmora. This idea was not well received by members of Lloyd George's Cabinet nor by the Northcliffe press, which raised an uproar. A division of opinion between England and America was precisely what Clémenceau desired.

French policy was motivated by a desire to regain its loans, English policy was conditioned by industrial interests that wished for trade, and American policy was prompted not only by President Wilson's hope for a liberal régime in Russia, but also by fear of Japanese aggrandizement in the Russian Far East.

Clémenceau, not wishing to have even the appearance of disagreement among the Allies, urged a statement that they had no wish to interfere in the internal affairs of Russia, and especially that they had no intention of restoring Czardom. Their object was to hasten peace in Russia and for that reason they proposed to summon representatives of all parties to the meeting in the Sea of Marmora. The proposal was drawn up by President Wilson and sent out by wireless to all Russian factions on the night of January 22, 1919.

But while Clémenceau was agreeing with his colleagues he jeopardized any possible result of the conference by assuring French support to the Ukrainian and other anti-Soviet governments if they rejected the proposal, stating that he would prevent other Allies from making peace with the Soviet Government. Accordingly, the governments of Kolchak, of Denikin, and of Northern Russia refused the invitation and the matter came to nothing.

Although the Reds have often been accused of torpedoing the Prinkipo peace proposal, such was not the case. The Soviet Government immediately replied that it was anxious to secure an agreement that would put an end to hostilities.

This was not quite the last heard of peace proposals. At the instigation of President Wilson in February of 1919, Mr. William G. Bullitt paid a hurried visit to Russia. Although unofficial, this visit had the interest of both Lloyd George and President Wilson. Bullitt secured from the Soviet authorities the terms of a peace proposal to remain open till April 10, 1919. The proposal was rejected by the Whites, owing to the great advance made at that time by Kolchak's armies.

A similar effort at peacemaking engineered by the late Fridtjof Nansen proved futile. When Mr. Nansen made his proposal, although the Soviet Government has been painted as refusing to have anything to do with his feeding project, as a matter of fact Moscow replied:

We are in a position to discuss cessation of hostilities only if we discuss the whole problem of our relations to our adversaries— that is, in the first place, to the Associated Governments. That means to discuss peace, and to open real negotiations bearing upon the true reasons for the war waged upon us, and upon those conditions that can bring us lasting peace. We were always ready to enter into peace negotiations, and we are ready to do it now as before.

While peace talk bred alternate hopes and fears, Denikin's forces were suffering reverses in the spring of 1919, at the time Kolchak was making his greatest advance. The left flank in the Donetz, under Mai-Maievsky, had been pulled in to Mariupol. Although in the southeast the line along the south bank of the Manych still held, the Crimean forces under General Schilling maintained their position on the Isthmus of Kerch only with the aid of Allied battleships on the flanks.

General Wrangel and others appealed to Denikin to concentrate on one column. They urged that he push through to Tsaritsin, join Kolchak's left flank, and press on to Moscow by the Volga route. But the commander-in-chief turned a deaf ear.

Matters of great significance to the Whites were now transpiring south of their base of operations. The British were pushing their own projects on the Caspian Sea, in Turkestan, Georgia, and Azerbaijan. Many of these activities were at cross-purposes with the avowed aims of the Whites. The boats which formed the Caspian fleet were seized by Colonel Bicherakhov, who was in the service of the English. Nevertheless, the crews of these vessels were unreliable. Accordingly, on March 1, 1919, they were disarmed, and Admiral Norris, commander of British naval forces in the Caspian, assumed all responsibility for operations against the Red fleet at Astrakhan and for provisioning the Ural front by way of the Caspian Sea. Wishing to keep control of the Caspian, as the French did of the Black Sea, they opposed every effort of Denikin's to restore the Caspian fleet and carried out the blockade of Soviet vessels at Astrakhan single-handed. It was rumored at the time that the English planned to seize Astrakhan and the Red fleet, as well as attack the Ural Red Army from the rear, a threat which was sufficient to tie up a number of Bolshevik troops at Astrakhan.

The English also held the city of Petrovsk, now renamed Makhack-Kala, which had been occupied by their agent, Colonel Bicherakhov; an important Caspian seaport, as well as a railway terminus connected with Vladikavkaz on the one hand and Astrakhan on the other. Its loss was a serious blow to the Bolsheviks. The collapse of the Second Soviet Army, which in November, 1918, operated in the region of the Kuban and Stavropol, was largely due to its inability to use the Vladikavkaz-Petrovsk Railway. The occupation of Petrovsk effectively balked for a time all efforts of the Red Army to retake possession of Baku and obtain its petroleum.

Meanwhile the English were exporting petroleum via Batum, Enzeli, and Krasnovodsk. Also, they easily obtained permission from the Turkestan Government for the export of cotton.

Denikin was not only worried by the semi-independent military and diplomatic policies of the Allies but by political affairs among the Don and Kuban Cossacks which were a thorn in his side.

The Don *Krug* had met at Novocherkassk early in February, 1919, and in the course of these sessions strictures were made upon the command of the Cossacks in the field. The Ataman, General Krasnov, considering the criticism directed against himself as well as the officers in charge of operations, resigned on February 14th, and five days later General Bogayevsky was elected Ataman of the troops of the Don.

Fighting which had died down at the height of the winter had flared up again as the armies rested and provisioned themselves for new attempts. Reds and Whites lost heavily in engagements along the fronts of both the Don Cossacks and the Volunteer Army as they grappled for possession of the Donetz Coal Basin during February and March. The Cossacks were compelled to retreat as far south as the River Manych, while the Volunteer Army succeeded in holding fast to the Donetz Basin. At the same time that Bolsheviks were launching a drive southeast against the Donetz Coal Basin, another Red column were forging south along the right bank of the Dnieper from Ekaterinoslav and driving before them the ranks of the Ukrainian Nationalists under Petlura.

Political events as important as operations in the field were occurring in the Red State. The Third Internationale convened in Moscow March 2-7, 1919, with representatives from Germany, Austria, Scandinavia, the Balkans, Switzerland, Finland, Poland, and America, followed on March 22d by the Eighth Convention of the Russian Communist Party. At this meeting there were scenes of wild rejoicing over news of a Red revolution under Bela Kun in Hungary.

The convention sought to deal with the middle peasant

problem by promises of improved machinery, seeds, fertilizers, and equipment for the farms. In addition, Kalinin, a peasant farmer, was elected President of the All-Russian Central Executive Committee to succeed Sverdlov, a Jewish apothecary, who had died.

The problem of nationalities was handled in astute fashion by granting autonomy to various groups on the outlying marches of the old Russian Empire. In this Lenin showed great wisdom. Many of these territories were already occupied by White armies and such recognition of local governments which were springing up was a bid for their loyalty. By a loose attachment to the Central Red Government which occupied a territory roughly corresponding to the Russian State of the sixteenth century, the Red Government was in a position to strengthen the tie once the White armies were out of its way. The Bashkir Republic, the Ukraine, Latvia, Lithuania, and White Russia were formally recognized. Meanwhile the Communist Party remained a single, centralized organization whose edicts were to be universally applied.

As speeches fulminated among the politicals in Moscow, the officers of the Soviets were hammering their forces into an effective instrument, eager to try its power against foreigners upon Russian soil or against the troops of Kolchak or Denikin. Everywhere the Red Army detachments were becoming better equipped and disciplined.

Events now proved that the policy of the French command in not allowing Denikin to move his headquarters to Sebastopol was a mistaken one. When the Bolsheviks began their approach into the Ukraine, the Directory of that region declared war on Soviet Russia. General Grekov went as the Ukrainian Directory representative to Odessa, where he entered into conversation with the French command. The French evidently believed General Grekov's story to the effect that the Directory could raise a force of 500,000 men, but they were soon to eat bitter bread for their credulity. The Bolsheviks attacked the French near Kherson on March

11, 1919. French and Greek troops in this region were augmented by a poorly equipped White brigade under General Timanovsky. After losing three hundred and eighty-six men and fourteen officers, the French and a small number of Greeks evacuated Kherson and sailed for Odessa.

General Lukomsky estimated forces on both sides about Odessa to be as follows: The Volunteer Army was represented by the brigade of General Timanovsky, composed of 3,350 bayonets, 1,600 swords, 18 light guns, 8 howitzers, and 6 tanks. The Allies had two French, two Greek, and part of one Rumanian division, a total of 30,000 to 35,000 bayonets and swords. Opposed to these forces were two Red regiments of local troops and some small and poorly trained units, which had been recently organized—in all about 15,000 bayonets.

The French command was badly shaken by its humiliating experiences at Kherson and elsewhere. The crew on a French naval vessel mutinied. What with Bolshevik propaganda and war weariness, French troops were no longer reliable, and in order to prevent decisive engagements and to insure safety, it was decided to make Odessa a fortified camp, such as Salonika had been made under General Franchet d'Esperey. These operations began on March 28, 1919. In view of a possible correlation of forces, the outlook for defense was reasonably promising.

To the east, disaster nearly overtook Denikin when on April 12th Red troops pierced the Manych position in a series of savage battles and began moving southwest toward the line of the Vladikavkaz-Rostov Railway. Denikin, in personal charge of the operation, pushed the Bolsheviks back across the Manych River but was halted. In these bloody encounters no quarter was asked and none offered by either side. Finally Wrangel was given charge of a large cavalry force and won a decisive victory on May 9th near the village of Velikokniazheskaia, wiping out the Tenth Red Army and netting 1,500 prisoners, 55 guns, and 150 machine guns, removing the threat of a separation between troops in the Caucasus and in the Donetz area.

Friction between the French command and Denikin continued. The former were obviously looking for a more submissive government. For a while they were toying with the idea of giving their support to Petlura, but the terms they offered amounted to turning the Ukraine into a French colony.

General Denikin received a shock when, on April 4th, the French authorities informed him that they had made the following decisions:

1. In Crimea and New Russia (Odessa Region) the French command is considered the Supreme organ, alone qualified to solve all the questions which may present themselves.
2. The French command undertakes to conduct in its zone all the operations against the Bolsheviks.
3. The French will take care of everything relating to the Russian commercial shipping in the Black Sea.

The general replied that the liberation of Russia from the Bolsheviks must be carried out not by foreigners, but by Russians themselves, and that all he desired of the Allies was to maintain a base for the formation of a Russian army. Such wrangling could not last much longer!

In spite of the contrary policies of France and England, substantial help was now forthcoming in the nature of surplus war supplies and a small personnel. Ships laden with munitions, rifles, guns, drugs, which were desperately needed, and clothing, began to arrive at Novorosiisk and with them some three hundred officers and noncommissioned officers of the British Army, as technical assistants.

Denikin also looked hopefully to Siberia where the White movement was promising success. In the spring of 1919 Admiral Kolchak was beginning his greatest advance, pushing the Bolsheviks from his base in Western Siberia. The Allies saw in him the hope of a Russia which might overset the Reds, recognize the old debts, and put the country back in the family of nations. Coincident with the recognition of

Behind the lines

Troops resting

General Petlura

the Omsk Government by the Allies on June 12, 1919, Denikin recognized Admiral Kolchak as the supreme ruler of Russia. Kolchak replied to Denikin:

I am deeply touched by the patriotic decision dictated by your high ideals of duty to the country. In the period of disintegration, general depression, and pessimism, you were one of the first to raise the standard of a united resurrected Russia. By your decision at the present moment you give the country another example of a soldier and citizen who considers above all the happiness of his country and its historic future. God bless you in your service to Russia.

After agonizing months it appeared some unity of command might coördinate the movements of various White armies.

To counterbalance the hopes raised by the recognition of Kolchak, an event occurred in April which astounded Denikin and lowered the morale of his soldiers. Paris had reversed its policy in South Russia. The French command received a wire ordering the removal of all French troops from Russian soil in three days. The commander of the Allied troops in the south of Russia, General d'Anselme, evidently eager to leave a land where he had had only painful experiences, acted with an alacrity which exceeded even his hasty orders. He ordered the evacuation to take place in forty-eight hours. It actually lasted four days, bringing on a panic among the civilian population, who dreaded the Red régime which began for them two days later, when the local Soviet of Workmen and Peasants' Deputies took control of the city. The last French ship left the roadstead of Odessa on April 8th.

The evacuation was carried forward in such haste and confusion that it closely resembled a flight. Only a small number of the civilian population could procure passage. Thousands lined the docks, begging the French to take them anywhere. Not a few committed suicide. Pandemonium reigned in the city, for all knew that Red troops were ready to march in as soon as the guns on the French cruisers were out of range. General Timanovsky's brigade sought refuge in Rumania, where they were disarmed by French orders. After many humiliations they were finally shipped by boat to Novorosiisk. These events largely destroyed faith in France on the part of the desperate men fighting in Denikin's army.

The evacuation of the French left suspended in mid-air certain Volunteer units, which had penetrated north of the Crimea into Taurida Province in order to save that rich food-producing region. They were wholly unsupported on their left flank, a situation which imperiled all the Crimea. Irregular Red troops penetrated the region on the left bank of the Dnieper and had the field to themselves, with the exception of the Volunteer units. At this moment the troops of the Ukrainian Nationalist Directory under General Grigoryev turned Red. These changes compelled the Crimean-Azov Volunteer Army to seek refuge within the Peninsula. A stand was made at the Isthmus of Perekop, but the Red forces were too powerful to be resisted. The Volunteers were compelled to retreat to Akmanai, in the vicinity of Feodosia, where they made a stand on April 14, 1919. This was a favorable position, inasmuch as they could receive protection on their flanks from English, French, and Russian naval vessels.

Following the flight from Odessa came the French evacuation of Sebastopol, which further deepened the misunderstanding between France and the armed forces of Denikin. General Franchet d'Esperey arrived at Sebastopol on March 26, 1919, declaring it was necessary to hold out for at least two weeks longer, giving assurance that the French would not quit Sebastopol. At this time the forces protecting the city consisted of two battalions of the 175th French Infantry, one Greek battalion, two batteries, and a small number of French auxiliary troops. In addition there was the personnel of the French cruiser, *Mirabeau*, which had run aground. There were also French, Greek, and English naval vessels which possessed some armament in the harbor. On April 12th hopes rose with the arrival of 2,000 French Algerian troops, and two days later with the landing of 2,000 Senegalese.

Colonel Trousson of the French Army was in command of the entire Allied force.

The order to evacuate Sebastopol on April 12th was given by Colonel Trousson, Admiral Amette of the French Navy, General Subbotin, the Russian commandant of the fortress, and Admiral Sablin, the commander of the Russian fleet. In anticipation of the move, civilians were being evacuated as early as April 2d. In the morning of April 16th Admiral Amette ordered the ships to get under way and all forces departed before the day was over. Another bitter disappointment was faced by the battered host beneath the flag of General Denikin!

Sebastopol was the base of the Russian Black Sea Fleet. In order to leave nothing for the Bolsheviks the French put out of commission even the obsolete Russian war vessels and sank over thirty submarines, some of which had been finished as late as 1917. Only four were saved by Russian officers who took them to Novorosiisk.

French intervention in South Russia lasted some four months, and involved a total of 70,000 men. From the Soviet point of view the operations were in the nature of an invasion. The same spoliation, devastation, drumhead court-martial, and wholesale destruction of goods occurred during the French occupation as under the Red or White troops. The damages caused by the French through the seizure and destruction of goods have been variously estimated at 125,-000,000 rubles.

Denikin's military strength continued to grow in spite of events which encouraged the Reds in the spring of 1919. The French had quit the Black Sea ports, a Red Government had been formed in Bavaria, but it was short-lived and was overthrown on May 5th. On March 22d a Communist state had been set up in Hungary under Bela Kun, with much bloodshed and looting. In early May the Hungarian Red Army was able to hold back Czechoslovak and Rumanian troops. Moscow decided to send soldiers from the southwestern front to strengthen Soviet Hungary, but was prevented from doing

so by the revolt of a former Czarist officer, Ataman Grigoryev, who was serving in the Red Army on the southwestern
front, and by the advance of Denikin's Volunteer, Caucasian,
and Don armies up the Volga and west and north into the
Ukraine. Grigoryev became little more than a brigand quar-
reling with his brother bandit, Makhno. Later, followers of
Makhno through a ruse succeeded in murdering their competitor. Although further quarrels broke out between Trotsky
and Stalin, Lenin was able to adjust matters in such a way
that the Red command was not fatally hampered.

In the midst of his preparations for a conclusive campaign,
Denikin was worried by the attitude of France and of England. Before the summer of 1919 set in, England evinced a
desire to extricate herself from Transcaucasia. On May 10,
1919, the British command notified the Georgian Government that Italian troops were to replace the British, but
Italy refused to undertake the responsibility. Nevertheless,
in the course of July and August, English troops evacuated
Georgia and Armenia, remaining only at Batum.

Denikin, discouraged but dogged, planned his attack
against Moscow. After the successful mending of the breach
in the Manych line by Wrangel's cavalry victory at Velikokniazheskaia on May 9th, the commander-in-chief was ready
to launch major operations northward against Kharkov and
Tsaritsin.

An electric atmosphere of expectancy hung over General
Denikin's armies. "Boots and Saddles" aroused men eager
to put their preparation to the test—to thrust at Moscow and
finish off the Reds. On the long picket lines men whistled
old folk songs of Holy Russia as they groomed their horses.
The blacksmith's hammer rang cheerily as mounts were shod
which should carry seasoned cavalry over the steppes to the
shining towers of the ancient capital. The infantry looked
to their shoes, repaired old rifles, and tightened their belts
for the march. Many had been fighting since August, 1914.
After this last campaign, after five years in the field, they
would go home to their farms, their gardens, their stores and

forests and professions. Soon they would be advancing from the Volga to the Dniester.

General Wrangel was given command of the attack on Tsaritsin with the Volunteer Caucasian Army. General Sidorin, with the Army of the Don, was on his left, and still farther west the Volunteer Army under General Mai-Maievsky was pushing toward Moscow.

The road to Tsaritsin was a bitter experience—three hundred kilometers of salty steppe land, almost uninhabited. For days, foot and horse went without food or water. The nights were sharp and the men suffered acutely from cold and damp as well as the lack of sufficient food. A few automobiles in the advancing army used ropes wound around the wheels when the sharp road demolished the tires.

General Wrangel's army contained many Moslem units which carried their green flag with a yellow crescent upon it. The Moslems of the Caucasus had declared a Holy War against the Soviets. Among their number were not a few brilliant officers, including General Ulagay and the brothers Agoyev, both generals.

Artillery and shells to destroy the wire entanglements before Tsaritsin, which Wrangel had been promised by Denikin, did not arrive, for headquarters were concentrating on the rapidly advancing columns to the west. Wrangel, haughty and imperious, conscious of the victories he had won for the cause and knowing the hopelessness of attacking Tsaritsin without artillery, wired Denikin on May 2d:

It would be criminal not to follow up our success. What we can do cheaply now will cost us huge losses in the future. Courage is not enough. The cavalry can do wonders, but it cannot remove barbed wire. If you do not send us infantry, guns, munitions, and more cars, without which I cannot move about and direct my troops as I should, our success will be but a Pyrrhic victory.

Two days later he sent an even more imperious demand. On June 1st an attack was made, but Wrangel was repulsed with the loss of five lieutenant generals, three brigadier generals, eleven captains, and hundreds of men. The Reds attacked, compelling General Wrangel to withdraw to the Tchervlennia River. Exasperated by the delay of the promised support, Wrangel wrote a harsh letter to Denikin asking to be relieved of all command after the conclusion of the campaign. General Yuzefovitch persuaded Wrangel to stop the delivery of the letter, which he did.

At last Wrangel's reinforcements for which he had been clamoring in strident telegrams to Denikin came, on the night of June 16th, and in a desperate battle of three days the Whites captured 2 armored cars, 131 locomotives, 10,000 lorries, 2,085 of which were loaded with ammunition, 300 machine guns, 70 field guns, 40,000 prisoners, and a huge fortune in booty. Denikin and Romanovsky came up for the parade of the troops and the *Te Deum* in the cathedral. Wrangel and his small Caucasian Army had covered themselves with glory.

The town had sunk beneath all semblance of civilization. Typhus and smallpox were raging. Thousands of corpses had been thrown into ravines on the outskirts and had remained unburied. Over four hundred carcasses of horses littered the streets. Drunkenness and orgies had been the custom day and night.

While at Tsaritsin, Denikin unfolded his plan of campaign for the taking of Moscow. General Wrangel was to take Saratov and move forward through Nizhni-Novgorod; General Sidorin, commander of the Army of the Don, was to move via Voronezh-Ryazan, and Mai-Maievsky, with the Volunteer Army, was to proceed direct from Kharkov by way of Kursk, Orel, and Tula. This fatal order dispersing the scanty troops of the commander-in-chief into three forces was the prelude to the eventual disaster.

At the time of Wrangel's operations on the right flank, Denikin's most westerly army, the Volunteers under Mai-Maievsky, were pushing steadily forward, capturing Kharkov on June 13th. When Denikin drove through the streets of Kharkov the population went wild with joy. Women sought to kiss his hand and many who could not reach him kissed his automobile. Deputations from the city and countryside, from civic and cultural organizations, greeted him as one who had saved their lives. Town after town fell to the advancing troops. By June 29th the Volunteer Corps of the Crimea had occupied the whole of the peninsula. On the map it appeared as if the White armies were sweeping irresistibly forward, but old staff officers knew that the weary soldiers were being hopelessly dispersed on an extended front without reserves. The advance pushed northwest and west until the provinces of Voronezh, Tambov, and most of Saratov came into the possession of Denikin's forces.

Far to the west, the Ukraine had been suffering under one government after another. On January 22, 1919, a delegation of the West Ukrainian Republic which composed Galicia accepted the authority of the Directory.

After the Armistice the West Ukrainian Republic in co-operation with the Directory of the Russian Ukraine centering at Kiev immediately entered upon a war with Poland and boundary controversies with Hungary and Rumania. Rumania, in alliance with Poland, invaded the Bukovina and Southern Galicia. Hungary was anxious not to lose Ruthenia, but the Ruthenian Rada voted to join the Ukraine and send delegates to Kiev. Ukrainian troops of the Galician West Ukrainian Republic moved into Ruthenia for a short time but were driven out by the Magyars. In the end, Czechoslovakia was awarded Ruthenia at the Peace Conference.

The Poles had invaded Galicia and in November, 1918, had seized Lemberg. Their army was stopped along a front which ran through Galicia from December of 1918 to July, 1919. Surprised by Ukrainian resistance in Galicia, the Entente sent a commission under General Bellamy toward the end of January, 1919. The Galician Committee at the Paris Peace Conference, under the chairmanship of General Botha, were offered recognition of the Ukrainian Republic in March of 1919 if the republic would abandon Lemberg to the Poles. This the republic refused to do and demanded Lemberg and a boundary line along the River San. Meanwhile, Po-

land set moving the army of General Haller and in May
threw it against the exhausted Ukrainian troops who were
compelled to retreat to the River Zbruch, the former boundary between Austria and Russia.

After some fighting the army broke up through an utter
lack of munitions and equipment. The remnant left Galicia
in July of 1919, crossing the River Zbruch into the territory
of the Ukrainian Republic. This army remained under the
authority of President Petruchevich, who was proclaimed
Dictator of the West Ukrainian Republic of Galicia in
July of 1919, fighting under General Petlura with the Ukrainian Army.

When the Germans had quitted the Ukraine, confusion
prevailed. Red uprisings had occurred in Kharkov and
Odessa and certain anarchistic military leaders like Zelenyi
and Grigoryev took the field with independent commands
which were little more than bands of robbers.

The Directory had displayed more statesmanship than
had the Central Rada, but was faced with a difficult situation. The Allies refused to recognize either the Ukrainian
Republic or its Directory. Thus, in the spring, summer, and
autumn of 1919, the Directory had a war on three fronts,
against Poland, the Reds, and Denikin, as well as incipient
social revolution within its territory.

Guerrilla bands roamed the countryside, robbing towns
and villages. During the year 1919 a weird figure arose in
the province of Ekaterinoslav: Nestor Makhno. Makhno at
the time of the Revolution had been serving a sentence in
Siberia. Returning, he organized a large band which perpetrated every conceivable horror upon the Jewish population. He flew a black flag and fought every army and government—Red, White, or the forces of the Ukrainian Directory.
When he was routed by one army he escaped into an
unoccupied area. He became a legendary figure, his very
name striking terror into the soul of peasant and townsman.
Not only did the Ukrainian bandits rob and kill without
mercy, they also had a penchant for destroying what they

could not use. Towns were burned to the ground, furniture and doors were used for bivouac fires. Vandalism laid its heavy feet upon museums, art institutes, and universities. The accumulations of decades were wasted in wanton destruction.

Lemberg was lost to the Poles, Odessa and Kherson to Denikin, Kharkov to the Reds, and in February, 1919, the Bolsheviks occupied Kiev, whereupon the Directory fled toward Galicia. In June and July of 1919 Poland occupied the whole of Galicia, and in August Denikin occupied the southeastern section of the Ukraine.

The Ukrainian troops were in a desperate plight, without adequate munitions, clothing, sanitary or medical supplies, or food. Typhus and typhoid fever carried away thousands of them.

General Petlura rallied his forces and in spite of every difficulty recaptured Kiev from the Bolsheviks in September of 1919, soon to lose it to Denikin, who a few days later lost it to the Bolsheviks. The Reds also captured Kherson and Odessa from Denikin. The Ukrainians recaptured Odessa from the Reds, who counter-attacked and drove them out.

The Ukrainian Directory was dissolved in the fall of 1919 and Petlura became Dictator. The principal cause of this change was a disagreement between General Petlura, who favored an understanding with France and the Allies, and Vladimir Vinnichenko, who stood for an alliance with the Bolsheviks.

Petlura had often been held responsible for the Jewish pogroms in the Ukraine during this period. Life for the Jew in Russia had always been a sharp and dolorous journey. During this period some twenty thousand Jewish men, women, and children were slaughtered. Eighty-three persons were murdered in Kitaigrod in one night. Bloody massacres occurred in Bardischev and Chelomir, for which the Jews maintained two officers of Petlura's, Colonel Korwenko and Colonel Palients, were personally responsible. In the town of Proskurov over 6,500 Jews were robbed and murdered and buried in a common grave. Dr. Arnold Margolian, a prominent Ukrainian Jew, formerly a Supreme Court Justice in Kiev, in his book, *The Jews of Eastern Europe,* more or less absolves the Ukrainians and places the blame upon the White armies of Denikin and Wrangel. But many of the most bloody pogroms occurred in areas where these forces were not in occupation. At any rate, years later, in 1926, when General Petlura was murdered in Paris, a French jury, after the defense's recital of Jewish sufferings in the Ukraine, acquitted the slayer, a young Jew who, by killing the Ukrainian general, sought to bring the plight of his people to public notice.

Many of the pogroms could not be blamed upon General Petlura, as they happened in regions where his forces were not operating. The country was overrun with detachments of marauders of all armies—Red, White, Polish, and Ukrainian. These, together with the forces of Grigoryev, Makhno, and Zelenyi, committed unspeakable crimes upon the Jewish population. Some Jews were killed by the soldiers of Denikin and later by Wrangel's men. However, a grave incident did occur which could properly be ascribed to Petlura's army. In the spring of 1919 a town in Podolia, with two thousand Jewish militia, turned Bolshevik and attacked the Ukrainian Army. In revenge the Ukrainians slaughtered without mercy the Jewish residents within the town. Anti-Semitism was especially strong in all territories occupied by anti-Bolshevik armies, who visited their wrath upon local Jews for miseries which they alleged were the results of vast Jewish international plots. All the time-honored prejudices against the Jews were refurbished and brought forward often in the interest of money and loot.

Petlura as Dictator was hard pressed by the Poles, the Reds, and Denikin. Disease, battles, and lack of supplies threatened the immediate collapse of his military establishment. Whereupon, Petlura entered into negotiations with Poland for the surrender of Galicia to Poland for recognition of the Ukraine and the promise of Polish lances against the Soviet troops. At the time a majority of Petlura's army were Galician Ukrainians, under the leadership of Dr. Petruchevich, who were outraged by what they called the betrayal of Galicia to the Poles.

Dr. Petruchevich, acting on behalf of the Galicians, immediately entered into negotiations with General Denikin, and an agreement was made in November of 1919 for combined efforts against the Bolsheviks. The breach between Petruchevich and Petlura was the death knell of both Petlura's forces and the units of the West Ukrainian Republic of Galicia. Typhus was raging in every regiment. The soldiers were poorly paid, hungry, and without munitions. They went where they would. A portion operated in coöperation with Denikin. Others stayed with General Petlura. Some regiments surrendered to the Bolsheviks. With some 20,000 men, Petlura retreated across the Zbruch River into Galicia, which was now Polish territory. Two divisions of the Galician republic's men staged a dramatic campaign of their own, fighting their way back across Galicia to Czechoslovakia, where they were interned and hospitably treated.

From this time on Petlura threw in his lot with Poland, who was anxious to have an ally on her southeastern marches. Petlura and Ukrainian soldiers were later to feature prominently in the Polish-Soviet War of 1920.

Separatism among the Cossacks flared up again during the summer months. General Wrangel, who was familiar with their mentality and whose victories had made him famous among them, was dispatched to the Kuban to persuade them to remain loyal to the White cause. Through his efforts, Denikin was able to secure an amendment to their constitution whereby power was concentrated in the hands of Ataman General Filimonov.

Having finished his Kuban mission, General Wrangel pushed toward Saratov, but Trotsky, seeing the danger of a union with Kolchak against whom the Red command was concentrating large masses of troops, repulsed his attempts with heavy losses, although General Pokrovsky had defeated

Budenny's crack cavalry in bloody fighting. When Kolchak's army began the retreat in June and July, the bulk of the Red Army, free now from any serious danger from Siberia, was directed against Denikin. With Kolchak retreating, all chance of liaison with his forces was gone. Wrangel's push toward Saratov came to a halt as superior Red forces were massed against him.

A general Red attack on the Army of the Don and on Wrangel's column began on August 1st. Wrangel retreated slowly toward Tsaritsin, where soon after the civilian population was evacuated. In ferocious battles before the city from the 22d to the 24th of August, the Tenth and Eleventh Soviet armies were defeated with a loss of 18,000 prisoners, 31 guns, and 160 machine guns. After remaining on the defensive until October 4th, the Caucasian Army began another offensive and advanced northward some fifty kilometers, but the chance to take Saratov on the road to Moscow was gone forever. General Erdeli, commanding a contingent on Wrangel's right flank, was retreating into Astrakhan, and the Don and Volunteer armies on the left were encountering resistance although continuing to move forward at a slower pace.

To the west and north during July, August, and September, Denikin's forces had been winning victories. Kiev, Kursk, and Orel were taken, White cavalry had reached Voronezh; but the lines were over-extended. The front had no depth or stability. It had become a series of patrols with occasional columns of slowly advancing troops without reserves. Exhausted men found themselves in the midst of a population growing less friendly as the gathering Red counter-attack became imminent. Odessa was captured by the Bolsheviks, but due to the presence of Allied warships on the Black Sea little use could be made of the port. By the 1st of September, Denikin's line ran in long, irregular curves from Poltava in the west, through Kharkov and Pavlovsk toward Kamyshin.

The high tide of the White movement against the Soviets had been reached in September of 1919. Yudenich was preparing to attack Petrograd with some hope of success. Kolchak's army might again cross the Tobal and strike for Moscow, and Denikin was pushing his advance with vigor.

But three hundred and seventy-five miles remained between Kharkov and Moscow. The Whites pushed on until by the middle of October White cavalry were beyond Orel, the farthest north of any city taken by the armed forces of South Russia. Even if the forward squadrons had constituted an advance guard of substantial armies behind them, there were still two hundred miles of hostile territory between Orel and the Kremlin. During this rapid advance in the summer of 1919 Denikin was reported to have captured 700 guns, 1,700 machine guns, 35 armored trains, and 250,000 prisoners. In spite of vast territories gained, in reality Denikin's forces were in a dangerous predicament.

The bulk of the White troops were concentrated in the direction of Kharkov, in the hope of reaching Moscow by the shortest possible route without reference to other White forces in the field in Western Siberia. On the extreme flank the Caucasian Army had occupied Kamyshin on July 28th and advanced to within sixty versts of Saratov, but could go no farther. Denikin's men were now in the center of the country, a third of European Russia embraced within their lines. Many believed that they would soon be within sight of the towers of the Kremlin.

Nevertheless, with a front reaching almost to Moscow and with advances which looked on large-scale maps like a sweeping victory, Denikin's officers slept fitfully by their bivouac fires. The old soldiers knew their lines would snap, should Trotsky release his full strength at any one point. The Caucasian Army under Wrangel was ordered to hold a defensive position before Saratov. Meanwhile, Trotsky on October 18th attacked and split open the junction between the Army of the Don commanded by General Sidorin and the Voronezh-Lisky front of the Volunteers. Orel and Kursk were hurriedly evacuated. The jovial but dissolute General Mai-Maievsky was not equal to the task before the Volunteer Army. While the Volunteer Army had become demoralized, the morale of the Caucasian Army was high. Mai-Maievsky condoned peculation. The Moslem commander, General Ulagay, hanged a round dozen of his own men for stealing chickens!

"Boots and Saddles" no longer aroused eager soldiers to the day's march. Petty jealousy between officers, division of opinion on politics and strategy, Cossack separatism, the lack of an adequate land policy to pacify the peasants, the loosening of moral restraints, the inevitable hardening of all feeling as the soldiers were compelled to forage off their countrymen, and the ferocity generated by fierce class warfare had dimmed the flame of patriotism in thousands of hearts. Resignation and abandon were displacing the high spirit with which officers and cadets had sought the Don. Risings and brigandage were occurring in many places in South Russia.

The handwriting was on the wall. October of 1919 saw the last advance of Denikin's armies. Had he accepted Wrangel's advice and concentrated large masses of cavalry behind Kharkov as an army of maneuver, he might yet have saved the situation, but his forces were scattered over a thin line which ran for nearly one thousand miles over the fields of Russia. Hundreds deserted either to the Red cause or fled to the Balkans, Turkey, or to the east and southeast. Those in the high command saw realistically the gravity of the situation they were now powerless to change, but were stayed in their despair by the faint hope that the Allies might still lend aid sufficient for their need.

Western journalists and diplomatic representatives wishing for victory for Denikin sent more optimistic reports than conditions justified. On the eve of the catastrophe, English, French, and American journals gave assurance that Denikin would soon be in Moscow.

The Red power consolidated its position as White influence among the civil population weakened. The stage was being set for the *dénouement* in the tragic drama of General Denikin's South Russian struggle. Homeric laughter echoed through the Kremlin. Lenin showed himself to the people and spoke to crowds upon the Red Square.

Chapter VIII

NORTH RUSSIA: FROM THE ARMISTICE TO THE ALLIED EVACUATION, OCTOBER, 1919

THE narrative now shifts from the steppes and mountain fastnesses of the south to the arctic zone. The story of anti-Bolshevik struggles in North Russia, which Chapter IV recorded down to the Armistice, is here resumed.

Local White Russian governments and regiments were artificial entities supported by the Allies. The Russians did not know when Allied troops would be withdrawn, leaving their meager forces to face the onslaught of the Reds. Under such conditions, with the indisputable knowledge of the growing power of the Soviets and the sketchy policy of Allied intervention, it was natural that Russian soldiers should have an eye to the future and be prepared to change sides in order to save their lives. Consequently, many hundreds deserted to the Soviets.

After the Armistice the forces in and about Archangel totaled 18,325, with a rifle strength of 11,195. The British had 6,220, the French 1,680, the Italians 25, Americans 5,100, and the Russians 5,300, as an integral part of the Allied forces. In addition the Russians had about 12,000 troops of an indifferent nature which were loosely coördinated with the Allied effort. By the 19th of January the Reds had massed against them 22,700 men, with a rifle strength of 18,300, which was nearly twice as many as they had at the time of the Armistice on the Western Front. In addition they had 66 field guns, 9 heavy guns, and some 150 machine guns. Red troops to the number of 17,900 were in direct contact with the Allied forces, while some 4,800 were held in reserve near Vologda and Viatka. In the Murmansk area at this period some 15,000 Russian and Allied troops were deployed against an equal number of Bolsheviks. Behind the Reds were the vast resources of Russia.

The morale among both foreign and Russian troops sank steadily, due to the inhospitable country, long nights, and gloomy arctic days. Friction was constant, not only between Russian and Allied officers, but with the civilian population. Among Allied troops the chief cause of depression was the lack of a clear understanding of why they were in Russia and what they were expected to do now that the Great War was over. The Russians, more accustomed to the climate and the melancholy forests, looked forward apprehensively to a future judgment day with the Soviets. Former Czarist troops were weary of war. The failure of their military machine to give them victory as well as the impossibility of mobilizing and equipping a large force in the North where there was little hope of concluding a decisive campaign had dimmed their zest for fighting.

Of the Archangel and Murmansk sectors the former was the more important one. There, the pursuit of Bolshevik forces had divided Allied troops into two main forces: the railway column with its base on the Vologda route, and the Dvina River column with its advance base at Bereznicheck. The farther these two columns advanced from Archangel the more widely they became separated. To gain security it was necessary to form semi-independent and auxiliary commands. Onega, on the right flank, which was in intermittent patrol contact with the Murmansk force, was protected by Chekuyevo, while the possession of Pinega on the opposite flank was necessary for the safety of Archangel.

Allied headquarters wisely determined not to extend already dangerously lengthened lines of communication and transformed the expedition from an offensive to a defensive operation in October of 1918. The Onega force, which was responsible for the right flank, retired on October 25th from the neighborhood of Kaska to Chekuyevo, though a week before it had compelled the Bolsheviks to retire upon Turchasova.

On the left flank a similar policy of consolidation led to the occupation of Karpagora on Thanksgiving Day, but on December 4th the Bolsheviks compelled a retirement on Pinega. Thus both flanks were consolidated and Allied forces

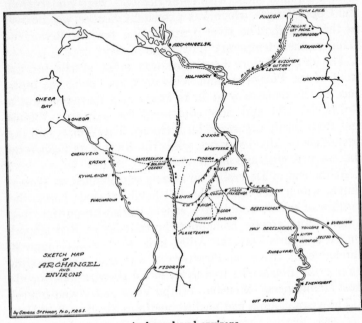

Archangel and environs.

were ready to meet attacks on their center, which soon was hard pressed both at Kodish and on the Dvina River.

The first day of November witnessed the opening of a determined attack on the Kodish front by the Bolshevik Army, reinforced by some of Trotsky's newly organized regiments, which succeeded in working their way to the rear of the Americans. Only luck and well-directed machine-gun fire saved the day. The Allies left Kodish and on the 9th of November were safely intrenched behind the Emptsa

River. Meanwhile, the main attack, directed at the Dvina column, was developing. On the day of the Armistice a bloody engagement began at Tulgas, lasting four days and ending in the retreat of the Soviet troops.

Both sides now prepared for winter; engineers built block-houses that were proof against anything except a direct hit from a six-inch shell; wire entanglements were constructed, and Upper Tulgas, which was a constant menace, was burned to the ground. The river froze, losing for the Red commanders their temporary advantage in river craft.

The month before Christmas was quiet except for the front of the Pinega column. This area was under the influence of the monastery at Lake Soyla; yet its mayor was a Bolshevik. Old and new contended for mastery; Whites and Reds busily organized local troops. The Whites had the advantage of Allied support, while the Reds were flushed by success at Kodish and on the Dvina.

At the end of December an attack was planned on Pleset-skaya, which was one of the Bolshevik advance bases, the capture of which would have relieved pressure on the river columns and greatly hampered the transfer of Red troops. On New Year's Day the Allies took Kodish but found it untenable. A drive on Plesetskaya was also unsuccessful, leaving the Bolsheviks free to carry on preparations for almost simultaneous offensives on the Vaga and Dvina forces.

The Vaga column had pushed out from Shenkursk to Ust-Padensk, nearly three hundred miles from Archangel. It presented a tempting salient to the Bolsheviks, but Shen-kursk was important from a political point of view and the position at Ust-Padensk served as a screen of protection. It was accordingly defended until the night of January 22d, when it was finally abandoned after several sanguinary clashes.

Moving forward, the Bolsheviks encircled Shenkursk. With the river frozen so that no relief was possible save along roads in the hands of the Bolsheviks, with food for only sixty days, with the marked infantry and artillery superiority of the Red Army, it would have been folly to remain until a well-organized siege should annihilate the garrison. A native disclosed a forgotten trail through the forest, and the retreat from Shenkursk began. At midnight of January 23d, the artillery, preceded by mounted Cossacks, were swallowed up in the darkness of the forest, followed by infantry and a rabble of refugees. Behind lay Shenkursk, full of stores, which it was impossible to destroy without betraying the evacuation to the encircling Reds. The artillery and Cossacks cut up the trail for weary infantrymen floundering on the half-frozen road. As daylight came through the pine tops, the fugitives heard the booming of artillery, bombarding abandoned Shenkursk some fifteen versts in the rear.

While the Vaga column had been driven back from Shenkursk and all but surrounded, the Dvina column was being similarly imperiled by encircling movements. But the Bolshevik attacks, though continued until April 5th, did not meet with much success there.

In conjunction with attacks on Shred Mahrenga, Morjagorskaya, and Tarasova, which last alone was taken by the Bolsheviks, renewed attempts were made to capture Tulgas at the end of January and beginning of February. Although the Reds did not succeed in their attempt to surround the Dvina force, they did succeed in pegging down to the Dvina a number of troops whose presence would have been very welcome to the hard-pressed Vaga column.

General Ironside was now perilously short of soldiers, his force totaling a rifle strength of only 11,195, of whom 5,100 were Russians of very doubtful quality, with thirty-five field guns, of which seventeen were in reserve at Archangel, and ten heavy guns, of which half were in reserve. Opposed to him were 18,300 Bolsheviks with sixty-six field and nine heavy guns.

It was obvious that reinforcements must be had, equally certain that they could not come, at least in numbers, until late spring. There remained only two measures by which to augment his forces: first, by training local Russians, who had so far proved disappointing; and, second, by withdrawals from General Maynard's forces at Murmansk. In February one battalion of infantry and half a machine gun company were under orders from the Murmansk coast for Archangel. The reinforcements were timely, for the Bolsheviks were preparing to attack once more.

Throughout February the Vaga column, which had halted at Vistavka, had been heavily shelled by the Bolsheviks. On the evening of March 3d, Whites holding Yevsievskaya took possession of a supply of English rum and while they made merry the Bolsheviks captured the town.

The Red Army now practically surrounded the Allies in Vistavka. Their artillery, reinforced by six- and nine-inch guns, opened up with renewed violence, and when on the afternoon of the 5th of March the barrage lifted from the town and fell on the Canadian artillery in the rear, the woods and frozen river swarmed with attacking Reds. The Allies and Russians at Vistavka were surrounded and almost given up for lost by headquarters at Kitsa, who, after an unsuccessful attempt, finally broke through to the beleaguered garrison. Although the Reds were repulsed, the smoking remnants of Vistavka were abandoned by the White forces, who moved to Kitsa under cover of darkness.

While the Vaga column was by no means secure and while the threat against Vereznichek, the keystone of the Vaga-Dvina arch, was still serious, a new surprise offensive against the Vologda Railway force demanded the attention of General Ironside.

The main line of lateral communication during winter was the Sorokskaya-Onega road, by which reinforcements had lately arrived from Murmansk. This road, a wagon track some eighty feet wide through the forest, continued from Chekuyevo, which was in Allied hands, to Bolshie Ozerki, thence to Obozerskaya, which was the headquarters of the railway force. The capture of Bolshie Ozerki would separate Onega from the railroad column and would endanger Obozerskaya, whose safety was essential for the railroad guards and highly desirable for the Vaga and Dvina columns. General Kuropatkin planned to take Bolshie Ozerki, drive through to Obozerskaya, and mop up the isolated Vaga and Dvina columns at leisure. On the night of March 16th-17th the Russo-French force holding Bolshie Ozerki was caught napping and was annihilated.

General Ironside hurried to Obozerskaya to take command in person. The *élan* of five hundred and eighty men that he had scraped together in Archangel was the direct result of his personal qualities of leadership.

All Fool's Day of 1919 found two hundred Americans and four hundred other Allied troops battling for their lives on the river fronts. Once the Red units with an enormous preponderance in numbers attacked front and rear simultaneously. It was impossible for machine gunners to miss the attackers nearly waist deep in snow. Rifle grenades blew holes in the Red platoons, leaving the snow stained with widening patches of crimson as bodies stiffened and froze in the arctic cold. That night many passed through the lines and surrendered. On the next day the attack was renewed, but without vigor. The spring thaw came to Ironside's rescue and the Bolsheviks, fearing for their artillery, withdrew to Shelaxa.

Bolshie Ozerki was the climax of the Red winter offensive, but the Vaga column was still under pressure. On April 5th Red soldiers attacked Shred Mahrenga, but were repulsed. As the ice on the Vaga was breaking, Ironside determined to leave Kitsa on April 19th for Ignatevskaya and to hold the line of Maly Bereznichek and Nizhni Kitsa. On the night of April 25th Tulgas was surrendered by White Russian troops but immediately recaptured. On May 1st and 5th the Bolsheviks launched their last unsuccessful attack on the weary Vaga column at Maly Bereznichek.

The Allies reoccupied Ignatevskaya on May 20th as soon as the gunboats arrived from Archangel, and the winter campaign was at an end.

A White patrol

Transport

British gun in contact with the Bolsheviks

On the Murmansk coast there had been little activity throughout the winter. On January 16th General Maynard captured Rugozerskaya, sixty-five miles southwest of Sorokskaya, and the following month carried out a successful attack on Segeja. Although Maynard had recently dispatched reinforcements to Ironside, who was being hard pressed on the Vaga front, it was necessary to draw off pressure from the Archangel front by a threatened offensive on the part of the Murmansk forces. At Segeja the Allied position was insecure, due to discontent among the Finnish and Karelian elements of the population. Nevertheless, Maynard nonplused the Bolsheviks by taking the offensive in the spring, precisely at the time when they imagined him to be hampered by mutiny and treachery.

General Maynard planned an advance in two bounds; from Urozero to Mezelskaya, and from Mezelskaya to Medvezjya Gora. The seizure of Medvezjya Gora had the advantage of materially reducing the front to be held and controlling all the avenues of advance northward. The first operation was carried out early in May. After a pause of some days, the attack was resumed and the town of Medvezjya Gora was occupied on May 21st. This advance of over sixty miles was made across a wilderness of forest, marsh, and lake, without the aid of aircraft or artillery, against an enemy entrenched in good positions with both flanks protected, an operation which raised the morale of the expeditionary troops and did much to counteract Bolshevik propaganda.

During June Maynard continued to push south, but his Russian troops proved disappointing. Moreover, his slender forces were further reduced by the withdrawal of a detachment of Royal Marines at the end of June. On July 19th the small contingent of Italians was withdrawn from the line and the promised French reinforcements had not arrived. He had therefore to remain content with occupying the Shunga Peninsula and with the capture of Kyapeselga on July 6th, which somewhat restored the morale of native

White troops. He was now in a position to threaten Petro-zavodsk, whence an advance on Petrograd was a possibility. But by that time the withdrawal of all expeditionary forces both from Archangel and Murmansk had been definitely decided.

In spite of some military successes, the winter campaigns had demonstrated the precarious condition of the interventionist and White Russian forces. In addition to the inherent difficulties of the enterprise, friction developed among the national contingents that made up the force, as well as between the Allies and the Russians whose cause they had come to champion. The hostility of the natives to the expedition as a whole became obvious early in its history. From the first the Allied military commands failed to agree with the Chaikovsky Government, the only one that could claim some popular support, choosing for their local allies General Miller and Major General Marushevsky. The former was a monarchist whose position as Military Governor of Archangel was entirely due to his standing with the British military establishment, and the latter had previously been commanding officer of the Russian Brigade in France, and was out of touch with affairs in Russia. The natural result of this alliance with avowed reactionaries was to throw the supporters of Chaikovsky more and more toward Bolshevism.

Bolshevik propaganda was further aided by the interest that the British showed in the resources of North Russia, the questionable honesty of arbitrary exchange fixing, the scaled depreciation of the old ruble, and unwise emphasis upon the sanctity of the old Russian debt which the Reds had repudiated. Such matters were capitalized by the Communists to show that the Allies came not to save Russia but to restore the Czar, recover the debt, extort concessions, and make a little on the side at the expense of the peasants by manipulating the currency. More potent in its influence upon the peasant than all talk about the natural antipathy of a capitalist toward a socialist state was the downright dishonesty of many among the Allied troops. Stealing from government stores was especially tempting to troops in Russia, for natives would barter valuable skins for a little rum or other comforts of the soldier's life. This thieving was condemned by the high command, but it continued to flourish. Moreover, Allied troops were so corrupted by the license of war that they are alleged by Russians to have robbed the bodies of the dead like ghouls, and to have stolen like common thieves. As days passed the common people who wanted land and peace were less inclined to support a movement which brought only requisitions, warfare, and hardship.

With the end of the war on November 11, 1918, Allied statesmen found difficulty in persuading voters at home that fighting in Russia was still necessary. Both in England and in the United States there was an outcry for the withdrawal of troops from Russia. As early as February, 1919, Senator Lodge, speaking before the United States Senate on the subject of the American forces in Northern Russia, declared that "it is the duty of the United States to take those troops out. They are too many to be sacrificed wantonly and uselessly, and they are too few to be effective."

On March 4th the War Cabinet of Great Britain decided to appeal to the Allied representative at Paris to evacuate the North Russian contingents as early as possible, news which put heart into the demoralized forces at Archangel and Murmansk.

The evacuation of Archangel began as soon as the port was open at the end of May. The first to go were French and American units, the latter leaving on June 26th. The cost of the enterprise to America had been 2,485 casualties. The transports that carried them brought British reinforcements under General Grogan, preparatory to the evacuation of the whole Allied force. Another relief force, under General Sadleir-Jackson, landed at Archangel in the middle of July.

Meanwhile, military preparations had not ceased. On May 4th, General Ironside was authorized by the British War office to prepare for an offensive in the direction of Kotlas, with the object of effecting a junction with Kolchak's Northern Army, then under General Rudolf Gajda, the Czech officer in the Russian service. The reinforcements that arrived in June and July were among the best in the British Army and were exceedingly well equipped. Their arrival materially improved the situation of soldiers who throughout the winter had had their backs to the wall. They now numbered roughly 37,000 men, of whom 13,000 were British. Therewith the Bolsheviks lost the advantage in numbers which they had enjoyed all winter.

In a telegram dated June 19th, General Ironside informed the War Office that his preparations for an advance on Kotlas were nearing completion, that if there were any wavering on the part of the Russians, the occupation of Kotlas would raise their morale, that he should be able to pull in Kolchak's right wing from the direction of Yarensk on the Vychegda and thereby greatly increase the strength of his Russian units. But events occurred which considerably dampened the expectations of those in command at Archangel and those in office at Westminster.

In the first place, as the summer advanced, Kolchak suffered heavy setbacks, destroying all hope of a junction with his forces. Furthermore, stubborn resistance shown by the Bolsheviks in a minor engagement made General Ironside hesitate as to how far it was wise to press the attack. In addition, continuous dry weather had caused the Dvina River to fall several feet, a circumstance which immobilized the Allied naval flotilla, upsetting all arrangements for the river transport of the force.

To add to his worries, two serious mutinies broke out, independently of each other, the first on the Dvina front, the second on the Onega. At Troitsa a mutiny took place in the Third Company of First Bn. Slavo-British Legion ("Dyer's Battalion") which was recruited from Bolshevik deserters and prisoners, and in the machine-gun company of the

Fourth Northern Rifle Regiment which was in reserve on the right bank of the Dvina. Several British and Russian officers were murdered, and two British and two Russian officers wounded. The mutiny was suppressed only by prompt action on the part of the flotilla. A number of the mutineers were tried by court-martial and shot; the battalion was disarmed and sent to the lines of communication as a labor unit.

The War Office sent a cable to General Ironside at Archangel on the 4th of April, 1919:

Will you please communicate, as you may deem expedient, the following message to the troops:

Although you are cut off from your country by the ice, you are not forgotten. Your safety and well-being, on the contrary, is one of the main anxieties of the War Office, and we are determined to do everything in our power to help you and bring you safely home. You were sent to North Russia to help draw off the Germans from attacking our armies in France, and undoubtedly you helped last year to keep large numbers of German troops away from the battlefield and so enabled a decisive victory to be won.

Whatever may be the plan of action towards Russia decided on by The League of Nations, we intend to relieve you at the earliest possible moment, and either bring the whole force away or replace you by fresh men. These reliefs are being prepared now, and will come through the ice to your aid at the earliest moment when the ships can break through. Meanwhile, your lives and your chance of again seeing your home and friends and your fellow-countrymen, who are looking forward to give you a hearty welcome, depend absolutely upon your discipline and dogged British fighting qualities. All eyes are upon you now, and you represent the British Army which has fought and won and which is watching you confidently and earnestly. You will be back home in time to see this year's harvest in, if you continue to display that undaunted British spirit which has so often got us through in spite of heavy odds and great hardships. Only a few more months of resolute and faithful service against this ferocious enemy and your task will have been discharged. Carry on like Britains fighting for dear life and dearer honour, and set an example in these difficult circumstances to the troops of every other country. Reinforcement and relief are on the way. We send you this personal message with the most heartfelt wishes for your speedy, safe, and honourable return.

During this dangerous period the governments represented in intervention in North Russia were being asked embarrassing questions. Owing to the extreme distaste which had grown up against every form of military life, the British Government was finding it difficult to receive support for any form of assistance to the beleaguered troops. Finally a contingent of two brigades of 4,000 each was raised, of men and officers who volunteered for this specific task.

A yet more serious outbreak occurred at Onega on July 22d. Without any warning, a regiment of the North Russian Army, not recruited from prisoners or deserters, mutinied and handed over the whole Onega front to the enemy. As Onega was essential for land communication between Murmansk and Archangel, it was evident that the safety of General Ironside's forces was seriously imperiled. Had it not been for the recent arrival of reinforcements, the whole expedition might have met with disaster.

Russian forces in August were reënforced with the arrival of over 700 officers from the old army who attached themselves to General Miller's forces. With them came General Kvetsinsky who accepted the position of chief-of-staff.

The Allies were discouraged with their measures to stabilize the population of North Russia and support them against the Reds. Their eyes turned toward the South where Denikin's effort gave greater promise of success. Sir Henry Wilson remarked in a memorandum:

The position had to be faced that the British Empire, in common with all Entente nations, was weary and exhausted, depleted in men and money, and incapable of further military efforts on a great scale. That being so, it behoved us to apply what resources were still available in the most profitable direction. North Russia offered no prospects of decisive results, and with Kolchak's failure any sustained military effort in that theatre was doomed to be barren. Moreover, the local conditions were entirely discouraging. In the words of Captain Althan, R. N., our senior naval officer on the Dwina, to whose ability, energy and whole-hearted coöperation the success of our operations is greatly due, "the instability of the Russian troops, the lack of discipline, organizing ability and military leadership of the Russian officers and Higher Command after a year of the most loyal and capable British support, soon made it evident that to continue that support would be fruitless." In the South, on the other hand, Denikin's operations, starting as they did with every conceivable disadvantage, by sheer determination, energy and patriotism had achieved already remarkable success, and offered a much greater prospect of decisive results.

Accordingly it was decided and, I am convinced, wisely decided, to concentrate all our remaining efforts in South Russia and to close down our commitments in the North.

But evacuation was no simple matter, with Red forces in constant contact with various small forces deployed over a wide terrain and a civilian population dependent upon Allied strength. Winston Churchill remarked in a speech to the House of Commons on the 29th of July, regarding evacuation:

I should like to say a word about the difficulties of evacuation. Although to us who sit here at home in England it may seem very easy to say, "Clear out, evacuate, and come away—" although it may seem very easy to arrive at that intellectual decision, yet on the spot, face to face with the people among whom you have been living, with the troops by the side of whom you have been fighting, with the small Government which has been created by our insistence, with all the apparatus of a small administration, with all its branches and services, when you get our officers and men involved like that on the spot, it is a matter of very great and painful difficulty to sever the ties and quit the scene. I do not disguise from the House that I had most earnestly hoped and trusted that it would be possible in the course of events for the local North Russian Government to have a separate life and existence after our departure, and with the fullest assent of the Cabinet and the Government, and acting strictly on the advice of the General Staff, we have been ready to hold out a left hand, as it were, along the Dvina River to Admiral Kolchak in the hope that he would be able to arrive in this district, and by joining the local Russian forces, which amount to nearly 30,000 men, stabilize the situation and enable our affairs there to be wound up in a thoroughly satisfactory manner.

Nothing could be gained by remaining any longer than was necessary to carry out the evacuation successfully.

Owing to the unreliability of Russian troops fighting in the White cause, the withdrawal of Allied forces was a difficult military operation, demanding a unified command.

Fearing the possibility of disaster in an exploit becoming increasingly unpopular in England and America, General Lord Rawlinson, a seasoned British officer, was appointed commander-in-chief of the entire expeditionary force, with orders to carry out its evacuation. Lord Rawlinson reached Archangel after a hasty trip to Murmansk on August 11th.

The Allies decided to evacuate Murmansk last for several reasons. In the first place, General Maynard could threaten Petrograd, should the Bolsheviks follow General Ironside's withdrawal too closely. Also, the possession of the Murmansk coast was necessary for sea communication between Archangel and England. Finally, as the Murmansk port was ice-free, it was not essential to evacuate it as early in the fall as in the case of Archangel. September 1st was set as the date for the evacuation.

On his arrival at Archangel, Lord Rawlinson was greeted with the news of a successful offensive on the Dvina, which had taken place on August 10th. This operation was in the nature of a disengaging blow carried out by General Sadleir-Jackson with British and Russian troops. All objectives were taken and an advance of twenty miles made, capturing Pulhega and Borok, Bolshevik bases on the Dvina.

However, the effect of this triumph wore off so rapidly that Lord Rawlinson decided to support another offensive to be launched by General Miller. For that purpose he put off the final evacuation till September 10th, and called out a reserve force that had been kept in readiness in England to cover the withdrawal. One battalion of infantry, two machine-gun companies, and several tanks went to Archangel, the remainder of the reserves to Murmansk. General Miller at first entertained the ambitious project of gaining the line Verkhotoimski-Shenkursk-Tarasova-Plesetskaya-Onega, but the morale of the Russian battalions on the Vaga and the Dvina was so poor that he resolved instead to undertake an offensive on the railway front in conjunction with a landing under Colonel Danilov at Onega.

On August 29th operations commenced with simultaneous attacks on the railway and Seletskoe fronts. At first the attack on the railway met with complete success: Emptsa was captured, together with ten guns and five hundred prisoners. But in the evening the Bolsheviks brought up armored trains and temporarily dislodged the Russian troops, who had relieved the two companies of Royal Fusiliers, which included many Australians. The attack on the Seletskoe front was halted by the Reds, and on September 1st the Reds launched a counter-attack at Bolshie Ozerki which was defeated only by the effective bombing of Allied airmen.

In the meantime Colonel Danilov's detachment met with surprisingly little resistance and Onega was reoccupied by the 10th of September, the day appointed for the withdrawal of all British troops. Loyal Russian forces had succeeded in reaching the line Tarasova-Shelaxa-Onega and General Miller and his troops were elated. These attacks so distracted the enemy during the period between the Dvina attack in August and the commencement of the Allied withdrawal in the middle of September, that the retirement went on almost unhindered. General Grogan's skillful employment of aircraft, both for reconnaissance and for bombing, broke up the enemy's attempt at encirclement. Except for a short engagement at the junction of the Dvina and Vaga rivers, caused by the failure of the Russians to cover the British retirement down the river, the evacuation was completed practically without incident. On September 12th, Troitsa was cleared and by September 23d the inner defenses of Archangel were reached.

General Ironside, acting on Lord Rawlinson's instructions, handed over quantities of military stores, including tanks, to the North Russian Government to help them continue their resistance to the Bolsheviks. By September 27th the Allied evacuation of Archangel had been completed, and by 6 P.M. of that day all transports had steamed off from the mouth of the Dvina, bound for England.

The evacuation of Murmansk, which proved more exciting, was completed some two weeks later. The Royal Marines and two companies of American Railway Engineers who had only arrived on April 7th had been withdrawn on June 30th, and the Italian detachment on July 19th. General Maynard was therefore short of troops until the arrival of reinforcements collected in England. In spite of Rawlinson's shortage, a force was dispatched to the Shunga Peninsula and the islands to the south were completely cleared of Bolsheviks.

News of the mutiny of Russian troops at Onega reached General Maynard on July 23d, when he immediately detailed a mixed force to watch the southern shore of the White Sea, especially in the neighborhood of Sorokskaya.

The question of the policy which the Russian forces should pursue now became acute, especially in view of the imminent withdrawal of Allied troops. General Skobeltsin, the Russian commander in the field, was opposed to any retrograde movement, but an advance was considered equally unadvisable until it was time to strike a disengaging blow; therefore the Bolsheviks were harried by raids and airplane attacks to prevent them from taking the offensive and to keep them in a state of anxiety.

Wishing to have the Murmansk offensive coincide with General Ironside's withdrawal to the inner defenses of Archangel, Lord Rawlinson decided that a general Allied offensive should be timed to start on September 14th. General Skobeltsin was advised to hold a defensive line around Medvezjya Gora, but he was anxious to press on to a line along the Suna River, although that meant the extension of already dangerously long lines of communication. A compromise was reached whereby Allied support was promised as far as the Nurmis River but no farther.

In order that the Russian command might have the credit

of a successful offensive, orders were issued in the name of the G.O.C. Russian Forces, General Skobeltsin.

The plan of campaign was for an advance down the railway of two columns, composed of British and Allied troops with Russians supporting them. Simultaneously, a flanking detachment of Russian regiments was to be landed from the Shunga Peninsula to prevent the destruction of bridges and the escape of the enemy's more northern garrisons. A third column, starting from Svartnavolotski, twenty-five miles west of the railway, had orders to take Koikori and to proceed on Konchozero.

The railway detachment met with success and by the 16th the Allies and Russians had occupied the line of the Nurmis River. The flanking detachment from the Shunga Peninsula met with even more striking success, but the failure of the third column to take Koikori destroyed any chance there might have been of reaching the Suna River. Over one thousand prisoners were taken in this short campaign. By September 20th the conduct of all operations was handed over to the Russian authorities.

The Allies now began their evacuation of Murmansk in earnest. On September 30th General Maynard was placed on the sick list, whereupon Brigadier General H. C. Jackson took command of the final stages for departure. The previous day Kem had been abandoned. Matters did not, however, run smoothly. Small parties of Bolsheviks and Red Finn deserters damaged the lines of communication, whereupon Lord Rawlinson instructed General Sadleir-Jackson to accelerate his program by embarking some of his troops at Popov and Kandalakshi and to secure his lines of communication by retaining two Serbian companies for some days longer. A small detachment of British troops which had been sent to Solvetsky Island on September 22d to arrest suspicious characters was attacked on landing and failed in its mission. General Sadleir-Jackson went at once to clear up the situation, with monitor M23 and the seaplane ship, *Nairana*.

One Ermolov, head of the Russian Civil Administration in the Murmansk theater, and General Skobeltsin were advised to approach the Finnish Government with the view of inducing them to send two companies of White Finns to round up the Red Finn deserters who were playing havoc with the railway. The Allies had come as friends of the Red Finns and foes of the pro-German White Finns; when they left, the rôles were reversed!

On September 25th the Bolsheviks effected a landing at Valenavolok and captured Lijma. If this attack had been followed up vigorously, General Skobeltsin's left flank would have been turned and disaster for the Allies might have followed. By October 4th all British troops were north of Kandalakshi. Although the evacuation of the Serbs was menaced by the destruction of bridges between Kandalakshi and Murmansk, nevertheless all Allied troops had left Murmansk by the evening of October 12th.

The total casualties, killed, died, wounded, and missing, sustained by British forces in North Russia from the commencement of the campaign in the spring of 1918 to the evacuation in October, 1919, were 196 officers and 877 other ranks, of which the killed numbered 41 officers and 286 of other ranks. The cost in treasure was just over 18,000,000 pounds sterling.

Immediately on his arrival in Archangel, Lord Rawlinson, after consultation with Generals Ironside and Maynard and Mr. Hoare, the acting British Commissioner at Archangel, had urged General Miller to agree to the following proposals:

(a) The abandonment of the defense of Archangel after our departure.

(b) The evacuation to other parts of Russia of those amongst the civil population who might be victims of Bolshevik reprisals.

(c) The transfer of the North Russian Government to Kem or Murmansk.

(d) The concentration of all the best elements among the Russian troops for the defense of the Murmansk front.

The advantages of this scheme were that it was far easier to defend Murmansk than Archangel, which after Kolchak's reverses had no particular military importance. Furthermore, a successful offensive southward along the Murmansk Railway would not only place General Miller in a position to threaten Petrograd, but might enable him, if all went well, to join hands with the army of General Yudenich in combined operations for its capture.

But General Miller was not eager to abandon Archangel, whose loss would be a severe blow to the prestige of the North Russian Government and the White cause. He exaggerated the improvement in the morale of local troops and minimized the rapid spread of Bolshevik propaganda. As a consequence, the North Russian Government was unwilling to recognize the perils involved in their plan of action when British troops should be evacuated, or to face realistically the fact that the great majority of the town population and the peasants looked upon the possible success of the Reds throughout the northern territory with indifference, if not with eagerness.

The North Russians had recognized Omsk as the All-Russian Government and Admiral Kolchak as the supreme ruler as far back as May 23d. A dispatch from Omsk on September 10th announced that Kolchak's Cabinet had ratified the provisional statutes of the administration of the northern region and gave the commander-in-chief of its armed forces, General Miller, the powers of governor. Miller, at Kolchak's order, announced that he would defend Archangel rather than evacuate his men and their families. This decision was to cost them dearly in the immediate future.

General Sir Henry Wilson, in his summary of the Allies' operations in North Russia, made several observations upon the operation:

It began with the landing of 150 marines at Murmansk in April, 1918. These were followed by 370 more at the end of May, which were in turn reinforced by 600 infantry and machine gunners on 23d June. From that time onward demands for reinforcement followed each other without intermission, and our commitments steadily grew without being able to resist them, until the British contingent numbered 18,400.

The Mesopotamian campaign started with the despatch of two brigades and ultimately absorbed nearly 900,000 men before it was terminated.

The six divisions with which we entered upon the Great War in France and Belgium swelled to sixty-three before victory was achieved.

I think the moral of this is easy to point. It is that, once a military force is involved in operations on land, it is almost impossible to limit the magnitude of its commitments.

Major General Sir C. Maynard leaves no doubt about his feeling in regard to his North Russian experiences in his account, *The Murmansk Adventure*:

What I have written in earlier chapters has, I hope, served to convince even the most skeptical that the Murmansk Force was sent to Russia to meet an urgent strategic need, and that it fulfilled its allotted task during the closing phases of the Great War with a measure of success fully justifying its despatch.

I trust also that I have satisfied the fair-minded that ample justification existed for continuing our assistance to the anti-Bolshevik elements after we had ceased to be at war with the Central Powers. Some there will be who dispute this last contention; but few of these are likely to be found outside the class that welcomed the access to power of Russia's disrupters, and welcomes still their maniacal creed. And with this class I differ gladly.

To my mind, our action at Murmansk in common with that in other parts of Russia, can give rise to no feeling of self-reproach, and to one only of regret—namely, that the help we gave fell short of that required to throttle in its infancy the noisome beast of Bolshevism.

The morale of Allied troops in North Russia was low, not because the men were cowards, for the fighting at Tulgas, at Bolshie Ozerki, and at Kodish called for both resolution and courage. The spirit of the men was due almost entirely to the rigors of the climate, the conditions which hindered a proper system of leave and reliefs, and the lack of high purpose in the expedition. Both Allied and Bolshevik generals were able soldiers. General Maynard showed energy and resourcefulness when in April, 1919, the Finns and

Karelians mutinied. General Ironside and his adversary, General Kuropatkin, displayed marked ability as strategists in the planning and execution of their campaigns.

The lack of a definite policy, clearly proclaimed and understood by the Allied and Russian troops at Archangel and Murmansk, was in itself a dispiriting factor. Sir Henry Wilson frankly acknowledged the lack of Allied policy in a Blue Book on December 1, 1919:

> The Allied Governments consequently found themselves committed to the retention of their contingents at Archangel throughout the winter, although they had not decided on any definite policy with regard to the Bolsheviks.
> The difficulties of the Entente in formulating a Russian policy have, indeed, proved insurmountable, since in no Allied country has there been a sufficient weight of public opinion to justify armed intervention against the Bolsheviks on a decisive scale, with the inevitable result that military operations have lacked cohesion and purpose.

The condition of the civil population was hazardous. Fear of Red reprisals was a serious handicap throughout the period of Allied and White Russian effort in the North. There was a continuous food shortage. On the Murmansk coast the Americans undertook in the summer of 1918 to feed 100,000. In the Archangel area the population of some 600,000 faced immediate want when the Allies should evacuate.

The evacuation was a difficult operation, ably performed, which reflected credit on Generals Maynard and Ironside who planned it and on General Lord Rawlinson who supervised and coördinated their schemes. From a purely military point of view, the expedition to North Russia was not discreditable.

This expedition, originally sent out to prosecute the war against Germany, alongside loyal Russians during the Kerensky régime, had changed its nature until it was at war with the Bolshevik Government, although no declaration of hostilities had ever been made. It would be easy to condemn all high officials responsible for their presence; it is also possible to understand the reasons for troops being kept in this inhospitable region for months after the Armistice. There were natural difficulties to evacuation during the winter months; commitments had been made to the anti-Bolshevik population who could not honorably be left to the vengeance of the Bolsheviks without adequate opportunity to emigrate if they chose, for the local governments had been constructed largely by the Allies.

General Miller's decision to hold Archangel facilitated the task of the Allied commanders, sparing them the trouble of wholesale evacuation of the population. Only 6,500 chose to emigrate and were set down on the shores of the Baltic states and South Russia. The project of putting the North Russian Government on an independent footing was an impossible feat, for the prerequisites, a junction with Kolchak's forces and the establishment of an efficient local White Army, were lacking.

After the withdrawal of the Allies, the North Russian Government had a precarious existence. Ample military stores and equipment were left in their possession. For many weeks General Miller's forces made a creditable defense, even capturing numbers of prisoners, guns, and considerable territory. But without a base of supplies and a terrain deep enough for maneuvers the end could not be far distant.

The Bolsheviks occupied Archangel on the 20th of February, 1920, and three days later they entered Murmansk. Heavy hands were laid upon those who had resisted the new Red order; in one case five hundred White officers were executed and buried in a common grave.

As a part of the grand strategy of the World War, the North Russian Expedition before the Armistice was justified and accomplished some results as a threat to Germany, holding German troops in the East, as well as preventing a German submarine base at Archangel. After the Armistice it accomplished little in the way of permanent help to White Russians in the North, and in no way materially balanced the scales against Lenin and his associates.

Chapter IX

THE BALTIC: YUDENICH'S CAMPAIGN; OCTOBER, 1918, TO DECEMBER, 1919

WHILE Kolchak's line swayed back and forth in Siberia and Denikin was stubbornly pushing his armies toward Moscow, figures were moving in the tragic drama of famine, pestilence, and bloodshed in Russia's northwestern provinces.

The Baltic campaign eventually commanded by General Yudenich was interwoven with the fortunes of Esthonia and Latvia. A brief review of the troublous times in that nation from the date of the Kerensky Revolution may prove helpful in understanding the origin, the exploits, and, perchance, the reasons for the defeat of the Russian Northwestern Army.

Kerensky, in April of 1917, had accorded Esthonia the right to form a representative legislative body and to recall for a defense force all soldiers whose homes were in her territory. Throughout the summer, efforts had been made to organize Esthonian civil institutions and the army. In this period many suffering from German occupation looked with favor toward revolutionary Russia, a feeling radically revised when Lenin seized power. All purely Esthonian nationals had worked for the defeat of Germany, but the Balto-Saxons who included the majority of the propertied classes placed their hope in a Teutonic victory.

When the Bolsheviks had overset the Provisional Government in Petrograd in November of 1917, Anwelt, the leader of the Esthonian Reds, had carried out a reign of terror with wholesale murder, robbery, and imprisonment, further alienating the Germanophile elements of the population, who, more than ever, doubted the ability of Esthonians to govern wisely. Whereupon they had invited Germany to deliver them. The German high command had moved at once, occupying Reval on February 25, 1918.

The retreating Reds carried away with them over one hundred hostages, including Baron Dellinghausen, marshal of the nobility. Many of these unfortunates had been sent to Siberia from whence the majority after much suffering were repatriated, due to the efforts of Germany.

A Provisional Government had been set up by Esthonia on February 24, 1918, some two weeks before the Treaty of Brest-Litovsk, and an independent republic again proclaimed. The German army of occupation did not recognize this government and had maintained martial law throughout Esthonia until the end of the Great War. Naturally the Germans favored the Balto-Saxons, a fact which created more antagonism between them and the older Esthonian stock.

The Treaty of Brest-Litovsk had placed the former Baltic provinces in hard straits. Lenin and Trotsky had agreed to the independence of their regions at the point of a German bayonet. By the terms of the treaty the Germans were to remain in control until order was restored. These uneasy new states found themselves between a still powerful German Empire and the restless masses of Russia. In addition, local groups of Reds in Latvia, Lithuania, and Esthonia seized control of towns and villages and pillaged the countryside.

The Germans offered aid to the Esthonians against the Reds on July 1st which was refused, the latter not wishing to obligate themselves further to a powerful nation which already had laid heavy hands upon them.

A small White force, the Russian Northern Corps, led by Czarist officers, had been formed in Pskov in September, 1918. This corps, later known as the Russian Northwestern Army, entered upon its struggles with Red forces in the Baltic region. These troops and the inhabitants of Pskov dreaded the withdrawal of German soldiers after the Armistice, for they surmised that such action would be a signal for an advance by the Red Army, which proved to be the case.

The Northern Corps, badly clothed, half armed, and hungry, and faced by far greater numbers, was forced to retreat into Esthonia. After hard fighting near the town of Walk, the corps was compelled to divide its forces. At the time a portion decided to pass through Esthonia to the Murmansk region, while others planned to journey through Germany and Poland to join General Denikin. This latter group succeeded only in reaching Libau via Riga, where they formed the nucleus of a body of troops under a Baltic noble, Prince Lieven.

The portion of the corps which had decided to go to Murmansk was commanded by Colonel Neff, who had formerly served in one of the Czar's sharpshooter regiments. This section was unable to carry out its original intention and allowed itself to be attached to the Esthonian Army, then in process of formation under General Laidoner. As part of the Esthonian forces, Colonel Neff's men received better treatment than their comrades in the Russian Northern Corps and were sent to the Pskov front.

Here in October of 1918 they were joined by Captain Bulak-Balakhovich and his forces. Bulak-Balakhovich had begun his military career in August, 1914, as a volunteer private of the Russian Army, securing promotion rapidly for bravery in the presence of the enemy. After the great German advance into Russian Poland, he organized small bands behind their lines and became famous as a guerrilla fighter. He had received seven wounds and at the time peace was signed at Brest-Litovsk he was a captain of cavalry. When the Bolshevik Revolution occurred he had secured permission of the Reds to raise a detachment of cavalry to prevent the encroachment of Germany on Russian territory. The regiment was formed in April, in the town of Luga. Bulak-Balakhovich turned against the Bolsheviks and in

October, 1918, removed to Pskov with more than 1,000 men, 4 captured machine guns, and 120 horses. The staff promoted him rapidly through various grades up to major general. Bulak-Balakhovich, who was something of a marauder, was popular with the White troops and was known by the sobriquet, *Batjko,* meaning father.

The rear of the army was under the direction of Major Krusenstein, who had the burden of finding food, not only for the soldiers, but also for the civil population. Under the Imperial régime he had been chief-of-staff of all fortresses in Finland and the Baltic provinces, an able and energetic officer. The commander of the First Corps was Major General Count Pohlen and under him was Major General Dzierojinsky, both of whom had had distinguished careers in the old army.

The Armistice of November 11th contained a clause requiring Germany to maintain order in Russian territory under her occupation. Later the Germans remained in spite of Allied protests. Nevertheless, the bulk of the German Army retreated, taking their stores with them, to the chagrin and disappointment of the Esthonian National Council, who were left to deal with their own nettlesome internal affairs as well as with Russian Bolshevism.

In these chaotic days no one person stood out who was capable of seizing command of the situation and unifying mutually suspicious factions. In addition to the Germans and the native Esthonians, several influential persons were in the field, including certain British officers. Colonel Prince Avalov-Bermondt, Colonel Virgolich, Prince Lieven, and various Russian officers of the old army, chief of whom, at the time, was Bulak-Balakhovich, were all violently anti-Bolshevik. The English were more anti-German than the other leaders they were attempting to weld into a unified fighting force.

The chief actor in the drama of German occupation at this time was the famous General von der Goltz, who attempted to combine anti-Bolsheviks and carry out the Eastern policy of Germany. He was one of the best drill masters in the German Army and prior to the Great War had reorganized the Turkish military. He had formed a force of some twenty thousand men in Latvia and Lithuania not only with the intention of fighting the Soviets but also of providing a refuge for such Germans as wished to flee the consequences of their own revolution.

Von der Goltz, in his book, *Meine Sendung im Finnland und im Baltikum,* published in Leipzig in 1920, remarks regarding the complicated situation:

Particularly active in the work of recruiting men for Prince Lieven's Russian Division—an anti-Bolshevik military body—was Colonel Bermondt, who having been adopted by his uncle, called himself Prince Avalov-Bermondt. He too, like Lieven, had found assistance in Germany, and so was an enthusiastic and sincere Germanophile. He recruited a small force of his own, which swore allegiance to him and which grew stronger as equipment and arms became available. Working in conjunction with him, Colonel Virgolich, a former officer of the Gendarmerie, also recruited a small volunteer corps of his own.

In both of these volunteer army organizations German units came into being. I had no confidence in them, partly because they lacked leadership and also because they were being demoralized by the German Bolsheviks who naturally feared the formation of a strong Russian anti-Bolshevist military organization. . . .

The problem of leadership was particularly harassing. In the end Colonels Bermondt and Virgolich recognized Prince Lieven as their superior. Then the kind English uncles took advantage of the situation, of which they had gotten wind early. They realized more quickly than the undiplomatic Germans the importance of the newly formed military body and sought to gain control of it.

The Esthonian National Council who again refused an offer of aid from Germany in November, 1918, could, at the time, muster two small units of some six hundred men, largely composed of Baltic volunteers under Colonel Weiss. General Laidoner was placed in command. His force was soon augmented by some three thousand Finnish volunteers under General Wetzer.

As the Germans retired the Reds followed them, driving

the Esthonian forces westward from the Russian-Esthonian frontier. For nearly a month the Bolsheviks worked their will upon fully three-fourths of the territory of the new nation. Hundreds of helpless civilians—men, women, and children—were massacred in Dorpat, Vesenberg, Narva, and other cities. Local people who had reason to fear or hate their former masters paid the debt with interest. Rape, robbery, and murder reigned for several weeks.

The Esthonians rallied and with the aid of a Finnish loan and British war material were able to expel Red troops who had advanced nearly to Reval in February of 1919. Admiral Sinclair and the British Navy prevented the Bolsheviks from taking the city. Although at the time of the German retreat the population was more pro-Russian than pro-German, Red activities turned them violently anti-Bolshevik.

Meanwhile Latvia went Red. Thus Esthonia was threatened east, south, and west and along the coast, as well as by local uprisings. With British coöperation this latter danger was alleviated.

Latvia had only an informal force of Baltic volunteers around Riga to defend it against the Red Army. When German divisions withdrew after the Armistice a few platoons had been left behind as a guard to protect the liquidation of the German administration. Retreating German soldiers had stripped the country of food. The Latvians had hoped that the Allies would intervene in force to protect them. As a move against Germany, the Allies blockaded Libau and other Latvian ports, permitting only food consignments to enter through the American Relief Administration. The inevitable result of the blockade was to force all trade into German hands and increase sympathy toward the Baltic barons party, which was largely German by both blood and culture.

A Red Army of some twelve thousand men entered Riga on January 2, 1919, retaining control for five months. The Bolsheviks pushed on and occupied Mitau, Libau, and Win-

General Yudenich (left) with Admiral Pilkin

Bolsheviks interned in Germany

"Uncle Tom," Esthonian armoured train

General Laidoner, commander of the Esthonian Army

dau, establishing a reign of terror over the whole region. The Soviet gunwomen were particularly brutal in the Latvian occupation. Some of them were workingwomen who were convinced Communists with a grudge to pay against the old order, many were prostitutes and criminals, who, in the unsettled times, found opportunity to indulge every impulse of sadism, lechery, and diabolism.

Although the Allies were not in a position to send large groups of troops they refused to employ available German battalions on the Prussian frontier. Peace had not yet been signed with Germany. The Allies' hesitation to coöperate with their late enemy is understandable, but their failure to do so not only jeopardized the Latvians but also the Esthonians and White forces along the Baltic. The Bolsheviks had trod heavily upon Riga and vicinity. Over fifteen hundred persons were executed in the city and more than two thousand in the country districts. More than eight thousand persons perished from starvation and malnutrition, and some thousands of citizens had languished in jails and concentration camps under famine conditions. Plunder and spoliation had added to the misery of the Latvians. Before fleeing the city Red officials brutally murdered a number of notables confined in the Central Prison. When the Volunteer and German forces took Riga, Red soldiers and officials captured in the operation were shot without mercy.

The Baltic Volunteer Corps of Latvia by the end of January, 1919, numbered no more than seven hundred men, under Major Alfred Fletcher, a German staff officer. Prince Anatol Lieven had already organized his Russian division. There were also a Lettish brigade under Colonel Ballod, and a body of German troops under Major Bischoff, who had remained in Courland after the Armistice. These German troops took the field against the Reds with the Baltic Volunteers in spite of the prohibition of the Allies. In addition, the First Guard Reserve Division from East Prussia was persuaded to enlist in the struggle. General Count von der Goltz was given an invitation to take supreme command of this combination of Baltic, Russian, Lett, and German troops, constituting the White Army of Latvia.

Von der Goltz quickly brought some semblance of order into these motley units. The Baltic Volunteer Corps were within a few weeks recruited up to three thousand men. By February they were prepared to take the field against the Reds, and cleared Windau and later Mitau of the Bolsheviks. Libau was liberated and finally Riga, on May 22d. The population were in a starving condition and hailed their deliverers with the wildest excitement. The American Relief Administration came to the rescue with a trainload of flour and in a few days the *U.S.S. Lake Mary* with a cargo of food, escorted by the *H.M.S. Vancouver*, made her way through dangerous mine fields into Riga harbor. Here, as elsewhere, the anti-Bolshevik forces made no room for liberal or even moderate opinion, and imprisoned scores who had already suffered under Red domination.

The White movement in Esthonia and along the eastern borders had been strengthened by the presence of General Rodzianko, a famous Russian cavalry officer who arrived in February of 1919. He had become a hero as the commander of a brigade under General Pavlov, always leading at the head of his squadrons. Shortly afterward he was placed in full command of the Russian Corps.

By mobilization and the addition of volunteers who had been prisoners the corps increased to almost five thousand men. Rations were provided for three thousand men in the White units, the remainder being supported on supplies and money taken from the Bolsheviks near Pskov.

There was much hard fighting during the early months of 1919. On February 15th, Trotsky announced that the invincible Red Army was about to drive the Esthonian bourgeoisie into the Baltic; but the attacks were repelled, and the Esthonian Army, now numbering about forty thousand, were successful not only in liberating their own land but also in driving Red troops from a portion of Latvian territory. Near the end of February, Bulak-Balakhovich made a raid on the town of Gdov but after holding it several days was forced to retreat.

General Rodzianko received aid from the Esthonians in May, 1919, when his troops had retreated from Pskov to Yamburg. The Esthonians attacked in the direction of Pskov and aided in the liberation of Northern Latvia. Esthonian troops next had a brush with von der Goltz's volunteer corps composed mostly of German soldiers, near Riga. Von der Goltz had meanwhile disbanded the Latvian Government at Libau. General Gough of the British Mission forbade von der Goltz to invade Esthonia and in a sharp conflict at Wenden-Ronneburg the German general was so badly defeated that he was forced to retire from Latvia.

During the spring of 1919, Reds, Whites, and Esthonians prepared for a drive. On May 13th the Northern Corps launched an offensive eastward from the Narva River, having as its aim the capture of the towns of Yamburg and Gdov. Red troops retired on the entire front and many voluntarily surrendered. At times whole regiments came over, bringing their arms with them. By this means the corps increased within three weeks to a strength of about twenty-five thousand. When Yamburg was taken, General Rodzianko addressed the populace, concluding with the words: "Go to the baths, cleanse yourselves from the life you would have been compelled to lead. In the morning go to church and pray God to help you start a new life."

The strong fortress of Krasnaya Gorka on the north was taken, and on the south the Reds were forced to evacuate Pskov and retreat along the railway toward Luga. No organized Red Army now remained in front of the corps. Ten Red regiments had been annihilated in ferocious fighting. 20 guns, 200 machine guns, 3 armored trains, 3,000 prisoners, and numbers of locomotives and vans had been captured.

The occupied territory, embracing more than two thousand square kilometers and containing an estimated population of almost 500,000 inhabitants, extended in a zone along the eastern and southeastern borders of Esthonia from thirty to sixty versts in width. It included Yamburg, Gdov, Pskov, and parts of the Peterhof and Luga districts. The front held extended from the Finnish Gulf southward for more than two hundred versts, to the point beyond Pskov where it joined the line of defense established by the Esthonians.

Their front was by no means a solid one. Much of the territory was swampy and heavily wooded, and with the small number of troops available it was possible to hold only about one hundred and eighty versts of actual fighting line and this mainly with patrols. Nevertheless, the front was sufficiently secure to permit the Northern Corps to establish something in the nature of a permanent administrative organization. A military commander was appointed for each of the three districts of Yamburg, Gdov, and Pskov, whose duty it was to develop some kind of civil organization.

Such an undertaking was beset with almost insurmountable difficulties. All previously existing institutions had been annihilated by the Bolsheviks, who had created nothing to replace them. Through months of terrorism—during which many villages were burned and many others robbed of all money, cattle, horses, and food supplies, including seed grains—the population was reduced to starvation. Never completely self-supporting, the inhabitants now stood face to face with death. Money had lost its purchasing power and commerce was reduced to a barter basis.

The difficulties of reconstruction were increased by the lack of experienced administrators. Nevertheless district commanders energetically attacked the problem and in a period of two months accomplished remarkable results. The first step was the restoration of local self-government, which had previously existed in the form of district Zemstvos or Land Councils. Town and village municipalities were also resuscitated wherever possible.

The direction of civil administration, under the military, was placed in the hands of a Chief of Civil Government, and for this important post Alexandrov, a former Petrograd judge, was chosen. Liberated districts were then divided into two provinces, north and south, and two former members of the Duma, Count Benningsen and Krüdner-Struve, were appointed governors.

The staff of the Russian Northern Corps was planning a drive upon Petrograd, but without the supplies and support to insure success. Although Esthonia had coöperated in driving back the Bolsheviks, relations between Esthonians and Russians were growing strained. Esthonia stated that Russian commanders were recklessly squandering their money and rendering no account of the expenditures. Moreover, no recognition of her independence had been accorded either by Denikin or any other White commander. So intense became the antagonism between the two groups that in June and July Esthonian newspapers were filled with anti-Russian articles. The Esthonians were not interested in the reëstablishment of Russia, "One and Indivisible." If victory for the Northern Corps meant a restoration of the *status quo ante bellum* they preferred the Red Government which they had reason to believe would recognize their independence.

The White Russians also had their grievances. To them it seemed that Esthonians were much more interested in driving Germans out of Esthonia and Latvia than in fighting the Bolsheviks. They also complained of Esthonia's unwillingness to sell potatoes to their army, which was entirely without them, at a time when they were selling as low as five marks the pood. Moreover, Esthonian customs officials refused to permit Russian soldiers and officers to carry small packages of cigarettes and food over the frontier, even when such articles were for personal use. Some Esthonian troops composed of Ingermanlanders had refused to advance. Petty annoyances, aggravated and multiplied, assumed significant proportion in the aggregate.

General Rodzianko tried to allay the bitter feeling by pointing out that the army was formed on Esthonian territory, that it enjoyed the hospitality of the Esthonian nation and was receiving assistance from its government. Despite these efforts, relations grew worse.

Finland might perhaps have been expected to fight the Bolsheviks, but Finland had powerful Socialist groups who were not disposed to coöperate with White Russians against the Reds. The Soviet Government had recognized Finland's independence as far back as January 4, 1918, and in spite of attempts on the part of the Finnish bourgeoisie, with the help of German bayonets to establish a White Government, the Red Finns, aided by the Soviet Government, triumphed temporarily. After the Treaty of Brest-Litovsk the Russian Red Guards were expected to withdraw from Finland, but they did not do so. Thereupon civil war ensued, with Germany helping the Whites, and the Allies supporting the Reds. The Armistice changed the complexion of affairs, and soon Finland was recognized by the Allies.

A broad constructive policy by the Allies and by Kolchak toward Finland would have assured Finnish coöperation with the White Russians on the Baltic. Although General Mannerheim had made an agreement to help them in May of 1919, recognition of Finland by Kolchak came only after the complete failure of the Baltic campaign. Sir Henry Wilson, in a memorandum on the 16th of April, 1919, remarked in this connection:

The lack of Allied policy in regard to Finland and the other Baltic States precluded the timely, effective (and perhaps decisive) action which might otherwise have been undertaken against Petrograd. In this connection, however, it cannot be too strongly pointed out that the news that the Allies were taking active measures to assist these States would undoubtedly prevent any great transference of Bolshevik forces from this front. Incidentally, such assistance would keep the Esthonian forces (of whose disinclination to continue the struggle there are persistent reports) in the field. The despatch of missions to the Baltic States is therefore highly desirable.

Great Britain was the prime supporter of the Northwestern anti-Bolshevik movement. General Gough, of the British Army, head of the Allied Military Mission to the Baltic

States, arrived in Finland on May 26, 1919. His chief-of-staff was Colonel Marsh, who took an active part in all British dealings with Esthonia and the White Russians.

Throughout the campaign the food problem was of vital importance, as little remained in the land which had been occupied for years. The Baltic Mission of the American Relief Administration brought timely assistance to the Northwestern anti-Bolshevik forces. On May 19th Colonel Krusenstein, chief of the general staff, Russian Northern Corps, appealed to the United States, through the American Relief Administration, as well as to Finland and the Baltic States, for food necessary to continue the struggle against the Bolsheviks.

Toward the end of May, Captain John C. Miller, then a member of the Mission of the A. R. A. to Finland, made an inspection of liberated districts, finding the direst suffering everywhere he journeyed. In a number of villages individuals who had not had bread for from three to nineteen days begged for food. Rations consisted of a pancake made from potato peelings and fish heads discarded by the troops, ground into paste and fried. Soup was made from fish heads and from sour grass. Farmers were somewhat better off in the Yamburg district, where many still possessed a few cows and sheep. Many who had stores hidden away refused to part with them for money. Only by barter could foodstuffs be obtained. In order to ameliorate distress as much as possible among the civil population, Rodzianko had deprived his army of its scanty stores of bread and had distributed it among the poorest inhabitants. Soldiers divided their rations with families where they were billeted.

At Gdov and elsewhere public kitchens were serving meals, consisting of soup made from grass, a hot drink from teaberry leaves, and meat and bread when they could be obtained. The local hospital at Gdov was giving a diet to its patients of one-half pound of bread per day, with fish soup. They had had no meat for two weeks past, and there was flour on hand for only four days. The usual bread ration in the villages and towns was less than one-half pound per day. The peasants were living on bread made from about one-quarter rye and three-quarters moss, husks, and flaxseed.

When the Esthonians under General Laidoner captured the city of Pskov on May 30th, he publicly invested the military authority in Bulak-Balakhovich. At the same time he announced that an American officer, Lieutenant A. A. Granstedt, had arrived to investigate food conditions. The starved population went wild with joy, for the citizens had no food save spoiled salt fish which was being sold for two rubles per pound. The entire municipality had only sixty cows furnishing milk for a hospital and ten asylums for orphan and refugee children. Because of lack of seed only one-third of the surrounding farm land was sown. The condition of children was pitiful. The American Relief Administration immediately sent shipments of flour to Pskov, as well as to the districts of Gdov and Yamburg.

Major R. R. Powers, Chief of the Esthonian Section of the Baltic Mission of the A. R. A., arrived in Reval on June 8th and immediately informed himself regarding the amount of food necessary to secure the successful occupation of Petrograd by the Whites.

A conference to consider the entire situation was held in Reval on June 11th which General Gough, American Relief Administration officials, and high officers of the Esthonian and Russian armies attended. An important agreement was drawn up between the Russian civil and military authorities of the liberated districts and the A. R. A., under the terms of which food supplies were to be furnished both to the civil population of liberated districts and to the army. Some timber land in the district of Gdov was pledged as a guarantee of payment for all foodstuffs furnished. In addition, the sum of 5,000,000 Finnish marks, or a corresponding sum in foreign value, was to be paid by representatives of the Russian Political Conference, headed by General Yudenich, to the Helsingfors office of the Relief Administration. Of this sum, 1,000,000 marks was to be paid immediately through the

American Legation at Stockholm, and the remaining 4,000-000 were to be paid without interest within one month from the date of the agreement. The British accepted responsibility for war materials. Public opinion in England did not permit of the dispatch of British troops in force.

The British promised that the first load of military material, consisting of 4 tanks, 6 airplanes, 15,000,000 cartridges, 3,000 automatic rifles, and complete equipment for 10,000 men, would arrive in Reval on June 27th. On the strength of this promise, the Northern Corps decided to postpone any further offensive action until July 1st.

As the military authorities possessed the only organization capable of handling transportation of supplies, it was decided to turn over to the Supply Committee of the Russian Northern Corps the food for the army and for the civil population. The number of troops which would have to be rationed was estimated at 40,000. This figure represented about 14,000 more than the actual number of men composing the army at the time, but in view of the fact that entire regiments had been coming over from the Bolsheviks it was deemed necessary to provide for such contingencies.

Food arrived on June 15th when the *S.S. Lake Charlottesville,* having on board 2,400 tons of flour and towing a barge containing 147 tons of bacon transferred from another vessel, put into Reval harbor. White leaders had high hopes that with hungry soldiers fed they would soon have munitions with which to take Petrograd and strike a body blow at the Soviet power.

In the period of quiet following the May offensive, the corps which had been under General Laidoner of the Esthonian Army had been re-formed into the Northwestern Army, with four divisions and a total fighting strength of some 26,000 bayonets and swords with a few batteries of small-caliber guns. Nearly all were engaged in holding the front line.

When the army left Esthonian soil General Laidoner gave

the command of the Russian troops to General Rodzianko. Soon thereafter the government in far-off Omsk appointed General Nicholas Yudenich commander-in-chief of all Russian armed military and naval forces operating against the Bolsheviks on the Baltic on June 15, 1919.

Nicholas Yudenich had become a hero in the Great War when he stopped the Turkish invasion pushing toward Tiflis in the battles of Sarikamysh and Ardahan. Yudenich was thoroughly Russian. Graduating from the famous Alexandrovsky Military School in Moscow, he had risen rapidly in the Imperial Army. After a course at the Military Academy in Petrograd, he had served on the staff of an army corps and was chief-of-staff of a brigade of Turkestan Rifles. Leading a charge at the head of this organization, he had been wounded in the Russo-Japanese War. In recognition of his valor and services he was made a major general, sent as chief-of-staff to the Caucasus, and five years later was made a lieutenant general. When the war broke out he was fifty-three and one of the youngest army commanders. His knowledge of Southeast Russia equipped him for the brilliant campaigns he had carried out against the Turks. Now he awaited anxiously the promised war materials from Great Britain.

General Yudenich no longer was commander of well-equipped divisions such as he had deployed against the Turks. Many of his men were barefoot, without uniforms or rifles, and not a few were ill. The troops, unsupported by heavy artillery, were scattered on a loosely held line from the Finnish coast to Pskov. Ambulances were almost non-existent, medicines were scarce. No adequate field hospitals or dressing stations existed for the care of the wounded.

In addition to the shortage of food, men, and equipment, Yudenich, as Kolchak and Denikin, found that he must address himself to the psychological front to which he, as they, was unaccustomed. Bolshevik propagandists were showering the Northwestern Army in the vicinity of Pskov with leaflets denouncing American and British imperialism and urging the White Russians to join their Red brothers in building up a new social and economic order in the old empire.

June 27th passed without the arrival of munitions! But rumors prevailed that tanks would be sent, and talk among both officers and men turned upon what would be accomplished when these monsters should arrive. Up to this date morale among the troops had been excellent, but as days wore into weeks without the arrival of supplies, Bolshevik propagandists took advantage to impress upon soldiers the fact that the Allies had not kept, and probably would not keep, their word.

The Reds now deemed the hour had come for an attack and began an advance early in July in the north which quickly developed into a general offensive along the entire front. Large Red reinforcements arrived from Eastern Siberia where the troops opposed to Kolchak were winning victories. Among them were many skilled Communist speakers who were employed by the Bolshevik staff to incite wholesale desertions to the Soviet armies. The Red attack continued day and night against the hard-pressed Northwestern Army which was compelled to yield to superior numbers at several points. By the middle of the month the Bolsheviks were threatening Pskov.

Toward the end of July, Esthonia in self-protection sent troops and two armored trains against the advancing Reds. With their aid Pskov was saved for the moment but later lost to the Bolsheviks. Meanwhile the northern portion of the White front continued to suffer reverses.

It was not until August 2d, over a month after the promised date of arrival, that the first British ship bearing munitions anchored in Reval harbor. The following day the fall of Yamburg sounded the death knell of the first attempt to take Petrograd.

Prince Lieven, often bitterly accused by White officers as tardy in coming to the assistance of Yudenich, at least made one sizable effort, for he now dispatched 3,000 of his troops from Libau. In spite of these reinforcements, the Northwestern Army was pressed back until the Reds were within striking distance of Yamburg. The continuous fighting, with odds almost three to one, the armored cars which persistently broke up the army's machine-gun nests, and the lack of sufficient munitions or equipment, told heavily upon Yudenich's soldiers. Yamburg was evacuated on August 3d after the railway bridge across the Luga River had been destroyed. The Luga River flows swiftly between high banks, and the bridge, which had only recently been rebuilt, was a vital feature of the campaign.

Yudenich now appealed to Major Powers of the American Relief Administration for armored cars and gasoline for motor trucks. A wire was dispatched to Major Powers in Paris that a British ship had arrived the previous day with shells and equipment for airplanes, but no gasoline, and that two more ships were due shortly. A plea was made that if the American Relief Administration would send armored cars and gasoline they might yet take Petrograd. Paris headquarters of the A. R. A. replied that 50,000 gallons of gasoline for the use of sixty motor trucks would be due in Reval about September 1st. The telegram from Paris was signed by Herbert Hoover, who requested Krusenstein to keep him informed as to "relative front powers."

To add to Yudenich's worries, Soviet Russia announced on August 1st that peace would be made with Esthonia as soon as the frontier towns of Yamburg, Gdov, and Pskov had been retaken. A separate peace between Esthonia and Moscow was not improbable at this point. Indeed, friction between Esthonia and Yudenich was such that some White officers talked of war upon Esthonia after disposing of the Bolsheviks. The Esthonians, on their part, having already won recognition from the Bolsheviks, asked themselves why they should continue a struggle in favor of White Russians who refused to recognize their country against Red Russians who had done so.

It was in an effort to keep Esthonia in the struggle that, on August 10, 1919, Brigadier General F. G. Marsh invited several Russian political leaders who were backing the White movement in the Northwest to a conference in his office. He told his guests that Esthonia's support was essential to the White cause, that it could be retained only by prompt and full recognition, and that such recognition must come not from one individual but from a Russian Government. Those present were invited to form a government for the Northwestern region which would act as he had suggested. He threatened the withdrawal of supplies to the Russian Northwestern Army by the Allies if this step were not taken, and gave them until seven o'clock (the time being then 6:20 P.M.) to form a government! He went as far as to give them a list, distributing the various portfolios, after which he withdrew from the meeting.

The meeting unanimously decided to accept this British ultimatum. General Marsh, upon being informed of the fact, required the Ministers of Foreign Affairs, of Finance, and of the Interior to sign a treaty with the representatives of the Esthonian Government recognizing the independence of Esthonia. The next day, after much discussion regarding formalities, a Declaration recognizing Esthonia and inviting her coöperation, together with that of the United States, Great Britain, and France, with the Northwestern Russian Army, was signed by the same group, at General Marsh's instigation. The Declaration read, in part:

In order to obtain real military assistance to the Russian North Western Army from the Esthonian Government and in view of the latter's avowed readiness to sign a treaty to that effect only with a democratic government for the North Western region, which must be created for that purpose, we, the undersigned, having estimated the conditions in which the task of saving our country from the yoke of the Bolsheviks is to be conducted—as explained to us in the course of a meeting presided over by Col. Marsh—conditions which, if continued, preclude the possibility of further assistance on the part of the Allies, hereby declare:

(1) That we have formed a Government for the North Western region of Russia, including the former province of Petrograd, the provinces of Pskov and Novgorod, and of such

regions as will be liberated in that part of Russia from the yoke of the Bolsheviks.

(2) That we have assumed full responsibility for the settlement of all regional questions.

(3) That we expect the Esthonian Government to assist the North Western Russian Government by armed force in the liberation of Petrograd, and the provinces of Petrograd, Pskov and Novgorod from the Bolshevik yoke, in order to enable the Government, upon the capture of Petrograd, to establish a firm democratic order and put into practice a democratic program, based upon respect for the rights and liberties of the individual.

(4) That we feel certain that the Allied Military Mission, which is supplying the Russian Army with military stores, will likewise continue to supply food, munitions, and other necessaries through the Minister of War, and will render us financial assistance.

(5) That apart from this, negotiations must inevitably be conducted with the Esthonian Government with a view to obtaining for the new region an outlet to the sea in one of the ports of Esthonia for the sake of ensuring mutual trade relations.

They further declared their belief that the All-Russian Government under Admiral Kolchak would agree with their decision and requested the representatives of the United States, France, and Great Britain to obtain from their governments the recognition of the complete independence of Esthonia.

The new government was headed by C. G. Lianozov, a Constitutional Democrat, who was also Minister of Foreign Affairs and Finances, while General Yudenich was in charge of the Ministry of War. The Cabinet included several radical members.

Great Britain had agreed to support the Lianozov Government in every way in its struggle against the Bolsheviks, and especially in its efforts to occupy Petrograd; to supply Lianozov with munitions and modern weapons of war, such as tanks and airplanes, to exercise pressure upon Germany to facilitate recruiting among the Russian prisoners of war in Germany; to furnish supplies to the districts suffering from the effects of Bolshevist rule, and to grant a special credit of 1,000,000,000 rubles, after the overthrow of the Bolshevik régime, for the purchase of machinery and raw materials for the restoration of Russian industry. In return, Great Britain demanded recognition of her special interests in the Baltic region, that the Baltic countries be given opportunity to exercise self-determination, that Russia declare her disinterestedness in the Persian question, recognize all debts of the former Russian Government, and forbear from making any important purchases in Germany so long as delivery agreements based upon the credit arrangements with Great Britain existed.

Esthonia, no doubt believing that recognition by Allied governments would follow for the White Baltic Government which was their puppet, agreed on August 12th to coöperate with Yudenich. Three days later Yudenich made a public announcement of his intention to advance on Petrograd.

The Northwestern Government on August 24th issued a detailed statement of the principles forming the basis of its impending activities. It pledged itself to:

A firm struggle against the Bolsheviks, as well as against all those who aspire to re-establish the old régime, the equality before the law of all the citizens of the Russian State, without distinction of race, nationality and religion.

All the citizens of liberated Russia were guaranteed inviolability of person and domicile, freedom of the press, speech, association, assembly, and strikes.

Steps were to be taken for the summoning of a new All-Russian Constituent Assembly to be elected by a general, direct, equal, and secret vote:

If after the liberation of the Petrograd, Pskov, and Novgorod provinces general conditions may not yet warrant the convocation of an All-Russian Constituent Assembly, there should be summoned, for the purposes of coördinating conditions of local life, a Territorial Popular Assembly in Petrograd, elected on the same democratic basis by the population of the liberated provinces.

Nationalities were to decide freely for themselves their form of administration:

The administration of the Russian State is to be founded on principles of wide local autonomy, Zemstvos, and municipal self-governments are to be elected upon a democratic basis.

The land problem was to be solved in the Constituent Assembly, in accordance with the will of the toiling agricultural population; until its solution, the land should remain in the hands of the peasantry.

The labor question was to be settled on the basis of the eight-hour day, the State control of industry, and the full protection of labor and of the working class.

The pronunciamento closed with a ringing appeal for support.

By September 1st the Northwestern Army possessed a strength of 17,000 men, including 3,000 bayonets, 600 swords, 6 tanks, 53 guns, 4 armed autos, and 4 armored trains. But the tanks and trains were out of commission because of the broken bridge at Yamburg. Opposed to the Northwestern Army was the Red Army, with a strength of 21,000, with 5,000 bayonets, 960 swords, 60 guns, 3 armored trains, and 4 armed autos.

Yudenich now decided that the moment had arrived to drive toward Petrograd. His troops were in as good condition as he could hope to place them before the coming winter. Kolchak's retreat was releasing more and more Red regiments and Yudenich was realist enough to see that little hope could be placed in a decisive victory by Denikin. He now made a counter bid to the propaganda of the Bolsheviks. The Northwestern Government issued an appeal to the army, stating that their White Government was composed "of men in public life, or representatives of all classes and of all the strata of the population," that Czarism was hateful to it, that it believed the land to belong "to those who toil upon it," and that it would preserve the eight-hour day and all other measures for the freedom and happiness of the people.

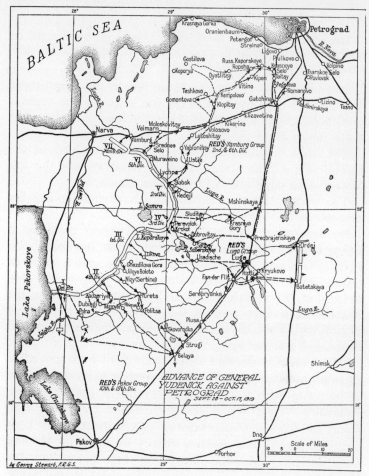

Advance of Northwestern White Army of General Yudenich against Petrograd, September 28–October 17, 1919. Arrows show White's attacks.

The Northwestern Army were close to the old capital. They had a limited and a possible objective. Although in itself the former capital possessed no conclusive importance, the capture of Petrograd would stun the Bolsheviks and perhaps raise the peoples in the interior of Russia to revolt. A memorandum was sent by Major Krusenstein to the American Relief Administration asking food for the population of Petrograd.

The drive began with minor engagements which were successful. Bulak-Balakhovich broke the Bolshevik lines at Bulata on October 1st, capturing hundreds of prisoners. White hopes were raised high.

Yudenich began an advance on a front of one hundred miles, risking everything in one effort to take Petrograd. Allied ships maintained a naval blockade against the old capital. On October 12th Yamburg was retaken by the Whites. Two days later Yudenich was approaching Gatchina, thirty-five miles south of Petrograd, White scouts in advance of General Rodzianko's army reached Kikerino, and the Reds were falling back in disorder on Petrograd. Southward, Pskov, which had been captured by the Bolsheviks August 27th, was retaken on October 15th. Three days later the cavalry of General Yudenich were in the suburbs of Petrograd. Not only White Russians but foreign observers felt that the fall of Petrograd was imminent.

But the troops were exhausted. They had been fighting day and night on scanty rations. Their spirit was weakened by the growing resistance of the Reds and by the adroit use of propaganda. The words Peace, Land, and Freedom were whispered into the ears of infantrymen whose frost-bitten feet made forced marches a horror, and to horsemen whose mounts could no longer respond to the charge. One of the White generals, in his eagerness to be the first in Petrograd, disobeyed orders and failed to cut the railroad at Tosno, an oversight which allowed the Bolsheviks to bring up reserves. Yudenich's force moved more slowly and finally stopped.

The Bolsheviks in Petrograd who had some 20,000 seasoned troops at their disposal, mustered every man who could bear arms, compelling the Northwestern Army to retreat toward Esthonia. By early November the White troops were driven back beyond Gatchina. The army was demoralized. Desertions were numerous. Many of the wounded were left behind. Spotted typhus broke out among the straggling regiments. Men lay down to die in road corners and barns as their comrades pushed on toward the Esthonian frontier. Red cavalry followed closely, by day and night, driving on Yudenich's forces who could scarcely provide rear-guard defense. It was another dolorous chapter in the annals of Russian White armies.

Hungry and despairing soldiers looked with dread upon another winter with starvation for a bedfellow and typhus to slay them should they escape Red bullets. The commander of the Baltic campaign had no organized rear in which he could recoup and prepare for another thrust. East of him was the Red Army, flushed with victory, and to the west and south were discontented secessionist states. Yudenich knew his hopeful army had ceased to exist as a combat organization and saw that White power on the Baltic was spent.

Esthonia dreaded Red reprisals for participating in the campaign. Her treatment of the retreating Northwestern Army was harsh. As White troops crossed the frontier they were disarmed, placed in scanty billets, and treated with disrespect.

In late November, Lianozov announced that a new offensive against Petrograd was being planned. The Supreme Allied Council asked Esthonia to cease disarming Yudenich's troops and to permit the reorganization of the army on Esthonian soil, but Esthonia, who began negotiating peace with the Bolsheviks, refused.

Yudenich was an unwelcome guest at Riga on December 20th. Latvia, too, refused to receive him and would not consent to the transfer of his troops to Latvian soil, fearing that this would ultimately mean a Bolshevik offensive. The refusal of Esthonia and Latvia to coöperate further in an attack on Petrograd snuffed out the last hopes of Yudenich and the Northwestern Government.

The Northwestern Army was left in sorry predicament. Crowded into a small space near Yamburg, the troops faced capture by the Bolsheviks or internment in Esthonia. Two thousand of Yudenich's men went over to the Reds. Esthonia denied the ancient right of asylum to the remainder of

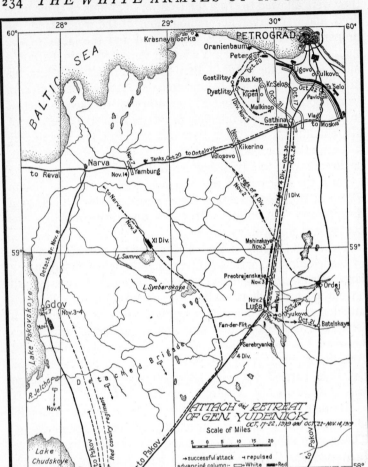

Attack on Petrograd and retreat of Northwestern White Army, October–
November, 1919.

Yudenich's force and the refugees that accompanied them.
Soldiers and refugees suffered in zero temperatures without
sufficient housing, clothes, or food. Thousands of soldiers and
civilians perished of typhus, exposure, and hunger. Finally

they were allowed to cross the frontier in groups of three hundred, and were given accommodations of the worst kind. All property of the army was confiscated and the labor of the soldiers exploited. When Yudenich departed from Esthonia in an automobile flying a British flag, taking with him his private fortune, he left behind some 12,000 soldiers suffering from spotted typhus and 21,000 starving refugees attached to his army. Later Yudenich negotiated for the transfer of his remaining troops from Esthonia to Serbia but was unable to secure the necessary aid. Those who escaped frost, hunger, or disease were finally disbanded in Esthonia.

With the collapse of the Northwestern Army, the *raison d'être* of the Northwestern Government ceased and it soon disappeared. The failure of the Northwestern campaign was consequent upon many causes.

The largest factor in Yudenich's disaster was his own lack of leadership. He was a brilliant fighter when fitted into a large war machine, but lacked those capacities to steady and encourage men when exalted to the position of sole commander of an independent operation. He was at odds with General Rodzianko, and was unable to settle differences between his subordinates. White officers complained that British coöperation in the naval attack on Kronstadt had not been carried out with sufficient vigor, but this charge was hotly denied by officers in the Royal Navy.

Another reason for failure was a refusal to use all available troops of whatever nationality in the common cause. There were thousands of seasoned soldiers who would have furnished stability to the improvised battalions Yudenich was compelled to use. Von der Goltz, smarting under the refusal of England to allow him to participate in the campaign against the Bolsheviks, remarked of the British:

They prevailed upon old General Yudenich—a highly honorable man, but totally under the influence of his Staff, which was pro-English and wholly dependent on England—to order Lieven to report with his corps on the Narva front.

Prince Lieven was an excellent soldier and believed it to be his duty to obey the order, although he was fully aware of the condition of affairs. The troops reported for duty, and their good equipment aroused universal astonishment. An English officer, in speaking to a Russian officer on the Narva front, expressed his displeasure at the fact that *boches* were in Russian service. "They are not *boches*, but Russians equipped by *boches*. As for the appearance of the Russian soldiers equipped by England, please look at this man, who stands near by." The other Russian soldier looked like an unkempt beggar. Thus Lieven's division on the Narva front made propaganda for the German cause and in addition was of real use. The English were then at last taking care of the Yudenich troops. Later, in the most unscrupulous and stupid manner, they egged on Yudenich to undertake an offensive against Petrograd, single-handed and totally unprepared, with the result that most of the so-called Northern Army, including Lieven's Volunteer Corps, was massacred.

The growing strength of Communist Russia would have made victory uncertain for any commander operating against Petrograd. Trotsky, directing the defense of the city, had issued a proclamation on October 18th reviling his enemies and calling on his troops to defend the Revolution. The determination of young workers, peasants, military students, and soldiers whom the Petrograd Soviet scrambled together astounded White and Reds alike. Five hundred and fifty Red seamen lost their lives when Admiral Cowan's gunners sank three Bolshevik torpedo boats in a naval engagement in the Gulf of Finland.

The coöperation of Esthonia was fraught with uncertainty. Her struggle with Germany distracted her attention from the Yudenich campaign. Esthonia was compelled to make peace with either Germany or Soviet Russia. Unable to withstand attacks from two sides, she chose to consider peace with Soviet Russia. Upon the failure of Yudenich, she felt released from all obligation to continue the struggle against the Bolsheviks. In September and October conferences of the Baltic states met at Dorpat to consider peace with Red Russia. Discussion of peace with the Soviets was resumed on December 1st and a treaty signed on February 2, 1920.

The lack of a unified command which could strategically

direct the movements of White troops in the East and South and Northwest against the Red Army was a disability in common with all White efforts. The assistance of the Allies was rendered in a haughty spirit which failed to elicit confidence.

The devastated state of the countryside made an adequate service of supply impossible. At no time were the men adequately fed or equipped. Hunger became an ally of the Reds. Foraging expeditions turned into downright raids alienating the peasantry. If it had not been for the assistance of the American Relief Administration many thousands of soldiers and civilians would have starved. Throughout the old Baltic provinces and Poland the Americans rendered an inestimable service not only in saving a multitude from starvation but in preserving the lives and health of hundreds of thousands of children.

Mud, snow, and frost added to the soldiers' miseries. Typhus slew over 14,000 White soldiers. Adequate hospitalization and care of the wounded were out of the question.

The spirit and loyalty of the troops was not high. Reluctant support by Avalov-Bermondt made it impossible for Yudenich to consider this force a working unit of his army. Here and there among ranks and officers courage and devotion flared up, but outbursts of noble patriotism were sporadic and group differed with group. Neither officers nor men were buoyed up by a clear purpose or led by a chief who in vigor and political sagacity as well as in military knowledge was adequate for the tumultuous times.

Every psychological and military advantage lay with the Red Army. It possessed a unique command from the outset. The Bolsheviks made use of the fact that England was backing Yudenich, describing the campaign as one of capitalist England against the workers of Russia. Many Red officers showed ability even with improvised battalions from the workingmen's quarters of Petrograd. They had a conviction that Yudenich stood for reaction while they were establishing a new world, ridding themselves of a top-heavy bureaucracy, the secret police, a mediocre dynasty, and a theory of the state which made church and press and school subservient to the crown. Such ideas furnished a social dynamic to Red troops who had been infuriated by defeats and the suffering they had endured under the Czar. Thus a grim and resolute group of men were able to stave off the White thrust which had progressed from Pskov to the city limits of the old national capital.

Chapter X

SIBERIA: KOLCHAK AS DICTATOR: FROM THE ARMISTICE TO THE RAILWAY AGREEMENT OF MARCH, 1919

THE Armistice, although it made practically no difference in Siberian conditions and in the factional strife of the Russians, did, as far as Allied troops were concerned, change their status. No excuse could now be found in danger from war prisoners for forming an eastern front against Germany, or for aiding the Czechs who long since could have been safely evacuated. English, French, and Japanese representatives had committed themselves to an anti-Bolshevik policy and carried on as before November 11th. Adopting a strict interpretation of his *Aide Memoir,* General Graves withdrew American troops to the vicinity of Vladivostok where they remained until the Inter-Allied Railroad Agreement of the following spring. With General Graves' view the representatives of the American State Department and the English and Japanese military were in disagreement.

The American State Department before the Armistice authorized consular agents in Siberia to give aid and advice to local governments, but stated that it was not prepared to recognize any government in Russia. Inasmuch as all the towns were in control of the Whites it was in effect a policy which aided only their interest.

The banquet at Omsk on November 6th to celebrate the establishment of an All-Russian Government, the Directory, was more successful than the thing it celebrated. The memory of it had not yet faded when Kolchak, as Minister of War, determined to inspect the front, accompanied by

Colonel Ward, senior foreign officer at Omsk, and a British guard. The deplorable conditions which he witnessed impressed upon Kolchak the weakness of the compromise government formed of Socialist-Revolutionaries and conservatives and the necessity for strong measures. On his return journey to Omsk he stopped at Petropavlovsk for a conference with General Boldyrev, who had suddenly left the Ufa front. Colonel Ward surmised that the Socialist-Revolutionary faction headed by Avksentiev, and the militarist group organized by Colonel Lebedev, once a staff officer of Kornilov's, were at odds and that Admiral Kolchak was being sounded by both from their own points of view.

From conversation with the admiral, Colonel Ward gathered that a movement was on foot to curtail Kolchak's control over the army. He suggested the resignation of Kolchak as Minister of War, but Kolchak believed that he could maintain his leadership.

In the evening of November 17, 1918, the admiral and his British escort returned to Omsk. During the night the telegraph line east was cut and the three Socialist-Revolutionary members of the Directory were arrested. This action was staged by Colonel Lebedev, a deadly enemy of the Socialist-Revolutionaries.

Toward midday of November 18th, Ward was officially informed that Admiral Kolchak had been offered supreme authority. Kolchak had refused to accept it. Ward was also told that the remaining ministers were anxious for their safety, which was threatened partly by Russian troops and even more by the Czechs, who, being democratic, were naturally hostile to any thought of a dictator. What added to the confusion was the fact that the chief actors were waiting to see what the British attitude would be before taking decisive steps. Colonel Ward, in view of the state of tension between the Czechs and the Cabinet ministers, issued a warning that any approach or collection of troops near the British cantonment would be treated as hostile.

Admiral Kolchak's personality and career equipped him

with qualities which made possible his sudden rise to power and his striking failure. He was a small, well-dressed, energetic man, moving about with quick, nervous gestures. His smooth-shaven face and smart appearance were more like that of a Western European officer than the traditional bearded and robust Russian soldier. His excessive excitability was calculated neither to inspire confidence in his officers nor steadiness in his troops. He was not as good a combat leader as Kornilov, nor did he possess the stubborn tenacity of Denikin.

Kolchak had won distinction on three scientific expeditions to the Arctic. He had served in the Russian fleet in the Japanese War and when the fleet was destroyed had been an officer in a land battery at Port Arthur. Later he had cooperated with the Duma in creating a general staff for the Admiralty to restore efficiency to the navy, which had been badly crippled. In the Great War he had accomplished more than any Russian officer, in mining and counter-mining operations in the Baltic and the Black Sea, to promote the security of the Russian naval establishment. In the troublous days of Kerensky's Government, like General Brusilov in the army, he knew how to make concessions to the revolutionary spirit and at the same time to preserve some semblance of discipline in the fleet. German agents circulated the report that as a landowner on the Black Sea he was only interested in the export of grain, a rumor which injured his influence. Mutineers had demanded his sword on the 23d of June, 1917. Declining to surrender his St. George sword of honor, he had thrown it into the sea. Kerensky recognized his value and wished to make use of him, but Kolchak demanded employment in a position where he would not be hampered by any army or navy committee. In the summer of 1917 Kerensky had ordered him on a mission to the United States, with the result that he was in Sweden when Kornilov attempted his *coup d'état*. On his way back from the United States, Kolchak arrived in Japan at the outbreak of the Bolshevik revolution. The admiral seems to have despaired of Russia's continuing the war, for he at once offered his services to the English War Office. A telegram from London asked him to report at Shanghai for Mesopotamia, but when he arrived at Shanghai he was told that he might return to Siberia.

The next few months Kolchak spent in obscure movements and negotiations in China, Japan, and Manchuria. Semyonov offered him command of the Harbin detachment, but Kolchak refused, and the relations between them were strained from that time forward.

At this period the admiral attempted to come to some agreement with Japan, but General Tanaka advised him to retire until a later date. In Siberia he met General Knox of the British Mission. This English officer befriended Kolchak throughout his tragic period of leadership but not always with the wisest counsel.

The small, square-shouldered naval officer, with a military air and energetic movements, was of too unstable a disposition to be the man on horseback in the ruthless days of the Siberian turmoil. His violent fits of anger revealed a fundamentally weak, if honest, nature. He lacked all suppleness, tact, and even prudence. One of his colleagues, Baron Budberg, who was close to him at Omsk, describes him as a "big, sick child, a pure idealist, a convinced slave of duty and of service to an idea and to Russia; certainly a neurasthenic, quick to flare up, very wild and uncontrolled in the expression of his dissatisfaction and anger, lacking in selfish interest and *amour propre,* he hates all violence and arbitrariness, but because of his rash temper he often goes beyond the limits of the law; always he is under another's influence. The practical aspect of life and its ruthlessness he does not know." Kolchak was destined to suffer from this fatal ignorance and to drag many to disaster with him.

British officers in Siberia were keeping His Majesty's Government informed of the position of the Directory and had not concealed its instability. Nevertheless, London had decided to recognize the Omsk Government and had actually drawn up the telegram of recognition when news came of Kolchak's *coup d'état*.

In the afternoon of the 18th of November, 1918, Kolchak assumed the supreme power, and early in the evening called on the French representative and later upon Colonel Ward. To the latter Kolchak explained the causes for his setting up a dictatorship, stating that the attempt of the Council chosen by the Ufa Assembly to combine all parties in the government of the country, and to bring order to troubled Russia, had failed utterly. He stated that the Central Committee of the Socialist-Revolutionary party had issued a proclamation which was bound to produce in the new Russian army the same calamitous lack of discipline that had ruined the Imperial forces eighteen months previously. In consequence of the proclamation the Cabinet had no alternative but to dissolve the old Directory of Five and centralize power in one person, to whom the ministers would be responsible.

Replying to the admiral, Colonel Ward stated to him that circumstances appeared to justify the Cabinet of Ministers in their action and Admiral Kolchak in assuming the supreme power. He believed, however, that the Socialist-Revolutionary members of the Directory and some others had been arrested, and that, if this were to result in their execution, the loss of the sympathy of the English, the Americans, and the French was inevitable. The outside world would interpret the proceeding as an attempt of old army officers to destroy a democratic régime and achieve a return to Czarism. Kolchak declared that his intention in assuming responsibilities as supreme ruler was to prevent extremists on either side from continuing a state of anarchy which made democratic governments impossible.

Since no information was forthcoming about the political prisoners, Colonel Ward followed up a letter addressed to the Russian authorities with a second emphasizing the grave injury that would be done to Kolchak's cause if these prisoners of state should suffer any harm without due process of law. He learned that three officers had reported to headquarters assuming entire responsibility for the arrest of the ministers, whom they had not injured and that they were prepared to hand them over, together with their papers and several million rubles, believed to be loot, to the proper authorities. The admiral placed the three officers under arrest, to be tried by court-martial, and safeguarded the political prisoners with a strong detachment of his own until such time as he could convey them out of the country.

The prisoners left Omsk on November 21, 1918, for the Chinese frontier on a British train and with a guard of British and Russian soldiers which accompanied them to Chang-Chun, near the Chinese-Manchurian frontier.

With the exile of these political leaders Admiral Kolchak's troubles began, which would have overwhelmed him at once if it had not been for British support. Colonel Ward, while remaining outwardly neutral, admits that he "constantly made representations and gave advice, when asked, about all manner of affairs, both internal and external. . . ." Kolchak was Britain's protégé, a fact which helped him in the days of the *coup d'état* and hindered him subsequently because of the jealousy of France. It was even rumored that a bargain was to be concluded between Great Britain and the supreme ruler where, in return for intervention south of the Urals, the English were to have a monopoly in exploiting the resources of Turkestan. The truth is that the English did not know of the plans for the *coup d'état*, but made the best of the accomplished fact.

The supreme ruler from the commencement of his term of office was hampered by the dissatisfaction and withdrawal of the greater part of the Czechs, by the opposition of the Japanese and their tool, Semyonov, by the suspicion of the French, who were backing the Czechs—distrusting Kolchak as a protégé of England, and by the hostility of General Boldyrev, the late commander-in-chief of White troops in the region.

These difficulties were quite unsuspected by the public outside of Russia. Even representatives of Allied govern-

Admiral Kolchak reviews Siberian troops

Admiral Kolchak praises boy for heroic action

A trio of Kolchak's soldiers

War prisoners during Kolchak's retreat

ments who were on the spot were slow to realize that mutual jealousies and petty suspicions, together with the faulty conduct of the army and a failure to understand the mind of the civil population, would inevitably lead to the overthrow of Kolchak. In the West the press and the governmental spokesmen hailed Kolchak as the savior of Russia. His *coup d'état* was pictured as a genuinely democratic measure supported by all the more stable elements of the population. Even when his forces were compelled to make disastrous retreats, these movements were described as strategic measures which placed his armies in even stronger positions than they had formerly held. Correspondents and statesmen wanted the White forces to win and their wishes colored reports coming from Russia and Siberia.

The *coup d'état* of Admiral Kolchak came as an unpleasant surprise to the Czechs. They were democratic, even socialistic, in their ideas and had little relish for the autocratic ways of many former high Czarist officers. They would have been far more congenial to Kornilov, Denikin, or Alexeyev than to the nervous, high-handed Kolchak and numbers of absolutist officers about him. General Syrový remarked when he received the news: "The change of Government has killed our soldiers. They say for four years they have been fighting for democracy and now that a dictatorship rules at Omsk they are no longer fighting for democracy." Gajda alone among the Czech officers of higher rank favored dictatorship.

General Syrový on November 20th, fearful lest hostilities break out between the Czechs and Kolchak's soldiers, ordered all political discussion to cease among the Legionnaires. On the 22d of November the Czech National Council condemned the *coup d'état* as:

"against those elementary laws which should be the foundation of all Governments, including that of Russia. We who are fighting for the ideal of liberty and the rights of the people, cannot give and will not give our help or sympathy to *coups d'état* which are in opposition to those principles. We hope that the crisis created by the arrest of the members of the provisional control Government will be overcome by legal methods; therefore we regard this crisis to be still existing."

On November 28th the *Official Journal* of the National Council stated:

Among others the detachment under Colonel Krasilnikov, which participated in the *coup d'état* at Omsk, has not been to the front since it was at Kirensk in the month of August. The detachments under Semyonov, Annenkov, and perhaps of Kalmykov are all at the rear. They are wanted at the front, we have a right to ask for them.

The British, apparently eager to pacify the Legionnaires, decorated three hundred officers and men. The King sent a wire to General Syrový, thanking him for his services in the common cause and assuring him that Great Britain would never forget her obligation to his soldiers for helping to restore peace and security in Russia. But these gestures could hardly satisfy the Legionnaires, who had served notice to the world that they were weary of Russia and Russian civil war and politics.

It was soon seen that if the Legionnaires were to line up with any Russian political party, it would be with the Socialist-Revolutionaries. They continued to establish Soldiers' Councils which were condemned among Kolchak's officers. The admiral commanded General Gajda to arrest the agitators, who were handed over to General Syrový. But General Syrový was submissive to the Czech Council and was compelled to release the prisoners, with the result that Gajda resigned his position in the Czech legions and joined Kolchak's army. As a reward for his loyalty to the Omsk Government and because of his proven ability Kolchak gave him command of the forces around Ekaterinburg and eventually of his entire Northern Army.

Disgusted with Kolchak's régime, Czechs began to withdraw from the line. The Soldiers' Councils were definitely Socialist in color. The ranks of the legions were now being filled by recruiting Czechs and Slovaks from among prisoners of war. They were weary with fighting futile battles, while the Russians, in turn, found General Syrový and his soldiers irksome to their pride and asked that they be sent to the rear. Finally it was decided that the Czechs should guard the Trans-Siberian Railway pending their evacuation.

Japan was the most energetic of all the Allies that intervened in Siberia. By August of 1918 her troops had occupied all strategic centers east of Lake Baikal. The Japanese viewed Kolchak askance, inasmuch as their interests would best be served by a buffer state in the Far East under leadership amenable to the Sunrise Kingdom. Although finally recognizing Kolchak, Japan, nevertheless, maintained Kalmykov and Semyonov who were thorns in the side of the admiral and whose position astride the Trans-Siberian at Khabarovsk and Chita controlled the only route by which supplies could reach his troops.

A convention between Japan and the former Government of the Directory placing certain railways in Japanese hands was on the point of being signed when the Directory fell and Admiral Kolchak was made Dictator. Kolchak, like many Russians after the Russo-Japanese War, was anti-Japanese. His first act as supreme ruler was to inform Tokyo that the change in the government involved a change in policy in regard to Japanese control over certain positions of the railway.

Japan immediately became alarmed lest Kolchak's authority threaten her position in the Far East, whereupon Tokyo ordered Semyonov to repudiate the supreme ruler's authority. The Japanese issued the same instructions to Ataman Kalmykov, on the Ussuri Railway. Thereafter, the supreme ruler was hampered by Semyonov and his Cossacks. Nothing in the way of brigandage came amiss to Semyonov. He interfered with the evacuation of the Czechs, who were only prevented from attacking him by the attitude of Japan. For the spoil from looted trains and villages he found willing buyers in the merchants of Chita and Harbin. Not only did he refuse to recognize Kolchak's authority but he also held up his supply trains, arrested his officers, and threatened to set up an opposition government. He was the one Russian commander in active power from Khabarovsk to Lake Baikal.

The supreme ruler ordered his forces to clear Semyonov and Kalmykov off the line, but was informed by the Japanese staff that these two Russian patriots were under Japan's protection. British and French protests proved futile to change the Japanese in this decision.

General Boldyrev, commander-in-chief under the Directory of Five, was at the Ufa front when Kolchak seized power; there he remained some five or six days, in consultation with the Czech National Council and members of the old Constituent Assembly. Learning that the English were behind the admiral, he understood that no successful retort to Kolchak's *coup d'état* was possible. Returning to Omsk, he was offered by Kolchak a position which he refused, and begged permission to leave the country, which he thought could not profit by a dictatorship. His request was granted, and from then on his leadership ceased to count.

Meanwhile the Socialist-Revolutionaries felt that with the Armistice they need no longer work against the Bolsheviks in order to defeat the Germans. Allied intervention appeared to them as support for Russian reactionaries and they became more sympathetic to the Red cause.

After Kolchak's *coup d'état,* the Constituent Assembly secretly formed an Executive Committee and proceeded to organize an attack. The admiral's assumption of power, they stated, had clarified the situation and revealed the true political complexion of all parties concerned. Unwilling to engage in civil war against workers and peasants, they tried to call together all troops attached to the Constituent Assembly in order to direct them against Kolchak, and to open negotiations with the commander of the Bolshevik troops.

Kolchak was by political associations a liberal but was faced with the inevitable enigma of dictatorship. Should he listen to reactionary opinion about him or obey his own judgment? In an effort to conciliate liberal sentiment he declared for the calling of a National Assembly to be elected by universal suffrage as soon as order was restored. This was intolerable to many of his officers, who hoped for the restoration of the monarchy.

A simultaneous uprising of monarchists and liberals occurred on December 23, 1918, in the midst of the Perm offensive in which nearly one thousand lives were lost. In this fracas some two hundred prisoners were released, among whom were a large number of political suspects including members of the former Constituent Assembly. Those who had been released were ordered to return within twenty-four hours on pain of being shot. The members of the Constituent Assembly with a few others surrendered themselves. That night a group of officers in Kolchak's command murdered the whole group and escaped punishment.

A typical small revolt broke out at Kansk on December 26th, the most easterly point of the disturbed area, in conjunction with riots at Omsk. Fifteen Bolsheviks succeeded in routing the railway guard of one officer and fifty men. After a short stay, enlivened by barbarities, drunkenness, robbery, and debauchery, they departed at the approach of a squadron of Cossacks, taking refuge sixty versts from the line, protected by the deep snows of a Siberian winter.

Siberia was now infested with bands of Ishmaelitish peasants, their hand turned against every one and every one's hand turned against them. These groups were variously composed, one element being persons who in Red days at the end of 1917 had murdered right and left, taking possession of lands, livestock, and chattels. They argued that the Civil War was not their affair, nor was there any reason why they should supply Kolchak with money or men. Along with them were many escaped criminals, who generally constituted the leadership of their guerrilla commandos. The seed of Bolshevism planted in such fertile soil, encouraged by the example of Semyonov's successful defiance of the supreme ruler, promised at any moment to bring forth a harvest of disruption within and behind Kolchak's lines. Handfuls of determined and half-starved men terrorized towns and temporarily paralyzed the railway with impunity, due to their mobility and the enormous distances to be covered by troops sent to punish them.

Tragedy laid heavy hands upon the Russian Far East in the abuses of the Cossack leaders provisioned and armed by Japan. General Graves in his amazingly honest and forthright book, *America's Siberian Adventure*, remarks of this period:

Semyonov and Kalmykov soldiers, under the protection of Japanese troops, were roaming the country like wild animals, killing and robbing the people, and these murders could have been stopped any day Japan wished. If questions were asked about these brutal murders, the reply was that the people murdered were Bolsheviks and this explanation, apparently, satisfied the world. Conditions were represented as being horrible in Eastern Siberia, and that life was the cheapest thing there.

Because of its strict neutrality in Russian affairs, the American command came in for bitter criticism both in officers' messes among the various Allied groups and in the Russian press. Charges ranged all the way from the Americans being pro-Bolshevik to moral degeneracy. General Graves sent word to Soukine, Minister of Foreign Affairs for Kolchak, that such vilification must stop or he would padlock the building of the journal at Vladivostok. At one time the American commander was approached by a Russian officer with the proposition that if he would pay $20,000 a month to two Czarist officers the defamatory articles would be stopped.

During this period and to the end of his stay in Siberia, General Graves, careful not to violate his written orders, encountered friction, opposition, and criticism from the American Consul General, Harris, acting under the State Department, who, with the Japanese, French, and English, was encouraging the Kolchak régime, in which the American commander had little confidence. This friction continued until General Graves' departure on April 1, 1920.

Statements have often been made that some one Allied officer was in command of the total Allied forces in Siberia. Such was not the case. Each contingent was under its own commander. General Graves was bound by explicit orders. General Otani and General Oi, of the Japanese command, General Knox, head of the British Mission, and other foreign observers had greater freedom of action.

The rampant brigandage of Kalmykov at this time gave no little worry to American headquarters at Vladivostok. General Graves remarked:

By December 1, 1918, the actions of Ataman Kalmykov, of the Ussuri Cossacks, had become embarrassing to me. The United States had asked Japan to join in the limited objects for which American troops were sent to Siberia and every act of Japan, or Japanese paid Russian agents, was, logically, a discredit or a credit to the United States; and Russians were sure to think, because the United States had invited Japan to join her in action in Siberia, that she must be working with her. Japan, in her intent to divide the people and prevent a strong Government from emerging in Siberia, soon had Semyonov and Kalmykov in her employ. It is hard to imagine a man like Kalmykov existing in modern civilization, and there was hardly a day passed without some report of the terrible atrocities committed by him or his troops. On December 1st, I reported to the War Department, in part:

"I, of course, under my instructions to take no part in the internal squabbles could do nothing, with the exception that I have reported to the Japanese Headquarters that the excesses of Kalmykov should be stopped and that his actions were a disgrace to civilization. I did this, and so informed them that I did it, because it is well known that he was being paid by Japan and, that if Japan should stop supporting him, his excesses would stop immediately."

It was almost impossible to remain strictly neutral and equally difficult to aid any section of the population without entering the Russian *mêlée* as a partisan. Kolchak and his supporters considered all who did not back them as Bolsheviks, a category in which they included many docile citizens and even moderate Zemstvo groups who were, on the whole, men of marked democratic views.

General Ivanov-Rinov, who had been sent to the Far East as one of Kolchak's representatives, commanded troops which plundered and murdered without mercy all who did not support the admiral. All officials were his adherents. Only persons of like persuasion could hope to have freight forwarded or receive the slightest assistance from the Kolchak Government. Japan continued to support Semyonov to the chagrin of Kolchak. Semyonov on a pretext refused to report at Omsk. Seated at Chita astride the Trans-Siberian, he and the Japanese who controlled him had Kolchak in their power.

In spite of protestations of liberalism, Kolchak was surrounded with many who were reactionary and blind to the rights and aspirations of the masses. Although Ivanov-Rinov and Horvath did not kill and murder in any such manner as the bandits Kalmykov and Semyonov, their troops assaulted and robbed throughout their territory, refusing to believe in the good faith of any save Kolchak's supporters. General Graves remarked concerning them:

> The fact of the matter is, it is rather unreasonable to expect the practice of centuries to be stopped suddenly by the Czarists and especially when there was only a slight chance that the ruthlessness practiced would be published to the world. The Allies in Siberia had become so enmeshed in Siberian affairs, in their determination to destroy Bolshevism, that they could protest only feebly against Czarist Russian excesses, if they protested at all.

An order tantamount to a general mobilization was issued from Kolchak's headquarters including all officers and soldiers of the old Russian army. Both the order and the manner of executing it aroused the resentment and destroyed the loyalty of large sections of the Siberian population. The bulk of the people saw no hope in the new dictator and were sick of bloodshed. The response was small, whereupon Ivanov-Rinov and other Kolchak officers used force, virtually setting up a reign of terror in many districts to muster the required forces.

The slightest resistance brought upon a family execution and robbery. Abuse of the populace continued, women were beaten with ramrods, men given the knout, dozens executed without trial simply because they were unenthusiastic regarding the régime at Omsk. One is at a loss to account for the motive of such sadism unless the Japanese-controlled leaders in the Far East wished a general uprising which would vindicate setting up an autonomous state or that the instigators of such atrocities thought the easiest way to control Siberia was to set up a terrorist rule. Certainly such foul treatment of the common people won no adherents for Kolchak and the White cause. No room was left for moderate opinion—all were considered either for Kolchak or for Red Moscow.

Kolchak's forces were so weak that arming them was virtually arming the Reds. A humorous turn was given to an otherwise tragic situation when General Knox, whose government was then clothing and arming one hundred thousand of Kolchak's troops, received a telegram from the Bolsheviks thanking him for equipment! General Knox had the humiliation of seeing hundreds of thousands of pounds of war material furnished by Great Britain fall from the irresolute hands of Kolchak's various contingents into the hands of the Red Army.

When the year 1918 closed, Admiral Kolchak's forces consisted of three semi-independent organizations directly responsible to him: The Southern Army, mostly Cossack units, under General Dutov; the Western Army formed around the nucleus of the People's Army raised by the Committee of the Constituent Assembly, under General Khanzhin; and the newly recruited Northern Army, under General Gajda.

A decision was reached by Kolchak's high command to open a drive against the Reds without waiting for the spring. In the face of opposition from the more cautious and competent army leaders, it was resolved to concentrate the main force of attack in a northwesterly direction toward Perm. The more ambitious of the admiral's associates welcomed this decision, as it offered the chance of reaching Moscow before Denikin and reaping the full glory of victory.

Kolchak, restless and worried, felt it incumbent upon him to justify his leadership by some major military operation, although his troops were in no condition to withstand a hard campaign. An offensive on Perm was perilous, but several reasons existed for making the attempt. It was necessary for the supreme ruler to show something for the *coup d'état.* If Perm could be captured, Kolchak's right flank might be able to carry on to Kotlas and Vyatka, achieving contact with the left wing of Allied and Russian forces operating from Archangel, while he planned that his left flank would touch the Orenburg Cossacks under Dutov and the forces of General Denikin farther south.

General Gajda, now commanding Kolchak's Northern Army, initiated the drive against Perm. He ordered the Fifth Czech Regiment to assist but met with a stout refusal. Syrový ordered all his units to the rear of Admiral Kolchak's front. However, Gajda met with a striking initial success, capturing Perm on December 24, 1918, with 31,000 prisoners and a vast quantity of war material. The advance of Kolchak's right flank then stopped at Glazov, just out of reach of Ironside's conglomerate forces on the rivers Dvina and Pinega. The halt was due partly to intense cold, partly to a thoroughly bad service of supply. By the end of January, 1919, all Czech troops were replaced at the front by Kolchak's soldiers. The White command was happy to be rid of them, a sentiment heartily reciprocated by the Legionnaires.

It was a misfortune for Kolchak that he was unable to establish tactical relations with Ironside's troops at Archangel. For seven months Gajda's associate, General Pepelayev, maintained his position at Glazov, but the Allied Expeditionary Force at Archangel was too hard pressed to join him there. When at length Ironside was reinforced in June, the hour had passed when it was possible to join forces. Kolchak's armies were in retreat and all chance of uniting forces against the Bolsheviks was lost.

General Pepelayev, brother of one of Kolchak's ministers, had the greatest difficulty in maintaining his advanced position, not so much because of the strength of Red forces opposed to him as because of the scarcity of medical supplies and food. Thousands of poor wretches died from exposure at a temperature of 60 degrees below zero, thousands more were in a ghastly condition from frostbite. The Omsk Government seemed either utterly indifferent to their sufferings or entirely inefficient. Supplies for the front were diverted by officers of the commissariat.

General Hepov on February 10th took stern measures to rectify this situation. Ten of the leading citizens in Perm were arrested and informed that since the Omsk Government was apparently ignorant of the fact that troops need food, General Hepov was compelled to request them to produce necessary provisions within ten days on pain of their lives. Owing to the disorganized state of the railways, Hepov granted a reprieve for a further four days, at the end of which time food trains arrived and the leading citizens of Perm slept soundly in their beds. The incompetency of the supply service accounts for the breakdown of the Perm offensive.

As for the second half of the plan, which was to join hands with Denikin in the south, this was even less successful than the attempt to make contact with General Ironside. The last day of December the Bolsheviks captured Ufa—temporarily, it is true—and thus prevented any very firm connection being made with General Dutov. Dutov's Cossacks were in sympathy with General Boldyrev, late commander-in-chief, in his opposition to a dictatorship and all contact with Denikin was made impossible at this time by the Reds of Turkestan, who were threatening Orenburg. The Bolshevik counterattack at Ufa was not pressed, but General Dutov reported that seventy of their best propagandists had slipped through his columns.

Kolchak received further blows to his leadership during the concluding stage of the Perm offensive, which was marked by risings of both Royalists and Bolsheviks and the Prinkipo peace proposal.

Reports of the futile warfare in Western Siberia were beginning to disturb the more realistic elements at London, Paris, and Washington. Anxious to withdraw from the Russian turmoil and having little faith in the success of the disunited and sometimes antagonistic White Army leaders, President Wilson and Lloyd George on January 23, 1919, sent an invitation by wireless to all the armies in Russia, proposing that they send representatives to a conference to be held on the Island of Prinkipo near Constantinople. Only the Red Government answered in the affirmative. This proposal had the effect of morally strengthening the Bolsheviks, who saw in it an intimation of retirement on the part of the Allies while among White leaders it was a source of bitter disappointment.

Without hesitation Kolchak refused the invitation to Prinkipo. Shortly before receiving the invitation a sympathetic message had arrived from the British Government and a communication from the French High Commissioner which contained distinct mention of help and recognition. Allied officers in Omsk were surprised by the Prinkipo proposal following these advances, while the Russians were horrified. A sudden reaction set in against the Allies, American and English prestige suffering severely, to the profit of Japanese and French diplomacy.

When Colonel Ward interviewed the supreme ruler on January 31st, he hinted that there must be some points connected with the proposal that were not fully explained. The admiral remarked: "While the British Government advise an arrangement with the Bolsheviks, they continue to furnish me with generous supplies for the Russian Army." As for the Americans, if Colonel Ward is to be credited, the suggestion of a peace conference "received the blessing of every representative, Jew or Gentile, of the United States of America in Siberia." Events aided Japan in persuading most of the Whites that the United States was not to be relied upon, for which both the French and English were grateful.

The Perm offensive, begun and carried on under great handicaps, had lost momentum by the middle of January. The remaining winter months of 1919 were occupied by political maneuvers arising from the Prinkipo proposal, by attempts to restore order on the Trans-Siberian Railway, and by sporadic efforts to organize a service of supply which quickly took the form of governmental requisitions at the point of the sword. Conspiracies flourished in the frustrated and overheated atmosphere about Kolchak. Every one was eager to blame his colleague for failure.

During this period, General Belov, General Boldyrev's late chief-of-staff, met in consultation with General Lebedev and General Antonovsky and others which boded ill for Kolchak's rule. General Lebedev was requested by Colonel Ward to insure the admiral's safety, for which, he was plainly informed, he would be held responsible. Other conspiring generals were then dispersed to different points of the compass. Meanwhile, Kolchak was being harassed by revolts behind his front.

But the Whites were not alone in their anxiety. By the beginning of 1919 the Bolsheviks were in desperate straits. Their armies on various fronts were calling for men, supplies, and food. Soviet Russia was in fact, as it declared itself to be, a military camp. Lenin drew power within his own hands, compelling all activities of the Red state to conform to the military necessities of the moment. Although preaching internationalism, he now seized upon the patriotic motive to inflame the masses against the White leaders. One of the most difficult groups with which he had to deal was the "middle peasants," who because of the food crisis compelled the Red Government to cease wholesale requisitioning. This group wanted a tax in kind instead of the commandeering which amounted to expropriation or downright robbery, to which they had reluctantly submitted since the early days of the Soviet régime. Nevertheless the needs of the armies had to be met. On January 11, 1919, the Council of People's Commissars, by a decree allotted to the peasants the amount of grain and fodder necessary to maintain their farms and claimed all the rest for the government. This measure further alienated the peasants, except the very poorest, whose loyalty the Soviet Government had consistently sought.

Red savagery in these months was matched by the ferocity of the Whites. Annenkov, with his base at Semipalatinsk, gathered round himself a like-minded crew of ruffianly Cossacks, Russians, Ukrainians, Magyars, Bashkirs, Prussians, Mongols, Tartars, and Chinese and proceeded to suppress the Reds. He requisitioned everything: safes from banks, silver, furniture, linen, clothing, and food—nothing came amiss. Systematic pillage, murder, and incendiarism constituted his simple plan of campaign. Kolchak, who was not strong enough to crush Annenkov, made himself an accomplice by recognizing him. It was alleged at the time that this bandit also had British support. When Kolchak sent Annenkov's troopers to the front, they distinguished themselves solely by massacring the Jews of Ekaterinburg.

Far to the East, not only the civil population but also Kalmykov's troops were growing restive under the intolerable treatment they received at his hands.

A serious revolt broke out in late January of 1919. The average Siberian citizen found difficulty in reconciling the fair words uttered at the beginning of intervention with abrogation of rights, the killings and pillage carried on by these White leaders under the *ægis* of Japan. Kalmykov not only flogged and murdered civilians, but practiced the same atrocities upon his Cossacks. Some eight hundred of his men mutinied on January 27-28, 1919, at Khabarovsk, three hundred and ninety-eight of whom sought asylum at the headquarters of the Twenty-seventh Infantry. The mutineers sent a message to their own *Krug* to explain their action under date of February 27, 1919:

To the Sixth Military Krug of the Ussuri Cossacks:

We, Russian citizens, belonging formerly to Ataman Kalmykov's division, not being desirous of taking any part in the bloodshed, have left Ataman Kalmykov's despotic yoke, for the purpose of taking refuge with the American commandant. The reasons by which we came to the decision to leave Ataman Kalmykov are the following:

Every person knows that more than 2,000 men were shot dead by Ataman Kalmykov. All these were killed without being sentenced or tried. All these murders cannot be explained by trying to protect the country or patriotic schemes; they served only the selfish purpose of a terror government. Some examples may enlighten the brutality evidenced in carrying out this bloodshed.

1. Eleven men shot dead, without reason, were left on the spot. Their naked corpses, unburied, were left to the prey of beasts. The sight of them was so horrid that American and Japanese soldiers took photographs of these horrid scenes.
2. Sixteen Austrian musicians, who were playing in the Chaska Chai, were executed in the public gardens in full daylight and their remains left there for public show. These musicians had not committed any crime deserving such bestial treatment.
3. By order of Ataman Kalmykov some employees of the Swedish Red Cross, among them one lady, have been shot. Ataman Kalmykov wanted to rectify this murder by charging them with espionage, but the real reason was that he got a chance to get hold of 3,000,000 rubles and a large stock of different goods.
4. Prisoners of war, who are detailed to work in town, have been forced to deal the last death-bringing stroke to wounded citizens for Cossacks.

All the examples mentioned above prove the horrible terror which was exercised by Ataman Kalmykov. Many women were left without husbands, mothers without sons, and children without parents. This went so far that the Allied commandants were obliged to place a guard at the prison in order to prevent further murder of Russian citizens.

Under the pretext of being bolsheviks peaceful Russians have been killed, with the sole purpose of robbing them.

Further, we want to describe the situation of the Cossacks.

More than six months we have lived without money and without fuel. The food, which was without any nutritive power, was so little that it did never still our hunger. And worst of all was the treatment by the officers, chiefly by Ataman Kalmykov.

Beating and constant use of the Nagaika were everyday occurrences. To all this came the worries for our families, left without means to keep them living, so that we left Ataman Kalmykov and looked for protection to the American commandant. We are not partisans to bolsheviki ideas, we were never bolsheviks, and we have no longing to become such. We are ready at any moment to defend Russia against the enemies who threaten her. We simply sought the protection of the American commandant, as we did not want to serve the command of such officers, who, while we are suffering, lavish our money on women and get drunk from champagne, for which they pay 350 rubles a bottle.

We deeply regret that Colonel Birukof was killed, but we are not guilty, as out of the 800 men who mutinied only 450 are here. We could have killed that night Ataman Kalmykov and his officers and massacred the peaceful citizens of the town, but not wanting to do such a thing we went to the American commandant to find such a protection which no other nation would have given us.

The present moment is such that in order to save the country Ataman Kalmykov, who causes such terrible bloodshed and robberies, must be forced to give up his power and relinquish it to his betters.

Nobody but he and his officers are responsible for the happenings which took place on that memorable night. Hunger, ill-treatment, massacres forced us to mutiny. Ataman Kalmykov makes every effort to explain the occurrences by saying that we are on the side of the bolsheviks, and he ventures to mix in this affair the Americans, our protectors. This is nothing else but a lie, and we are glad to avail ourselves of the opportunity to declare openly to the Krug that no American had anything to do with that mutiny. Not only that they did not incite this mutiny, but they were unaware of what was to happen, and when we surrendered to them they took charge of us only for the reasons of humanity and to prevent further bloodshed. The treatment we receive in Krasnaya Rechka is good. We are well fed; our quarters are clean and warm, and everything is done to keep us in perfect condition. We owe every gratitude to Colonel Styer and Lieutenant Colonel Morrow and to his officers, who are treating us as soldiers. Our parents, wives and children may be tranquil; our present condition of living is more than satisfactory.

Hunger, bad treatment, and cold do not make a man better, but worse. We, who are loyal subjects of Russia, could not stand any more to be in the service of Ataman Kalmykov and left him. We who know his conduct, his deeds, declare openly to the Krug that an usurper, a butcher of this kind, can not remain any longer in power. He discredited the name of Cossack. His hands are covered with the innocent blood that he has shed.

Kalmykov complained loudly that the Americans had instigated the mutiny. Japan insisted upon the release of the men who had surrendered themselves to Colonel Styer and Lieutenant Colonel Morrow. But the American command was loath to give them up to Kalmykov, to meet death by firing squads or worse. Later, Japan demanded the arms, equipment, and munitions of Kalmykov's mutineers on the ground that they were furnished by Japan, that some were from arms captured by Japan, and that some were purchased with money from Japan. The incident was ended by the release of the men to go where they would and the Japanese giving a receipt for the arms and equipment which the men had surrendered.

The people began to stiffen their resistance. General Oi on the Amur section of the railway was suffering losses in February of 1919 in the section west of Khabarovsk and called upon the American command for aid. General Graves asked to be informed as to whether the "so-called Bolsheviks" were not Russians resisting unjust treatment by troops. The Japanese chief-of-staff replied for General Graves to do nothing until further notice. Shortly afterward a Japanese command of two companies was nearly wiped out in encountering a superior force of Russians, an incident which called forth much unsavory comment against the American military for refusing to coöperate. Two things must be said in all fairness: the Japanese themselves had one entire division at Khabarovsk, while the American force was only two battalions.

Throughout Siberia, Japan was astutely pressing her advantage. Her representatives, of whom General Mato was chief, pointed out to Kolchak and his officers that in view of the unreliability of the other Allies it would be well if he should accept Japanese aid. Kolchak himself realized the dangers and the impossibility of one Ally acting alone, but some of his officers did not.

When the Prinkipo peace proposal had come as a bombshell to the politics in Siberia, negotiations for an agreement regarding the control of the Trans-Siberian Railway were progressing. Some agreement respecting the protection and management of the line was imperative to check the demoralization of traffic.

The Trans-Siberian Railway was in ghastly confusion by the winter of 1918-1919. To maintain service, each military group was compelled to seize and run the road in its own territory, not infrequently to the disadvantage of adjacent groups. Freight trains had been suspended in favor of military trains since the 28th of December, 1918. Engines, carriages, and equipment fell into disrepair. The one all-important artery of communication was being closed at many points.

At the end of 1918 the railroad was divided into military zones for purposes of protection. The Japanese extended roughly from Verkhneudinsk to Chita, Semyonov's headquarters, on to the Amur Railway, from Karamskaya, north and east through Khabarovsk and southward to Iman, and another outlying section. The Japanese, by agreement with the Chinese, coöperated in guarding the Chinese Eastern Railway from Manchuria to Pogranichnaya. The Czechs extended westward of Irkutsk as far as Omsk. Semyonov, along with the Japanese, had detachments extending from Lake Baikal to Khabarovsk and down to Manchuria. Thus the railway and its accompanying facilities for telephonic and telegraphic communication were ruled by many masters. From the Armistice to the Railway Agreement which was drawn up in the spring of 1919, the American troops were concentrated near Vladivostok.

Strange incidents occurred in these days. A mission from the United States was sent to Siberia in 1918 to secure a large amount of platinum, and went as far inland as Chelya-binsk. With $1,250,000 in bars lying in the top bunk of an American Red Cross car, the train lay opposite Semyonov's train throughout the greater part of a day. Men who had murdered peasants for a dozen kopeks visited the train, not knowing that treasure enough to fill their skins with wine for a lifetime in Harbin or Pekin lay within reach of their hands.

Kolchak was preparing in the opening months of 1919 for his supreme effort to capture Moscow while Denikin had like hopes in thrusting up from the south. There was no liaison and no concerted action between the two and no one general strategic plan considered for all the counter-revolutionary forces.

Kolchak's offensive was being prepared under the most ill-starred auspices. His ragged, hungry, and poorly armed troops lacked both spirit and discipline. Red propaganda was reinforced by the stern reality that Communism was gathering strength with peasants and townspeople in Siberia. War fatigue of soldiers and civil population, the tantalizing policy of the Allies in withholding recognition of his government, dissension among foreign commanders whose troops were astride the Trans-Siberian for thousands of versts and the lack of an organized base, gave Kolchak the same worries Denikin was facing. His front was a mere series of patrols, his armies but specters of the solid phalanxes of the Belgian and French fronts. Well-meaning but lacking either the ruthlessness to drive out contradictory counsels, or force of character to subordinate his officers to his own will, out of touch with the rank and file of the people, Admiral Kolchak made ready for his thrust at the capital of the Soviets.

Chapter XI

SIBERIA: KOLCHAK'S RÉGIME—THE ADVANCE;
FROM THE RAILWAY AGREEMENT OF MARCH,
1919, TO THE RED ATTACK OF JUNE, 1919

KOLCHAK prepared his offensive under dangerous circumstances. Astride the railway, his one means of supply, was Semyonov and his cohorts from Lake Baikal eastward. The admiral was at the mercy of the Cossack leader and the Japanese. Although England was sending shiploads of supplies and promising more, hostile elements in the population more than offset this advantage. The insubordination, the excesses, and the incompetence of many of his commanders, who did as they pleased, once away from headquarters, rendered a closely coördinated action almost impossible. Added to this was the menace of a Red Army with all the material and psychological advantages of fighting on inner lines against a foe identified in the minds of a large section of the common people with the worst features of the Czarist régime and doing little to correct that impression.

Any sizable military operation in Siberia is dependent upon the railway. By late winter of 1919 the Trans-Siberian was in such confusion that some regulation was imperative. After extensive negotiations an Inter-Allied Agreement was signed in March. The Agreement was largely the result of a request for railway experts which had been made by the Kerensky Government in 1917. John F. Stevens, an able engineer, had been dispatched to Russia in the summer of 1917 and made adviser to the Ministry of Communications. An American Railway Service Corps had been organized of men of unusual capacity, mostly from the Great Northern

Railroad. When the Red Revolution came it found a number of other railway experts en route to Russia in Japan or in Harbin, where they remained for several months until the Agreement gave them opportunity for work. Two organizations were arranged, a Technical Board, and an Allied Military Transportation Board to coördinate military shipments under the order of proper military authorities. It was stated that "The protection of the railways shall be placed under the Allied military forces. At the head of each railway shall remain a Russian manager or director with the powers conferred by the existing Russian law."

In the assignment of railway experts to any station the Agreement read that, "the interests of the respective Allied powers in charge of such stations shall be taken into due consideration." Mr. Frank L. Polk, acting Secretary of State, emphatically pointed out that the word "interests" in the above clause did not imply "any political or territorial rights or spheres of influence." This definition, however, was not observed by either Kolchak or the Japanese and their protégés, Kalmykov and Semyonov. The Railway Agreement came too late and was too much of a compromise to enable Stevens' commission to create an efficient transport service.

Kolchak immediately appointed Ostrougov, his Minister of Communications, as chairman and it was not long until every station agent was an adherent of the government at Omsk. Although the United States went on record as favoring the move to aid "all Russians," as a matter of fact the railway was used for Kolchak and his friends almost exclusively as far as Russians were concerned.

United States troops which had been sedulously protected from fighting the Bolsheviks or being partisan in Russian affairs were, by the working of the Agreement, keeping the right of way open for Kolchak to the detriment of those of differing opinion, of whatever political color. The Chinese took over the guarding of the Chinese Eastern, while the Russians pleaded they were in no position to furnish guard troops. The British and French were unable to guard any of the line for lack of men. The English and Canadian forces went to Omsk in June of 1919. Later these troops, with the French, were withdrawn, leaving only the Americans, Japanese, and Czechs. Colonel C. H. Morrow and two battalions of the Twenty-seventh United States Infantry were sent to Transbaikal to take over a sector extending west of Verkhneudinsk to Mysovaya on the shore of Lake Baikal, their other sectors being near Vladivostok, including the line between Vladivostok and Nikolsk, Nikolsk to Suchan, and Spasskoe to Iman on the Ussuri line leading northward to Khabarovsk.

A proclamation was posted along American sectors, to the chagrin of Whites and pro-Kolchak Allied representatives, stating that:

Our aim is to be of real assistance to all Russians in protecting necessary traffic movements within the sectors of the railroad in Siberia assigned to us to safeguard. All will be equally benefited and all shall be treated alike by our forces, irrespective of persons, nationality, religion, or politics. Coöperation is requested and warning given to all persons, whomsoever, that interference with traffic will not be tolerated.

The American command first had trouble with Semyonov after Colonel Morrow's force arrived in the Transbaikal region in April of 1919. Semyonov had approximately two thousand men at Verkhneudinsk and Beresovka and the Americans about an equal number at these places.

The Cossack leader regarded every one who was not favorable to him as a Bolshevik and constantly operated armored cars and trains, of which he claimed to have had fifty-seven, from his headquarters at Chita westward to Lake Baikal and eastward over the Amur River route to Khabarovsk. In his process of terrorizing the countryside he arrested railroad employees and shot them without trial or mercy. Colonel Morrow, once he had taken over his section of the railroad, informed Semyonov categorically that he would not be allowed to come within the territory under his control and either arrest people or interfere with the traffic

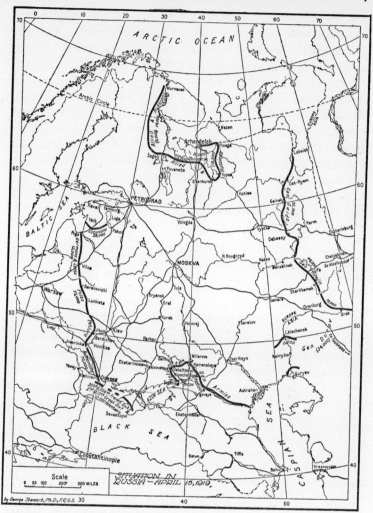

Situation in Russia, April 15, 1919. The Soviet Armies menaced on every side.

of the railroad; that the Americans within their sectors were obligated under the Railway Agreement to protect traffic from all parties. Morrow backed up his statement with a threat to open war upon any armored trains that came within his reach. The extent and nature of White Russian atrocities, after Siberia was cleared of the Reds in 1918, can be explained only on the supposition that Semyonov and his ilk were attempting a terror government.

Semyonov not only interfered with ordinary citizens but acted in the most traitorous manner toward Kolchak. In April of 1919, Colonel Tomlovsky, commander of the engineers' company of the Ninth Siberian Division, requested Lieutenant Colonel William C. Miller, of Colonel Morrow's command, to give him assistance in reaching the front, stating that twice he had been ordered to the front but had been prevented by Semyonov. Colonel Tomlovsky came to Colonel Morrow the middle of May and made the same request, saying that Semyonov's command at Verkhneudinsk would not furnish him with transportation. Colonel Morrow informed him that as soon as the Americans had taken over their sector he would be given assistance. Later, on June 1st, the armored train *Merciless* attacked the command of Colonel Tomlovsky.

Colonel Morrow constantly received reports of the activities of Semyonov's armored trains. Many railroad employees and civilians who were not actually shot were beaten with chains, dying within two or three days after such treatment. One of Morrow's reports stated:

On May 5 (1919) men from the armored train *Merciless* whipped the master mechanic of the railroad, Mr. J. K. Aphanasiev. The armored trains of Semyonov, by their continual whipping of the railroad employees, the terror which they inspired in the officials as well as the employees of the railroad, their constant interference with passenger and freight traffic, were daily and hourly growing worse. The interference had reached such a stage that it could no longer be tolerated if the American command was to enforce the proclamation of General Graves of April 21.

Again:

Throughout the month of May continual reports were received regarding the interference of the forces under the command of Ataman Semyonov with the operation of the railroad, also of the enormous number of executions which were taking place at various points between Manchuria City and Verkhneudinsk, notably at Adrianovka, Olovyannaya, Borzya, and Makkavyeyevo, as well as whippings of railroad employees at other points in the sector.

The armored trains had names emblematical of their performance: the *Merciless,* the *Terrible,* the *Master,* the *Horrible,* the *Destroyer,* the *Ataman,* and other kindred sobriquets. The *Destroyer* had fifty-seven officers and men aboard her, which was a typical contingent. The armor plate was one-quarter to one-half inch in thickness, with eighteen inches of reinforced concrete behind it. There were ten machine guns aboard, two three-inch guns, and two one-pounders. Each train wrought its will upon the population of the towns as it patrolled the line. The fleet of armored trains was commanded by a major general.

In an effort to stop these incidents, Colonel Morrow arranged a conference at the headquarters of Japanese General Yoshie with two Russian officers, Major General Mejak and General Panchenco, at Beresovka on June 8, 1919. He reported the various incidents and demanded that one of Semyonov's armored cars that was in Verkhneudinsk should move within twenty-four hours or he would fire upon it. After various telegrams back and forth with Semyonov, who was at Chita, the car was finally moved.

Weary of the Russian quarrel, the Czechs were hostile to Kolchak's reactionary officers who were themselves antagonistic to any liberal sentiments of their chief. The admiral was unable to carry out any policy of conciliation toward the aspirations of underprivileged and Left Wing groups. He in turn suspected the Czechs of being incarnadined by their contact with the Bolsheviks. Neither he nor many other Czarist officers could understand the legionnaires' apparent lack of discipline in addressing each other with the familiar "thou" and the easy manners between officers and men.

The Czechs had been viewed by the Allies and especially by the French as a body of troops of proven capacity in combat who would be serviceable against Germany and who, because of their control of the Trans-Siberian, were preventing the repatriation of some hundreds of thousands of prisoners of war. Now that the German war was done, their presence in Siberia was useless, save as they might be utilized to aid Kolchak or forward the plans of the Allies. These soldiers were an immense distance from their home, cut off from all moral and material support usually forthcoming to any army fighting near its base.

In order to preserve the Czechs' Allied orientation, buoy up their spirits, and keep them from becoming infatuated with Red doctrine, the Allies sent General Janin as their commander-in-chief, superior to General Syrový, who was their senior officer. With him came General Stefánik, a Slovak. With Masaryk and Beneš, Stefánik was a member of the triumvirate which guided the whole Czech movement. As has been mentioned, Stefánik had been made a French general and on his arrival in Siberia incurred no little unpopularity by his efforts to introduce the stiff discipline of the Western Front among the informal but loyal legionnaires. He made himself still more unpopular by dismissing General Dieterichs, who joined up with Kolchak. Janin, who laid claim to be commander-in-chief of all Allied forces in Siberia, suffered a rebuff.

General Maurice Janin was probably as familiar with the Russian situation as any Allied officer. During the Great War, he had been stationed at Great Headquarters of the Eastern Front at Mogilev. This French general, as early as July 25, 1918, had been appointed by Clémenceau commander-in-chief of the Czechs, who had declared themselves part of the French Army. His intention was to organize a strong force, officered by foreigners. As a matter of fact, few foreign officers ever served with the Czechs.

The British were, throughout, energetic in their support of Kolchak. General Knox of the British Mission had been training and equipping Russian troops to fight the Bolsheviks. France feared that if England was to be made re-

Chinese soldiers

Admiral Kolchak (left), General
Pleshkov, and Mr. Popov

General Otani

Youthful guerrillas

A motherless child

Refugees

sponsible for the successful reorganization of the Russian Army the new Russia would rely upon the English rather than upon her. Due to French pressure, Knox's orders had been canceled and he was compelled to mark time until Janin's arrival.

When Janin arrived at Omsk in the spring of 1919 with the Allied Council's orders to take command of Allied and Russian forces in Siberia, he was met with a stout refusal. The Russian Army, already formed, held it would be an insult to the national dignity to obey the commands of a French officer. Janin remarked in his journal in April, 1919, regarding the strained situation between the legionnaires and Kolchak:

"I shall have," says Kolchak, "to disarm them forcibly. I shall place myself at the head of my troops and blood will flow. . . ." He talks for a long time about their disregard of the Russian authorities, their want of respect for those at Irkutsk. He charges them with insolence because, for the protection of the railway, they ask for the right to act over the whole zone as they think fit and, if need be, to place certain districts under martial law. I answer mildly but plainly, that his fears are unjustified. . . . With regard to him personally there is not the least ill-will. As for Gen. Artemer, on the other hand, who is Commandant at Irkutsk, I cannot blame the Czechs. They treat with hostility a man who proclaims himself to be their foe, and declares that he would sooner see German officer prisoners walking about in Irkutsk than the Czechs. I would add that towards the end of January Artemer expressed himself to me in a way that was fully in accordance with these wishes.

Kolchak was using every available means to increase and equip his forces in the spring of 1919. Hundreds were forcibly enlisted into his unstable battalions. The methods adopted were often so harsh that recruiting expeditions resembled punitive measures rather than the effort of a friendly government to win the support of its subjects. Because of the difficulty in receiving and verifying information, it was almost impossible for the outside world to know either the number or quality of Kolchak's men.

Early in March Kolchak's offensive was under way, meeting with a series of successes. The plan of campaign was to exert pressure on the northern or right wing, which had been most successful in the Perm offensive, in the direction of Vyatka, thus threatening a junction with the forces of the northern region under General Ironside. Meanwhile, the left wing was to press toward Samara and Saratov, with the intention of cutting off Red forces in Turkestan and eventually joining Denikin, who was operating in the Don Basin. The center was to attack at Ufa and Sterlitamak in the direction of Kazan.

On the right wing, the Bolsheviks were unable to hold the line of the River Kungur and were compelled to evacuate the Kama Basin. On the left wing, Kolchak's troops succeeded in capturing Buzuluk, Uralsk, Nikolsk, and Yershov, thereby threatening Samara and Saratov. Orenburg remained uncaptured, a pool left by the ebbing Red tide, but a potential danger if ever that tide should rise in full flood.

Fighting was fiercest and most decisive in the center. Deep snow finally made active warfare impossible—except for a few skiiers—save along the roads, enhancing danger of encirclement. If the highways to the rear were cut, no possibility of escape existed through field or forest. The Bolsheviks therefore retreated rapidly rather than risk capture. When the snow melted in May, the position at once changed. It was as though the line had been enormously extended. Where before it had been sufficient—indeed, only possible— to move along and guard the roads, after the ground had dried following the thaw it was easy for cavalry, infantry, and light artillery to maneuver almost at will through forests or across the plain.

The army of General Khanzhin, with its base at Chelyabinsk, contained two remarkable shock battalions, one the Ufa Rifle Division, under Colonel Kozmin, and the other, the Izhevsky Brigade, under Colonel Molchanov—the latter composed of men from the Izhevsky works, who were bitterly opposed to the Bolsheviks. Both sides depended for serious fighting on shock divisions, since their ordinary troops were apt to consider carefully the result of a battle before engaging in it.

Colonel Kozmin broke the Soviet front in the direction of Biisk on a branch line some two hundred miles south of Novonikolayevsk and was at once joined by two Red battalions, who went over to what was obviously the winning side. Ufa fell on March 13th and Sterlitamak on April 4th. The Bolsheviks continued to retreat until the thaw came to their rescue—as it was coming to the rescue of Ironside at Bolshie Ozerki—by turning streams into rivers and rivers into seas.

At the end of the first week in April the line ran west of Glazov, Urzhum, and Malmyzh, and one hundred and thirty kilometers east of Kazan. In the center it rested on the River Vyatka; in the south it ran west of Bugulma, Buguruslan, Buzuluk, Uralsk, Nikolsk, and Yershov, retaining this position for several weeks.

The whole front actually, though not apparently, was in a very unsound condition, since the advance had been pressed too rapidly for the creaking supply service. One of the fatal preoccupations of every White commander was to include as much territory as possible within his lines without adequate organization of the rear. Footsore and hungry troops became more wavering in their loyalty to the admiral as they tightened their belts.

Graft and inefficiency grew steadily worse both at the front and in the service of supply. On May 30, 1919, Gajda's army was estimated at 120,000 men, on June 9th, 100,000, when they were drawing rations from Omsk for 275,000. He stated that his whole staff was implicated in this falsification and that on June 1st he had only 60,000 men and by the end of the month only half that number. The percentage of supplies which failed to reach the front was appalling. Although Gajda took what measures he could to correct the abuse, little came of it. The British furnished 100,000 uniforms to Kolchak forces, a large number of which found their way to the backs of Red soldiers, either by capture or because the wearers deserted.

During these critical weeks Kolchak showed himself incapable of statesmanship in his treatment of Finland. Even before the Great War and the peace of Brest-Litovsk it was evident that Finland would some day strike for independence. By recognizing Finland's independence the Omsk Government could have won the sympathy, not only of the Finns but of other secessionist populations in Poland and the Caucasus. This course was strongly urged upon Kolchak, but M. Sazonov, with a Bourbon blindness to realities, persuaded him to reject the proposal. Kolchak maintained that he had no power to declare Finland independent without the assent of the Constituent Assembly. The Finns on their part were unable to see why a man, who could declare himself Dictator without reference to any legal basis, could not by the same token take cognizance of an accomplished fact. As a result Finland categorically refused to coöperate in Yudenich's operations for the capture of Petrograd. Recognition, which Kolchak finally made, came too late to be of any significance to the White cause.

Moved by Kolchak's rapid advances in March and April, realizing that rebellion to a successful chief might mean a firing squad for him as soon as Kolchak was free to turn his bayonets eastward, Ataman Semyonov made a belated pledge of loyalty to the admiral. Semyonov was assisted in his repentance by British pressure which had been brought to bear upon the Japanese to modify their financial and moral support of the Ataman. When Colonel Ward arrived at Chita to speak for the British, it was officially announced that Semyonov had submitted to Kolchak and the proposed remonstrance was changed into congratulations. Semyonov's submission was not whole-hearted, for he cherished the hope of setting himself up as sovereign of Mongolia, his loyalty to Kolchak depending entirely upon his own plans.

Kolchak's armies slowed up, halted, and were soon beginning a retreat which, save for sporadic rallies, never ceased until his promising military machine ended in complete disaster. General Khanzhin, who commanded the Western Army in the center of Kolchak's line, decided to retire on the River Belaya at the end of May, 1919. Troops were fatigued by long marches and depleted in strength. Regiments of seven hundred men were quite common, and owing to scandalous pilfering by the commissariat, in some regiments as high as 85 per cent of food, clothing, tobacco, and other necessities for the soldiers failed to reach the front. There were no reinforcements, no leaves, and no reserves, except untrained ones.

As black news came from the front the nervous Dictator awaited cables from the West regarding recognition. Once he had the full confidence of powerful nations he might be able to secure enough aid to decide the struggle between White and Red.

The old Directory Government was about to be recognized when it had been overthrown by Kolchak. It might have been expected that Kolchak would have received the recognition which was to have been accorded the preceding government, but that recognition had long been withheld. Statesmen at Paris were confronted with problems enough, studying maps to discover the difference between Cilicia, Silesia, and Galicia, without making their confusion worse confounded by questions regarding unpronounceable localities which sounded like place names in Asiatic folklore and by discussions regarding fine political distinctions for which Russians seemed willing to die but which Western minds found difficult to understand.

The Big Four felt that it would be foolish to recognize a régime which might disappear, like its predecessor, in the course of a few weeks. Again, recognition of the Omsk Government in the winter of 1918 would have meant, almost inevitably, the presence of Russian representatives at the Peace Conference; and their presence, though fitting, would have complicated an already involved situation. Still further, both the French and the Japanese were chary of recognizing England's protégé. Finally, it was possible that Kolchak's régime might be the prelude to the restoration of Czarism, for which no great Power wished to be held responsible. The principle of "self-determination" proclaimed by the Peace Conference further complicated matters as far as Russia was concerned, as it was yet to be determined who were the authentic Russians, the Bolsheviks, the Whites, or some third group such as the Socialist-Revolutionaries.

In spite of all that stood against it, hints of recognition had been conveyed to Kolchak by the French Mission as early as January, 1919. The Prinkipo proposal set the clock back. On May 5th, however, a dispatch from London arrived at Omsk concerning recognition of Kolchak's Government. It was the subject of lengthy conferences between Colonel Ward, General Knox, and the admiral. On May 7th General Knox and Colonel Ward began to draft a reply, the articles of which had been agreed to by the supreme governor, which was hurriedly completed on the morning of May 9th. Old line officials fought over the proposals, and two of them, Women's Suffrage and Universal Education, were rejected, although the admiral assented to a sufficient number for negotiations to proceed apace. Kolchak's position at this time was strong, as his success was still unbroken while both Denikin's and Yudenich's attacks were developing.

The Supreme Council, on May 26, 1919, notified the admiral that the Allied and Associated Powers were willing to supply him and his associates with munitions, supplies, and food, that they might establish themselves as the government of Russia, on these main conditions:

1. A Constituent Assembly elected by free, secret, and democratic franchise, to be called.
2. No revival of the privilege of any class or order.
3. Independence of Poland and Finland to be recognized.
4. The Peace Conference to assist in the settlement of other boundary disputes.
5. Russia to accept the liability for the Russian national debt.
6. Russia to join the Peace Conference.

Kolchak sent a satisfactory reply on June 4th which was accepted on June 12th. The Omsk Government was not technically given *de jure* recognition even by these notes—the United States was still opposed—but it received *de facto* recognition. Such action upon the part of the Allies was not, however, followed up by consistent support, either moral or material, of such a nature as to assure Kolchak's success. This diplomatic triumph presaged little as far as the White armies in the field were concerned. The news of recognition coincided with gloomy telegrams from the front which told of crumbling battalions and Red strength.

The spring thaw, which swelled the streams and turned the countryside into a slough of despond, made the Bolsheviks' task of defense an easy one. Treason also played its part, as it did so often in these Russian campaigns. The English had armed and trained some Ukrainians without suspecting that the desire to return home might prove stronger than loyalty to Admiral Kolchak's government. An entire regiment of these well-equipped but dispirited troops had deserted to the Bolsheviks at Buguruslan, others had most of their casualties wounded in the index finger—only explicable as self-mutilation. Desertion is bound to be frequent in a civil war, but it was peculiarly demoralizing for White officers who never knew when they would be abandoned to the most atrocious tortures. But the men were not alone in their disloyalty. Many officers skulked behind the lines who should have been at the front with their regiments which further demoralized the common soldier.

Even under these grave conditions, Kolchak possessed enough talented officers to have reorganized his forces behind the Tobol, the Ishim, or the Irtish River had it not been for the disloyalty and unrest of large segments of the population both west and east of Lake Baikal. The single line of railway over which he had no direct control east of Lake Baikal, the depredations of several White leaders which created hatred for White rule, the undercover activities of Bolshevik agitators, and the poverty and suffering of the war-weary Siberians united to create nearly as much danger in the rear as there was from the Red Army at the front.

The struggle between the Soviets and Kolchak had entered into a second phase, the disintegration of the rear because of the disappointment of the workers and peasants in the Omsk régime. Lenin, realistic if ruthless, accommodated his theories to the necessity of pacifying the peasants, while Kolchak was hampered by the landlord class, who officered his peasant army. No radical land policy was ever promulgated to receive the loyalty of the tillers of the soil. Consequently, after severe reverses, Kolchak's White army began to melt away like spring snow, because the peasant wished to plow his land in peace.

In extenuation of the admiral it can be said that distance, the turbulent period, the need of supplies which could not be furnished by a well-served supply organization, and the semi-independent character of several leaders rendered disciplined control almost impossible. Ataman Annenkov, of the Semipalatinsk Cossacks, whose operations were in the nature of ferocious brigandage, was only one of the many White leaders of a like kidney who had taken the field to wage private wars of their own. During operations in May of 1919 against a Red commando at Krasnoyarsk, Major Beil, a Czech officer, discovered a detachment under a Russian named Krasilnikov pillaging a village. In response to Major Beil's objections, the head of the detachment replied: "It is Kolchak's order."

The Civil War had loosed men from every restraint of culture, religion, or common decency. Life for all hung by a thread, hundreds were shot on mere suspicion. In such an atmosphere, a spirit of diabolism made monsters out of even quiet and formerly moderate men. Massacres, rape, and pillage by the followers of Semyonov, Annenkov, and Kalmykov drove thousands toward the Bolsheviks—the Reds could be no worse and would at least give them the land. In one instance Ataman Kalmykov, upon the refusal of a village in Amur Province to give up some educated refugees, broke holes in the ice and thrust under all the inhabitants. Kolchak made many mistakes of his own and was not infrequently unwise in his decisions, but he was in no sense the brutal tyrant that many of his followers proved to be and over whom he could exercise no effective curb.

Partisan bands of peasants who turned against Kolchak were favored by the vulnerability of the Trans-Siberian Railway with its numerous small wooden bridges easy to burn. So immense are the distances that it would need a large army to guard the right of way effectively. Guerrilla organizations of no particular color, composed of peasants, fugitives, and deserters from Kolchak's army, raided the countryside. A few had rifles, some carried shotguns, most of them were armed with sticks and pikes and scythes. It was a Jacquerie, the rioters losing heavily whenever they encountered the Czechs; but Russian troops, especially when they were in small detachments, fell easy prey to the attacks of these Partisans. It is estimated that these bands numbered some 3,000 between Novonikolayevsk and Barnaul, 4,000 between Barnaul and Semipalatinsk, and 12,000 around Biisk.

General Graves refused to allow his command to become implicated on account of these depredations. His unwillingness to consider himself at war with the Bolsheviks earned for Americans the reputation in very White quarters of being Bolsheviks themselves. Colonel Ward considered the behavior of the Americans hostile to Kolchak and favorable to the "forces of disorder." The fact seems to have been that England's representatives exceeded their orders to remain neutral and were often angered by the Americans' reluctance to follow in their steps. Many Allied officers, adopting the terminology of the White Russians, called Partisan, Socialist-Revolutionary, or other anti-Kolchak troops "Bolshevik" and treated them as mortal enemies.

The magnitude of the country and the meager transportation facilities made a consolidation of an advance into a solid front almost impossible. Kolchak's great drive never reached within four hundred miles of Moscow and once retreat began it could not be stopped until it had reached two thousand miles east of the point of beginning. Looking eastward, the distance from Moscow to Kazan was four hundred and fifty, from Chelyabinsk to Petropavlovsk three hundred, from Petropavlovsk to Omsk one hundred and eighty, and from Omsk to Irkutsk thirteen hundred. From Vladivostok to Moscow was forty-two hundred miles. The whole of the United States could be laid upon Russia and Siberia and only reach from Petrograd to Irkutsk.

Although reports were hailed in the Western world of great drives which to the unknowing indicated that Kolchak was on the verge of taking the capital of the Soviets, in reality his forces had extended themselves along railways that fan out from Siberia into European Russia, with little real threat at Moscow.

Troops were already pouring back toward Omsk. Officers absented themselves from their regiments and sought safety. Hungry soldiers were murmuring sourly over wounds and hardship. If Kolchak offered only death and privation, why not cast in their lot with the Reds? Thousands among them were seasoned veterans. They knew the White armies of Siberia would never again advance!

Chapter XII

SIBERIA: KOLCHAK'S RETREAT; FROM JULY, 1919, TO THE DÉBÂCLE OF FEBRUARY, 1920

Moscow was now ready to strike. Although Yudenich was threatening Petrograd from the old Baltic provinces and Denikin was pushing up from the Don, the Red command knew the Northwestern Army had no resources for a long campaign and that Denikin's forces were being dangerously extended.

The line of the River Belaya should have been almost impregnable, but the lassitude of General Khanzhin's troops made insecure even a front protected by natural advantages. The keystone of this sector was the short stretch of line from Ufa to Chisma, the junction of the Ufa-Samara and Ufa-Simbirsk railways. Once the Dioma bridge was in the hands of the Bolsheviks, the fall of Ufa was almost a certainty.

The Reds attacked at two points. They drove toward Ufa and toward Krasny Yar where the stream made a salient in General Khanzhin's line, and where the river was most easily crossed. The Belaya was forced in two places on June 6th and the loss of Ufa and a retreat to the River Ufimka was inevitable. The great bridge at Dioma was blown up and by that act the White Army proclaimed its belief that it would pass that way no more!

Red commanders had succeeded in driving a wedge into Kolchak's center. Their main attack was now directed toward Krasnoufimsk. The capture of this town would imperil Ekaterinburg and would compel General Gajda to retreat from Perm and so prevent any chance of a junction

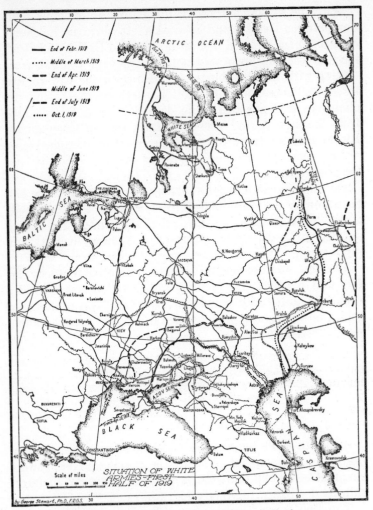

Situation of the White Armies in the first half of 1919.

between Gajda and Ironside, who at that moment was planning an offensive on the Dvina toward Kotlas with the intention of joining the North Russian forces with those of
Kolchak.

With the similar purpose of preventing an effective junction between Denikin and Kolchak's left wing, the Bolshevik high command pressed their attack toward Uralsk and Orenburg, whose capture would not only prevent Denikin from uniting with Kolchak but would also open the way to Red forces in Turkestan, and to cotton! Between these two main offensives Red generals planned to develop another attack from Sterlitamak and Verkhne-Uralsk toward Chelyabinsk. By the close of June Kolchak confronted the Bolsheviks on a line that ran, Perm-Kungur-Krasnoufimsk-Sterlitamak-Orenburg.

On the diplomatic front a victory of some importance had been won by the Omsk Government. President Wilson made a statement on June 12, 1919, that the United States had decided to "assist the Government of Admiral Kolchak and his associates with munitions, supplies, and food."

But this promise was more than counterbalanced by the fact that Kolchak was facing a growing Red Army amid a decidedly unfriendly population. General Graves quotes a report on the loyalty of the region to the Omsk Government which asserts:

It is estimated that on July 1, outside the office-holding and military class, the Omsk Government had less than 1 per cent of followers. It was estimated that the Red followers were about 45 per cent, Social Revolutionists about 40 per cent, with about 10 per cent divided among other parties, giving 5 per cent to the military, office-holders, and Kolchak followers.

Although these percentages constituted only a rough appraisal of the state of mind of the population, they were eloquent testimony that Siberia was weary of war, dictatorship, and all that these entailed.

The Red drive toward Krasnoufimsk was firmly pushed home. Ufa fell on June 11th. The River Iren was crossed on July 2d, and Perm was lost on July 3d. Fighting in this area was now rapidly approaching a crisis. Kolchak's Third Division, under General Rakitin, was astride the Kungur-Ekaterinburg road flanked on the north by the "Immortal

284 THE WHITE ARMIES OF RUSSIA

Regiment of General Gajda," British-trained and equipped, and on the south by other picked troops. Rakitin hoped to nip out the head of the salient that the Bolsheviks were forcing in the direction of Ekaterinburg. At the crucial moment the Immortal Regiment determined to live up to its name by flight. It was disarmed a few days later, but it had involved the retreat of the whole line from Atchitskoe.

All efforts at counter-attack by Gajda's troops proved futile and the Bisert was forced by the Bolsheviks on the 5th of July. On July 17th victorious Red troops entered Ekaterinburg and some days later Chelyabinsk was in the hands of the Bolsheviks. By the first of August, Kolchak, alarmed, was preparing to move his government to Irkutsk.

The retreat rapidly threatened disaster. Railways broke down, Ekaterinburg, Chelyabinsk, and Troitsk were abandoned. Between the fleeing armies and Omsk lay three rivers, the Tobol, the Ishim, and the Irtish. A stand was possible at each. The line for some two months ran along the River Tobol, five hundred kilometers west of Omsk, where 20,000 men were lost in killed and wounded. Moscow, now distracted by Denikin's advance, was unable to press the offensive with decisive strength.

White troops were reformed in three new armies behind the Tobol under the command of General Dieterichs, who replaced General Lebedev as chief-of-staff. The first army was commanded by General Pepelayev, the second by General Lokhvitsky, and the third by General Sakharov. Ataman Ivanov-Rinov was called west from Omsk to recruit the Cossacks.

Although it was announced that Pepelayev had 20,000 men in the north, Lokhvitsky 31,000 in the center, and Sakharov some 50,000 on the left or southern front, these numbers were exaggerated. General Graves on a tour of inspection to Petropavlovsk in July was able to discover only a negligible number of troops. Soldiers and officers were throwing away arms and clothing and making for the rear.

The sick and wounded were often untended and died where they fell.

Behind the Tobol the retreat became somewhat more orderly, but the condition of the common soldier made any prolonged resistance to the Reds impossible. All Kolchak could hope for was escape for his men and for the multitudes of refugees. Fear of reprisals seized upon tens of thousands who made their way east by rail, foot, and horseback. Farms were looted of their last pound of bread. Horses and forage were taken. Peasants who resisted were shot. By this time the men wore every kind of uniform, including peasants' dress. Many of them had rags tied around their feet. On one occasion when Kolchak visited the troops he was given a guard of honor which walked barefoot by his side.

The armies and the refugees retreated slowly toward Petropavlovsk. In this operation and in evacuating the city, only resolute action by Kappel's rear guard prevented the capture of the main units of Kolchak's forces. Kappel enjoyed a reputation for integrity and fighting capacity unattained by most of the admiral's high officers.

In two months the Bolsheviks had dealt a mortal wound at Kolchak's armies and extricated themselves from the chain with which Ironside, Kolchak, Yudenich, and Denikin threatened to encircle them. They had also captured the abundant cornfields of the governments of Perm and Akmolinsk and rich booty from the White armies' supplies.

In the United States and Western Europe the defeats of Kolchak were minimized. He was even reported to be in a better position than when he was moving forward against the Reds. This optimistic note was held months later even in the face of facts, which undeniably indicated that the force of the White movement in Siberia was spent.

White officers who had placed faith in consistent and effective aid from the Allies after their government had been recognized were doomed to bitter disappointment. Although the Allies and especially England had furnished Kolchak with some 100,000 tons of war materials, there was no concerted, steady policy of support. Lord Curzon, on August 16, 1919, remarked in a draft memorandum:

The situation is so complex and the difficulties of arriving at a decision which is acceptable to all are so great that, in some instances, it would be no exaggeration to admit that there is no policy at all.

The Allies' forces in Siberia were doing little that could help in a final solution of the situation. Sixty thousand Japanese were stationed along the Trans-Siberian east of Lake Baikal, between the lake and the Manchurian border, then north over the Amur Railway to Khabarovsk, and southward on the Ussuri line to Vladivostok. Over eight thousand Americans were on the short stretch east of Lake Baikal from Mysovaya to Verkhneudinsk, at Vladivostok, and on the three other short sections near Vladivostok which they were guarding. Some fourteen hundred Italian, fourteen hundred British, and eleven hundred French officers and men were scattered at various points, mostly west of Lake Baikal and near the seat of the Omsk Government.

The commander of American troops was frequently put in an embarrassing position. It was impossible for him to obey his *Aide Memoir* literally. There was some truth in assertions current in Siberia at the time that by not supporting Kolchak he was giving aid to the Bolsheviks. By the same token, in helping to guard the railroad, which was a purely Kolchak affair, he was working to the disadvantage of the Reds.

Semyonov continued to be as great a worry to Kolchak in the east as was the Red Army in the west. He made a practice of holding up trains over the Chinese Eastern Railway when they passed out of Manchuria into Siberia. A Chinese general complained to General Graves on his trip to Omsk in July, 1919, that the Ataman had held up all trains on July 4th, 5th, and 6th at Dauria, a small town thirty miles west of the border. The general asserted that Semyonov had taken

Retreat

Confusion

Kolchak officials examining prisoner

American Y. M. C. A. officials on the job

Wounded being treated by American Red Cross

14,000,000 rubles from Russians and Chinese. When General Graves reached Omsk, General Kreschatski confirmed the report and said that the admiral would have to adjust the matter, as the Cossack leader gave no receipts and that it was robbery. Kreschatski pointed out that because of the effect such action would have internationally, Kolchak would be forced to pay.

During this period, Semyonov had several well-known stations east of Chita where he conducted wholesale executions—at Makaveyevo, Adrianovka, Borzya, Dauria, Oliviannaya, and a place called Post 159, located some six versts east of Chita. On August 19, 1919, fifty-two carloads of prisoners were slaughtered by Colonel Stephanov and his command and upon the following day he was able to report to his chief, Semyonov, that he had killed sixteen hundred people on the day previous. These human slaughter yards continued in operation throughout the period when the railroad was guarded under the Inter-Allied Agreement. In such turbulent times severe measures were inevitable, but hundreds of innocent peasants, townsmen, laborers, and railroad employees who were neither Reds nor bandits nor disturbers of the peace and who were in no sense a danger to the White cause were murdered. The American commander remarked of this period:

I doubt if history will show any country in the world during the last fifty years where murder could be committed as safely and with less danger of punishment than in Siberia during the régime of Admiral Kolchak.

Local Bolsheviks were fomenting uprisings along the railway. At Krasnoyarsk they seized control, spreading their power eastward, threatening to cut off all escape for the fleeing soldiers and refugees. The Amur Railway between Chita and Blagoveshchensk was suffering from many attacks. Three groups of insurgents—Cossacks who desired to re-establish their semi-independence in revolt against Semyonov, a group of genuine "revolutionaries" under Partenov and Namakonov; finally, professional brigands, some one hundred and fifty desperadoes whom Abram Boika had collected in the hills of Manchuria by the promise of lavish plunder—raided stations and stole freight from cars and warehouses.

The methods of these gentry were forthright. They would swoop down upon the railway, burn bridges to prevent reinforcements, and demolish garrisons, as, for example, at Mogocha, where Japanese soldiers stood a siege early in October until rescued by Colonel Umeda. Zilovo, the headquarters of the Reds since early September, was occupied October 20th, and the uprising, though not put down completely, was restrained. The Transbaikal district was like the Italy of Guelph and Ghibelline; an ordinary cutthroat would have blushed to commit some of the atrocities that were perpetrated wholesale along the railway. Women were ripped open, children bayoneted, and men flayed alive. Brutality made Bolsheviks where none had been before.

The tension between Kolchak and Gajda, which was characteristic of the situation between the admiral and his other commanders at the time, is revealed by the entry of General Janin, then commanding the Czechs, in his Siberian diary, under date of July 12, 1919:

This evening Gajda came to ask for my signature for a Czechoslovak passport, as well as for an encouraging word. He had had a violent quarrel with the Russians who wanted to break up his train, and he intimated that he would offer armed resistance. A peace was patched up, owing to the mediation of General Burlin. That's shabby treatment, after all he's done for Siberia and for the Admiral (Kolchak) himself. With the latter he exchanged words bare of amenities (I have confirmation of this from another source). The Admiral threw up to him the fact that he had democratic tendencies, that he favored Socialist-Revolutionaries, that he counted in his armies and General Staff officers of progressive views. Gajda replied that the reactionary orientation was a dangerous thing; the promises made to Siberia had not been kept; hence the trouble, and this was becoming dangerous. Kolchak accused him of deficiency in military science. Gajda replied that the Admiral, having merely commanded three ships in the Black

Sea, could have no pretensions to knowing anything about it. To the threat of court-martial Gajda replied that he was a Czech and therefore was not his subordinate. He asks for my protection on and for the eventual support of the Czechoslovak troops; he seems to fear that they will arrest him.

A spirit of frustration and of jealousy was abroad among the admiral's officers. Recriminations were telegraphed back and forth along the Trans-Siberian, messes were disturbed by violent quarrels. Some officers demanded that their honor be satisfied by duels.

General Gajda, after being cashiered by Kolchak for his criticism of the Omsk régime, made his way east, arriving in Vladivostok on August 8, 1919, after many adventures. Between Chita and the Manchurian frontier he found the bridge over the Onon River destroyed. In two weeks a causeway was constructed which allowed the passage of his train. At a small town called Ossa Ochansk he witnessed the results of a Red massacre in which some three thousand men had been put to death. In a long report to Admiral Kolchak full of spleen and accusation he stated:

The acuteness of the situation demands special precautions. It is imperative to trace a clear and democratic course of state policy, follow it with unswerving strictness, and in the assurance that you can count upon the majority of the people and on the Army. The Government must clear away doubts as to its democracy and its desire to establish civil law and order. The Government must cut away from its own agents who do not hesitate to profit by their own position. The Government must declare that its final aim is to call a Constituent Assembly, on the basis of universal, equal, direct, and secret suffrage. A meeting of the representatives of the Government and district Zemstvos and municipal Dumas, as well as representatives of social organizations. It is necessary to take steps to prevent such defects as shooting without trial in all Russian territory. It is necessary, also, to work out a system of freedom of assembly as in European countries.

Measures should be taken to restore the authority of Zemstvos and municipal Dumas, and start investigations as to administrative punishments inflicted upon members. Steps must be taken to arouse the sympathy of the peasant masses, and the development of agriculture.

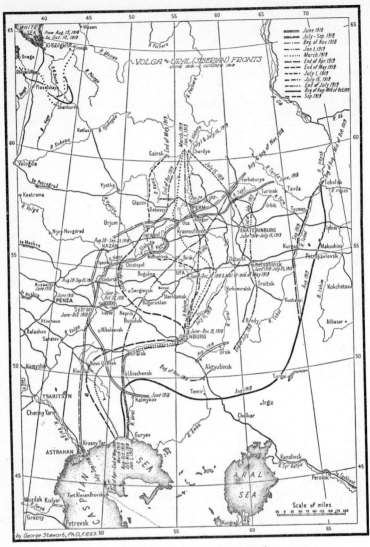

Volga and Ural Fronts, June, 1919–October, 1919.

In an interview which he gave to the press on the day of his arrival at Vladivostok, Gajda did not conceal his disillusionment with Kolchak's government. He said:

The Kolchak Government cannot possibly stand and if the Allies support him they will make the greatest mistake in history. The Government is divided into two distinct parts, one issues proclamations and propaganda for foreign consumption stating that the Government favors and works for a Constituent Assembly, the other part secretly plans and plots a restoration of monarchy. This is perceptible only to those who are part of the Government. It is a hypocritical government which attempts to convince the peasants that their cause is being fostered and yet looks for the psychological moment to restore monarchy. Kolchak has surrounded himself with old régime officers whose only salvation for future existence depends on restoration of monarchy.

Relations between the Czechs and Kolchak continued to grow worse during the summer of 1919. General Janin, who also took a critical view of the supreme ruler, remarked in his journal dated August 16th, concerning the action of Colonel Krejčí, who commanded the Czech division at Tomsk:

For a long time, Krejčí, out of consideration for his troops, has been warning the local natives that he would hold them responsible if they did not take steps against those persons who wanted to destroy the line, or if they did not give information about them. From the moment when he issued this order nothing had happened. Some villages had even asked for arms, so that they would be the better able to protect the line. But when the Russian authorities heard of the existence of the order they were astonished; I received from the Minister of Tellberg a memorandum announcing that "Legality Committee" (an institution which ought to have a good deal to do, since atrocities are being committed wholesale) has revoked this order and sent the necessary information to Krejčí. I replied through the Minister of Foreign Affairs that Krejčí was not under them but under me, and that this annulling of the order was beyond their powers, also that I would notify the Colonel to this effect. Thereupon they requested me to revoke the order myself. I refrained from replying in the peremptory fashion of an ataman; these people might have a trap for me. On the other hand, I don't like to be ordered about. The Czechs are benevolent towards the natives, and the supervision of the Trans-

Siberian line is an enervating task for them. I asked Krejčí if he
thought he could get on without the warning he had issued; he
answered in the negative. So I told the Russians that their General
Rozanov had on March 16th issued an order at Krasnoyarsk
which declared that for every attack on the railway line one would
take a certain number of the political prisoners who were lying in
the nearest prison, they would be hanged at the spot where the
line was damaged. Their corpses would be left upon the gallows.
I added that this order had been executed, and that it had been a
great deal talked about, and that, before annulling Krejčí's order,
I should have to know that Rozanov's had also been annulled, as
I would otherwise be damaging the Czech morale. Soukine (the
Secretary of Admiral Kolchak) replied that Rozanov's order had
been withdrawn. But I know perfectly well that this was not the
case. I demanded the date of this, the confirmation in writing, the
proper references, and so forth, in order to be able to place them
in my own order. That was as far as we got. . . . Anyhow, Krejčí
did not hang any one.

Rifles began arriving for Kolchak at Vladivostok in September of 1919, pursuant to the agreement made by President Wilson on June 12th. On September 16, 1919, General
Graves refused $1,000,000 in payment for rifles which he
felt justified in not delivering because of the activities of
Rozanov, Kalmykov, and Semyonov, whom he believed were
planning to attack the Americans. In this refusal he had the
approval of the American Ambassador to Tokyo, Mr. Morris,
who was then in Vladivostok. A furore arose in the press,
aided by the criticism of General Knox, the matter being
settled finally by arrangement for the Americans to deliver
the rifles at Irkutsk.

The second shipment, in charge of Lieutenant Ryan and
fifty soldiers, was held up at Chita. Semoyonov placed an
armored car on each side of the American train and demanded
15,000 rifles. The lieutenant wired for instructions to General Graves, who ordered him not to surrender a single gun.
After being held up for forty hours under threatening circumstances, Semyonov finally allowed Lieutenant Ryan and
his train to proceed westward.

General Rozanov was sent by Kolchak in early September

of 1919 to command his troops in the Russian Far East. Because of the arrest of an American captain and a corporal immediate friction sprang up between American headquarters and Rozanov. British, Japanese, and French officers lost few opportunities to aid Rozanov, but General Graves clung rigidly to the terms of his orders. Rozanov was little better than Kalmykov and Semyonov. Whatever his record had been in the Imperial Army, as a White commander in the Civil War his actions were no better than a common brigand.

General Graves cites instructions which Rozanov had given his troops on March 27, 1919, as indicative of the character of this officer when the latter was associated with Kolchak in Western Siberia:

1. In occupying the villages which have been occupied before by bandits (partisans) to insist upon getting the leaders of the movement, and where you cannot get the leaders, but have sufficient evidence as to the presence of such leaders, then shoot one out of every ten of the people.
2. If, when the troops go through a town, and the population will not inform the troops, after having a chance to do so, of the presence of the enemy, a monetary contribution should be demanded from all, unsparingly.
3. The villages where the population meet our troops with arms should be burned down and all the full-grown male population should be shot; property, homes, carts, etc., should be taken for the use of the Army.

"We learned," states General Graves, "that Rozanov kept hostages and, for every supporter of his cause that met death, he would kill ten of the people kept as hostages. He spoke of these methods used in Krasnoyarsk as handling the situation with gloves, but declared his intention of taking off his gloves when he came to Vladivostok, and handling the situation without the consideration he had shown the people of Krasnoyarsk."

By late September, Kolchak's army had lost all semblance of a fighting force and had become a mass of refugees fleeing toward Lake Baikal, overcrowding the towns, paralyzing such transportation in Western Siberia as the Czechs did not control, and filling the towns with dispirited troops. "The army," writes Miliukov, "was running eastward, abandoning supplies and equipment on the way, fearing nothing so much as to be overtaken by the Reds, and putting tens of versts between themselves and their pursuers."

The forces were suffering heavily from frost, lack of food, disease, disorganization, and the attacks of the oncoming regiments of the Red Army. Omsk, where Kolchak's retreating soldiers had crowded together in a stampede to escape the Red Army, was a lonely city in the midst of a vast steppe surrounded by Tartar villages. As Kolchak's fall became more and more imminent, the normal population of one hundred and twenty thousand was swollen to well over half a million. Every building was crowded, full of soldiers and refugees, dirty, lousy, infected with spotted typhus and typhoid fever.

When the main body of the troops arrived at Omsk they found unspeakable conditions. Refugees overflowed the streets, the railroad station, and public buildings. The roads were hub-deep in mud. Soldiers and their families begged from house to house for bread. Officers' wives turned into prostitutes to stave off hunger. Thousands who had money spent it in drunken debauches in the cafés. Mothers and their babies froze to death upon the sidewalks. Children were separated from their parents and orphans died by the score in the vain search for food and warmth. Many of the stores were robbed and others closed through fear. Military bands attempted a sorry semblance of gaiety in the public houses but to no avail. Omsk was inundated in a sea of misery.

In the midst of this pain, several *trains de luxe* awaited at the railroad station with steam up to carry away Allied diplomatic and military missions and the rear echelons of the Czechs, a fact which further embittered Kolchak's suffering troops. White officers and men growled to one another that the disastrous attempt of Kolchak to overthrow the Soviets would never have been attempted if it had not been for the urging of various Allied officers and their promised help.

The condition of the wounded was beyond description. Suffering men often lay two in a bed and in some hospitals and public buildings they were placed on the floor. Bandages were improvised out of sheeting, tablecloths, and women's underclothing. Antiseptics and opiates were almost non-existent. Only in the larger bars and cafés did there seem to be money and food and drink. Winter had set in and hundreds were dying of exposure.

Bolshevik forces followed closely upon the retreating Whites, occupying Petropavlovsk on October 30th. By the end of October it became imperative to prepare for the abandonment of Omsk. General Knox, with the staff of the British Military Mission, left the city on November 7th, and on the next day the French and Japanese missions followed. Two days later government officials began their departure, but many received too short notice for withdrawal and fell into the hands of Red troops. Kolchak's government moved to Irkutsk immediately, as it could only be a matter of days until the Red Army should capture Omsk.

The Czechs in their trains escaped the consequences of overcrowding and the moral débâcle. Ten thousand were held by General Syrový as a rear guard while the rest of the echelons moved toward Vladivostok. A picked company was used as a personal bodyguard for the admiral.

Day and night, roads leading to the east were jammed with horses, camels, and donkeys dragging guns, sleighs, and carriages. Men, women, and children stumbled over the snowy waste leaving crimson stains on the road as a testimony of their suffering. No serious officer could hope to re-form the sullen and dispirited troops.

The retreat was carried out in utter confusion. Troops recruited in the provinces of Perm, Ufa, and Akmolinsk deserted by regiments. Brigades of only a few companies were not rare. One brigade consisted of one hundred and eighty-four men. The workmen and officials of the Trans-Siberian line, which alone was the avenue of safety, were thoroughly discontented with Kolchak's government, and for the best of reasons: they had not been paid for months. No wonder, then, that strikes were frequent and that engines broke down. With amazing lack of foresight the Omsk-Novonikolayevsk section of the line, nearest the oncoming Bolsheviks, was heavily stocked with coal, while the Taiga-Krasnoyarsk sector was almost denuded of supplies.

The straw that broke the back of the Trans-Siberian was the quarrel between the Czechs and Kolchak. Since they had left the Ural front some ten months previously the Czechs had assumed the task of guarding the railway between Omsk and Lake Baikal and had rigorously abstained from all participation in Russian internal affairs, save to protect themselves. This neutrality exasperated Kolchak. The determination of the Czechs at the end of September to retire to Vladivostok had inflamed him to the point of madness. If they took precedence on the railroad, it would, of necessity, delay the retreat of his troops.

The Czechs, on November 16th, through Dr. Girsa, issued a statement to the effect that they considered their presence on the Trans-Siberian useless, since they were unable to cope with the conditions.

The intolerable position in which our Army is placed forces us to address ourselves to the Allied Powers to ask them for counsel as to how the Czech Army can be assured of its own security and of a free return to its own country, which was decided with the assent of all the Allied Powers.

The Army was ready to protect the railway in the sector which was assigned to it and it has fulfilled its task conscientiously. But now the presence of our Army on the railway to protect it has become impossible because the activities of the Army are contrary to its aspirations in the cause of humanity and justice.

In protecting the railway and maintaining order in the country, our Army is forced to act contrary to its convictions, when it supports and maintains an arbitrary, absolute power which at present rules.

The burning of villages, the murder of peaceable Russian inhabi-

tants by the hundreds, and the shooting, without reason, of democratic men solely because they are suspected of holding political
views are daily facts: and the responsibility for this before the
Courts of Nations of the entire world, will fall upon us because,
being an armed force, we have not prevented these injustices. This
passiveness is the direct result of our neutrality and noninterven-
tion in Russian internal affairs, and thanks to our being loyal to
this idea, we have become, in spite of ourselves, accomplices to a
crime.

In communicating this fact to the representatives of the Allied
Powers to whom the Czech Nation has been and will be a faithful
Ally, we deem it necessary to take every measure to inform the
nations of the whole world in what a moral and tragic position the
Czech Army is placed and what are the causes of it.

As to ourselves, we see no other way out of this situation than
to evacuate immediately the sector which was given us to guard,
or else to obtain the right to prevent the injustices and crimes
cited above.

Czech leaders saw clearly the futility of the White effort,
as did Lloyd George, who declared on November 8th that
the Reds could not be conquered by force of arms.

The following week an attempt at an uprising against the
Kolchak Government took place at Vladivostok. Gajda,
who had been cashiered after his break with the admiral,
moved to the Maritime Province and attempted a *coup
d'état*. As early as August, General Gajda discussed the plan
for an anti-Kolchak armed revolt with some progressive
Siberian leaders who belonged to the secret Committee for
the Convocation of a *Zemski Sobor* (Parliament). Baron
Aleksey Budberg, who held several important posts under
Kolchak, had written in his diary, under date of September
12, 1919, that at the session of the Cabinet of Ministers the
Secretary of War reported:

According to advices received from Vladivostok, the leading
Socialist-Revolutionaries who had gathered there were making
ready for the overthrow of the Omsk Government, after which
they intended to convoke a *Zemski Sobor:* it is known that the
agents of England and the United States have already notified
their governments of the impending events, and that in the opinion
of these foreign observers, the reactionary Omsk Government is

on its last legs, and power will pass into the hands of a new Government, which will be all-Siberian and popular. . . . The coup will be headed by Gajda, who is at Vladivostok and who promises the Socialist-Revolutionaries the active help of the Czechs stationed at Vladivostok and Irkutsk and the complete coöperation of the chief Czech commissioner, Dr. Girsa. The matter is considered so certain that the British representative interviewed the members of the would-be Government and discussed with them the details of the convocation of the *Zemski Sobor* . . .

The Czech general hoped by a coup to seize Vladivostok and set up a more liberal government. In this he was associated with Socialist-Revolutionaries. Neither the Czechs nor the local Zemstvos were active in these arrangements. General Gajda agreed to accept the military command, provided the coup was performed by Russians. Although many foreign officials were in sympathy with the enterprise, they kept hands off. Gajda staged his attack on the night of the 16th-17th of November, with some three hundred men, but within twenty-four hours he was decisively defeated. The handful of his followers which remained were captured in the railway station and promptly shot. Many of his wounded were neglected and allowed to die without succor. Gajda was arrested, but went free because of the presence of large numbers of Czechs. He was ordered to leave Siberia within twenty-four hours and not to return.

Anything was possible in these days—*sauve qui peut* was the preoccupation of Russian and alien alike. Missions with every variety of axe to grind imposed upon one another, upon local leaders, and upon the civil population. Every one turned wistful eyes toward Vladivostok. One canny Scot secured a freight van to himself and painted across the sides *Anglesky Missia* (English Mission), fitted it up with a cookstove and living quarters, and by persuasion and threats to station masters and trainmen succeeded in being carried three thousand miles east to the Maritime Province!

Admiral Kolchak had left Omsk on November 13th in the third of five trains which moved slowly toward Lake Baikal, carrying with him the imperial treasure. Although little order had reigned in the city, nevertheless some excesses had been prevented out of respect for the supreme ruler's presence. After his departure, the town was seized with a mad delirium of drunkenness and debauchery. Hundreds of soldiers turned Bolshevik in an effort to escape the Red doom which was approaching from the west. As the troops left Omsk, they fired munition dumps and destroyed factories.

When Omsk fell on the night of November 15th, Kolchak's government had become so unpopular that local Zemstvo and city officials refused to confer with his Council of Ministers. After the loss of Omsk, Admiral Kolchak sent out proclamations promising a more liberal government, but the hour had passed when promises would mend damage already done.

The railway was clogged with trains whose locomotives were frequently out of repair. From the middle of December, when the last semblance of a rear guard vanished, these trains were liable to raids, not only from Soviet soldiers, traveling swiftly in sledges, but also from Partisans, who gained in boldness with the rapid approach of the Red Army. Engines often had no water save that obtained from melted snow. Peasants and townsmen hid their food as the horde of soldiers and refugees approached. The dead were thrown along the tracks to rot and contaminate the district! Families were separated, girls sold themselves for a meal. Mankind was adrift, fighting for life. Those who died from disease and exposure numbered far more than those who died in battle and in the innumerable small massacres that marked the Civil War in Siberia.

More profound than the wounds of saber and shell was the mutilation of the souls of these men. Associated with Kolchak were many democratically minded officers who deplored the cruelty of some of his commanders. They foresaw the fatal results of Kolchak's policy, but, even as he, they were powerless to fight against the general mood of those who surrounded the admiral. Most of the common soldiers were trusting muzhiks who had not only been disappointed in the Czar and his officers, but now, in a new day which they had hailed as their time of deliverance, were being subjected to physical and spiritual travail through the incompetence and egotism of other leaders to whom they had lent their bayonets. Such minds, rendered incapable of confiding in White leaders, were ripe for the Red harvest which was swollen by discontent born of erratic leadership.

Retreat by train was luxury compared with the horrors of flight by roads which ran along both sides of the line. Sleighs pushed on their endless journey drawn by starved horses which died like flies. Peasants' homes were robbed of food, their farms plundered of horses to help in the ghastly exodus. Troops clothed in rags stripped corpses of tunics and boots to warm their frozen limbs. None knew who were Reds and who were Whites. At times men from both armies traveled on the same train! Villages would present the oncoming Red armies with batteries of British guns, with which General Knox had equipped the White Army. Men with undressed and infected wounds were left upon the roadside to be slain by the frost. Generals who a month before had been fighting the Reds were now serving them. Never had the steppes and forests of Siberia, accustomed to the spectacle of gangs of Czarist prisoners moving into exile, witnessed such confusion and misery.

When the exodus reached Novonikolayevsk they found hundreds of thousands of refugees. The troops were further dejected by the news of the collapse of Yudenich's army in November, 1919. Spotted typhus was rife in every regiment and among the vermin-ridden hordes of civilians. When the city fell on December 14th, over 30,000 men, women, and children lay dead in the streets and buildings of the city.

Between November of 1919 and April of 1920 over 60,000 died of typhus in Novonikolayevsk alone. In the echelon of the Izhevsky Division, half of the men died on the way from Omsk to Krasnoyarsk. Sick and dying refugees and civilians added to the macabre dance of death. Napoleon's retreat from Moscow in which he lost 70,000 men was orderly in comparison with the flight of Kolchak's army from Omsk!

As the sufferings of the men intensified, so did their hatred of the Czechs and the Allied representatives in their comfortable trains. Their comrades were sick or dying of starvation, their hospital trains without locomotives. By night, bivouac fires were made on the steppe of branches of trees, packing cases, and broken or abandoned sleighs. By day the column of fleeing soldiers and civilians wound out of sight east and west on either side of the railway. Every station was a graveyard, with hundreds and in many places thousands of unburied dead. At Taiga, where the branch line runs north to Tomsk, over fifty thousand were slain by hunger and disease. Thousands of horses and Mongolian ponies were beaten forward until they dropped in their tracks. Small wonder that Kolchak's soldiers bore ill will toward any more fortunate than themselves!

No order could be maintained in the retreat. Companies and regiments hung together out of sheer self-protection. The staff and many high officers made their way as best they could. The mass of doomed humanity moved eastward at the rate of twenty to twenty-five kilometers a day, leaving behind to mark its dolorous passage the bodies of children, men, women, and dead horses.

Reaching Krasnoyarsk, which had turned Red, the army moved around to the north of the city to prevent a battle they were unprepared to fight. The Bolsheviks attacked and only desperation enabled the fatigued White troops to break through, leaving their dead and wounded by the hundreds upon the snow and ice behind them.

In this city were many thousands of starving Germans and Austrian prisoners of war who saw with melancholy eyes the change in masters, longing for the Russian madness to cease and to return to their homes. In the pandemonium of the Civil War scant care was given these victims of the world conflict.

Although the admiral protested violently to the Czechs

for taking precedence upon the Trans-Siberian they paid as little attention as when Semyonov demanded that Kolchak's staff, with his sick, wounded, and the gold reserve, be allowed to pass the Czech echelons. It is true that the evacuation of the Legionnaires encumbered Kolchak's retreat, yet it is difficult to see what other course General Janin and General Syrový, of their high command, could have taken when, in mid-December of 1919, they had ordered that the transport on the railway in Czech sectors should be regulated entirely by the Czechs.

After the Kolchak Government had moved to Irkutsk it made a feeble attempt to keep the admiral's promise to institute a more liberal régime. The premier, Vologodsky, resigned and was succeeded by V. N. Pepelayev, brother of the general, and later by Tretyakov. Portfolios were offered to Socialist-Revolutionaries and leaders of the Coöperative Movement, but the offers was rejected. The Kolchak régime was now thoroughly discredited both at home and abroad.

Liberal elements were preparing a conference of Zemstvo and municipal leaders at Irkutsk, which planned to invite the admiral and his ministers to resign and to form a new government. Towns were beginning to revolt ahead of the retreating army.

The Allies had wanted Kolchak to win and had hoped until hope was impossible that he would rout the Bolsheviks. News of the exact state of Kolchak's armies and the mind of the civil population leaked out but slowly or was suppressed. On December 2, 1919, when it was obvious to realistic observers on the spot that Kolchak's force was spent, an editorial in the *New York Times* remarked: "His Government should be more solidly established hereafter." But thousands of starving and bitter troops with frozen wounds trudging toward Lake Baikal compelled Kolchak to see that his army no longer existed as an organization.

In his desperate situation, the admiral turned for help to the Japanese and to Ataman Semyonov. On December 19th, Premier Tretyakov went to Chita to negotiate with both.

The following day the Ob front, near Taiga, between Novonikolayevsk and Mariinsk, collapsed and with it the last remnants of a rear guard. Many Polish soldiers, less fortunate than their Czech brethren, were captured by the triumphant Red Army.

Finally, all hope of coöperation between the Czechs and Kolchak was dashed by the latter's reckless order of December 24th, to the effect that the army heads must prevent the evacuation of the Czechs by blowing up the tunnels, if necessary. The commander-in-chief of the Legionnaires could only reply by warning his subordinates of their danger, which was real enough, as General Skipitrov was encountered attempting to blow up the Baikal tunnels and prevented from doing so only in the nick of time. This dramatic episode further enraged the Czechs and strengthened their determination to shake the dust of Russia from their feet.

Uprisings had thrown the territory between Krasnoyarsk and Irkutsk into the hands of the rebels. The movement was headed by the so-called Political Center, a *bloc* composed of Socialist-Revolutionaries, the Menshevik wing of the Social Democrats, and the League of Toiling Peasantry. This *bloc* favored peace with Soviet Russia, opposed foreign intervention, and refused to fraternize with political representatives of the propertied classes. The peasant had come to believe that Russia was being sold to foreign interventionists and preferred Bolshevik rule to either foreign or White domination.

The anti-Kolchak revolution reached Irkutsk, the seat of the government, on December 24th, ahead of the admiral. A section of the garrison situated on the left shore of the River Angara, which flows through the city, rebelled, and the ranks of the rebels were swelled by civilians. A large detachment and all the government offices were on the right bank. The river had not frozen, the bridge across it was out of order, and all river craft were in the hands of the Czechs, who affected strict neutrality. Under these circumstances, troops on the right bank, who had remained loyal to the government, were powerless to make a move against the rebels. When the commander threatened to use artillery against the latter, General Janin vigorously opposed this measure.

Kolchak, on December 24th, was in Nizhneudinsk, about two hundred and ninety miles west of Irkutsk, forsaken by nearly all of his forces and officers. He now had little left save his title, and, for protection, gave himself into the hands of a battalion of Czechs who by this time had little cause to be grateful to the admiral for their sufferings in the Russian turmoil. Kolchak then had in another train, in gold bricks and bullion, some 650,500,000 rubles, and 500,000,000 rubles in securities and valuables, the treasury of Imperial Russia. Upon a rumor that Red forces were advancing to capture the gold, General Janin sent a telegram ordering the Czechs to retreat to Irkutsk.

General Janin was now faced with a difficult task. Could he save the Czechs and save Kolchak also? What was he to do with the gold for which he had accepted responsibility? The rebel government at Irkutsk, strongly Socialist-Revolutionary, was growing redder daily, as the Bolsheviks advanced eastward. Janin was receiving telegrams from Allied representatives farther east that they could not see their way clear to aid him if he remained at Irkutsk. The air was full of rumors and confusion.

To avoid bloodshed, the Zemstvo and municipal leaders, who were largely in sympathy with the program of the Political Center, opened negotiations with the Cabinet of Ministers. The revolutionists demanded the retirement of Admiral Kolchak, a drastic change in the composition of the government and the convocation at Irkutsk of a Constituent Assembly, or *Zemski Sobor*. The Cabinet was willing to accept these conditions and was ready to transfer the local governmental authority to the *Zemski Sobor*. It was stipulated, however, that there should be freedom of movement for Kolchak and for the remnants of his army.

But negotiations were broken off on December 28th, when news reached the Cabinet that Ataman Semyonov was on his way westward to rescue Irkutsk, to be followed by Japanese reinforcements. That day the rebels attacked the government forces, but were beaten off by a unit which had remained loyal. Characteristically enough, within the next twenty-four hours soldiers who had saved the day for the government shot their officers and joined the revolutionists, but when the latter placed them on the firing line they again changed their allegiance.

Kolchak's officers looked anxiously eastward. Perhaps at last the White chiefs of Transbaikalia would come wholeheartedly to the support of their leader. But when events at Irkutsk demanded the support of every adherent of Kolchak, one of Semyonov's generals was busy in private plunderings a short distance east of Lake Baikal in the Selenga Valley. In December, Semyonov had sent General Levitsky with his Wild Division to Verkhneudinsk. This organization consisted of some two thousand Mongols, mounted on Mongolian ponies and camels, and some five hundred Cossacks. Immediately there began flowing in to Colonel Morrow's headquarters piteous cries for help from the Russian villages.

Village Sheraldai, January 3, 1920.

Friends, Americans: The people implore your help and request you to protect them from Semyonov's Wild Division, who burn villages, bread, and the property of peasants; who kill old men, women, and children, and who have mercy on no one.

We beg you to help us for the sake of the babies and old men. Have mercy and help us. Upon your arrival, you can be convinced by your own eyes of the true facts, through seeing the remnants and ashes of our homes.

(signed by thirty-eight peasants.)

Another petition read:

General Verdict of Kharashibersk Rural Assembly

January 17, 1920.

We, the undersigned citizens of Zai-Baikal Oblast Verkhneudinsk, Mukhorsibersk Volost, village Kharashibersk, association, being at meeting this date in the presence of our president, Nikita Varfalemieva, we were discussing our political standing, when we decided to go to citizen American Consul with this verdict to protect us from Japanese and Semyonov's bands. We all, like one man, together with other associations of the various villages and districts, arise against the above-mentioned Japo-Semyonov's insolence which forces us to obey them. With the help of arms they got into our village and killed about thirty men. They were finishing the wounded and were robbing house owners, taking their money and properties. They raped women and burned down fifty-five houses with four wives and children in them. Request you, citizen, American Consul, come with protection to our helpless, in which we are signing.

(Two hundred and two signatures.)

After devastating the village of Bobkina on the 10th of January, 1920, killing some fifteen unarmed people, a mixed investigating committee composed of the former American vice consul at Chita, Mr. Fowler, and Lieutenant Davis, of the American Army, Lieutenant Fuji and Captain Keda of the Japanese Army, Major Doctor Marland and Major de Latour Dejean of the French Army, reported:

A dozen corpses, with the hands cut off, were lying heaped up in a pile half destroyed, all the bodies more or less cut up by saber wounds. The greater part bore many wounds made while living by saber blows, particularly on the face and back. All the corpses were burned. Many bore evident traces of having been burned while still living. From this last observation it must be admitted that the greater part, severely wounded only, must have died of asphyxiation as an inspection of the wounds shows not one was immediately mortal.

Several of Semyonov's armored trains had arrived at Irkutsk on the 29th of December, gave the rebels battle, were repulsed, and did not renew the attack, while the expected Japanese rescue party did not materialize.

Allied representatives, headed by General Janin, continued to plead with the government to hand over authority to the revolutionists. "General Janin," writes a member of the Kolchak Government in his memoirs, "relying on Czech reports, pointed out the inevitability of the rebels' success. The Allies declared that the Socialist-Revolutionaries were a legitimate political party, having nothing to do with the Bolsheviks, and that the Allies did not wish to oppose them."

An armistice was concluded, and, urged by the entire Allied diplomatic corps, representatives of the government met delegates from the Political Center, three Socialist-Revolutionaries, one Menshevik, and two representatives of the military command of the rebels. The Political Center demanded Kolchak's resignation, Semyonov's dismissal, disarmament of all military units, surrender of the valuables and supplies, and trial of all those who were responsible for the policy of the Kolchak Government. While the ministers parleyed, government troops left their positions and the revolutionists occupied the city.

The supreme ruler still had reason to hope that he would be allowed to leave Siberia with the honors of war, for on January 2d the Czechs had transmitted word to him that efforts would be made to save all his troops, but failing that he would be escorted safely to the Far East. Whereupon Kolchak, on January 4th, sent a wire to the authorities at Irkutsk stating that he had surrendered his person to the Czechs. The imperial treasure was delivered to the Allies on the same day and placed in the custody of the Czechs. Upon Kolchak's private car were placed the flags of England, Japan, France, America, and the new state of Czechoslovakia.

On the morning of January 5th, Irkutsk awoke to read a manifesto of the Political Center declaring that "by the will of the people and the army, the régime of the Dictator Kolchak has been overthrown," that the plenitude of governmental authority was now vested in the provincial Zemstvo and in the municipalities, that a Provisional Siberian Council would be called on January 12th and would be followed by a Siberian Constituent Assembly made up of representatives of local self-governing bodies, peasant congresses, Cossack organizations, and trade unions, and finally that the instigators of Kolchak's reactionary policy would be brought to trial.

On the same day Admiral Kolchak resigned he issued an ukase transferring his power in European Russia to Denikin and in the Far East to Semyonov. Some two weeks later the Ataman proclaimed himself temporary ruler of Siberia.

Kolchak, at Nizhneudinsk, separated from the remnants of his army and government, was at the mercy of the rebels who had seized the city. Having been notified that his ministers wished him to resign, he did so, disbanded his bodyguard, and formally placed himself under the protection of the Czechs. Before resigning, at the instance of the Allied representatives, the supreme ruler transferred the gold reserve of the empire to the Czechs for safekeeping.

Maddened by the fact that the Czechs were escaping to safety—an escape which inevitably hindered the freest use of the Trans-Siberian and its equipment—Colonel Siroboyarsky, representative of Ataman Semyonov on Admiral Kolchak's staff, sent General Janin a long and bitter telegram from Verkhneudinsk on January 23d. This message had wide circulation, copies having been sent to all principal Allied and Russian officers in the Far East, and represented the point of view of many of Kolchak's officers toward Janin, Syrový, and the Legionnaires. The Whites and the Czechs had ceased to be comrades-in-arms. The telegram read:

Your Excellency:

As a representative of Ataman Semyonov, attached to the staff of the Commander-In-Chief of the Russian Armies, I have done my duty, to the best of my ability and knowledge, up to the last day. As a true Russian officer, who received the highest decorations of war, who was wounded many times, and whom you knew personally during the last war, I take the liberty to tell you of the unbelievable high treason of our former brothers, who were delivered from the Austro-German yoke by many thousands of our best patriots, who sacrificed their lives on the battlefields of Galicia. This unheard of betrayal of the Slavonic common cause struck horror into the hearts of the Russians who witnessed it.

I, myself, was wounded in front of the trenches of one of the Slavonic regiments of the Austrian Army at the time of its deliverance from bondage. This regiment is now in Siberia. Last year it seemed that we had received the justly earned help of our former brothers, the Czechs, who, saving only their own lives, tore the

Bolshevik chains asunder; the chains that held the Russian nation captive in a living tomb. The news was spread over Siberia and the whole world with lightning rapidity, arousing highest respect and admiration for the Czech Falcons and liberators. By one move, by a short victorious struggle, the Czechs became legendary heroes, Knights without fear or blame. Their exploits made them immortal. The Russian people looked upon them as their saviors.

Your appointment as the commander-in-chief of all Slavonic troops in Siberia, the greatest honor given to you as a representative of France, was welcomed everywhere with greatest satisfaction. But, since your arrival, the Czech troops were being taken from the front to the rear, supposedly for a much needed rest. The suffering Russian patriots, the officers, the volunteers, and the soldiers, having fought for more than three years with Germany for the same ideals as your country did, shielded the retreating Czechs with their own bodies. It was with a feeling of sadness that we watched the echelons moving eastward, laden heavily not so much with military equipage as with so-called war booty. . . .

After leaving their brothers in the rear, thousands of impassable versts behind, the Russians began to retreat because of the unbearable blows received by the Bolsheviks. Here the Knives of the Cains, the Czechs, were raised to strike mortal blows in the backs of their exhausted and helpless brethren. I do not know how and by whom the telegrams of the patriotic Russian leaders were received. The messages were full of despair, invoking pity and mercy for the innocent Russian fighters, who were perishing, arms in hand, while trying to secure a passage through the lines of the treacherous Czechs for the sick and wounded, for families left without food and shelter, and for thousands of women and children dying from cold and exposure. . . .

Time, the best judge of mankind, will supply to future history the real facts of the rôle played by the Czechs in the present, most trying days of Russia. Now when the agonizing cries of the dying armies and of their heroic leaders are in all probability silenced, when there is no one to ask you in vain for mercy, I take the liberty to tell you all that I witnessed during the two months of the evacuation of Omsk while, as a representative of Ataman Semyonov, I was with the Supreme commander-in-chief.

The Czechs, after some preliminaries, made a deep thrust into the rear of our armies, and seized and paralyzed the only railroad which was supplying our forces. At the same time they were supporting the unorganized social revolutionary element, better to say, the Bolsheviks. A group of these scamps, led by Ensign Krylenko, taking advantage of our concentration of forces in the front and the weakness of our rear, succeeded in creating chaos and demoralization. The Czechs were openly abetting the Bolsheviks, giving them full freedom of action, at the same time refusing similar concessions to the representatives of the existing government. After declaring the railroad neutral, they granted the full use of the same to the insurgents, but denied the same privilege even to the Supreme Head of the Government. At some railroad stations, from the first days of the insurrection, the Czechs were giving out weapons from their armored cars to the so-called people's army. They had an agreement with the latter regarding a mutual neutrality till their departure. Our officers, going to the East, were being captured and executed. . . .

Now it is clear to everyone the new, and perhaps the last, effort of the forces which are under your command. These forces are moving wavelike, since a long time, from the West, with the intent to inundate the last bulwark of our government, and to extinguish the last lights of the sacred cause of the regeneration of Russia. These lights are glimmering, yet in the Far East and in Trans-Baikalia, jealously guarded by the valiant Ataman Semyonov, who was the first in whole Siberia, long before the Czechs, to raise the banner of battle against those who trampled on right law and order. You, the commander-in-chief of the Slavonic troops, since the very day of your arrival, not being acquainted with the new surroundings, have shown a hostile attitude toward Ataman Semyonov on account of his misunderstandings with the head of the government. Now you and all your army look upon him as an enemy, because he remains faithful to the very government to which you were formerly urging him to be loyal, and from which you yourself turned away suddenly, leaving it without help and support.

It is simply stupefying to see to what indignities you, our allies, are subjecting our grief-stricken Russia. Are the horrors of the surrender of Odessa so soon forgotten? And yet, all that which takes place in Siberia is ten times worse than the treason in Odessa, where all that was good, honored and ideal perished. Can it be that in Siberia also such an implacable decision should prevail, whereby even single fighters, whom you were supplying with arms and clothing, thus supporting them in their fight against the Bolsheviks, must die? . . .

Tell us, at last, what is your standing in relation to the horrors which are now taking place? If you are the leader of the Czechs, over whom as is openly said by everyone, you have no power, then all the events now taking place will not be connected with your name as a representative and the executor of orders issued by the

French Government. In this case, tell distant France that the Russian patriots who saved Paris for her do not believe that she is deaf to their sufferings. And if we cannot ask France to help us, let her at least not give protection to those who at present prove to be the betrayers of our holy cause—the regeneration of our Fatherland.

Janin received not a few such messages, but held to his decision, feeling that no good end could be served by entangling Czech soldiers in the *débâcle* into which White forces in Siberia had fallen.

Meanwhile, Semyonov's troops at Verkhneudinsk and Beresovka had become such a threat to the Czech and American forces who were guarding the railroad that they had been compelled to disarm fourteen hundred. Skipitrov throughout his campaign had committed the same crimes which had marked Levitsky's depredations in the Selenga Valley. His passage was marked by the same sort of killings, rape, and plunder as occurred when the armored trains of General Bogomoletz passed up and down the line. When Irkutsk fell, Skipitrov retreated eastward with twenty-six hostages promising to return them if his forces were not pursued by the Bolsheviks. However, he had the whole group taken to the upper deck of the ice-breaker, *Angara*, where his Cossacks killed them with mawls and threw them into the lake. Skipitrov also fired upon a Czech echelon, which compelled the Czechs to disarm his entire force and seize four armored cars.

On the night of January 10th four of Semyonov's armored trains had passed through Verkhneudinsk on the way westward to relieve Irkutsk. The fifth armored train, the *Destroyer*, had stopped at Verkhneudinsk. The station master had been arrested and taken aboard the *bronevick*, as the armored trains were called. His clothing and that of his wife had been taken away and the furniture in the house destroyed. Upon being informed of this outrage, Colonel Morrow had boarded the *Destroyer* and informed General Bogomoletz that he was passing through the American sector by special permission and that he would not be allowed to arrest any one or to execute them. Bogomoletz had replied that he would do as he pleased. After a sharp argument, the station master was released. Having proceeded westward some sixty miles, the *Destroyer* came to the station, Posolskaya, where Lieutenant Paul Kendall was in charge of a detachment of thirty-one men guarding the railroad, who were sleeping in wooden box cars at the time. The weather was forty degrees below zero. Approaching the box cars where the Americans were, the armored train opened fire, killing two men and grievously wounding another one. Rallying to the attack, the Americans damaged the locomotive with rifle fire and hand grenades. The train retreated some five versts, where the Americans captured, with the commander, General Bogomoletz, five officers and forty-eight men.

General Bogomoletz and his command were brought under guard to the headquarters of Colonel Morrow, who immediately notified Semyonov and demanded a trial. No trial ever occurred and on the day that Colonel Morrow left Verkhneudinsk, January 29, 1920, he had the doubtful pleasure of seeing Bogomoletz released and riding through Verkhneudinsk in an automobile, knowing that he was to be given a banquet at the Russian Club that evening.

A revelation of what life aboard the armored trains was like is contained in the testimony of Assistant Surgeon Michael Morosov as set down by Lieutenant Colonel Gillem of the Twenty-seventh Infantry, and quoted by Lieutenant Colonel Charles H. Morrow, U. S. Army, during hearings before the Senate Committee on Educational Labor relative to the Deporting of Undesirable Aliens:

1. Q. How long have you been of the bronevick? A. Since September, 1919.
2. Q. Have you got a family? A. A wife and child. I was forced to work on the bronevick; I wanted to commit suicide, because I couldn't stand the horrors of Semyonov's men.
3. Q. Did you see any Americans at Station Posolskaya? A.

No; I was asleep at the time. Friends say that the bronevick fired first.

4. Q. What did the bronevick do after the fighting? A. The engine couldn't go at full speed, so it backed up slowly about three versts and stopped.
5. Q. Why do the people call the bronevick "destroyer" not only in name but also in action? (No answer reported.)
6. Q. How many executions did you see at Station Oloviannaya? A. Fifteen men and one woman were taken into the car and whipped, then taken to the ice hole and killed one after another. In most cases they were lashed and hit with the bayonets and then thrown in the ice hole alive. All took place January 1, 1920.

At the last trip, from Chita to Verkhneudinsk, there were killed about forty men only because they were suspected of helping the Bolsheviks.

At the same expedition one woman was killed because she wouldn't give herself up to the military commandant of the station. All these cases can be verified, as the bodies were never buried.

All executions were committed by order of the general himself, because it was a punitive expedition.

The provodnick of the general's car was so badly whipped that he died two days ago.

The general had mercy for nobody. He was also the only judge.

Before his service on the bronevick he worked on Station Adrianova and took part in executions of one group of Bolsheviks, three hundred and seventy men, and small groups of fifteen and twenty men.

Everybody on the bronevick knows very well that the general would continue his executions up to Irkutsk. My opinion that the most men killed were peasants who knew nothing about politics.

Q. Did the men like the service on the bronevick? A. About six did, the rest were forced to do it. For the least offense people were whipped and killed. One man tried to leave the bronevick at Manchuria. He was caught and whipped. He died two days later.

On the armored train, *Destroyer*, Colonel Morrow's troops found one hundred and seventy-seven pocketbooks and a half million rubles which they turned over to General Myssura. At Troitskasavsk in January Semyonov's officers executed over eight hundred political and military prisoners, each day employing a different method.

Months later, Mr. Sayres, Secretary of the American Railway Corps, in an address in June of 1920 in San Francisco, remarked:

General Semyonov is a Buriat, a half Tartar, and a robber. He was financed by the Japanese and the Allies. His train lay alongside of mine for more than ninety days, so that I knew the gentleman quite well, and when you hear stories about the "nationalization" of the Russian women (all of which have been disproved) I want to tell you this—and I do not think you are going to see it reported in the newspapers—General Semyonov had thirty of the most beautiful women that I ever saw held in his train. He ran back and forth over the Trans-Siberian railroad, robbing and pillaging. He robbed the Chinese banks and custom-houses. In three days' time in Chita he took sixty million rubles and stripped every man, woman and child, taking every bit of valuables that they had about them. I was there at the time.

In the same speech, Mr. Sayres described Kalmykov:

Another of these marauders was Kalmykov. He was about twenty-five or twenty-six years old. That gentleman shot, without trial, in fourteen months, four thousand, two hundred men and women. Day before yesterday I met in the streets of Los Angeles a young fellow who was a member of the Twenty-seventh Regiment. One day Kalmykov came through the district where this young soldier was stationed and threw a bomb into a schoolhouse when there were eighteen or twenty children in it. This boy helped to carry all that was left of them away in a coffee sack and buried them.

The Allies and America saw that further efforts were futile. By January 1, 1920, even the British War Office, which had hoped so much from Kolchak, was compelled to report that he had "ceased to be a factor in Russian military affairs." President Wilson, on January 12, 1920, had ordered the evacuation of the United States forces as soon as possible after the departure of the Czechs and the safety of the Stevens Railway Commission was assured. The Supreme War Council officially terminated the blockade of Red Russia on January 16th. The first American transport sailed on January 17th.

Colonel Morrow and his troops entrained the last of January, moving slowly eastward with echelons of the Czechs, happy to leave Transbaikalia behind them. They left behind some ten thousand Czechs with General Janin and three American railroad engineers to facilitate their evacuation. En route, the Czechs and Americans were forced to disarm four thousand, five hundred of Semyonov's men before they dared to move through his territory. Had it not been for the influence of the Japanese they would have disarmed all of his command on whom they could lay hands. During their passage, Semyonov did all in his power to inconvenience them through interfering with the telephone and telegraph facilities.

In the Russian Far East, General Rozanov fell from power with only slight resistance on January 31, 1920. Rozanov in his short command in the Russian Far East, from November 18, 1919, until the time he was driven from power, had killed between five and six hundred people with only the sketchiest of trials, many of them merely memoranda after the act.

The Allies having despaired of raising another White Army in Siberia, nevertheless were anxious to secure Kolchak's personal safety. Although the supreme ruler had needlessly offended the Czechs, Janin attempted to save the admiral until in his opinion he was jeopardizing the safety of the echelons for which he was primarily responsible. General Janin came to an understanding with the local Socialist-Revolutionaries whereby they would facilitate the evacuation of the Legionnaires and he would surrender to them Kolchak and the imperial treasure. Admiral Kolchak received this news, tantamount to a death sentence, with equanimity. To the complaints of high Allied officials, safe in the Far East, General Janin replied that he was solely responsible to the government in Prague and the Inter-Allied Council in Paris.

The Socialist-Revolutionaries who now had custody of Admiral Kolchak had a particular score they wished to pay. In the first days of the uprising at Irkutsk, General Sychev had arrested thirty-one Socialist-Revolutionaries. The Allied commissioners had insisted that they should have fair treatment. Notwithstanding his promise to the Allies, however, Sychev had left Irkutsk with the prisoners and on January 8th had drowned them in Lake Baikal. This action had sealed Kolchak's fate!

The drama of Siberian dictatorship as far as Kolchak was concerned rushed swiftly to its close. As the Czechs moved slowly toward Irkutsk, the miners of Cheremkhovo on January 13th demanded that the admiral be handed over to them. Blahos, the commander of the train, promised to surrender the admiral to the proper authorities at Irkutsk. The following day the train reached the Irkutsk station and was drawn up between two others. Many of the admiral's officers tore off their epaulets or donned Czech uniforms, others crawled under neighboring cars, and were thus able to save themselves. Possibly Kolchak, too, might have escaped by such a ruse, but the supreme governor preferred dignity to safety. Blahos delivered him up, together with V. N. Pepelayev, and the admiral's former minister, at the demand of the local authorities, who locked them in the city prison. The Czechs also handed over the gold reserve to the Irkutsk authorities: 5,143 boxes and 1,680 bags, with an estimated value of 1,150,500,000 rubles, all in good order with the exception of two small thefts of unknown origin.

Between Irkutsk and the pursuing Red Army was a small force of some ten thousand of Kolchak's soldiers, chiefly officers commanded by General Vladimir Oskarovich Kappel, one of the admiral's best commanders. Kappel had an honorable record in the World War. Following the Czechoslovak rising in the summer of 1918, he held high posts under the Samara Government, the Committee of the Constituent Assembly, and later under Kolchak. Two Czech officers gained contact with Kappel and urged him to make a detour of the city on his way east, lest his disillusioned soldiers take vengeance upon Kolchak. As Kappel's ragged soldiers approached Irkutsk, the Democratic régime, knowing that they would sooner or later have to account to the Bolsheviks if they either let Kolchak or the gold reserve slip through their fingers, the local authorities did some rapid thinking.

By the time the forces of Kappel and Pepelayev reached the last station west of Irkutsk the pink government turned Red, handing over the administration to the local Soviet of Workers and Peasant deputies. The reign of the Political Center had lasted only sixteen days.

Admiral Kolchak's trial, begun under the Political Center, was now concluded under the Soviets. The proceedings of the special commission which investigated his case were published five years later by the Soviet Central Archives and is a remarkable document of the Civil War. That the Revolutionary Committee, as the court was called, would return a verdict of capital punishment for both Kolchak and Pepelayev was a foregone conclusion.

The admiral's tragic administration ceased in the early morning of February 7, 1920. The White leader faced the end with sublime courage. The sentence of death was carried out against Admiral Kolchak and Pepelayev by a detail who blew out their brains with automatics.

With the death of their leader, the White forces of Siberia were completely adrift. No Russian officer alone and no group could command the power to again take the field.

Two weeks after Kolchak's execution the Red Army occupied Irkutsk, on its victorious progress toward the Pacific. One of its first acts was to take possession of the imperial gold reserve.

Kappel's desperate and dilapidated army saw the futility of attempting to take Irkutsk and passed around the city, crossing Lake Baikal on the ice, leaving behind them corpses of men and horses to mark their passage. General Kappel himself had his legs so badly frozen in this campaign that he soon afterward died of his injuries.

Immediately after the execution of Admiral Kolchak, Allied officials in Siberia began bombarding General Janin with telegrams of remonstrance and blame. He records in his journal in this period:

The High Commissioners of the Allied Powers and two White Russian dignitaries from their peaceful havens at Vladivostok or Harbin follow the Admiral's career with a far-off solicitude, are displaying a beautiful indignation at the idea that I have not allowed the Czechs to be killed on his behalf. . . . With regard to the High Commissioners I send them an additional telegram. The only concrete thing that they have done at Irkutsk has been to demand locomotives of Skipitrov and, after obtaining them, to depart—not, I am sure, because they are afraid, but because the whole affair appears to them to be tedious and uninteresting. Despite my efforts to persuade them to do so, they have not intervened between the two parties, neither with respect to the gold nor the Admiral's safety. They have not even been able to bring the latter to accept a form of abdication in which one could believe, nor to take in hand while there was time the question of the hostages whose fate has determined his own, as I had warned them. After having promised to intervene energetically in the case of Semyonov, all they have done is to transmit with their approval the lying assurances of this chief of a band of assassins. Here we are in the midst of enemies; the Japanese, moreover, are an uncertain quantity and Semyonov is a menace. The Czechs and others are exposed over two thousand kilometers to the assaults of the Reds, who have recently forced the Poles to capitulate. The rear guard fights under difficult conditions; there is a deficiency of locomotives and of coal. They (the White Russians) have been massacring to their heart's content around Lake Baikal, and have flung thirty-one hostages into the water, while the hordes of Semyonov continue to loot and murder. Nothing of all that seems to trouble these gentlemen. The sole matter which torments them is that I—acting, by the way, as I told them I would do—have not set myself against the instructions I received so as to risk the destruction of the Czechoslovak Army for the sake of that man who, having lost Siberia, had recommended the blowing up of the tunnels in order to bring about likewise the annihilation of that army. What is most extraordinary, is the fact that the Japanese High Commissioner seems to be astonished at not finding in me an obedience which his own mission has refused to render him. . . . Anyhow, they will know what I think. . . . When I reflect on the fate of Nicholas II and his family! They had not intrigued with the Boches, and yet they (the Allies) did not put themselves out to this extent in order to save them. The ambassadors dis-approved of the efforts that we wanted to attempt at Mogilev with a view to rescuing them. . . .

In the years that followed Janin was often accused of treachery, as were the Czechs. Janin finally wrote a book to vindicate his actions in Siberia.

No retreat in history equals in misery the sufferings of Kolchak's men and of the refugees who accompanied them. In the long fifteen hundred mile trek from the River Tobol to Lake Baikal 1,000,000 men, women, and children had per-ished. Horses fell exhausted and the occupants of sleighs froze in the arctic cold. Women holding their children in death were often robbed of their coverings and those stricken with typhus were cared for by comrades who were them-selves soon to perish. Starving men ate snow and dead horses. Fear, which increased as the Red rulers came closer, drove the multitude forward until one by one they fell exhausted.

Included among the fleeing mass were some hundreds of prisoners of war who had either joined up as soldiers as a way of escape from bondage, or had been impressed in serv-ice corps. A poignant narrative of the privations and misery of German and Austrian prisoners caught up in the retreat of Kolchak's armies has been written in Eric Dwinger's *Between Red and White.*

The spent remnants of Kolchak's battalions gradually made their way through Transbaikalia. At every station gaunt soldiers and refugees begged for bread. Men sold their arms and their clothing for a meal. The more fortunate dis-posed of furs and jewels and bought passage to cities in the Orient. Some joined up with Semyonev, others with local Bol-sheviks. High officers escaped where they could. General Lebedev fled to China, General Sakharov with British help made his way to the Maritime Province. Sakharov later wrote a book, *White Siberia* (Belaya Sibir), which was grossly un-fair to General Knox and to the British when it is remem-bered that seventy-nine shiploads of British war material had been the mainstay of Kolchak's service of supply.

Many causes had operated to bring disaster to the Kolchak régime. It had been founded upon a dictatorship which lacked the realistic outlook and the iron will necessary to rule under such conditions. Kolchak's government and the Directory which preceded it had been conceived in compromise, leaving unsatisfied the more liberal and radical elements in the population.

Kolchak completely misapprehended the mentality of Siberia. He failed to make use of the nascent desire for autonomy and to appraise a social background which was antipathetic to high-handed measures which in former days were possible in old Russia.

His officers, with such notable exceptions as Kappel, Sakharov, and Pepelayev, were by no means the best of the old army. Many regimental and divisional commanders had been sensitive regarding their positions, slack in the performance of duty, and self-serving in escaping the dangers of campaign.

The staff was over-large, and in spite of the presence of many hard-working and honorable officers it was an inefficient organization. Over nine hundred officers constituted the admiral's staff, who, in turn, had many times that number of subordinates about them.

The disorganization of the rear had been a fatal obstacle that even an aggressive front could not rectify. The total absence of any radical land legislation to win the allegiance of the peasant and civil administration capable of assuring townsmen of a just and stable government estranged the common people.

Kalmykov, Semyonov, Annenkov and Rozanov did the admiral irreparable harm by their thirst for blood and booty, while wholesale forced mobilizations conducted by such officers as General Ivanov-Rinov bred hatred and fear of the Omsk régime.

Claims were made that Kolchak's retreat was due to the failure of the Allies to furnish sufficient war material. Lloyd George in the House of Commons on November 8th denied this by saying: "We have given real proof of our sympathy for the men of Russia who have helped the Allied cause, by sending one hundred million sterling worth of material and support of every form."

The failure of the supreme ruler cannot be laid to the Czechs nor to the diminishing support of the Allies, although the occupation of the railroad by the Legionnaires slowed up the disastrous retreat, and the gradual cooling of Western enthusiasm for intervention in Russia gave notice that the Russians must depend upon local resources. The Czechs in the formative stages of Kolchak's army rendered valuable assistance, and the Allies, especially England, furnished munitions enough for a much more formidable campaign toward Moscow if a single route had been selected and the campaign pushed along a narrow front.

The decision to attack Perm had been a major strategical blunder, for even if contact could have been achieved with Ironside's forces at Archangel, although it would have looked well on a map, it would have meant little from a military standpoint, due to the state of transportation and the relative unimportance of these regions. Moscow was the important center, the one altogether appropriate objective. The failure to concentrate on a well-organized campaign on Moscow was equaled only by Kolchak's failure to attempt a union with Denikin, a point Wrangel never tired of urging upon the commander of the armed forces of South Russia as they were struggling up the Volga from the south.

Frost, disease, enormous distances, scarcity of transport, the necessity of using the creaking service of the Trans-Siberian whose operations were in the hands of many masters, and the fact that their opponents possessed the rich supply base of central European Russia, had all been against the success of Kolchak's enterprise.

The chief cause of failure was Kolchak himself. He was one of a company of not unusual men whom revolution and civil war had raised to power. At the end he manifested superb dignity in the face of disaster. But he was upheld neither by outstanding capacities nor popular support. He had neither Kornilov's power to win the affection of his men, the strength of character of Denikin, nor the *verve* of Wrangel. He was aloof from the people, with little knowledge of their needs or how to meet them. Having been trained in marine warfare he could lay no claim to excellence as a land strategist, nor did his conduct of his campaigns reveal any aptitude to take the best military advice available. Theoretically he was a Democrat, but the times demanded resolution, clarity of mind, and determination of unusual strength. The admiral was a man of honor, but possessed no adequate combination of poise, iron will, and personal qualities of leadership for the task events had conspired to lay upon him.

Chapter XIII

SIBERIA: FROM KOLCHAK'S DEATH TO THE FOUNDING OF THE FAR EASTERN REPUBLIC, APRIL 6, 1920

WITH Kolchak dead Siberia lay prostrate—a corpse for whose flesh fierce chiefs were still battling. The Red Army, merciless toward those even suspected of White sentiments, halted for a time at Lake Baikal and then moved slowly eastward never again to be repulsed. Communist ideas preceded them, taking root in disillusioned cities and villages. To advance quickly would invite attack by either Semyonov or the Japanese, or both.

The Whites, after Kolchak's execution, were in disagreement regarding their future chief. Some acknowledged Semyonov, others Kalmykov, still others the sinister Baron Ungern-Sternberg. The local population reflected every shade of political opinion from the purest white of ultramontane monarchism through deepening pinks of social democracy to the veriest scarlet.

Transbaikalia was without law or order. Uprisings and midnight frays were constantly occurring. Neighbor was turned against neighbor in the struggle to survive. Peasants, woodsmen, and town dwellers became a law unto themselves. Food was scarce and prices were rising. Typhus, typhoid, and tuberculosis were raging in the remotest villages. In confusion and despair, monstrous acts of reprisal and brigandage were committed. Criminal elements rose like a bloody froth on the boiling cauldron of politics and class animosity. Any one who could command a few rifles and a machine gun was a law unto himself.

The common people, the gray background of all conflict, awaited desolately what each day should bring forth. They had been penalized by both Red and White, and, in many instances, had suffered at the hands of foreign troops presumably sent to aid them. They knew not when a Bolshevik or Partisan rising would plunder their homes or a White liberator would carry away their last cow or the tools from their workbenches. Thousands fled to Mongolia, Manchuria, or took shipping to Asiatic ports. Those who could not escape knew they must risk death by sword, disease, or famine. In abysmal misery they waited for the armies to spend their fury.

In the Amur Province the whole fabric of the government, which had been nominally controlled by Admiral Kolchak but actually by Semyonov, had fallen to pieces on February 4th and a Revolutionary Executive Committee took charge.

Scattered through towns along the Trans-Siberian were numbers of Socialist-Revolutionaries growing more friendly to the Soviets as it became clearer that the Red Government in the end would prevail. Local Zemstvos who had suffered under Kolchak's régime were favorable to any new order that promised justice. The presence of foreign troops discouraged responsible citizens, the overwhelming majority of whom would have welcomed any decent government that gave peace and bread.

Provisional governments were set up in several towns and cities east of Lake Baikal. West of the lake the railway uninterruptedly was Red. Citizens of Blagoveshchensk, once Japanese and White Guards under Kuznetzov had discreetly retired, created a Red Government without much disturbance, except the execution after a rather sketchy trial of twenty-four Cossack officers. Towns in the Kamchatka peninsula went Communist and organized a Soviet Government. Irkutsk had long since yielded to the Communists.

When Rozanov had been driven from power in Vladivostok in January, instead of creating an entirely new administration responsible elements persuaded the accredited Zemstvo authorities to assume control under the name of the Provisional Government of the Maritime Provincial Zemstvo. Medvediev, the President, was a Socialist-Revolutionary; Nikiforov, the Prime Minister, was a Communist. Although the new government was hampered in the full exercise of authority by the presence of Allied missions and troops and the general uncertainty of their situation, they immediately set about establishing an orderly and lawful régime, to the relief of nearly all classes.

The Zemstvos, realizing the mistakes in the government which had preceded their assumption of authority, put forward an honest effort to meet the social and political needs of the population. Medvediev as presiding officer of the Zemstvos stated officially:

Russia has already spilt too much blood. As long as I am the head of this Government, no person will be deprived of life, liberty or property except by decree of our civil courts. We will no longer permit the military to decide to kill someone, and then convene a military tribunal so as to make this murder legal in the eyes of the civilized world.

I want to call your attention to the fact that we have not changed a single judge, and we do not intend to make any changes. The Chief Justice here was appointed by the Czar and has been on the bench for eighteen years, and the Zemstvo is willing to abide by the decrees of the civil court.

With singular sincerity of purpose he and his associates carried out the implications of this proclamation.

The population of the Maritime Province was now ready to take vengeance upon Ataman Kalmykov at Khabarovsk. One Bolgakov-Belsky organized a force of Partisans and marched up the valley of the Ussuri. Kalmykov feared being caught between Partisans of the Maritime Province and those of the Amur Province, and fled from Khabarovsk on February 12, 1920, after plundering the city. Three days later a Revolutionary Autonomous Administration was established at Khabarovsk.

Kalmykov made his escape into Chinese territory on February 17th and a week later arrived at Fugdin, where he surrendered his arms to the Chinese authorities and on March 8th was placed under arrest. Those of his forces that did not melt away were turned over to the Bolsheviks. After more than one attempted escape, Kalmykov was shot by his Chinese escort.

At the end of February, Japan, whose occupation of the Amur region had been particularly severe, began to evacuate her soldiers. Some were dispatched west to Transbaikalia, others were concentrated at Vladivostok.

The spearhead of the Red Army continued to advance. The repeated failures of anti-Bolshevik generals to create an ethical government and provide anything save starvation, massacres, and death, led thousands to throw in their lot with the Revolution, believing that the White cause was a forlorn hope which could not be saved.

Russians, White and Red, were not the only groups which had been suffering during the Siberian Pentecost of calamity. Alien eyes had been watching the course of events amid terrible poverty and woe—the prisoners of war, some 450,000 of them, concentrated in large and small cantonments. They had been initiated into the delusions of military conflict; they now had time to scrutinize the shibboleths of revolution and counter-revolution mouthed by numberless speakers and splattered over posters and banners in bold announcements. After the peace of Brest-Litovsk many were compelled to forage for themselves as the prison camp guard and commissariat organizations dissolved. In some cases after the Revolution the guards simply walked away, leaving the prisoners to fare as they could. Many months passed before any large number were repatriated. Allied missions did all in their power to prevent the return of prisoners until after the Armistice. White and Red leaders alike were employing the railway beyond its capacity and little attention was given the prisoners.

The pitiable condition of these unfortunate men had been made more tolerable by the efforts of various relief organizations. In some districts the camps were well equipped and

British gun on the Ural Front

Russian bath train

Siberian types

German and Austrian officer prisoners, 1,000 in a room

large liberties were allowed. Many worked upon the land, in lumber and mining villages, in shops and factories. Various Red Cross societies and the American Y. M. C. A. did work of inestimable value in organizing recreation, schools, workshops, and canteens where tea, coffee, dried fruits, sugar, condensed milk, canned foods, and tobacco could be purchased at low prices, in furnishing writing materials, libraries, postage, and in facilitating the slowly moving exchange of letters and packages. Carloads of musical instruments were utilized, some camps having orchestras composed of musicians who were famous in their home lands. Professors and teachers conducted courses in over one hundred branches of science, letters, and art. For these improvised schools the Association purchased and reprinted hundreds of thousands of texts. Theatricals, religious services, lectures, musicales, all strengthened minds strained to the breaking point in the tedium of incarceration. A record of an extraordinary enterprise of compassion toward the prisoners is covered in the Y. M. C. A.'s record of its activities, entitled *Service With Fighting Men.*

The American Red Cross under Dr. Teusler also did a notable work in furnishing clothing, medical supplies, and food to many districts. All relief organizations were in a difficult position due to the extreme partisan feeling among opposing groups of Russians. A neutral position was almost impossible to achieve, as both groups looked upon aid to the other as an inimical act.

In coöperation with relief agencies the soldiers organized shops, bakeries, tailoring establishments, and crude studios where much creditable artistic work was accomplished. In the years of waiting, every ingenious idea was exhausted by the prisoners to save themselves from the mental, physical, and spiritual deterioration inevitable where men are cut off from their culture, their work, their homes, their womenfolk, in a land growing daily more barbaric in the throes of social upheaval.

Thousands of the prisoners were shamefully exploited by

their Russian masters, who employed them in factories, for various private enterprises, and upon public works. Not only was there graft in the administration of their scanty rations, but also in the wages they received under international conventions dealing with prisoners of war. During the long retreat of Kolchak's forces some hundreds were impressed as labor troops and perished miserably on the steppes or in the forests. Neither Red nor White were concerned with the unfortunates who were of no significance in the Russian class struggle.

Only a few thousand of the prisoners of war ever took arms in Siberia and then largely in the cause of self-protection or in the hope of recouping themselves for their years of penury. The possibility of escape in a land of such distances was so slender that not infrequently friendly relations grew up between captor and captive. There were love affairs and marriages in remote corners of Siberia and upon the Turkestan steppe.

The morale of the prisoners, in general upheld by heroic efforts, perceptibly declined after the Revolution of 1917, and with the development of brigandage and civil war. When the proclamations of a new order were read in the camps the distinction between the prisoners of war and the Russians was lessened. Slowly the bureaucracy began the work of repatriation after Brest-Litovsk, although the prisoners often took matters in their own hands and went home as best they might. A few turned Red and fought with Trotsky's armies. Some thousands settled in the country where they had been so long confined. Multitudes died of starvation, typhus, malaria, or nostalgia for their own country.

Before the Armistice of November 11, 1918, in Western Europe one of the chief arguments of Allied statesmen for intervention in Siberia had been the presence of hundreds of thousands of German, Austrian, and Hungarian prisoners of war, as well as smaller bodies of Austrian and German Poles, Rumanians, and interned civilians who might be reformed in fighting units by Germany or Red Russia. This peril was in reality slight, inasmuch as relations had been strained between Germany and the new Soviet power after Brest-Litovsk and months went by before there was any sizable exchange of prisoners. The Trans-Siberian Railway was crowded with the trains of Czechs, Whites, Reds, and brigands of dubious colors which made any wholesale repatriation impossible until the Civil War should cease.

After the Armistice, the prisoners had only one wish—to return home as quickly as possible and escape the chaos of Russian civil war. From the Czech prisoners who had fought in the Austrian armies the Allies had nothing to fear, as with the exception of a few hundred who turned Communist, they either lost themselves in Russian life or joined up with the Legionnaires as laborers. Thousands of prisoners of war made their way to China and Mongolia. Many died en route, others stumbled into the coast cities of China on their slow pilgrimage to Europe. Over ten thousand perished after the Armistice from disease, starvation and exposure.

The prisoners found their way home over a period of three and a half years after the Revolution, having been absent for periods of three to seven years, thin streams from the stagnant reservoirs of humanity which had been confined hundreds of miles eastward. With faded uniforms and clothing made of meal sacks and blankets they crossed their frontiers, gaunt specters out of a land prostrate beneath the iron heel of war. Comrades led their blind by the hand, carried their cripples, buried those who had died on the way in unmarked graves by the track, or dumped them from moving trains. On reaching their homes, many who had looked out of abysmal sorrows hopefully toward the west were doomed to disappointment. Their old countries were split to pieces, their wives and children estranged by years of separation. Like Enoch Arden, hundreds came to farms and villages where another had supplanted them. Newly arisen politicians and self-seeking bureaucrats, having quickly forgotten the lessons of war, were preparing the way for another catastrophe. Selfishness, greed, and pleasure were the order of the day. Such was the tragic lot of the prisoner—a dead man who was suddenly thrust back into life!

Two pictures, poignantly drawn, of life and ideas among the prisoners of war who beheld the break-up of old Russia occur in Rodion Markovits' *Siberian Garrison* and Ferdynand Goetal's *From Day to Day*.

The Czech Legionnaires, admired by most of the foreign representatives, came to be cordially disliked by Russians, who blamed them and General Janin for handing over Admiral Kolchak to his enemies. They were unjustly accused of pilfering gold from the imperial reserve, and in many quarters hated because of their command of large sections of the railroad. Weary with fighting, incensed by misunderstandings, disgusted with White leaders, they awaited their turn to embark for Europe to carve out new careers.

When the Czechs passed Lake Baikal and entered the American and Japanese zones, they were relieved from guarding the railway lines. The evacuation began under the command of General Raše, a medical officer. First to be sent home were the wounded, the sick, and the insane. Cholera, spotted fever, dysentery, and typhus had claimed many of their number. Tuberculosis was rife. Some three hundred of the men had lost their reason. The ferocity of the Civil War in Siberia was calculated to disturb even the strongest minds. Neurasthenia and spiritualism were prevalent, and many séances held in which the spirit of Ziska was invoked for an answer to their problems!

Along with the Legionnaires were several hundred Czech and Russian wives and not a few babies. Even in war men fall in love. While in the Ukraine the soldiers were allowed to marry. Later, marriage was forbidden but the ban was finally released. Over 1,600 officers and men married during the migrations of the echelons back and forth over the railways of Russia and Siberia. Most of the marriages were solemnized by a priest, one Chadim, who accompanied the Legionnaires.

The first transport, the Italian ship *Roma,* left Vladivostok harbor on January 15, 1919, on a two months' voyage around India to Naples, where it arrived on March 11th. Allied ships conveyed the remainder of the troops during the years 1919 and 1920, some landing at Trieste and others at Marseilles. The American ship *Sheridan* sailed via the Philippines to the United States where the men were transferred across the country and sent to Europe. General Stefánik arranged through the American Red Cross for the carriage of the larger group of the troops. The steamship *Heffron* struck a submerged rock off the Japanese coast. Its contingent was quartered at Kobe and cared for by the American Y. M. C. A. while the vessel was being repaired. Seven Japanese and two Russian vessels were also used. So many were the disabled and the sick that twelve vessels sailed before the line troops could be embarked. One of the last ships to depart was the Czech vessel *Legie,* purchased by the Legionnaires' Bank in Vladivostok, a ship which was destined to be the first Czechoslovak merchant vessel. By August of 1920 nearly all the Legionnaires had been repatriated.

As Red governments crept nearer to Vladivostok all foreigners saw that intervention was a failure. The British and the French knew the time for departure had arrived. American soldiers remained near Vladivostok awaiting the order to embark. By March of 1920 little was left for the American contingent to do except to guard the railway until echelons of the Czechs and their own outlying contingents should reach Vladivostok. The last United States troops sailed on April 1, 1920, happy to leave a land where they could do little to help the general situation and gain no glory for themselves, leaving the Japanese and the Russians to settle their accounts. Among the few American representatives left were members of the Inter-Allied Technical Board of the Trans-Siberian.

Many representatives of Allied governments had acted *ultra vires* in the Siberian tangle. In extenuation and fairness it must be said that distances from home governments preoccupied with the Great War demanded personal initiative and freedom of action. No foreign group appreciated the violent nature of Russian class hatred which burned like a forest fire across the melancholy length of Siberia.

America's action in Siberia was almost wholly negative. Of all the foreign military groups the Americans retained the strictest neutrality. The bitterness with which Allied officers on the spot condemned the Americans for their stand was somewhat mollified by the results of Kolchak's policies which in the end ruined his effort. The American forces suffered throughout because of the lack of a clear explanation to foreign officers and to all sections of the Russian population as to why the United States had soldiers in Siberia. The divergent policies of the State and the War departments, and the fact that few knew the strict terms of General Graves' *Aide Memoir,* caused many to think the Americans were either pro-Red or reluctant to assume obligations which all other Allied and Associated Powers were accepting. The temptation for all parties was to take sides in the months of tantalizing waiting and guarding of the railway.

Although the American contingent did maintain a close watch on other parties, this failed to accomplish anything except perhaps to forestall the seizure of the Chinese Eastern Railway by Japan. The appointment of an able man as American High Commissioner, coördinating the efforts of all American representatives, might not only have produced a more constructive policy but might have materially aided the establishment of a stable government in Siberia. Any blame for the negative attitude of the American Expeditionary Force, whose officers and men felt keenly the futility of their presence, must be laid on President Wilson and Secretary of State Lansing rather than upon the command, the personnel of American troops, or the War Department.

During the whole Siberian episode the Americans, Czechs, Canadians, Italians, and Chinese found themselves squarely aligned in policy against England, France, and Japan. The only case in which America was forced into backing any one faction was in the early Ussuri River campaign launched before General Graves' arrival in August and September of

1918 and after July 12, 1919, when President Wilson issued an order to aid Kolchak with munitions, supplies, and food, an action which was in fact irreconcilable with the *Aide Memoir* to General Graves. This order was interpreted in the light of the State Department utterances of November 7, 1919, that "This Government does not propose to depart in any way from its principles of non-interference in Russian internal affairs." America had been willing to send war supplies, but was not willing to take the field with Kolchak against the Soviet order.

Intervention in Siberia was understandable in view of the general situation on the Western Front in the summer of 1918. Troops and war material were sent to aid the White movement as part of the grand strategy of the World War and because of the dread of Communism held by all the nations of the West. Newton D. Baker remarked in his foreword to General Graves' *America's Siberian Adventure*, regarding the action of the United States:

Detached from its world implications the Siberian adventure seems mystifying. Indeed, even General Graves himself has "never been able to come to any satisfying conclusions as to why the United States ever engaged in such intervention." But if one looks at the world situation, the explanation is adequate and simple. The world was at war. The major focus of the terrific military impact was on the Western Front, from the English Channel to the Swiss Frontier, but the shock of the conflict reached throughout the world, and in outlying places, everywhere, strange collateral adventures were had. All of these "side shows" were, in one way or another, peripheral spasms from the profound disturbance at the center of the world's nervous system. Some of them were designed to sustain Allied morale, during the stagnation of the long-drawn out stalemate on the Western Front, with the thrill of romance, as when Allenby captured Jerusalem and swept the infidel from the holy places of Palestine. Some of them were mere surgings of restrained feeling, in semi-civilized populations, due to the withdrawal of customary restraints by remote governments which were centering their efforts on the battle in Europe and had neither time nor strength to police faraway places. . . . On the Western Front the nations engaged were dominated by a single objective, but in places like Siberia both the comprehension and concentration of European opinion was absent. Siberia was like Sergeant Grischa, who had no conception of what it was all about but knew that the once orderly world was in a state of complete and baffling disorder.

This statement applies as well to the action of other nations.

The Czechs had been in danger, even though at the time of Allied intervention in force they were no longer so. Throughout, one of the main reasons for Allied intervention was the unconfessed fear of Bolshevism.

The British were thoroughly disillusioned regarding intervention in Russia. A Committee to Collect Information on Russia was appointed on the 17th of May, 1920, with the Right Honorable Lord Emmott as chairman. Its first published report in 1921 stated:

When the intervention of the Allies in Northern Russia was continued after the German danger, which evoked it, had disappeared, and Allied military assistance was given to the armies of Denikin and Kolchak in the civil war, the Soviet Government began to look upon itself as the defender of the world revolution against the attacks of capitalist countries, which attacks they regarded as unprovoked.

With regard to the effects of intervention, the abundant and almost unanimous testimony of our witnesses shows that the military intervention of the Allies in Russia assisted to give strength and cohesion to the Soviet Government, and, by so doing, achieved the opposite of what it was intended to effect.

We are informed that the military intervention of the Allies in Russia was always regarded with misgivings by the majority of non-Bolshevik Russian Socialists, notwithstanding the fact that a bitter persecution was directed against the latter by the Soviet Government. Later, when, following the military success of the anti-Bolshevik forces, the White leaders showed themselves unable to organize a Democratic Administration, their rule was undermined and finally overthrown by the very population which had welcomed them as deliverers from the Bolsheviks. Owing to these events the Soviet Government rallied to itself larger numbers of other classes. This event was accompanied by another change in the attitude of Russians towards the Allied countries. There is evidence to show that, up to the time of military intervention, the majority of the Russian intellectuals were well disposed towards the Allies, and more especially to Great Britain, but that later the attitude of the Russian people towards the Allies became characterised by indifference, distrust and antipathy.

Japan because of her Korean possessions and her special interest in all Far Eastern affairs, viewed the whole Siberian situation with anxious eyes although she had been unwilling to go west of Lake Baikal unless the expense was paid. Tokyo viewed with disfavor a possible Kolchak government of real strength and permanence. If, however, Kalmykov, Semyonov, Rozanov, or some one else could have been set up as puppet governors of an autonomous state in the Russian Far East, Japan's purposes would have been served and her interests safeguarded. To these ends she expended 900,000,-000 yen and many lives, and caused manifold sufferings in Siberia. Japan had little interest in Western Siberia or European Russia, her desire being for influence in the East which might afford outlet for manufactures and serve as a zone of protection against Communist influence.

Japan's policy was confused by intrigues between the War Office and more moderate leaders. All parties were agreed in their hatred of Bolshevism. The military were concerned to use every means to prevent the Russian Far East from becoming a unified territory. Japan's generals laid down the principle that the Red Army should be allowed to come only as far as Lake Baikal.

The idea of a buffer state east of Lake Baikal was in the air and offered a pleasing prospect of peace to both Moscow and the Far Eastern provinces. The Soviet power had difficulties enough on the economic front without assuming additional military commitments which might prove hazardous.

Lenin, presiding over the Council of People's Commissars, working day and night in the smoke-filled imperial suites, and Trotsky, poring over war maps in his peripatetic train that was continually making the rounds of different fronts, were content to bide their time and support any scheme which would deny power in the East to Japan or Semyonov or any one save the rulers in the Kremlin.

Chapter XIV

SOUTH RUSSIA: THE RETREAT OF DENIKIN; OCTOBER, 1919, TO MARCH, 1920

THE scene now shifts from the snows of Siberia to the vast steppes of South Russia. The turning point in the military fortunes of the armed forces of South Russia had come in late October of 1919. Denikin had been unable to give sufficient depth to his extended front, and by November the retreat was in full swing. The front, now twelve hundred miles long, was an imaginary line upon the commander's military maps, intermittently patrolled by half-loyal Cossacks and weary infantry, unable to resist the onslaughts of Bolshevik cavalry and machine-gun units. Hundreds were intellectually incapable of withstanding the plausible arguments of Trotsky's teachers who penetrated the White lines and desertions daily plagued nearly every regimental commander. The Volunteer Army was sharply pressed.

Having forced the Caucasian Army under General Wrangel to retreat from before Saratov to Tsaritsin, the Reds hurled their main force against Denikin's left wing along their southern front in defense of Moscow, entering the city of Orel on October 20th. To relieve pressure at this point, two Kuban cavalry divisions, followed by a division and a half more, were shifted from the right flank of the Caucasian Army under Wrangel to aid the hard-pressed Volunteers in the vicinity of Kharkov, but these reinforcements were unavailing. Harassed by General Budenny's crack cavalry units, White forces began a retreat which never ceased until they reached the Black Sea.

Red troops which had been smashing the thin front of the

White armies since the beginning of October, 1919, now threatened Kharkov. Mai-Maievsky's directing of the Volunteer Army was unsatisfactory. Many officers were clamoring for his dismissal. In some respects he was an able soldier and a hard fighter, but during the Civil War he had given way to unrestrained license and his orgies had a demoralizing effect upon officers and men. His burly, rotund figure, his pink face with the bulbous nose of a clown, his jovial spirits, and undoubted courage endeared him to his men, but they had lost confidence in him as a combat leader. Denikin was forced to consider a change of commanders.

Kuban separatism had reached such proportions that General Denikin had sent an armed force in November, and, in violation of the Constitution, surrounded the Rada meeting at Ekaterinodar and arrested twelve of its members. One of them was straightway court-martialed and hanged, on the charge of high treason. The same day General Wrangel arrived in Ekaterinodar and brought with him a new and greatly curtailed Constitution which the Rada was forced to adopt. The extent to which the local population was outraged by these actions cannot be exaggerated!

Wrangel had been in Taganrog on November 23d, whence headquarters had removed from Ekaterinodar, and was summoned by Denikin and Romanovsky to command the Volunteer Army. Two days later he left for Kharkov with General Shatilov as chief-of-staff, but that city was even then being captured by the Red Army, Wrangel's former command, the Caucasian Army, being given to General Pokrovsky, with General Siegel as chief-of-staff.

Conditions behind the Volunteer Army were in utter confusion. Retreating units were often mixed. Nearly every regiment had its own trains clogging the main line. The sick and wounded were in a pitiable state. Many hospitals and hospital trains were without doctors, nurses, or medicines. Starving, infected, and delirious patients staggered about in quest of food. The cavalry, all important in the warfare of movement, were unable to fight—their spirit was exhausted.

Broken communications and a lack of discipline rendered efficient staff work impossible. Kharkov was abandoned and the population and institutions evacuated without direction or destination. Railways and roads were inundated with a mass of humanity fleeing southward.

Incensed over the situation, Wrangel, on December 9, 1919, wrote a long dispatch to General Denikin describing the chaotic condition in which he found the army, and delivered it personally to the commander-in-chief. The dispatch condemned in harsh terms the strategy which had jeopardized the army and drew attention to his communication of April 4, 1919, wherein he advocated the shortening of a front from Tsaritsin to Ekaterinoslav, with the right flank on the Volga and the left on the Dnieper. Transport had broken down, the rear was now too vast to organize, continual advance and fighting had exhausted the troops, and most of the horses had gone lame. He stated that:

The war is becoming a means of growing rich, re-equipment has degenerated into pillage and speculation. Each unit strives to secure as much as possible for itself. What cannot be used on the spot is sent back into the interior and sold at a profit. The rolling stock belonging to the troops has taken on enormous dimensions— some regiments have two hundred carriages in their wake. A considerable number of officers are away on prolonged missions, busy selling and exchanging loot. The Army is absolutely demoralized, and it is fast becoming a collection of tradesmen and profiteers.

The troops are over-fatigued owing to incessant marches and to the bad condition of the roads; the horses utterly exhausted; the artillery and field trains are often abandoned, as the horses fall by the way.

The cavalry is in a pitiful state. The horses are unshod, and lame in consequence; many of them are like skeletons owing to lack of forage, and have sores on their withers.

The Commanders of Corps and Chiefs of Divisions report that the majority of the units have entirely lost their fighting capacity.

This is the bitter truth. The Army has ceased to exist as a fighting force.

He wrote of banquets and debauchery among the officers, the bad police and counter-espionage system, the departures of ill-paid railway workers, the subjection of an enthusiastic liberated population to the horrors of pillage, violence, or despotism. Risings were occurring in the rear of the army.

Wrangel considered it indispensable to choose one direction, to evacuate Rostov and Taganrog at once, to choose and fortify bases behind the line, to cut down the general staffs, care for the officers' families, put down drunkenness and marauding, reinforce horse and foot, organize and amalgamate the police and espionage system, and place the railways under military control.

This long and biting dispatch, imperious to the point of insubordination, could not have been pleasant reading for General Denikin. Many of the conditions save those caused by major strategical mistakes could not fairly be laid at the door of the commander-in-chief. The lack of discipline among his generals and the breakdown of morale accounted for much which was blamed upon the sober and hard-working general at Taganrog, who had assumed a task which no Russian officer could have carried to success without consistent aid from sources outside of Russia or with the loyal and coördinated support of all Russian forces in the field.

Wrangel reported to headquarters that the Reds were operating between the Don Army of General Sidorin and his own forces, seeking to drive the Volunteers to the sea. He advocated retreat to the Crimea, but Denikin insisted this would be desertion of the Cossacks and forbade it.

Cities and towns fell daily to the advancing Bolsheviks. By the end of November, Red troops had penetrated one hundred and twenty miles south of Orel and within three weeks had taken Kharkov and Odessa.

By December of 1919, Trotsky had 51,000 bayonets, 7,000 swords, and 205 guns in the Red Army opposed to Denikin, with fresh regiments training and in reserve and with the resources of Russia behind him; Wrangel had 3,600 foot, 4,700 horse, with only half the number of guns of the Soviet artillery. The Alexeyev Division which had been sent to the rear to be re-equipped and recruited to battle strength numbered only 300 bayonets. The new commander began fighting rear-guard actions with footsore infantry and Cossacks spurring spavined horses into an unequal fray. Retreating slowly, the Don and Volunteer armies converged on Rostov, with Red troops between them striking at their flanks. By the middle of December, Sidorin's and Wrangel's forces united after daily fighting throughout a march of over three hundred kilometers in the biting cold, lacking every necessity for winter operations in the field. Cities and villages of the Ukraine were daily falling into the hands of the Communists.

The wounded and the sick suffered terribly from lack of medical care. Pitiful scenes were enacted upon the evacuation of hospitals. Prisoners and soldiers would seize as many sick men as they could place upon doors, shutters, and stretchers, hurrying them to the railway where many died from lack of care and the bitter cold. Practically half of the army and the local population were contaminated with typhus. The unfortunate men who were left behind the retreating army could expect only death.

Thousands of soldiers, refugees, and local civilians who decided to stay in their towns and villages were hungry and many hundreds in a starving condition. The retreating regiments and companies supplied themselves by forced requisitions from towns and villages, while the peasants, growing more hostile, hid their food.

Officers and men ate bitter bread as they retreated over the endless steppe toward the south, harassed and outflanked by the Bolshevik forces. Deserters by the hundreds went home to their farms and families. Many officers lost all sense of responsibility for their commands. There was little order or planning in the retreat. The troops straggled slowly toward the sea, pressed by the Reds, with no adequate rear guard and no safe base upon which to retire.

General Wrangel's appointment as commander of the Volunteer Army was followed by a number of civil reforms which Denikin promulgated to liberalize the régime and win

Infantry

The backwash of war

The path of glory

American naval officer on the dock at Novorosiisk

Russian lancers

Irregulars

favor with the population. The Special Council was replaced by a Cabinet of Ministers, with General Lukomsky at the head. Due to the complete economic and social disorganization of the whole of South Russia the reform movement remained a feeble and ineffectual gesture.

Two courses were open to Denikin's forces—they could make for the Crimea or for Rostov-on-Don. Although the Crimea afforded excellent protection, movement to such a haven would destroy contact with the surviving fighting organizations among the Don, Kuban, and Tersky Cossacks. General Denikin chose Rostov and centered the retreat upon that city. In the Rostov area he hoped to reform and rest his troops, to hold the crossings of the Don and a line roughly described by the River Manych. A small portion of the army sought refuge in the Crimea.

While high officers disputed about praise and blame, the miserable remnants of corps, divisions, and regiments continued their hurried and disorderly retreat southward. Orders from the commander-in-chief were no longer carried out and the Bolsheviks met with feeble rear-guard resistance.

Transport by road and rail was clogged by a lack of schedule for movements; all groups moved when they could, by day or night. Men broke away from the columns daily, making their way across country to rescue their families and perchance carry them to safety. Thousands of refugees in every city packed their valuables in bundles and trudged toward the coast—a discouraged, desperate, savage multitude, glancing nervously back as they heard the crack of Red carbines in the outskirts of towns which were not yet abandoned. "Many Cossacks," writes Denikin in his memoirs, "threw away their arms or joined the Green bands by the regiment; utter confusion prevailed everywhere, the connection between staffs and troops was lost, and the train of the Commander of the Don Army, who was already powerless, ran the daily risk of being captured, and slowly made its way through a sea of men, horses and vehicles." During the long retreat, over 200,000 soldiers and refugees, men, women, and children, had perished from typhus and exposure. In several cases whole trains were silent, with every occupant, including the crew, slain by fever and cold.

At Rostov on December 19th General Holman, of the British Army, brought news that his government stood ready to aid the evacuation and protect the families of the military as well as the sick and wounded. It was apparent to all that an evacuation must take place sooner or later under increasing Bolshevik pressure.

The Volunteer and Don armies were united under General Sidorin and General Wrangel was sent to the Kuban and Terek to raise troops. Disgruntled when he discovered General Schkuro had been sent on the same mission and irritated over an accusation that General Shatilov had not been authorized to accompany him, Wrangel returned in wrath to the commander-in-chief—another episode in the long chapter of disagreement. Later Wrangel was sent to aid Lukomsky in converting Novorosiisk into a fortified camp.

General Schkuro, a Cossack from the Northern Caucasus, was typical of not a few adventurers who were not only difficult for any army head to manage but who created distrust and enmity among peasants and townspeople within the White lines. He began his career in South Russia with a small force of seven hundred men and soon came to command a division. "The Wolves of Schkuro," as his men were called, wore caps of wolfskin and a wolf's head was employed as their insignia upon their uniforms and equipment. His raids were bloody affairs in which pillage played no small part.

No sooner did the troops reach Rostov-on-Don than they were forced to move on. Novocherkassk was captured by the Reds and the following day Rostov was evacuated. The Caucasian Army had by then already lost Tsaritsin and was retreating south. Denikin's entire military organization was collapsing.

In an effort to gain favor for his government, the commander-in-chief began to make political concessions, yielded his right of absolute veto, gave a ministerial portfolio to the Socialist, Chaikovsky, and replaced General Lukomsky by General Bogayevsky, Don Cossack Ataman, as premier. This latter appointment was a sop to the Cossacks, who were becoming violent in their criticism of Denikin's régime. But the moment had long since passed when any change of political front could forestall the inevitable results of the policy of the commander-in-chief over a period of eighteen months.

Black news was coming from the Crimea and Southwestern Russia at this time. General Slashchov, a drug addict and a heavy drinker, in command of the Crimean troops, was suffering reverses, General Schilling had hastily evacuated Odessa and left the civil population to their fate. All discipline broke down when General Schilling's forces left Odessa; refugees slaughtered each other to reach the boats, numbers threw themselves into the water or blew out their brains. Shops and houses were looted by Reds and Whites alike. From the cellars and slums the underworld emerged, breaking open dwellings and robbing food supplies. No shipping could be found for General Bredov's forces, who made their way westward toward Rumania. This disastrous affair had raised a storm of opposition against General Schilling and made his subsequent appointment as governor of the Crimea very unpopular both with the troops and the civil population.

The problem of authority in the Crimea was acute. A Captain Orlov added to the unrest by fomenting an uprising against Denikin, causing nearly as much anxiety as if it had been a Red attack. Orlov operated in the hills with a small command of men of doubtful political colors.

An attempt was made by Schilling himself, who realized his unpopularity, to persuade Wrangel, who had arrived in the Crimea from Novorosiisk in late January of 1920, to accept the position of commander of the troops and Governor-General of the Crimea. General Lukomsky had advised Schilling that the course of wisdom was for him to talk over a special wire with Denikin, and, if possible, receive his per-

mission to turn over his post to Wrangel. Wrangel would not
consider the post and Denikin flatly refused his consent. He
anticipated the removal of the remnants of his armies into
the Crimea, and in that contingency he would himself become
Governor of the peninsula.

Denikin was burdened with grave problems. His armies
were threatened by the chameleon-hued governments of
Transcaucasia, by the pursuing Reds, by the possibility of
the Allies refusing further aid, and by the mob of discontented soldiers and officers growing more ill-natured as they
approached the crisis which awaited them at the seacoast. It
was obvious that his only course was to prepare for evacuation.

Hungry troopers, suffering from frost and wounds, discussed reasons for their failure as they whipped their spent
horses toward Rostov. Limping infantry magnified their
grievances as Red cavalry drove them forward day by day.
Officers complained sourly of what might have been, while
Denikin saw remnants of his promising armies, which once
had numbered 300,000 bayonets and sabers, return in companies where they had gone forth in regiments and divisions.

In order to appease the anger of his subordinates, officers,
and the public, General Denikin dismissed a number of high
officers, including Romanovsky, and appointed General Markov in his stead as chief-of-staff. Several high officers were
cashiered at their own request. But these actions failed to
satisfy public opinion.

As Denikin's prestige waned, owing to the *débâcle* in the
field, that of Wrangel rose. General Wrangel had consistently
opposed the official policy in matters of strategy and otherwise. As the hero of Tsaritsin, Wrangel was popular with the
troops, for again and again, sword in hand at the head of
cavalry charges, he had led them to victory where others had
failed. He was proud and impatient, a born cavalry leader
and a man of no mean strategical capacities. Gradually he
attracted a large following who openly advocated him as
Denikin's successor.

From Constantinople where Wrangel had retired he addressed a bitter letter to General Denikin:

You saw that your prestige was melting and that power was slipping from your hands. As you clung to it blindly, you began to imagine sedition and rebellion around you. . . . Poisoned by the venom of ambition, drunk with power, surrounded by low sycophants, you thought not of saving the country, but of preserving your authority. . . .

Of the troops, he said:

The Army, brought up on arbitrary rule, plunder, drunkenness, under the leadership of men who demoralized the rank and file by their example—such an Army could not recreate Russia.

Finally, about himself:

The eyes of the public began to be opened. . . . More and more loudly were acclaimed the leaders whose names remained unsullied among the general corruption. . . . Both the Army and the citizenry . . . saw in me the man capable of giving them what they longed for. . . .

While officers exchanged hot words, the wreck of the White movement in South Russia stumbled dejectedly toward the sea, too weary and too disheartened to offer more than an erratic protection to the unorganized multitude which now contained thousands of women and children.

For weeks the population at Novorosiisk had been mounting, as soldiers and their families crowded in by rail, by horse, and on foot. The military were surrounded by a sea of wounded and sick soldiers and refugees. To add to the torments of hunger, uncertainty, and disease, the famous "Borah," a terrific wind which is the curse of that coast, searched out the bodies of emaciated sufferers under their ragged uniforms and coverings. Ships in port were covered with tons of ice, some sinking under the burden. The gale swept through railway vans where soldiers and their families were shivering together, often blowing the cars from the tracks. Upon the sidewalks lay the blue, frozen bodies of the dead, with no one to bury them, usually stripped of boots and overcoats by the desperate population.

Hospitals were besieged by the sick and hungry. Despairing of medical care, soldiers stricken with typhus stayed wherever they happened to be at the onset of the disease. One colonel battled through two and a half weeks of fever crouching on the floor of a discarded telephone booth.

The full weight of the human avalanche reached Novorosiisk at the end of March, 1920. A nondescript mass of soldiers, deserters, and civilian refugees flooded the city, engulfing the terror-stricken population in a common sea of misery. Typhus reaped a dreadful harvest among the hordes crowding the port. Every one knew that only escape to the Crimea or elsewhere could save this heap of humanity from bloody vengeance when Budenny and his horsemen should take the town; but the amount of shipping available was limited. For several days people fought for a place on the transports. It was a life-and-death struggle. "Many human tragedies," writes Denikin, "were enacted on the streets of Novorosiisk in those terrible days. Much brutality came to the fore in the case of imminent danger, when naked passions drowned the voice of conscience and man was enemy to man."

On the morning of March 27th, Denikin stood on the bridge of the French war vessel, *Capitaine Saken*, lying in the harbor of Novorosiisk. About him were the vague outlines of transports which were carrying the Russian soldiery to the Crimea. He could see men and women kneeling on the quay, praying to Allied naval officers to take them aboard. Some threw themselves into the sea. The British warship, *Empress of India*, and the French cruiser, *Waldeck-Rousseau*, bombarded the roads on which Red cavalry were waiting. Amid horses, camels, wagons, and supplies cluttering the dock were his soldiers and their families with hands raised toward the ships, their voices floating over the waters to nervous commanders, who knew that once their decks were full those who remained on shore must face death or flee where they could. Some fifty thousand were embarked. During the panic and confusion, criminals slunk abroad to prey like ghouls upon the defenseless. Refugees who could not secure passage were compelled to await the grim judgment of Red columns which were already raising dust along roads into the city.

The same day on which the evacuation occurred, Novorosiisk was occupied by the Bolsheviks and hundreds of White Russians, both civil and military, paid with their lives for resistance to the sickle and hammer of the new régime.

Only the Volunteer Army, with a portion of the Don Cossacks, was evacuated from Novorosiisk. No transports were available to accommodate most of the Kuban Cossacks, some forty thousand of whom, together with half as many Don Cossacks and numerous refugees, pushed along the coast toward the frontier of Georgia, harassed by the Red cavalry.

The Volunteer troops and Don Cossacks landed at Feodosia. Denikin immediately made his way to Sebastopol, knowing that he was discredited as the leader of the White cause. Yielding to the pressure of an election by a Military Council of Superior Officers, he issued an edict which appointed Wrangel commander-in-chief of the armed forces of South Russia. Therewith he took leave of his comrades-in-arms and sailed for Constantinople.

Denikin left behind him in the Crimea a land seething with politics, a horde of bitter soldiers, and a population which at any moment might turn Red and refuse assistance to the army. Civil institutions and trade were in confusion. To many, the narrow confines of the peninsula seemed a prison house into which the Red armies might pour at any moment, for the demoralized troops could offer little resistance. Schilling's Corps held the passes to the Crimea, protecting the troops which had arrived on transports and war vessels from Novorosiisk. How long could they retain their positions, was the question on the lips of the whole military and civil population.

On arriving at the former imperial embassy in Constantinople, Denikin was prostrated by the news that his former chief-of-staff, General Romanovsky, had been assassinated by a Russian officer in another part of the building. Hatred

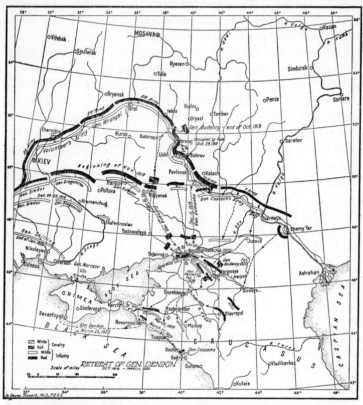

Retreat of General Denikin, October, 1919–March, 1920.

of headquarters which had accumulated among Russian officers thus found an outlet. An English guard was introduced into the Russian Embassy to protect General Denikin. From Constantinople he later sailed to England, accompanied by his family and General Kornilov's children, having played his part in the mightiest social upheaval of modern times.

During the last days of 1919 and the first quarter of 1920,

as Denikin and Romanovsky were attempting to bring order out of the bedraggled columns of the Caucasian, Don, and Volunteer armies, officers, soldiers, and civilians had vented their spleen upon the high command. Any leader who might have taken the field against the Bolsheviks would have been confronted with grave obstacles. The abdication of the Czar, for himself and his son, and the resignation of Grand Duke Nicholas as generalissimo, to which post the Czar had appointed him, left a vacuum in the thinking of every Russian soldier. The monarchical principle on which they had been reared had perished, and with it the authority and sanctity of their military oath. Enthusiasm could not be sustained by rapidly changing committees or by any self-appointed White Government.

The unorganized condition of the country in the rear of Denikin's forces had been enough in itself to spell defeat. All available men for the civil institution were steeped in the bureaucratic traditions of the old régime, a creaking device characterized by delay and not infrequently riddled by dishonesty. No civil administration in the ordinary sense had existed. One of the members of the Council thus described the situation in a memorandum quoted by Miliukov: "The new régime was being discredited by violence, flogging, plundering, drunkenness, abominable conduct of the men in authority; it was being undermined by criminals and traitors who went unpunished, by cowardly, dissolute officials who brought to the new post their old vices, the old incompetence, laziness, and self-assurance." Allowing for prejudice, this picture of the situation is not unduly derogatory, although numbers of honest and patriotic men served in the civil institutions.

The administration of justice had degenerated into abrupt trials by military tribunals, with little orderly legal procedure and few safeguards for the accused. The dictatorship of the sword and the haste with which affairs were moving had not favored long trials or nice distinctions. From the standpoint of the civilian, there was an utter absence of a strong legal government.

The finances of the White command had always been in a precarious condition. No one knew when subsidies of money, munitions, and equipment from England and France would cease. The inadequate taxgathering machinery had either failed to collect sufficient funds or developed into wholesale expropriation. Both the old Romanov rubles and the new paper money turned out by the army printing presses had steadily declined.

Politically, the high command and its bureaucracy had been neither able to gain sufficient countenance from the powers of Western Europe nor were they able to convince the population of the justice of their cause. Townsmen and especially the peasants, untrained in independent thinking, had given themselves over to an orgy of talk and failed to exercise initiative on their own part or give adequate aid to the army. In the promulgation of measures which depended for success upon the good will of the people, little consideration was shown for their feelings, a circumstance which had rendered them susceptible to the promises of Moscow. Denikin lacked the elasticity and clarity of mind which makes a statesman. His unbending use of the slogan, Russia, One and Indivisible, well enough for a rallying cry for die-hard Czarists, was a stench in the nostrils of the Ukraine, Finland, the Baltic States, the Poles, the Cossacks, and the peoples of Georgia and Azerbaijan, gratuitously offending those who might have been his allies if he had early announced a liberal policy and recognized the new states formed after Brest-Litovsk. As a result, the Transcaucasian republics gradually drifted toward a Soviet orientation, Georgia for a time having a Menshevik Government which later became Red.

The sullen attitude of populations among whom White officers had formed their base of operations often flared into treachery ⸱nd open hostility. Small wonder that a plain soldier was unable to do otherwise than exercise force when gentler means would have meant endless delay with the likelihood of failure in the end. All Denikin had tolerated by way of a legislative body, until near the very end of his service as commander-in-chief, was the so-called Special Council, which acted in an advisory capacity, since he possessed the power of absolute veto.

At heart Denikin was a liberal, but circumstances compelled him to rule occupied territories in a high-handed manner. The straits in which his troops had found themselves emphasized the blunt qualities of a soldier until in civilian eyes he seemed an autocrat. His armies had been fighting for their lives against not only the Reds but also against forces of dissension within their own ranks, and he could not regard too carefully the wishes of a public opinion that might change overnight with the winning or losing of a battle. His treatment of the Cossacks seemed to them severe. The cavalry, composed almost entirely of Don, Kuban, Terek, and Astrakhan Cossacks, were not only disturbed by political separatism but also aggravated by the custom of officering them with Czarist Russians. From the beginning the Cossacks had reciprocated the distrust of headquarters.

The agrarian question was never settled. The absence of any statesmanlike effort to deal with the matter in a land where ninety per cent of the population were tillers of the soil, lost for the White movement the sympathy of the peasant whose ear was caught by the mystical words from Moscow—Land and Freedom!

The fact that many nobles and aristocrats, scions of old governing classes, were in high positions, even though Kornilov, Alexeyev, and Denikin were men of humble birth and well known for their democratic tendencies, had given a class color to the armies which sprang up on the Don. The common people never forgot that it was Lenin who had stopped the war with Germany, nor did Red propagandists allow their memories to flag on this point.

Landowners had been allowed to take possession of estates of which the Revolution had deprived them. Gradually the conviction grew among the masses that they were being ruled by an army and a government subservient to the interests of the landowning class. Hence the Green movement sprang up, composed of peasants but augmented by individuals little better than brigands, who aspired to power in the rural districts, corresponding in raids and marauding expeditions to the Partisan movement in Siberia.

With the passage of months the moral fiber of the White troops and officers had deteriorated. They had long ceased to be volunteers moved by patriotism and self-sacrifice. Their ranks had become demoralized with conscripts, and with adventurers of every sort. Thousands of prisoners had been impressed into the service. Many fought beside the White leaders with enthusiasm, but others sabotaged the operations whenever possible. Coupled with unbridled license in many quarters were the unending quarrels, jealousies, and disputes which disrupted staffs and still breathe through the memoirs of every participant who has left a record of those bloody days when unity, obedience, and discipline were indispensable elements for success. Orgies among officers, many high in power, had been followed by drunkenness and debauchery among the men.

The civil population of small merchants, artisans, farmers, and their families had suffered alike from White and Red. Devoid of the ordinary source of supply of an army in the field, forced requisitions inevitably became pillage and robbery. Towns whose streets had been lined with cheering crowds as White soldiers liberated them from Trotsky's units soon found that the deliverers must be fed, that their constant campaigns made larger and larger demands for food, money, and every kind of material equipment.

Reprisals had led to distrust until in many operations no prisoners were taken on either side. Suspects had been shot by drumhead court-martials which were little better than outright assassinations. There was wholesale abuse of both civil and military authority. The befuddled peasant and townsman knew not which to fear most—a White friend or a Red foe!

The policy of the Allies was another cause of Denikin's defeat. He had never been able to depend upon promises made because of the shifting of interest among Western statesmen. Nevertheless, Britain had sent him 250,000 rifles, 30 tanks, 200 guns, airplanes, and several hundred English officers and noncommissioned officers as technical helpers. Some idea of British commitments to the White Russian cause may be gained from Winston Churchill's memorandum of September 15, 1919, just before the beginning of Denikin's great retreat, when he observed that up to that date Britain had expended nearly one hundred million pounds and France between thirty and forty million.

British personnel and munitions rendered immense moral and material support until public opinion at home prevented any further effective aid other than assistance in evacuation. The French never took Denikin's efforts seriously and had been less than half-hearted in any moral support from Paris, although aid to Denikin would have been the surest way of protecting their interests in Poland. France, like Britain, had followed a hesitating policy of recognizing one secessionist country after another, with no comprehensive plan in dealing with either Bolshevik Russia or with the White armies. The British, however, could maintain that if all they had sent had been wisely used Denikin might have won to Moscow and have vanquished the Bolsheviks.

Denikin and his chief-of-staff, Romanovsky, had been lacking in any outstanding gifts of strategy when the whole burden of mapping campaigns was laid upon their shoulders. Headquarters had been largely composed of infantry officers not sufficiently conversant with the problems of employing large masses of cavalry in the open warfare which characterized their campaigns. The basic military principle of massing troops for a limited and possible objective had been disregarded when they launched their all-important thrust toward Moscow.

With Kolchak and Yudenich, General Denikin shared the disastrous results of not having a unique command when a total strategy was necessary if White armies on several fronts were to overthrow Trotsky's forces, which were able to strike at one White advance and recoup their strength before falling upon another.

Humiliating and inquisitorial methods employed by Committees of Rehabilitation, and the suspicion under which officers and soldiers were held who had once willingly or unwillingly fought in the Red Army and later found themselves in the armed forces of South Russia, robbed Denikin of the services of numbers of able men.

In addition to the human causes of defeat, disease stalked unhindered across the steppes. Hundreds of thousands died of typhus, malaria, and smallpox. Surgeons were without instruments and hospitals, medical men lacked drugs and appliances. Hosts died who in a normal country could have been saved by careful attendance. Typhus was no respecter of persons. It struck down generals and slew the common soldier, it invaded hospitals and finished off the wounded, attacked villages and left them silent with their dead.

Denikin had been unable to catch the imagination of the great mass of his soldiers. Deluged with reports and memoranda, not only of field operations but foreign politics, finance, risings behind the lines, and quarrels among his officers, the commander-in-chief had seldom come in contact with his troops in action in such a way as to forge those bonds which made for *esprit de corps* and personal loyalty.

The commander-in-chief had often been over-sensitive and suspicious of those capable of giving him wise counsel. In a day of rapid changes in political complexion it was natural that a leader should show caution toward his subordinates, but a widespread feeling was abroad that the chief of the army was unduly jealous of his power and unwilling to listen with patience to the opinions of those who differed on military, economic, and political matters.

Thus the proud hopes of Kaledin, Alexeyev, and Kornilov, hopes which had been placed in the hands of General Denikin, were finally frustrated amid a welter of bloodshed, ruined cities, and despairing populations. No Russian general under the circumstances could have done much better than did he. Many could have done far worse. In spite of any blunders or weakness, Denikin was an honest man and a dogged fighter, in character and ability far above many of his associates. Perhaps his cause had been lost for him years before he had fought in it, in days and years when the Czarist régime had forfeited the loyalty of large sections among the people.

Only one other Russian soldier remained acceptable and willing to continue the war against the Bolsheviks, the newly appointed commander-in-chief, General Baron Peter Wrangel.

Chapter XV

SOUTH RUSSIA: GENERAL WRANGEL TAKES COMMAND, MARCH TO NOVEMBER, 1920

SHORTLY after General Wrangel arrived in Constantinople, upon leaving Russian territory at General Denikin's order, Admiral de Robeck, of the British Navy, showed him the dispatch the British Government had sent Denikin. Great Britain wished Wrangel to be under no illusions should he become commander-in-chief of the armed forces of South Russia.

Secret.

The British High Commissioner in Constantinople has been ordered by his Government to make the following communication to General Denikin:

The Supreme Council (of the Allies) is of the opinion that, on the whole, the prolongation of the Russian Civil War is the most disturbing factor in the present European situation. His Britannic Majesty's Government wishes to suggest to General Denikin, that, in view of the present situation, an arrangement with the Soviet Government for an amnesty for the Crimean population in general, and the Volunteer Army in particular, would be in the best interest of all concerned.

The British Government is absolutely convinced that the abandonment of this unequal struggle will be the best thing for Russia, and will therefore take upon itself the task of making this arrangement, once it has General Denikin's consent. Furthermore, it offers him and his principal supporters hospitality and a refuge in Great Britain. The British Government has, in the past, given him a large amount of assistance, and this is the only reason why he has been able to continue the struggle up to the present; therefore they feel justified in hoping that he will accept their proposal. If, however, General Denikin should feel it his duty to refuse, and to continue a manifestly hopeless struggle, the British Government will find itself obliged to renounce all responsibility for his actions, and to cease to furnish him with any help or subvention of any kind from that time on.

Constantinople,
April 2, 1920.

BRITISH HIGH COMMISSION.

This was a staggering blow to Wrangel, but he replied resolutely that even if he had doubts before, his mind was now clear and he would accept the appointment. He received a wireless message from Denikin, saying that a Military Council was to be convened at Sebastopol to elect a new head for the army, and requesting Wrangel to participate in it. Denikin had refused to appoint his successor, writing General Dragomirov on March 20th:

COMMANDER-IN-CHIEF OF THE SOUTH RUSSIAN ARMY

Feodosia.   No. 145.   March 20, 1920.

My dear Abram Mikhailovich,

For three troubled years of Russian history I have been foremost in the struggle, devoting to it all my strength, and bearing the heavy burden of power, as destiny decreed.

God has not given my troops victory. Faith in the Army's vitality and in its historic mission is still alive, but the intimate ties binding the Chief to his men are broken, and I have no longer the strength to elect a suitable man to whom I can delegate my power and my command.

Yours truly,

A. DENIKIN.

Wrangel arrived on March 22, 1920, on the British man-of-war *Emperor of India* and transferred to the cruiser, *General Kornilov.* Deciding that so large a conference would end in confusion, the officers under the presidency of General Dragomirov reduced their number into a Council of Superior Officers of Army Corps Commanders and higher officers which elected Wrangel commander-in-chief, whereupon Denikin issued an edict stating:

Lieutenant General Baron Wrangel is hereby appointed Commander-In-Chief of the Armed Forces of South Russia.

Sincere greetings to all those who have followed me loyally in the terrible struggle. God save Russia and grant victory to the Army!

In his reply to the British communication of April 2d to General Denikin, Wrangel wrote on April 4th in his official capacity as commander-in-chief:

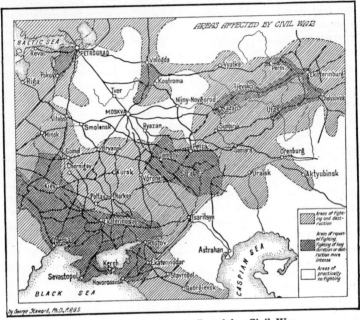

Russia in Europe. Areas affected by Civil War.

The British Government's categorical demand that we cease fighting makes it impossible for my Army to continue. I put upon the British Government the moral responsibility for the consequences of the decision they have made. I do not admit the absolute possibility of direct negotiations with the enemy; but I leave the fate of the Army, the Navy, the population of the occupied territory, and all those who have actually fought on our side, to the good offices of the British Government. I consider that those who have deprived the Armies of South Russia of their support at the most critical moment, even though these Armies have in the past shown constant loyalty to the Allied cause, are in honour bound to ensure the inviolability of every member of the armed forces, of the population in the occupied regions, of the refugees who wish to return to Russia, and of all those who have fought the Bolshevists and are now in the Soviet prisons of Russia. I have the right to ask my subordinates to sacrifice their lives for the safety of their country, but I cannot ask them to accept an amnesty from the enemy and profit by it, if they consider it dishonourable. Therefore it is absolutely necessary that the British Government should be prepared to offer a refuge outside Russia to the Commander-In-Chief and his principal colleagues, and also to all those who prefer expatriation to the clemency of the enemy. I am ready to accept the simplest living conditions for these people once they are abroad, in order to ensure that only those whose sentiments prevent them from accepting the amnesty will take advantage of the opportunity. It is understood that I give myself first place amongst the above. It is necessary that the armistice question be settled as soon as possible, so that work may be put in hand immediately by the agents of the English Command attached to my General Staff. The Crimea must not be handed over to the Soviet Command for at least two months from the time when the negotiations are completed, in order that the operations connected with the cessation of fighting, and the liquidation of the administrative, military and civil organs, may be accomplished peacefully. During this period the Allies must continue to furnish the Army and the population of the occupied region with everything that is necessary for them.

When General Wrangel took over the high command of White forces now concentrated in the Crimea, the situation appeared hopeless. He found his motley units in a state of utter collapse.

"Nearly twenty-five thousand Volunteers," he writes in his memoirs, "and ten thousand Don Cossacks, including those from behind the lines, had been sent down into the Crimea. The Cossacks had arrived without horses and without arms. Whilst they were landing they had actually thrown away most of their rifles. The regiments were absolutely demoralized. . . . The Volunteer regiments had arrived in a similar condition of complete disorganization; the cavalry had no horses, and all the units lacked transport, artillery, and machine guns. The men were in rags, and felt very bitter; for the most part they refused to obey their officers any longer."

This untoward situation did not prevent the new commander from deciding to continue the seemingly futile struggle. General Wrangel had no illusions about his chances for success, but he wished to save the honor of the army and by force of arms win better terms from the Red command in case his troops should remain on Russian soil, or more aid from France and England should they be compelled to evacuate. Wrangel had the foresight immediately to elaborate a plan of evacuation. Without delay he wrote to Prince Alexander of Serbia, asking for shelter, if he and his fellow soldiers should be forced to expatriate themselves.

Several measures were adopted to salvage at least a portion of the army and to put the civil administration of the province in order. At heart General Wrangel was a thoroughgoing conservative, but circumstances compelled him to see the mistakes of his predecessor and to put forth efforts to correct them. Associated with him was Peter Struve, who had attended the First Congress of the Russian Social Democratic Labor Party held secretly in Minsk in 1898. Struve wrote the manifesto which that meeting sent forth by secret channels throughout Russia and among the exiles abroad. In this document he said:

The Russian working class will carry on its powerful shoulders the burden of winning political freedom. This is necessary, but it is only the first step toward the realization of the great historical mission of the proletariat; the creation of a social order in which there shall be no place for the exploitation of man by man. The Russian proletariat will throw off the yoke of autocracy in order to continue with increased energy the battle against capitalism and the bourgeoisie until the complete victory of socialism.

The ways of war and revolution had thus thrown into cooperation a radical and a conservative!

Wrangel also employed A. V. Krivoshein, an intimate associate of Stolypin and an authority on agrarian matters in Russia, as an adviser. The commander-in-chief made a serious attempt to institute several democratic reforms, but often military necessity compelled him to undo with his left

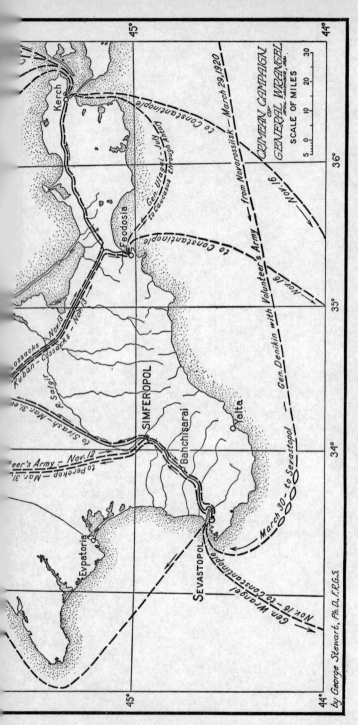

CRIMEAN CAMPAIGN OF GENERAL WRANGEL, APRIL–NOVEMBER, 1920.

by George Stewart, Ph.D., F.R.G.S.

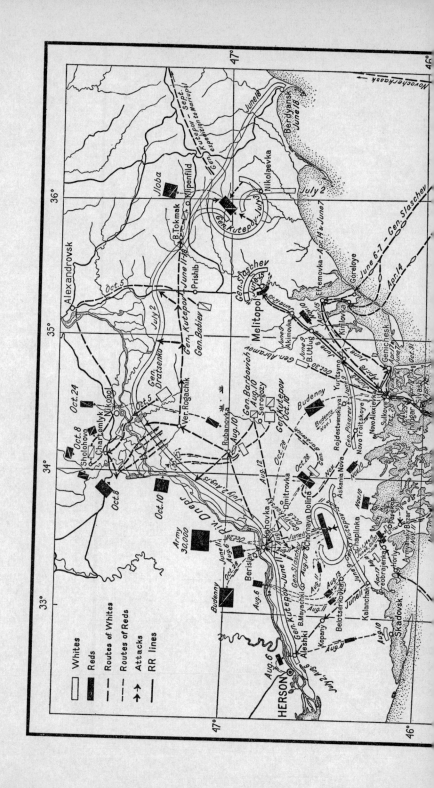

hand what he accomplished with his right. General Lukomsky represented General Wrangel before the Inter-Allied High Commission in Constantinople. In the minds of many, disturbed as they were by the more thoroughgoing revolutionary ideology of the Bolsheviks, these men, able and conscientious, were reactionaries. As before, the army behaved as in a conquered land.

A major portion of supplies was left behind in the ill-managed evacuation from Novorosiisk. Tanks, guns, planes, ammunition, and thousands of rifles had been abandoned. The artillery was without harness and the cavalry devoid of mounts. Only General Morozov's cavalry division, which had joined Slashchov's corps overland from the north, had horses. As a result, the Crimea was overrun with panic-stricken refugees constantly menaced by Green bands who roamed the hills. Demoralized by years of war and civil strife, the province was unable to feed its own population, much less the army, which with its followers numbered as many as one hundred and fifty thousand, of whom only a fraction might be considered as combatants. No fuel was available for the fleet and the railroad, and no clothing or arms with which to re-equip the army. There was a shortage of tea, sugar, tobacco, fats, bread, and clothing. It was necessary to purchase all materials from Constantinople with Allied gold which had ceased to flow into the treasury of the White armies of South Russia. The price of bread rose daily as the paper currency suffered inflation.

At the front, General Slashchov's Crimean Corps, an amalgamation of various shattered units, held the Red Army in check. With 3,000 bayonets and 2,000 swords Slashchov kept at bay the Thirteenth Soviet Army composed of 6,000 bayonets and 3,000 swords, which were being slowly but steadily reinforced.

The fleet under Admiral Gerassimov was in as serious straits as the army, with no reserves of coal or oil. Although sufficient tonnage was anchored at Feodosia, Yalta, and Sebastopol for an evacuation which was always impending, the ships were in no condition to put to sea. If the Red Army broke through, the population would be at their mercy, and of mercy there was little in either camp.

Civil institutions had almost ceased to exist. Wrangel placed upon M. V. Bernatsky, a former Minister of Finance, the task of forming a Cabinet and of organizing the apparatus of government.

The Crimea itself had little with which to support an army, and less after months of military occupation. The army had now some one hundred and fifty thousand mouths to feed, not over twenty-five thousand of whom could be counted upon as fit to take the field. They included the sick and wounded and pupils in the military schools.

As a result of their hardships and the succession of disappointments they had suffered, morale was very low both among men and officers. Pillaging, drunkenness, and frequent killings occurred in the areas where troops were located. The new commander-in-chief remarked: "Dissoluteness had also affected the Higher Command. They interfered in politics, intrigued, and mixed in undignified quarrels. The atmosphere was highly favorable to adventures of all kinds, both on a petty and a large scale."

Wrangel had few regiments which were whole-heartedly loyal. The tantalizing Cossack question remained unsettled. General Sidorin and his chief-of-staff, General Kelchevsky, developed a separatist policy. General Slashchov, who was defending the Crimea at the passes, became more and more erratic from drink and drugs. Captain Orlov's brigand commandos were making raids on unguarded towns and Red agents were landing from small vessels at night or filtering through the front. Wrangel faced an almost impossible task of taking both a civil and military population, equally demoralized, and organizing them for action, with every financial, military, and psychological factor against him.

In order to deal conclusively with Cossack separatism General Wrangel on March 29th issued a statute for the administration of territories controlled by the armed forces of

South Russia. He assumed unto himself absolute powers over all civil and military affairs. The Cossack lands were to keep their autonomy, but their troops were to be subject to Wrangel. Meanwhile, dissension was rife among the Cossack leaders. In the Kuban itself were some forty thousand troops, who retreated toward Tuapse when no transports were available for them at Novorosiisk when the wreck of General Denikin's armies put to sea. General Ulagay and General Starikov, of the Don Army Corps which had been left in the Caucasus, were having their own troubles in that area. Bitter recriminations characterized all intercourse between the Ataman of the Kuban, General Bukretov, the Rada, and the generals in the field. At Wrangel's order, Bukretov was made commander, with Generals Ulagay, Schkuro, Naumenko, and Babiev as his subordinates. But little came of the effort.

The Red army attacked in the Perekop area on March 31st and were repulsed. After bloody fighting, the Crimean passes were taken and fortified by the Whites. During the operation before Djimbuluk Station, Wrangel walked along the skirmish lines encouraging the men while Bishop Benjamin, who was with him, blessed them with his cross before General Anguladze led them in the storming of the Red positions.

So acute had the Cossack question become that due to diatribes in their press against the administration, a military tribunal under General Dragomirov sentenced General Sidorin and General Kelchevsky to hard labor, which was commuted to dismissal from the army and prohibition to wear the Russian uniform.

The political situation was becoming more and more trying. The high officers of the army awaited cables eagerly for news from England and France. What help might be forthcoming or what countenance their enterprise would receive they could not foresee.

Admiral Seymour, of the British Navy, sent a note to the commander-in-chief on April 19th:

The Admiralty begs to inform you that on Saturday, April 17th, Lord Curzon sent a telegram to M. Chicherin saying that although the Armed Forces of South Russia have been defeated, they cannot be allowed to go on to disaster, and that should M. Chicherin not reply without delay that he is at least ready to accept Lord Curzon's mediation and suspend all further offensive action in the south, His Majesty's Government will be obliged to order His Majesty's Fleet to take all necessary steps for the protection of the Crimean Army and the prevention of the invasion of their place of retreat by the Soviet forces.

On the same date, General Mangin, Chief of the French Mission, wrote to Struve who was in Paris:

As a result of our conversation of today, I have the honour to enclose an extract from the telegram from the Minister of Marine of the French Republic, which I have already sent to General Baron Wrangel:

"The French Government will act in concert with the British Government in supporting General Wrangel with material help, so that he will not be forced to make an armistice with the Soviet on their conditions, but will be in a position to make a proper treaty on behalf of his Army."

Wrangel's diplomatic representative in Constantinople, Neratov, wired on April 24th:

According to a Bolshevist radiogram, Curzon has sent an ultimatum to Moscow; an armistice is to be signed with the Volunteer Army, and if hostilities continue, he threatens intervention by the English fleet. Chicherin has agreed to begin peace negotiations immediately.

Later, on April 29th, Brigadier General Percy, Chief of the British Military Mission, sent a note stating that British efforts had failed to receive satisfactory terms from Chicherin and that "Should General Wrangel prolong the struggle, it can have only one result, and we cannot encourage it by subsidies in money or kind."

Aid denied from Western Powers was now forthcoming in the threatened outbreak of war between Soviet Russia and Poland. Although such a conflict would feed neither Wrangel's guns nor his men, it would relieve Red pressure upon his front. Also France, deeply interested in Poland, might be stirred to aid Wrangel who was in a position to divert Red forces should Poland be hard pressed. The Whites had long wished for an outbreak of hostilities between Moscow and the Poles, who hated each other not only for ancestral reasons but also because of constant frontier incidents— stealing, smuggling, and raids. Denikin's watchword, Russia, One and Indivisible, had made the Poles chary of enlisting upon any campaign the success of which might rob them of their nationality. During the whole course of 1919 diplomatic communications had passed between Warsaw and Moscow which at any time threatened to lead to a declaration of war, but the Poles held off while the Reds were defeating Denikin, whose purpose conflicted with their aspirations.

Poland deemed the hour had come to strike when, by the first of the year 1920, it had become obvious that Denikin's cause was lost. Polish troops by late January had already penetrated one hundred and eighty miles across the frontier in Red Russia, continuing to advance as far as Dvina and Berazina. Flushed with the prowess of their new state, the Poles were eager to make aggressive demands upon the Soviets. The Polish representative in Paris in early March refused to transmit to his government the demand of the Allies that Polish troops withdraw to the ethnographic frontier fixed by the Allied Supreme Council. Although the news treated the situation otherwise, Poland rather than Soviet Russia was the aggressor in the war of 1920.

The Polish-Soviet War was a complicated affair, with many cross-currents of personal jealousy, politics, and sectional feeling. This new war by an ancient foe aroused the dormant enthusiasm of thousands of soldiers and officers of the Czarist régime who had remained in the territories of the Soviet passively during the Civil War. General Brusilov accepted an invitation to the Revolutionary War Council and invited all old Russian officers to unite against the attack on Russia by the Poles. Hundreds came forward, eager at last to be of use. General Petlura, who had traded Galicia, which contained 4,000,000 Ukrainians, for recognition of the Ukraine, lent his sword to Poland. The Polish forces advancing toward Kiev contained many thousand Ukrainian soldiers.

On April 25th the advance began. By rapid strides the Polish Army pressed toward Kiev, capturing the city early in May.

Lenin made capital of the Russo-Polish conflict, proclaiming it a war against the imperialism of the White Poles, urging their overthrow and the erection of a Polish Soviet Republic.

The problem of deploying a Red army on the Polish border was a grave one. Soviet transportation was disorganized and was brought into a semblance of order only by militarization of the railway employees. A Red counter-attack was begun on May 14th which forced the Poles, who were overextended along the whole line, to give way.

The sudden collapse of the Polish Army was in large measure due to the attitude of the Polish troops in Kiev and the Ukraine. While Ukrainians had welcomed the advance against the Bolsheviks, a sudden reversal of feeling occurred when Poland was in occupation of Western Ukraine. Instead of developing cordial relations with the people, the Polish military treated the territory as a conquered land and insulted Ukrainian national pride. Large masses of the population who had greeted the Poles and their countryman, General Petlura, as saviors from the Reds, now turned against Petlura's new allies. The rapid retreat of the Polish forces was as much due to Ukrainian hostility as to the Red Army. Thousands of Ukrainian soldiers who had been fighting under General Petlura and Polish officers deserted. Budenny and his Red cavalry followed the fleeing army into Galicia until Petlura's troops stopped them before Lublin.

In consequence of the collapse of the right wing of the Polish Army the left wing in White Russia was compelled to retreat rapidly toward Warsaw. The advance of Pilsudski's forces to Kiev was in large part due to Ukrainian troops and retreat was largely due to Polish lack of moderation and the bad behavior of the troops of General Haller and General Shepicky. The Ukrainian regiments serving under Poland were interned and disarmed. General Petlura was obliged to leave the country and took up his abode in France.

The Red Army continued to advance in two columns, one in the south in the direction of Lvov commanded by Budenny, and the other in an encircling movement north of Warsaw headed by Tukhachevsky.

France became nervous for her protégé, Poland, and conveyed to Maklakov, who had been appointed as ambassador to France by Kerensky and was still recognized by France as the Russian envoy in Paris, its sympathy toward Wrangel's plan of defending the Taurida north of the Crimean passes, the only territory from which he could hope to obtain food and horses.

General Wrangel searched the horizon for more effectives. He not only needed, but also felt responsible for, the Kuban troops, which had been compelled to retreat along the coast toward Georgia when Novorosiisk was evacuated. These Cossacks were now feeling severe pressure from the Bolsheviks who had occupied Sochi. General Morozov, their commander, and some of the Rada were opening negotiations with the Red command with the knowledge and consent of the Ataman, General Bukretov. Wrangel, with the assistance of the British Navy, sent shipping to the port of Adler to embark all who refused to deal with the Bolsheviks. Because of the shallow water only small boats could be used for the purpose, all horses, guns, and machine guns being left behind. As the Don Cossacks had been embarked first at Novorosiisk, the Kuban Cossacks were now first to be taken aboard and were landed at Feodosia on April 21st. Bukretov resigned, and several of the Rada, including the president, went to Georgia.

The commander-in-chief immediately regrouped the reinforcements into his existing units. The Kuban troops with

the Terek and Astrakhan Brigade were put under General
Babiev at Eupatoria, one of the ablest cavalry generals in
the Civil War. He had received nineteen wounds, was devoid
of all fear, an excellent horseman, and possessed outstanding
qualities for leadership among the Cossacks. The Don Army
Corps was placed under General Abramov, a resourceful and
courageous general, a severe disciplinarian and incorruptibly
honest.

In an effort to disentangle their future from the mistakes
of "Volunteerism" in the past, the troops were renamed the
Russian Army, in an edict of April 28th. "Of the two armies
fighting in Russia," Wrangel wrote, "the right to the name
'The Russian Army' belonged to the one composed of the
men who had been loyal to the national flag, sacrificing
everything for the welfare and honor of their country."

The army was suffering because of a lack of more seasoned
soldiers and officers. In an effort to draw such men to his
colors, Wrangel took a more liberal policy with those of
differing views and toward those who had been forced to
fight with the Bolsheviks, or who had been advocates of
Georgian or Ukrainian independence, than did Denikin. He
complained bitterly of the policy of his former chief. "This
insane and cruel policy provoked a reaction, alienated those
who had been ready to become our allies, and turned into
enemies those who had sought our friendship. We had not
brought peace with us, but the cruel sword of vengeance.
An incredible number of officers who had welcomed us as
their liberators came under our command only to fall a
prey to our suspicions and to languish under interminable
inquiries. The same relationship had been established with
the civil population in the recently occupied territories." By
an edict dated April 29th, Wrangel freed all officers and men
who came over from the Red Army from every service disability and issued an appeal to the officers of the Bolsheviks
which was distributed from planes.

Wrangel, who saw realistically that he was engaged in a
warfare of ideas regarding social and economic life as well

as a warfare of sword and bayonet, now made an attempt to gain the allegiance of the peasants by a more liberal land policy and civil administration. He had hopes that news of this measure might arouse restive peasants in Soviet territory and be more effective in winning victory for the White cause than any force he could place in the field, but it is doubtful whether many beyond the confines of his front heard much of the new laws. An Agrarian Reform Commission under the presidency of Senator Glinka was set up at Yalta, which worked with an Agrarian Reform Commission in Simferopol aiming to give the peasants security and ownership of the land and thus wrest from the Reds their most attractive doctrine for enlisting the peasant under their banner. In a Prikaze issued by Wrangel's government in May, land settlements were placed under direct local administrations which became known as Agrarian Soviets who gave hereditary titles, breaking up large estates upon a graduated system of time payments. Local men were to deal with the local problems. Had such an organization and policy been set up eighteen months previously it might have done much to pacify the rear of the White armies and enlist the support of the tillers of the soil. Such action might also have reassured Western statesmen who never ceased to suspect counter-revolutionary leaders of monarchistic and reactionary purposes. The peasants became favorably disposed and in six months ninety of the one hundred and seven districts under occupation had made use of this new device for the division of land.

The time now seemed ripe for an offensive to wrest Northern Taurida from the Reds. Wrangel had 40,000 men in fighting trim, well armed, possessing 10 tanks and 22 planes. He now mobilized the classes of 1900 and 1901. Opposed to them was the Thirteenth Soviet Army under a former Lettish staff colonel, Pauka. While the English were urging the cessation of hostilities and some sort of peace or armistice with Moscow, the French, anxious for their ally, Poland, were sympathizing with Wrangel who held many Red troops on the Crimean front. A proposal was made to form a Russian force which should coöperate on the right flank of the Polish and Ukrainian troops, but events moved so quickly nothing came of it.

By May 25th the Red command had 15,000 foot and 4,000 horse opposed to the White forces, with the daily possibility of large reinforcements. Wrangel had at the moment a slight superiority in numbers and regrouped his troops into four army corps under Generals Koutepov, Slashchov, Pissarev, and Abramov, with 25,000 men and horse and the assistance of the fleet.

In a series of bloody battles, with the cavalry performing prodigies of valor, between the 25th and 30th of May, Wrangel captured 8,000 prisoners, 30 guns, 2 armored cars, and hundreds of machine guns, with ammunition, supplies, and horses in great quantities from the Thirteenth Soviet Army. By June 4th Northern Taurida was freed and food was assured for some time to the anxious population of the Crimea. Meanwhile, the Reds were winning a series of battles against the Poles.

Great Britain urged that Wrangel should maintain a purely defensive operation at the Isthmus of Perekop and warned him on June 2d that if he should go beyond and attack the Bolsheviks His Majesty's Government would be unable to concern itself further with the fate of his army.

In his reply to the British ultimatum, Wrangel pointed out that in order to feed his troops it was necessary for him to occupy the rich agricultural area of Taurida Province just north of the isthmus. He was confronted with a dilemma: should he abide by the British ultimatum and remain on the peninsula, facing annihilation for want of both food and remounts, or should he cross the isthmus and obtain food and reinforcements in the Taurida region, at the price of British support? He chose the latter course.

A series of sanguinary battles now occurred in the Taurida. Between June 15th and 23d the Russian Army had penetrated Bolshevik territory as far north as Orekhov and Alexandrovsk, taking 11,000 prisoners, 60 big guns, 300 machine guns, 3,000 horses, 2 armored cars, and huge booty, wiping out Zhoba's famous cavalry force.

Weary officers and men were cheered when on July 7th France offered *de facto* recognition of Wrangel's government upon the following terms: Recognition of the old Russian debt which should pertain to that part of Russia occupied by the White armies; recognition of the division of land among the peasants which took place during the Revolution; confirmation of the peasants in their ownership, and a promise to call a popular assembly elected on a democratic basis at the first suitable moment. Wrangel immediately made a request for *de facto* recognition on these stipulations.

This diplomatic triumph was offset by news of Polish victories in the north. Soviet forces had advanced in two columns. Due to personal animosity between Trotsky and Stalin, who was the War Commissariat's representative with the southern force, there had been little coördination of effort. On July 10th the Poles had wired Paris for Allied help, and General Weygand had been immediately dispatched as head of a French military mission. Warsaw had been so near capitulation that a Provisional Revolutionary Committee of Poland was organized on July 31st to administer the territory when it should come into Red hands with Dzerzhinsky in the chair. The roads were choked with refugees fleeing toward Prussia as they had been in the days of the great German advance eastward in 1914.

Wrangel, knowing that sooner or later Red troops which had been employed against the Poles would be loosed upon him, pressed his attack in Northern Taurida, a movement which compelled the Red command to shift troops from the Polish front against him.

Then occurred what is known in Polish annals as the Miracle of the Vistula—the catastrophic defeat of Red forces aligned against Poland. Several causes contributed to the Red defeat; the poor state of the service of supply, the improvisation of many of their regiments, the distance from

their base, lack of reserves, the desperation of the Poles, the
élan of their commander, Pilsudski, the insubordination of
the Red general, Tukhachevsky, who led his army westward
toward Lvov instead of obeying the first principles of
strategy by joining with Budenny in encircling Warsaw, and
the presence of an unassuming French general, Weygand,
whose advice and personal influence turned an imminent
débâcle into a ringing victory. The Poles attacked before the
Red columns could join and rolled them back into White
Russia as far as Minsk, capturing thousands of prisoners,
rifles, munitions, wagons, and artillery. Some of the Red
soldiers in the northern units fled over the frontier into East
Prussia and were there interned.

In these summer weeks General Wrangel cast an apprais-
ing eye along the Black Sea coast for a more hospitable
place d'armes. The Crimea was a prison house. A raid on
the Kuban had been conceived as a possible means of assuring a food supply and forming a less hazardous base for
the army. The overcrowded Crimea was short of everything
and the Taurida front was menaced by growing Red forces.
It was now possible for Moscow to send between 250,000 and
300,000 troops. Fighting was continuous throughout July
and although White troops captured more than 5,000 prisoners, 30 big guns, over 150 machine guns, 4 armored trains,
and large dumps of ammunition, their victories were deci-
mating the threadbare battalions. The constant warfare of
movement resulted in hand-to-hand fighting, with enormous
losses in killed and wounded. The eyes of both officers and
men turned eastward to the fertile Kuban. Maybe once again
they could clear it of Bolsheviks, secure a base, and press
northward!

General Ulagay, in charge of the expedition, embarked
4,500 foot and horse, 25 big guns, armored cars, 30 machine
guns, and 8 planes at Feodosia and Kerch on July 29th and
made for a landing near the village of Primorsko-Akhlar-
skaya with the plan of advancing rapidly on Ekaterinodar.
Ulagay allowed refugees and the soldiers' families to go with

them, the total number, including troops, being 16,000 men and 4,500 horses. The refugees proved a fatal hindrance from the outset, holding up the rapid movement of the forces and worrying officers and soldiers who were compelled to leave them near the coast, within striking distance of the Red Army.

Ulagay, after repulsing the Bolsheviks and having several victories to the credit of his squadron, became dismayed at the Red strength and indecisively fumbled the whole expedition. Overloaded with refugees and an enormous and unorganized staff, he encountered the enemy on the road to Ekaterinodar and wired for ships to evacuate his forces which were embarked at Atchuiev on August 17th. Although the expedition was a failure, in spite of heavy losses in killed among men and horses, the troops came back with their number increased by several thousand soldiers who had joined up in the Kuban, and hundreds of remounts.

France made good her hope of acknowledgment by giving *de facto* recognition to Wrangel's government on August 12th, at the moment when the tide was turning and she need no longer have feared for the existence of Poland. The Poles during August, strengthened by the presence of General Weygand and French staff officers, were disastrously defeating Trotsky's armies, who had penetrated to within sight of Warsaw. Nearly a quarter of a million Bolsheviks were captured by the Poles or interned in Germany. Wrangel's command waited nervously lest an early peace should release the remaining Red armies against him, knowing that France would probably cease to give material assistance once her ally was safe. During September the Russian Army was able to hold the Taurida through a series of bitter fights which cost heavy losses to both sides.

Taking advantage of the Polish victory, Wrangel, in late September and October, carried out an operation across the Dnieper against concentration of the Red Army at Kahovka. After a favorable development against the Soviet Second Cavalry Army, supported by regiments from the Sixth and

Thirteenth Soviet armies, Wrangel's troops captured several thousand prisoners, much ammunition and material, and inflicted heavy losses. But General Babiev was killed, and Naumenko, who succeeded him, badly wounded. The cavalry lost heart. General Dratzenko, commander of Wrangel's Second Army, maneuvered badly and the whole expedition came to naught.

On the same day as this disaster, October 12th, the expected treaty of peace between Poland and Soviet Russia was concluded. Sorrows were coming not singly but in battalions! Wrangel knew then that he must look to his ships, for no force he could muster could hope to hold out against the Red avalanche which would soon sweep southward.

Trotsky now began moving his best troops toward the Crimea. Even the brigand Makhno, who had fought alike against Red and White, enlisted for the final *coup de grâce* to the White armies of Russia. Wrangel, searching feverishly for aid, had sent an emissary to Makhno whom that worthy promptly shot. The Ukraine had been made a desert, but there was still rich booty in the peninsula.

Trotsky was ready by October 15th and his troops attacked all along the Tauridian front, crossing the Dnieper, striking at the flanks of separated forces, penetrating between armies. Budenny's cavalry harassed the lines day and night. For a few desperate hours Red horsemen cut off retreat to the isthmus, but it was recovered in time to save the army. Trotsky had three and a half times the effectives of Wrangel, with unlimited supplies. Harassed by their opponents, the White troops suffered severely from unseasonable frost; hundreds stumbled forward with frozen feet, their bodies padded with straw and moss beneath their ragged shirts. Both Abramov's and Kutepov's forces were fighting within the passes by October 20th, with nearly half their forces dead on the frozen steppe now occupied by the Red armies. By November 2d they had taken up fortified positions and entrenched themselves across the isthmus. The Reds had won back the Taurida and captured immense

General Budenny

General Wrangel

The last stand

Mongol chieftains at Chita

Transport in Siberia

Siberian peasant woman and children

booty. Only one order could now be given—evacuation into exile!

The commander-in-chief called together representatives of the various Allied Missions on October 28th: Count de Martel, the French High Commissioner; Admiral McCully, of the American Navy; Colonel Walsh, of the British Army, and Major Takahashi, of the Japanese Army. In consequence, Admiral Dumesnil, of the French Navy, promised to render all assistance under the agreement that the Russian mercantile marine and warships should be held by France as security for the expense involved.

Wrangel gave the orders for embarkation, when the troops should disengage themselves from Trotsky's armies. The First and Second Army Corps should make for Eupatoria and Sebastopol, General Barbovitch's cavalry should embark at Yalta, General Fostikov's Kubanians at Feodosia, the Don, Terek, and Astrakhan Cossacks at Kerch. He issued the following order to the population:

ORDER FROM THE REGENT OF SOUTH RUSSIA AND THE
COMMANDER-IN-CHIEF OF THE RUSSIAN ARMY

Sebastopol,
October 29, 1920.

People of Russia! Alone in its struggle against the oppressor, the Russian Army has been maintaining an unequal contest in its defence of the last strip of Russian territory on which law and truth hold sway.

Conscious of my responsibility, I have tried to anticipate every possible contingency from the very beginning.

I now order the evacuation and embarkation at the Crimean ports of those who are following the Russian Army on its road to Calvary; that is to say, the families of the soldiers, the officials of the civil administration and their families, and any one else who would be in danger if they fell into the hands of the enemy.

The Army will cover the embarkation, knowing that the necessary ships for its own evacuation are ready and waiting in the ports according to a pre-arranged plan. I have done everything that human strength can do to fulfil my duty to the Army and the population.

We cannot foretell our future fate.

We have no other territory than the Crimea. We have no

money. Frankly, as always, I warn you of what awaits you. May God grant us strength and wisdom to endure this period of Russian misery, and to survive it.

GENERAL WRANGEL.

Breaking away from their adversaries, the ragged regiments made for the designated ports. The embarkation was begun on October 31st and by November 3d all the troops and such of the civilian population as feared reprisals were on board.

General Wrangel on the *General Kornilov* received a wireless message from the French flagship, *Waldeck-Rousseau*:

TO GENERAL WRANGEL FROM ADMIRAL DUMESNIL

For the last seven months the officers and soldiers of the South Russian Army under your command have given a splendid display of gallantry. They have fought an enemy ten times more numerous than themselves, and have striven to free Russia from shameful tyranny. The struggle was too unequal, and you have been compelled to leave your country. I realize the anguish this step has cost you. But you must find some satisfaction in the knowledge that the evacuation has been conducted in an exemplary manner. The French Fleet, which has given you its whole-hearted support, rejoices to see the evacuation so brilliantly terminated. Your struggle has not been in vain; the population of South Russia will soon begin to compare your just and beneficent rule with the vile government of the Soviets. Thus you will be instrumental in awakening and regenerating your country. I most sincerely hope that this awakening may come about as soon as possible. The Admiral, the officers, and the sailors of the French Fleet do reverence to General Wrangel and pay homage to his valour.

On the 14th and 15th of November a hapless armada of one hundred and twenty-six ships of all sorts, ranging from passenger steamers, transports, men-of-war, and destroyers, to one tiny lightship, steamed out of Sebastopol, Feodosia, and Kerch. They bore 145,693 persons, of which 30,000 were women, 7,000 were children, and 100,000 were soldiers of all the services of the Russian Army. With what agony of spirit did many strain their eyes for the last gleam of lights over the slate-colored waters!

The Red Government was now in undisputed possession of

the territories of the old empire save Poland, Eastern Siberia, small sections of the Caucasus, and the Baltic States.

The Bolsheviks also had their travail and anguish. Ruined cities, demolished by shellfire, conflagration, and wilful destruction, lay across the path of the campaigns. Railroads with thousands of carriages and locomotives hopelessly out of repair, once the arteries of Russian trade, were capable only of the feeblest traffic. Industry had decreased to a small percentage of previous production, inflation had wiped out all savings and security values, the early crude experiments of Communism had reduced trade to a fifteenth-century level, hunger everywhere, a hunger which was to increase until the apocalyptical famine of 1921-1922. Hospitals were stripped of equipment and medicine, leaving the door open to malaria and typhus which claimed multitudes throughout the land. The dead moldered in a thousand wheatfields across the steppe from Rumania to Astrakhan, from the Baltic to Vladivostok, or rotted unburied under the winter sky. Orphans and widows mourned in every village of Russia. The wounded crowded the public buildings of every city, the *mutilées* and sick starved and begged upon the streets. The land was exhausted. There had been stout hearts, valor, and sacrifice on both sides, along with pillage, rapine, and wholesale butcheries which would have made Tamerlane turn pale. Along with the criminal element that raises its head in every revolution, a mighty host saw in the new government the hope of a better day. Thousands fought in the ranks of the Red armies from compulsion or fear, many more thousands from a sincere desire to defend the Revolution. Weak from bloodletting, the Reds were now to work out their own salvation within the smoking ruins of the Russian Empire, amid the almost universal hatred and suspicion of the West.

Chapter XVI

SIBERIA: THE RISE OF THE FAR EASTERN
REPUBLIC, MARCH TO JULY, 1920

AFTER the defeat of Kolchak the project of a buffer state was an intriguing idea to Moscow, to Tokyo, and to large numbers of responsible citizens east of Lake Baikal. The Soviets controlled the land west of Lake Baikal, but were unable to press on rapidly to the Pacific. Lenin's policy had been to allow autonomous governments friendly to the Soviet to spring up and then gradually to attach them with iron bands to the central Soviet Government.

The Russian Far East had suffered heavily from the absence of leaders of outstanding caliber and moral force. The White commanders of the region were by no means the best of the old Imperial Army, although their forces contained numbers of officers who had spilt their blood in loyalty to their country. No person in the Civil War suffered more heavily than the officer of moderate opinion, for in the fierceness of the strife there was no one to whom he could lend his saber. To many such officers the prospect of peace and security from Whites, Reds, and the Japanese was particularly pleasing.

Representatives of foreign Powers had not only been working for their national interests but were also at variance with each other. Many had lacked political and military capacities which the situation demanded. Foreign intervention was characterized by opportunism and disunity. Only the Red leaders had a clear-cut idea of campaign, a unified command, and a ruthless will to win.

In the battle of slogans and ideas the Bolsheviks had

378

proved themselves psychologically superior, not only to foreign representatives but also to every White leader. They possessed a sure sense of the weak places in the ideology of the Whites, and a gift for employing winged words. Above all else they possessed a flexibility in understanding and adapting themselves to situations they were, at the moment, powerless to correct. Therefore, when the idea arose of a new liberal state in the Far East, which they hoped eventually to control, they gave it a hospitable reception.

The conception and erection of the Far Eastern Republic was the result of the energy of one man, Alexander Krasnoshchekov whose real name was Tobelson. He was a man of humble Jewish parents, born on December 19, 1880, in the province of Kiev. At school he was the pupil of Uritsky and from that moment was connected with the revolutionaries. As a boy of eighteen he was arrested and sent to prison for six months; at the expiration of his term he was exiled to Nikolayevsk on the eastern seacoast of Siberia, where he renewed his revolutionary activity under the leadership of Leon Trotsky. His brother was hanged in the troublous days of 1905. Once more he was arrested and imprisoned, and soon after his release he left for America, where he remained until 1917. After working at the trades of tailor and paper hanger, he entered the University of Chicago, from which institution he received his B.A. in 1912. Shortly afterward he graduated in law, the "bread strike" prosecutions of 1913 brought him many clients. During this period he conducted a labor school in which he taught revolutionary doctrine. Krasnoshchekov also took part in the organization of the Industrial Workers of the World, though he does not appear ever to have been a member of it.

Immediately after receipt of the news of the Revolution, Krasnoshchekov joined the crowd of exiles that were returning to Russia. Early in August, 1917, he landed at Vladivostok almost penniless. By a curious accident he was named Menshevik member of the City Council of Nikolsk-Ussuriski, although he had never concealed his Bolshevik sympathies. In October, 1917, he became Vice President of the first Workers' Conference held in the Far East, and drafted the first by-laws for the labor unions there. At that moment the Bolshevik Revolution broke out.

Immediately Krasnoshchekov began to work for the victory of Communism in Siberia. He was instrumental in summoning a meeting of the Soviets of the Far East to meet at Khabarovsk, December 11, 1917. The Zemstvos summoned a rival convention, with Krasnoshchekov elected a delegate to both. At Khabarovsk, Krasnoshchekov attempted to reconcile the Reds and the Zemstvos. Suddenly confronted with the danger of opposition from Japan and her Russian troops, he urged the Zemstvos to arrest the commander of the Russians and join with the Soviets in a coalition. The Zemstvos representatives did arrest the commander but refused to share their power with the Soviets, whereupon Krasnoshchekov effected the dissolution of the Zemstvo Convention. This act led to immediate action on the part of Japan, one of her warships appearing in Vladivostok harbor on December 30, 1917.

For a period Bolshevism had flourished along the Amur. Krasnoshchekov was elected president of an association of Soviets, known as the Far Eastern Council of People's Commissars. A clash had occurred with the Japanese in March of 1918, but by May even Vladivostok had joined the Soviet confederation. It was at this time that the Allies decided to intervene.

Once Allied troops had landed, in the summer of 1918, Krasnoshchekov had recognized that resistance was useless. He and his staff had gone up the Zeya River to the hills on the approach of the Japanese, who searched for them in vain. Through a workman, Krasnoshchekov had obtained a passport which enabled him to set up as a merchant at Nerchinsk, where he joined the Chamber of Commerce. Disguised as a merchant, he traveled and spread revolutionary propaganda. In May, 1919, he had been arrested at Samara as a Bolshevik spy. He had escaped from his escort, but was rearrested on the less dangerous charge of being a vaga-bond and was imprisoned at Irkutsk in September. Mean-while Kolchak's power was crumbling, and on December 28, 1919, Krasnoshchekov was among several political pris-oners who were released, enabling him to continue his ef-forts for the Red power.

Krasnoshchekov's experience on the Amur in the first days of Allied intervention had convinced him that the Allies would not tolerate a Communist State in Eastern Siberia; moreover, he had come to believe that conditions in Eastern Siberia were not suitable for Communism. The solution was a democratic buffer state, but it was necessary to have the agreement of Soviet authorities, now victorious west of Lake Baikal, if this plan were not to be treated as counter-revolu-tionary. A mission led by Krasnoshchekov had been sent to the Soviet general staff then at Omsk to outline a plan of action. The Soviet Army was to halt at the River Oka, two hundred and fifty versts west of Irkutsk, and Krasnoshche-kov was to organize the remainder of Siberia into a demo-cratic buffer state between Soviet Russia and Japan. The boundaries of the new state and Russia were to be the Oka River from the Mongolian border to the Angara River, down the Angara to the Yenesei, and down the Yenesei to the Arctic. The Soviet general staff convinced, the approval of Moscow was promptly secured over long-distance telephone!

At the moment, Kolchak's broken armies were fleeing and the Supreme Ruler was a captive. Krasnoshchekov had left Omsk as the accredited representative of Soviet Russia. The Reds gave him full power to put into execution his plan of a buffer state. By the time he reached Krasnoyarsk he learned that the Bolsheviks in Irkutsk had decided to over-throw the government of the Political Center.

Irkutsk flatly declared for Bolshevism. But Krasnosh-chekov refused to forsake his idea. In March of 1920 he left Irkutsk in a prison car, the only available accommodation at that time on the railroad, with six Mensheviks and Socialist-Revolutionaries as coworkers, looking for a town in which to found a state. They arrived at Verkhneudinsk on the Selenga River on March 7th, at the very moment bands of Partisans were driving out Semyonov's soldiers. The Japanese garrison received Krasnoshchekov, who at once began organizing his government. The Partisans who had captured the town were naturally piqued at Krasnoshchekov's coming to govern it, but after two days of heated argument he convinced them that the establishment of his projected buffer state was to their advantage and the Temporary Local Self-Government of the Baikal Region was organized on March 9th. Krasnoshchekov did not become a member of the government but remained as "the ambassador of Soviet Russia at the court of the Baikal Region."

All parties saw in Japan a possible obstacle to their hopes. A note was sent to Tokyo by the Provisional Government of the Maritime Provincial Zemstvo on March 2d, demanding the withdrawal of all Japanese troops, pointing out that since the Czechs were departing in good order the last excuse for remaining was gone. The note openly declared that any further intervention by Japan could be regarded only as a violation of the sovereign rights of Russia in the Far East.

As the Japanese still maintained that the evacuation of the Czechs necessitated their present or even an augmented force in the Far East, the local government requested the Czech representative to state in writing whether the Legionnaires considered Japanese troops necessary to their safe evacuation. To this query, Dr. Vaclav Girsa, Czech plenipotentiary, immediately replied in the negative.

Japan's excuse for intervention henceforth scarcely ranked as a pretext. Her policy was dictated purely by fear of Bolshevik power on the Pacific and an eagerness to protect or further Japanese commercial interests. Although official protest was made against alleged atrocities committed by Japanese troops, no notice was taken of such memoranda save for a statement implying that Japan would withdraw when she chose.

In addition to the problem of Japanese intervention, the

movement for a Far Eastern Republic was faced with the remnants of several White armies. Although General Rozanov was overthrown by the time the republic came into existence, Ataman Kalmykov was at Khabarovsk and Ataman Semyonov at Chita. Semyonov's hold over the junction of the Amur and the Chinese Eastern railways divided the Far Eastern Republic into the Baikal Region and the Amur Province. Some twenty-five thousand to thirty thousand Partisans were collecting for an attack on Chita, beginning their advance on April 20th. They arrived within four miles of the city, when the Japanese were ordered out, shielding Semyonov from a vengeance he so richly deserved, compelling the anti-Semyonov forces to retreat to Mogzon.

Japan alone prevented Transbaikalia from following the lead of Vladivostok and the Pri-Baikal provinces in revolting. Her arms, used to save Semyonov from the fate of Kalmykov and Rozanov, were now employed as a threat to Red troops not to advance farther east at the end of March. The Japanese command ordered withdrawal of Bolshevik units from Gyrshelun to Khilok forthwith.

The Far Eastern Republic was formally established on April 6, 1920, due to the activities of Krasnoshchekov, by the Verkhneudinsk authorities. The territories included were Transbaikalia, Amur, the Maritime Province, the north half of Sakhalin, Kamchatka, and the right of way of the Chinese Eastern Railway. It proclaimed "a democratic Government, representing the will of the whole people, as expressed through its duly elected representatives, and guaranteeing to all classes of society the democratic liberties which are the safeguards of peaceful development of social forces," and stated that representatives of all political parties and nationalities, residing in the territory of the republic, would participate in the Provisional Government. It looked forward to the early convocation of a General Constituent Assembly "for the purpose of laying down the fundamental law and framing the Constitution of the Far Eastern Republic." An appeal was made to officers and soldiers of the armies of Kol-

384 THE WHITE ARMIES OF RUSSIA

chak and to Semyonov to lay down their arms, and to the
nations of the world for assistance in peaceful reconstruction. The democratic basis and the representative character
of the Far Eastern Republic were emphasized and property
was guaranteed security.

Emissaries were sent from Verkhneudinsk to persuade
the people of Vladivostok to join the Far Eastern Republic.
Jealousy quickly arose between the two cities as to which
should be the capital. Nevertheless, on the eve of the departure of the last transport with American troops, it was
obvious that the common people of the Far East were bent
upon peace and unity.

A shooting incident occurred in Vladivostok early in April
which further diminished confidence in the Japanese. On the
night of the 4th-5th of April, with the last of the Americans
three days away on the high seas, citizens were awakened by
the sound of firing and in the morning found all public buildings flying the Japanese flag. Russian guards had been disarmed, some thirty persons killed, and many injured. General Oi published a proclamation stating that while Japanese
plenipotentiaries had been negotiating with the Russian
authorities regarding a peaceful settlement of the question
of the stay of Japanese troops in the district, Russian troops
had attacked their quarters. In self-protection the Japanese
had demanded the disarming of Russian military units. They
neglected to mention that the day before the outbreak the
Japanese had posted notices in railway stations and had
mailed to Russian garrisons a demand that they surrender
their arms immediately.

The Russian version of this affair was issued by those
members of the Provisional Government who were fortunate
enough to find asylum with the Czech general staff. These
members made a statement to the Inter-Allied Diplomatic
Conference and a protest to the diplomatic representative
of Japan, claiming that the Japanese attack was unprovoked,
begging the Conference to propose to the Japanese command
that their imprisoned colleagues be released, government

buildings be evacuated, an apology be tendered, and their arms restored to the Russian detachments. No attention was paid to those protests.

Disturbances at Nikolsk-Ussuriski, Spasskoe, Iman, Okeanska, and Sedanka occurred simultaneously with the trouble at Vladivostok. Khabarovsk was bombarded on the same date, April 5th, suffering heavily from shell and machine-gun fire. Atrocities of every nature flared up. Japanese troops opened fire on the market place in broad daylight and slew many men, women, and children. A Japanese naval craft had bombarded Vladivostok. Government buildings and the edifice of the Board of the Zemstvo of the Maritime Province were seriously damaged. All who wore Russian uniforms were suspect and scores hunted down without mercy. Hundreds were imprisoned.

The coincidence of the Japanese attack on the Russians at Vladivostok with a series of attacks on Russians elsewhere on the same date, along with the general policy of Japan in Siberia, adds weight to the Russian version of the incident. In all Russian quarters there was a settled conviction that the Japanese command had determined to prevent the unification of Eastern Siberia, an opinion widely shared by Allied officers on the spot.

A desultory warfare again broke out along the Amur. Japanese forces sent west from Khabarovsk met with a stout resistance. Finding themselves unable to crush the continuous uprisings, the Japanese entered into conversations looking toward peace.

The Russians were too weak to resist Japanese aggression. An armistice was signed at Vladivostok on April 29, 1920, by which it was agreed that both sides were to cease fighting. Russian troops were to move thirty kilometers from Vladivostok and Khabarovsk and to maintain only a small force of militia along the railway. Russian troops so withdrawn were not to be sent to Transbaikalia, Semyonov's preserve, nor to Sakhalin, the Naboth's vineyard that Japan coveted, and a Russian-Japanese Conciliation Committee was to be established. All these provisions were to be temporary. This agreement, viewed realistically, put the Maritime Province entirely in the hands of Japan. Nevertheless, forays broke out daily near Khabarovsk and in Transbaikalia, where Semyonov was operating.

The actions of Japan had so disturbed the operation of the Chinese Eastern Railway that the Inter-Allied Technical Board, which was responsible for its operation, issued a sharp protest. The Japanese diplomatic representative at Vladivostok, anxious to distribute the odium, declared on April 28th that Japan was acting in conjunction with the other Allies. The American Consul published his government's reply on May 12th, categorically denying any new arrangement whatsoever since the Inter-Allied Railway Agreement of March, 1919.

As a result of Japan's action, liberal elements in Vladivostok became chary of committing themselves to a government having its seat at Verkhneudinsk. Citizens feared that a misstep in Russo-Japanese relations in Verkhneudinsk would have to be paid for in the Maritime Province. Conservative elements even went so far as to suggest a compromise with Semyonov and advocated a scheme whereby the Maritime Province should be in complete control of its own relations with Tokyo.

Krasnoshchekov almost despaired of the life of his offspring, when suddenly help arrived from an unexpected quarter. Japan had no wish to drive the Far Eastern Republic into the hands of Soviet Russia; she hoped rather to make the new government her tool, or at least to play the jealousy of one group against that of the other.

Suddenly, on May 11th, General Oi issued a declaration in which he bestowed a somewhat qualified blessing on the Far Eastern Republic, provided it did not turn Red. He suggested the formation of a neutral zone and prophesied the ultimate evacuation of the Japanese. An immediate armistice was drawn up relating to hostilities near Khabarovsk, and Japanese advances along the Amur Railway were halted.

The revolutionary government at Khabarovsk immediately gave its allegiance to the Far Eastern Republic.

Relying upon General Oi's statement, a preliminary conference was called at Gongotta Station on the Transbaikal Railway between Chita and Verkhneudinsk, composed of representatives of Japan and the Far Eastern Republic. Little came of this meeting, due to the refusal of Japan to allow free communication between Transbaikal, the Amur, and the Maritime Province, and because of the open preparations which were being carried on by Japan to foster reactionary attacks against Khabarovsk.

The Japanese did not, however, cease to fear the political situation in the Russian Far East nor to plot against the infant republic. They were assisted in their designs by the Nikolayevsk massacre, an incident which played into the hands of the Japanese and was useful in silencing public opinion abroad.

Nikolayevsk had been occupied by two companies of Japanese infantry—about six hundred and forty in number —as early as September, 1918. Exactly upon what pretext Japan justified the presence of her troops in this northern town, which was many miles from Manchuria, is hard to surmise. Some three thousand Partisans, led by a young Triapitzin who was half patriot and more than half brigand, attacked Nikolayevsk with its composite garrison of Russian White Guards and Japanese. The Partisans met with initial success and proceeded to besiege the town for a month. The first two men Triapitzin sent forward under white flags to treat for the surrender of the town were tortured and slain by the Japanese and White Guards. Upon a threat by the Partisans to bombard the town with long-range guns from the fortress, the Japanese consented to negotiate an agreement to cease supporting the White Guards and to retire to quarters in the town assigned to them. The Partisans entered the town on February 29th, to whom the White Guards surrendered their arms.

By a surprise attack in the early morning on March 12th,

the Japanese suddenly surrounded the headquarters of Triapitzin's Partisans and put it to the torch. The astonished
Partisans rallied and—as they heavily outnumbered the
Japanese—regained control of the situation. Three days
later the remaining Japanese detachment numbering one
hundred and thirty men were taken prisoner.

Triapitzin informed the Chinese Consul on May 22d that
he intended to burn the town rather than let it fall into the
hands of the Japanese relief force which was advancing from
Alexandrovsk. The Chinese Consul protested this proposed
act of vandalism, which would render four thousand Chinese
homeless, and inquired after the fate of the Japanese prisoners in jail. Triapitzin gave the Chinese residents three
days in which to leave and promised to return his prisoners
to Japan. Nikolayevsk was evacuated on May 25th and two
days later burned to the ground, the Japanese prisoners, one
hundred and thirty in all (not six hundred and forty, as the
Japanese declared), having been massacred to the last man!

Japanese relief forces arrived in Nikolayevsk on June 3d.
This unfortunate incident was widely utilized in the press
to arouse public opinion favorable to the military in Siberia,
as powerful elements in Japan were growing restive at the
continued and expensive stay of Japanese troops. On June
24th a great public ceremony was held in Tokyo in memory
of the dead. No effort was made in any quarter of Japanese
opinion to distinguish between Partisans and the troops of
the Provisional Government of the Far Eastern Republic,
though the forces of that government captured Triapitzin
and his bloodthirsty chief-of-staff at Kherby and tried and
executed them with twenty-two companions on July 25th.

The Japanese Government on July 3d published a declaration to the effect that, in view of the massacre at Nikolayevsk and the unsettled state of affairs, they would occupy
such parts of Sakhalin as they thought necessary, and that
Vladivostok and the city of Khabarovsk, an important point
on the way to the Sakhalin district, would be under their protection.

The Russian half of the Island of Sakhalin was occupied on July 4th, the Nikolayevsk massacre having provided Japan with an ample excuse. Meanwhile, Tokyo had been negotiating an agreement with the government at Verkhneudinsk.

Japan's policy, dictated by apprehension and confused by indecisiveness of an embarrassed Cabinet in Toyko, encouraged alternately the government of Vladivostok and Verkhneudinsk. It was evident from the commencement of negotiations with the Far Eastern Republic that Japanese delegates would oppose all proposals tending to union of the Siberian provinces. They refused to include the Transbaikal front between the Reds and Semyonov in the terms of the armistice, and denied a permit for the passage of delegates from Verkhneudinsk through Chita to the Amur region, upholding Semyonov as the authority in Transbaikalia.

The Amur region which had accepted the Verkhneudinsk Government on May 25th was separated from it by Semyonov's lair at Chita—a consequence both foreseen and desired by Japan. Both at Blagoveshchensk and at Khabarovsk Japan assisted reactionary elements, threatening military action if the Amur region would not treat with Semyonov as an equal. As soon as it was apparent that the people of Amur Province were determined to support no reactionary, Japan prepared to enforce her wishes at the point of the bayonet.

The Russian people believed that the government least in the power of Japan would be best for them and in this case it was the government at Verkhneudinsk. A conference in the Maritime Province passed a resolution in June in favor of union with Verkhneudinsk, and the Japanese, despite strenuous efforts, were unable to shake this resolution.

Following this episode, Japan stirred up dissension by insisting that Semyonov be treated as the lawful authority in Transbaikalia. Both the Verkhneudinsk and the Amur governments balked at negotiating with this brigand of whose heavy boot they had recent and painful remembrance.

The local Maritime Government at Vladivostok, however, agreed to receive a delegation from Semyonov and proposed that he call a National Assembly at Chita and surrender to it his civil and military power. This Semyonov declined to do and negotiations broke down.

Washington was becoming anxious regarding the continuation of Japanese troops in Siberia and early in July dispatched a note stating plainly that while the United States Government reserved, for lack of information, its opinion on the Vladivostok affair, yet it entirely failed to understand the reason for Japanese occupation of Sakhalin, which, since it is not on the mainland, had no connection with the Nikolayevsk massacre.

All parties were longing for peace. A second conference was held at Gongotta, which terminated on July 15, 1920, with an armistice arranged by General Takayanagi acting for Japan and Shatov for the republic, giving definite limits of operation to Japan and the Far Eastern Republic, with a neutral zone whose civil government was left in the hands of the Far Eastern Republic. The term of this agreement was to expire on the completion of the work of the Conference of Representatives of the population of the Russian Far East. An interesting note to the treaty read: "Troops under the command of Semyonov recognize this treaty which is guaranteed by the representatives of the Japanese Expeditionary Army in the territory of the Far East."

Both delegations agreed that an independent buffer state was the best means of securing peace, that this state should be in close friendship with Japan, and that it should be democratic but not communist. The Japanese delegation declared that at the conclusion of the work of the Conference of Representatives their military command would cease direct relations with local authorities; moreover, it promised to aid in summoning the conference and in hastening the evacuation of Transbaikalia. The Russian delegation, for its part, declared that the armies of Soviet Russia would not trespass on the territory of the government of the Far

Eastern Republic, nor even be allowed to pass through it. Moreover, it promised safety to Japanese citizens in the territory of the Far Eastern Republic.

The Japanese, true to their announcement, began the evacuation of Transbaikalia in July, an action which filled Semyonov with visions of firing squads and reprisals, for he was entirely dependent upon their support. In his anxiety he wrote the Japanese Crown Prince, entreating him "to insist . . . before his mighty parent, His Imperial Majesty, on the cessation of the evacuation of the troops from Transbaikalia, at least for four months." But the Japanese flatly denied the Ataman's request. They were growing weary of their *enfant terrible*.

A subsidiary but not unimportant cause for the more favorable position of the Far Eastern Republic was the temporary success of Soviet armies in Poland. In the beginning of the year the Poles had made such an effective onslaught as to raise the hopes of those who the previous year had expected Kolchak to march on Moscow. By the beginning of August the Poles were for the time being decisively defeated and the Japanese military command calculated that Red Army battalions would soon be moving over the Trans-Siberian to assist the Far Eastern Republic if need should arise. Although Poland eventually won this war, with the aid of French officers, the threat from Red troops in Siberia was very real at the time.

Japan was finding the Far Eastern Republic a difficult nut to crack. She was spending millions of yen, losing troops, incurring displeasure at home, and succeeding in gaining no real advantage to either her government or her people. The republic had united the Russian Far East and had refused to make terms with Semyonov. The United States had frankly expressed its opposition to Japan's policy, and the Allies were unwilling or unable to give Japan their support.

The hands of the Red Army were now freed by the treaty of peace with Poland, and Moscow was eager to send her soldiers along the Trans-Siberian.

Chapter XVII

SIBERIA: THE RUSSIAN FAR EAST GOES RED!
JULY, 1920, TO OCTOBER, 1922

THE agreement concluded at Gongotta on July 15, 1920, between the Far Eastern Republic and Japanese representatives relative to ending hostilities in Western Transbaikalia and the Amur Province meant peace. But war-weary muzhiks and townsmen, disillusioned with the assurance of Red and White Russians and the fair promises of foreigners, wondered whether peace was possible in a land where bloodshed had become habitual.

Three major tasks lay before the Far Eastern Republic all of which demanded immediate attention. The new government was compelled to achieve a *modus vivendi* with Moscow, to organize an army and civil institutions within its territory, and to deal conclusively with Japan and various chieftains who were under her control. Now, as in all other periods of the Civil War, politics, social and economic theory played as large a part in the campaign as did man and horse in the field.

The new republic came to terms immediately with Soviet Russia. A boundary treaty was signed by Karakhan on behalf of Soviet Russia, and by Krasnoshchekov for the Far Eastern Republic, which was approved by the government of the latter on January 24, 1921. Roughly, the territories east of the Selenga and the Yenisei rivers, including the Transbaikal, Amur, and the Maritime Provinces, with some of the adjacent districts and all the islands of the Okhotsk Sea south of the cape, including the Russian half of Sakhalin, were assigned to the Far Eastern Republic.

Officials now addressed themselves to the second task, consolidating their rule over the lands east of Lake Baikal and organizing their military and civil establishments. It had been agreed at Gongotta that a Conference of Representatives from the provinces in the Russian Far East should meet at Verkhneudinsk. Finally, in September, 1920, the Conference met, after a delay due to interception by Semyonov of delegates from the Maritime Province.

Semyonov caused the delay in hope that he might be appointed commander-in-chief of the new government. Although Japan used pressure to secure the inclusion of the Ataman in the newly formed government, his hopes were vain. A full agreement was reached by the Conference regarding the bases of unity and the formation of a single democratic authority. The Japanese Information Bureau accused the Verkhneudinsk Government of bad faith and of provoking disagreement among local Russian governments, an accusation which failed to prejudice the success of the Conference.

Another significant event in this period of calm was Japan's declaration of September 18, 1920, that in view of the settlement of the political situation in the Khabarovsk district, her troops would be withdrawn. The statement concluded with an expressed desire that the Russian Far East achieve unity.

With the withdrawal of Japanese soldiers from Transbaikalia, Semyonov's position became untenable. He retired from Chita, but finding that the forces of the Far Eastern Republic did not advance, he sent General Verzhbitsky to reoccupy the town. Verzhbitsky gathered a large force about him and tried to arrange terms with the Far Eastern Republic and with the "National Assembly," Semyonov's improvised and belated concession to the forms of democratic government, but external events moved faster than Verzhbitsky's negotiations. Taking matters into their own hands, Partisans seized Sretensk and then turned their attention to the Borzia-Dauria sector, east of Chita. The Partisans, forming an auxiliary force to the official troops of the Far Eastern Republic, invested Chita, and Semyonov departed in haste by air. His troops had the harder task of cutting their way out on foot. On the night of October 20th-21st Partisans occupied Chita and the same week the Far Eastern Republic transferred its seat from Verkhneudinsk to that city. Revolutionary troops took the station of Dauria on November 18th and the last vestige of Semyonov's power in Transbaikalia disappeared. The Ataman's final order of the day before leaving his army stated:

The Japanese military command guarantees to the Far Eastern (Semyonov's) army the transfer to the Maritime Province, but at the present time Colonel Isome does not have at his disposal a sufficient number of armed forces to cover our retreat. Therefore, in order to create a precedent of international character, and to give the Japanese command a reason to decidedly advance its troops, and to close the frontier to the Reds, after removing the Chinese who stand in the way, it is necessary, if the situation on the front will force us to do so, to penetrate as far as possible into alien territory without paying any attention to the Chinese troops on the border.

The remnants of his followers, after their defeat at Dauria, took refuge in Manchuria, faring as best they could. Their chief was taken by the Japanese to Vladivostok and later sent to Port Arthur. He remained there for several weeks before again emerging on the Siberian stage. His men were soon afterward transferred across the Chinese-Eastern to Grodekov and other points along the Ussuri Railway.

Chita was selected as the place for the final Unity Conference of the representatives of the provinces. The Conference, which met on October 29th, had the one purpose of establishing unity among the several provinces, after which it was to call a Constituent Assembly. A Declaration proclaiming the union of all territories of the Russian Far East in terms similar to the declaration of independence made at Verkhneudinsk on April 6th was issued, and on November 1st a further Declaration stated:

Be it known to all provincial authorities, civil and military government organizations, to detachments of Partisans and to all citizens of the Far East:

1. By the will of the entire people, expressed at the Chita Conference of the representatives of the United Provinces of the Far East in the declaration of October 29, the territory from Lake Baikal to the Pacific Ocean is declared the independent Far Eastern Republic.

2. According to the declaration of October 29 and the unanimous decision of the Conference on October 30, all the civil and military power is vested in the Provisional Directory of the Government of the Far Eastern Republic until the formation of a definite Directory.

3. Beginning November 1, 1920, the Provisional Directory takes upon itself all governmental power, by reason of which circumstances all the governments existing on the territory of the Far Eastern Republic lose their governmental functions and become organs of provincial administration.

4. All the regular armed forces are placed under the authority of the Supreme Command of the Republic of the Far East.

5. All the armed forces, such as partisan bands, remnants of the armies of Kolchak, Semyonov, and Kappel, no matter in what section of the Republic they are found, are requested immediately and unconditionally either to put themselves at the disposal of the Supreme Command or to surrender their arms.

The document was signed by President Krasnoshchekov and members of the Provisional Directory.

The same manifesto named Citizen Eiche, a Lett by birth and a Communist by conviction, supreme commander of the armed forces of the republic. His chief-of-staff, however, was an ex-Czarist officer with no political affiliations, one of a number of White Guard officers to whom on two occasions the Far Eastern Republic solemnly guaranteed safety if they should surrender their arms. Some of Semyonov's men accepted the amnesty, but the major part put their trust in Japanese support and elected to follow their leader.

Another solemn declaration was issued by the Conference on November 9th. It reiterated the demands of the republic as to territory, claimed the rights of the former Russian Empire to the Chinese Eastern Railway, promised to establish a democratic form of government, ordered the submission of all armed forces to the Central Government, offered an amnesty to the White Guards, promised to convoke a Constituent Assembly, and elected a government to last until the Constituent Assembly should meet. Chita was selected as the capital.

The position of the delegates from the Maritime Province was not without embarrassment, for a false step on their part might plunge the provincial authorities into new difficulties with the Japanese. However, their doubts were set at rest, and on November 12th the Maritime Zemstvo Board ratified the action of their delegates and decided "to consider its sovereign authority in the Far Eastern Republic as terminated, and from this date to commence the performance of its direct duties in the capacity of the Provincial Zemstvo Administration," thus acknowledging the sovereignty of the Far Eastern Republic.

The hesitation of delegates from Vladivostok was not unwarranted. The Japanese Information Bureau circulated rumors discrediting the work of the Conference which, however, failed in their object. General Takayanagi warned the Vladivostok People's Assembly of the dangers of unconditional ratification of the action of their delegates in recognizing the Far Eastern Republic. General Oi summoned members of the same Assembly to meet him and handed them a declaration containing the following remarks:

As the political situation in this territory has become serious, in connection with the Conference in Chita dealing with the unity of the country, I wish to point out to you that I have repeatedly announced that in order to prevent undesirable conflicts and to preserve peace and order in the country, a Communist administration will not be allowed in those regions in which Japanese troops are stationed. But judging from what is here going on under the influence of the Chita Unity Conference, the situation is rather serious; I am afraid that in the regions in which Japanese troops are stationed, peace and order may be disturbed.

The Vladivostok administration was not, however, to be

intimidated and ratified the action of its delegates at Chita.

The Chairman of the Japanese Section of the Russo-Japanese Adjustment Commission addressed to the Chita Government a long letter on December 2d in which he inquired whether the recognition of the Far Eastern Republic by the Maritime Province involved any change of attitude to Japan; also, whether the Far Eastern Republic was based on democratic principles to the exclusion of Monarchism and Communism alike, whether it was fully independent of Soviet Russia in its foreign policy, and whether it would admit the principle of the "open door" and the free investment of capital by foreigners.

The Maritime Provincial Government replied that its attitude toward Japan was not altered by recognition of the Far Eastern Republic; that its political system was based on democratic representative parliamentary institutions; that "the new state created in the Far East is conceived by our Government as entertaining treaty relations with Soviet Russia, excluding, however, the putting into effect of Communism in political and economic matters, and presupposing that the policy conducted will be along the lines of a bourgeois-capitalist system"; that the Far Eastern Republic was strictly independent of Soviet Russia; that the principle of the "open door" and free investment of foreign capital was guaranteed; and that the government did not permit the possibility of changing the fundamental principles of its program.

The date for the convocation of the Constituent Assembly was set at a meeting on December 12, 1920, as the 25th of January, 1921, and the election of delegates was to take place on January 9th, thus completing the work of the Unity Conference at Chita.

Elections to the Constituent Assembly were completed by January 20, 1921, and there seems little reason to doubt that all had an opportunity to exercise their right to vote without hindrance. Even reactionaries took part and elected two White Guard generals, Verzhbitsky and Molchanov. These two delegates, however, deemed it prudent to abstain from appearing at the Assembly. Protagonists of the Far Eastern Republic affirmed that the percentage of voters was nowhere lower than sixty per cent and in some localities ranged as high as eighty per cent. The members returned for Vladivostok were twelve Communists, one Socialist-Revolutionary, one Menshevik, one Progressive Democrat, seven National Democrats, and one Democrat.

At the preliminary session, three hundred and fifty-one members were present who elected a presidium of thirteen. This presidium, headed by Shilov, had as its other members six peasants, three Communists, two Socialist-Revolutionaries, and one Buriat Mongol.

Proponents of the Far Eastern Republic were distressed by rumors circulated in Vladivostok in January of 1921 to the effect that the consular body entrusted the defense of foreign interests to Japan. On January 28th the newspapers published a stout denial from the American consul:

> The Government of the United States of America has not applied to any other Government with the request to collaborate with its representatives or the local authorities for the defence of the life and the property of American citizens in Siberia, and has not counted upon such protection. The Government of the United States is also unaware of the fact that any other Government has made such a request or counted upon such help, or would like to commit to any Government whatsoever the protection of the interests of other nationalities or to accept the task of protecting the personal safety or the property of any other nationalities in Siberia.

The United States had learned a lesson not to be repeated.

The Constituent Assembly held its first meeting on February 12, 1921. Proceedings began with the singing of the Internationale, after which Krasnoshchekov made 'a speech in which he insisted upon the independence of the Far Eastern Republic and the desire of that government to entertain good relations with Russia.

Shortly after the opening of the Assembly a new Japanese

mission arrived under Major Miké, the old having left
Chita hurriedly when Semyonov was expelled. Major Miké
must have noticed with regret that all parties, except a mere
handful of reactionaries, were heartily opposed to Japanese
intervention. After statements by political parties, the Assembly settled down to frame a Constitution, the principles
of which are set forth in a Declaration of the Constituent
Assembly published in April. These principles included
democratic parliamentary government and the recognition
of the right of private ownership, except in the natural
resources of land and water, and a guarantee for the rights
of national minorities.

This Declaration was followed by appeals to the Great
Powers, rehearsing current objections to intervention and
claiming recognition. Since Japan was then preparing to
make a last assault with the help of several White officers
of high rank, these appeals were not without significance as
propaganda, as they played cleverly upon differences between Japan and the United States. The Constituent Assembly adjourned on April 26, 1921, at a moment when
enemies of the new republic were preparing their last effort against its life.

Was the Far Eastern Republic a Bolshevik state? Most
of the men in power were Communists, but the form of the
institution created was democratic and not after the pat-
tern of Soviet Russia. The sympathies of most of the high
officials of the government were indubitably with Moscow,
but it was not convenient to proclaim them too openly.

The republic had now achieved a workable relationship
to Moscow, and had molded her territories into a passable
political unity. She was forced to stake everything in her
third task—achieving a satisfactory solution with Japan and
the White generals who still threatened the peace of the
Russian Far East.

In the spring of 1921 Japan once more backed White
Guard officers in an ambitious enterprise. Three separate
columns were to participate. A plan was formulated in

June whereby Baron Ungern-Sternberg was to march from Mongolia, whither he had fled before the fall of Chita, to seize Troitskasavsk, Verkhneudinsk, and Chita. This advance was a daring conception, for the baron's resources, at least in men, were limited, but if success should attend his effort, the Far Eastern Republic and Soviet Russia would be effectively severed and the republic open to an attack in the rear. General Sychev was to advance from his base on the Chinese side of the Amur, cross the river, and capture Blagoveshchensk. Semyonov was to attack from Grodekov in the Maritime Province toward Iman and Khabarovsk. Until the convocation of a People's Assembly, the full civil authority was vested in Semyonov.

The Japanese appear to have promised the Whites abundant munitions and supplies, and to guard the port and fortress of Vladivostok, as well as to control the lines of the Ussuri and the Chinese Eastern Railway, until order should be established.

Chita under Semyonov's administration had formed an effective barrier separating the Baikal region from the Amur and Maritime provinces. The Japanese now resolved to use Semyonov to form a new barrier at Grodekov for the purpose of dividing the Maritime from the Amur Province, while other White Russians were located at Nikolsk-Ussuriski to separate the Maritime Province from Manchuria and access to the Chinese Eastern Railway. It was the nearly unanimous opinion of Russian moderates and foreign observers that the accomplishments of the three White generals, if successful, were intended to be but the skeleton of a new state dominated by Japan. Krasnoshchekov, in the name of the republic, protested to Japan against her continued support of the White Russians, but received no satisfaction.

At this juncture a Russian officer named Tirbakh, a former adjutant of Kolchak, came from Paris to Shanghai to arrange on behalf of the French authorities for the transfer of the remnants of Wrangel's shattered army to the Far

East. To this the Japanese readily assented. Negotiations with Semyonov were begun at Port Arthur but came to nothing.

Baron Ungern-Sternberg's command was a mixed crowd of Mongoloids and White Russians. Ungern-Sternberg was a Baltic baron of incredible ferocity. He was of average height, a rather weak-looking individual, with yellow hair and a long, reddish Cossack mustache. As a boy he left school and joined the Russian infantry, fighting against the Japanese at Port Arthur, receiving many wounds and special mention in dispatches. At the close of the Russo-Japanese War, his relatives placed him in a military school where he barely passed his officer's examinations. Unconventional and careless in his habits, he left the formality of the regular army and joined up with a Cossack regiment in Siberia, eating with his men and sleeping with them on the floor. There during a debauch he received a saber blow on the head which accounts for much of his later eccentricity. At one period in his career he made a year's trip on horseback alone from Vladivostok to Harbin. Upon the outbreak of hostilities between the Mongolians and Chinese he became chief of cavalry for the whole Mongolian Army. In the World War he served as a sub-lieutenant in a Nerchinsk regiment of Siberian Cossacks under General Wrangel, receiving many wounds and being decorated with the Cross of St. George for valor. He had not the slightest rudiments of common decency or military discipline. His appearance, behavior, flights of temper, and licentious habits had made him a marked man among the officers with whom he served. Only his reckless courage prevented his being cashiered by various commanding officers under whom he had served in the Imperial armies.

When Ungern-Sternberg entered a café other occupants retired, for he was an expert with his gun. In his drinking bouts he slew many of his own officers. The baron is alleged to have seen a pretty Jewess and offered a thousand gold rubles for her head; the head was brought and paid for. The medical service in his army was primitive—on the outbreak of typhus he ordered all those who fell ill to be shot.

On the collapse of Semyonov's power at Chita in the autumn of 1920, Ungern-Sternberg, accompanied by Japanese officers and a handful of troops, set out boldly for Mongolia—in the opposite direction to that taken by Semyonov. While in this region he married a Mongolian princess.

Geographically, Mongolia is a barrier between Siberia and China proper, and contiguous to Manchuria. After the Russo-Japanese War and the consequent frustration of Russian hopes in Manchuria, Russia had turned her attention to Mongolia. According to the terms of the Russo-Mongolian-Chinese agreement of 1915, outer Mongolia owned suzerainty to China, but for all internal purposes was autonomous. The collapse of Russia and the distractions of China encouraged Japan to push forward her sphere of influence from Manchuria to Mongolia. Such a policy was as dangerous to Red Moscow as it would have been to Imperial Petrograd.

The immediate political importance of Mongolia in the summer of 1921 consisted in its being the haunt of remnants of Russian White Army detachments under the command of General Bakich and General Gnoyev. Left to themselves, these detachments were helpless, but a vigorous leader like Ungern-Sternberg might conceivably employ them against the Far Eastern Republic in the Verkhneudinsk region, while Semyonov's men might sally from the east. Japan liberally supported the savage baron with money and encouraged him in his project of establishing himself in Mongolia.

As far back as November, 1920, the Soviets had attempted to secure a footing in Mongolia. The Russian Commissar for Foreign Affairs alleged that, at the request of the Chinese authorities in Mongolia, Red troops were to be despatched to drive out the forces under General Bakich and General Gnoyev. However, on November 27th, Soviet authorities had declared that as Chinese troops in occupation had already driven out these bands, the orders to Russian troops to cross the frontier had been canceled.

Such maneuvers quite naturally alarmed the Japanese and impelled them to support Baron Ungern-Sternberg, who promptly took Akcha, an important road junction. With no small skill he utilized the latent nationalism of the Mongols and turned it against the Chinese administration and army which, in violation of the 1915 agreement, was in occupation. By resolute action in February of 1921, he captured Urga, threatening the communications to the Far Eastern Republic with Soviet Russia. The baron at this stage employed national feeling, and Soviet Russia supported a foreign invader, the Chinese—a reversal of the usual Bolshevik policy.

Although China was preoccupied with a threatened civil war, Marshal Chang Tso Lin, though under orders from Pekin, made no effort to reassert Chinese suzerainty over Mongolia. He was anxious to keep within striking distance of Pekin lest any rival satrap should seize the advantage, and was equally concerned to keep on good terms with Japan. Also the honor of reconquering Mongolia was tempting to a soldier. Being a wise man, Marshal Chang determined to put the whole affair on a business footing. According to common report, he agreed with the Pekin Government to "obey" in return for some $10,000,000 (Mexican). He then suggested to Ungern-Sternberg that a retreat before the marshal's advancing hosts would be worth $600,000 to the baron, who demanded $1,000,000 while Chang received $3,000,000 on account from Pekin. At the same time the Far Eastern Republic officials at Chita entered into negotiations with Pekin for permission to send an expedition across the frontier against Ungern-Sternberg. Pekin haggled until the Far Eastern Republic took matters into its own hands.

Meanwhile a troop of Red Mongols equipped by Russians took the post of Maimaichen and proclaimed a Red Mongolia on March 21, 1921. It was an astute move, for just as Ungern-Sternberg had turned Mongol nationalism against the Bolsheviks, so now Mongol internationalism, such as it was, came in useful, at least as a pretext for an "invitation" to Moscow to enter Mongolia. Red troops attacked General Bakich at Chuguchak on May 24th, who extricated himself and attemped to join with the forces of Ungern-Sternberg in Mongolia.

In this semi-civilized countryside warfare became a series of raids leaving in their wake smoking villages and unburied corpses upon the steppe. The defenseless country people and herdsmen were helpless before every group. Between opposing forces no quarter was asked and none given.

Late in May the baron advanced northward from Urga in three columns. One followed the west bank of the Selenga River and was promptly disposed of by Soviet troops sent to meet it; another entered the territory of the Far Eastern Republic, where it was dispersed by troops of the republic; the strong center column attacked Troitskosavsk and after a prolonged fight was driven back to Mongolia in June of 1921 with Soviet and Far Eastern Republic troops acting in concert. Urga was recaptured on July 20th, and about the same time the Mongolian People's Revolutionary Government appealed to the Moscow Government "not to withdraw the Soviet troops from the territory of Mongolia until the complete removal of the menace from the common enemy, Ungern-Sternberg, who is now seeking reinforcements in the steppes." To this request Chicherin sent an immediate reply protesting Soviet friendship for Mongolia and hostility to Baron Ungern-Sternberg.

After the loss of Urga, the baron retreated into Western Mongolia, where he was captured by Soviet troops in August, brought to Novonikolayevsk, and in September, 1921, was shot—a bold brigand to the last.

The attack by the second column came to nought. General Sychev moved upon Blagoveshchensk, with a view to creating a division in the Amur Province. He operated from Chinese territory, was unsupported by sufficient strength, and his men were eventually disarmed by the Chinese.

The third column at Grodekov under Semyonov engaged

in desultory guerrilla warfare during the spring and summer of 1921. By this time these soldiers had been transformed into outright bandits under Japanese protection. They lacked all color of courage or patriotism—the riffraff of a dozen commanders, ready to rob, massacre, and burn any town where drink, women, food, or loot might be secured. An unsuccessful attack was made toward Khabarovsk and several engagements were fought in connection with Japanese efforts to secure a foothold in Vladivostok.

Japan had been making a determined effort to secure a monopoly on the long-coveted Sakhalin fisheries. The salmon catch alone runs into thirty thousand tons a year. Under the Portsmouth Treaty, Japanese subjects were allowed to participate in the fishing trade along the coast, and the Russian Fisheries Convention of 1907 defined more particularly the general principle admitted by the Portsmouth Treaty. The Japanese were specifically prohibited from fishing in the mouths of rivers and in fifty or more bays and inlets; moreover, the whole coast of the Sea of Okhotsk, many sections of which are still unexplored, was subjected to the general restriction that the Japanese could not fish in inlets the indentation of which exceeded by three times their width at the mouth. Outside these prohibited areas concessions were offered by auction to both Japanese and Russian citizens. The fisheries question had been brought to the fore in 1916, when the Czar's government was negotiating a secret treaty with Japan.

As early as December 16, 1920, Consul General Kikuchi had informed the Director of Foreign Affairs of the Vladivostok Government that certain fishing rights hitherto not under Japan's jurisdiction should be placed under her control. This communication was followed by an exchange of notes between the Japanese authorities and the Far Eastern Republic. The Japanese further irritated the Russians by publishing in Japanese without translation into Russian the regulations they had drawn up for fisheries they had appropriated from the Russians! It was in connection with the fisheries dispute that on March 21, 1921, Lieutenant General Kosina, of the Sakhalin District, had announced the forthcoming occupation of Nikolayevsk, De Castri, Mago, and Sofiisk, and the installation at these points of a civil government "for the re-establishment of peace and order."

Conditions had been unsettled throughout the spring and summer of 1921 in the vicinity of Vladivostok. White Guards under General Lokvitsky on March 30-31, 1921, had attacked the government offices at Vladivostok, attempting a *coup d'état*. Although the Japanese disarmed the government militia, Lokvitsky and his group lacked the numbers and power to establish themselves.

A second and more successful attempt by White troops at Vladivostok had taken place at the end of May, 1921, when local authorities received information that Japan had decided on the evacuation of the Maritime Province. Simultaneously rumors gained credence in Russian circles that the Japanese command, in order to prevent evacuation, were anxious to provoke further disorders. About that time the Japanese had discontinued all service on the Vladivostok-Khabarovsk telegraph line, except for their own messages. After a vigorous protest from Russian authorities, this service was renewed. This discontinuance was connected with an attack on Khabarovsk by Semyonov's troops. The assailants were at first successful and captured the city, but in a few days Republican troops arrived and drove the White Guards to shelter behind the Japanese.

Republican militia despatched to Nikolsk-Ussuriski were disarmed by the Japanese, and later Semyonov's men were allowed to take the town. On May 26th, the Japanese disarmed the Russian militia in the city of Vladivostok, whereupon White Guards promptly occupied the city, setting up the Government of Spiridon Merkulov.

At first sight it appears that Japan's policy was to establish once more a reactionary government in Vladivostok, but close scrutiny of her tortuous diplomacy, dictated by fear more than by desire for military and trade advantages in

Eastern Siberia, indicates that her main desire was disorder, as that alone gave pretext for the continued stay of her army.

It is difficult to determine precisely what part was played by Japan in the Merkulov *coup d'état*. At the end of May or the beginning of June, Yurin, the Far Eastern Republic's Minister for Foreign Affairs, in a note to Tokyo, plainly suggested that Japan had encouraged Merkulov. He demanded a definition of the Japanese attitude and permission for the Far Eastern Republic to put down the revolt. Chicherin, on June 1st, openly charged Japan with setting up reactionary governments at Vladivostok and Nikolsk-Ussuriski, including England and France in his indictment. Strangely enough, the Japanese actually concealed three Communists, Anton, Zeitlin, and Maslennikov, from the reactionary Merkulov Government!

Gradually Semyonov's men deserted him. The Merkulov Government refused him any subsidies. Opportunities for loot were not as plentiful as when Kolchak was west of Baikal. Now the Red Army was there threatening any day to move eastward. He was compelled to leave his troops and find asylum with the Japanese. Thus all three expeditions against the Far Eastern Republic led by White generals ended in futility. It looked as though the Far Eastern Republic had accomplished its three major tasks.

Without followers or influence, Semyonov had no further value to Japan. Consequently he retired to Shanghai and later found his way to America. His landing was questioned, and in the examination of his activities before the Senate's Committee on Education and Labor it not only revealed his barbaric treatment of all elements of the population in the Russian Far East, but also his intimate association with the Japanese high command in Siberia. Colonel Charles H. Morrow testified before the Senate investigating committee to his pillaging and wholesale murders of men, women, and children. Whole villages were slaughtered and trainloads of prisoners shot without reference to any human consideration or the laws of warfare.

After Semyonov's departure, the Merkulov Government slowly weakened, though the Japanese did what they could to revive it and, in fact, during negotiations with the Far Eastern Republic at Dairen, obstinately supported the "Provisional Government of Merkulov." In September, November, and December of 1921, Japanese soldiers and munitions were used without results to reinforce the crumbling White units. Although antagonism continued to flare up daily between adherents of different leaders, suggesting some strength, every week it became more evident that the Red Army would eventually occupy the whole of the Russian Far East. The White movement had spent its force.

Events had conspired to aid the Far Eastern Republic in its struggle with Japan, Semyonov, and Ungern-Sternberg. Nevertheless, the solidarity of citizens of the republic had contributed in no small measure to their final liberation. The Constituent Assembly had proved the ability of Russians in the Far East to rise above theoretical discussion and achieve some workable compromise. They had voiced energetic and unanimous protest against the presence of foreign troops. Armed forces of the republic had little difficulty in destroying Baron Ungern-Sternberg, while the fate of Semyonov was partly a consequence of his own brigandage. The Merkulov Government in Vladivostok confirmed Russian hostility in all quarters toward Japanese intervention in Russian internal politics. When the conclusion of the war with Poland and the evacuation of General Wrangel's forces from the Crimea rid Moscow of its last embarrassment in the West, the Far Eastern Republic knew it could rely on help from Soviet Russia. The possibilities of military aid from the Red Army had been demonstrated in the expedition against Ungern-Sternberg. Japan could not ignore this threat.

Neither was Tokyo likely to disregard the importance of a mission of investigation sent to Chita by the United States Embassy in Japan. This mission left Chita on July 1, 1921. Rumors circulated to the effect that a report was sent to

Washington favorable to the Far Eastern Republic and therefore hostile to Japanese policy.

Another factor in the Far Eastern situation was the invitation by President Harding to a conference at Washington, where the problems of Far Eastern policy were to be considered as part of the disarmament problem. This invitation was notoriously unwelcome in Japan, but could not easily be refused, and therefore, after some deliberation, was accepted. Participation in the Washington Conference meant that Japan must make a frantic effort to put the best possible complexion on her policy in the Far East. Accordingly the government at Chita was informed that Japan was ready to begin negotiations for the withdrawal of her troops from Siberia.

Negotiations between the Japanese command and the Far Eastern Republic opened at the station of Dairen on August 26, 1921. Japan's delegates refused to discuss the question of the evacuation of Sakhalin, which they alleged was a matter for negotiation with the All-Russian Government. At the same time they illogically considered the Far Eastern Republic competent to revise, in favor of Japan, the Fisheries Convention of 1907. For four months negotiations dragged on without result, and with many interruptions.

Once more in December of 1921 Japan resorted to her method of using Russian troops to carry out Japanese designs. The ragged remains of various White forces were assembled for a raid on Khabarovsk, which was driven off. The delegation of the Far Eastern Republic on November 17th had submitted to the Japanese delegates a note from their Minister of Foreign Affairs, calling attention to the aid still given by the Japanese command to White Guards and reiterating the demand for the withdrawal of Japan's troops from the territory of the republic. This protest had met with no response and a second statement denouncing Japan's activities had been issued by the Assembly on December 9, 1921.

Red forces had advanced slowly over the Amur Railway, occupying town after town. Khabarovsk was captured on February 18, 1922. It was evident that the Bolshevik War Office was only awaiting the propitious moment to move on Vladivostok.

Several months passed with no comment by Japan. The press on April 9, 1922, bore notices that Japan and the Far Eastern Republic had come to an agreement at Dairen, but on April 16th, the Conference was broken off because Japan would not fix a definite date for evacuation. Later, on June 24, 1922, Japan announced that her troops would leave Siberia before October 30th—the Foreign Office at Tokyo issuing the following statement:

The decision to evacuate is intended to place Japan on record as a non-aggressive nation, striving to maintain the peace of the world. It had been a matter of regret that various circumstances prevented Japan from carrying out her desire to withdraw her troops from Siberia. It cannot be said that political conditions there have attained full stability, but a change has occurred in the general conditions of the whole of Russia. Communistic measures seem to have been modified. The powers have altered their attitude toward Russia, as attested by the invitations to the Soviet Government to attend the Genoa and the Hague Conferences, and the conclusion of non-aggressive and non-propaganda agreements with Moscow. . . . Japan believes that with this removal of cause for suspicion by the Chita Government, the Far Eastern Republic of Siberia will strive to reach a commercial agreement with Tokyo.

No reference was made to evacuation of the northern half of Sakhalin.

Japan on July 29th invited delegates from the Far Eastern Republic and Soviet Russia to a conference, and on September 4, 1922, this conference, which was a successor to the Dairen Conference, met at Chang-Chun. Japanese demands included the internationalization of Vladivostok, a revision of the Fisheries Convention of 1907, the policy of the "open door" for Japanese merchants in the Far Eastern Republic, the destruction of fortresses in the territory of the Far Eastern Republic, and the neutrality of the Far Eastern

Republic in the event of Japan's going to war with a third Power. These conditions aroused a storm of protest from the Russian delegates. On September 25th the Conference broke up because Japan refused to evacuate the northern half of Sakhalin.

Finally when the Red commanders were fully prepared, the White Government of the Maritime Province crumbled like a child's sand castle before the rising tide of Communism. Moscow was now openly supporting the Chita Government, and troops of Soviet Russia were operating under Republican officers. It was clear that if Japan continued to support the White Government at Vladivostok, a break with Soviet Russia would follow. Desultory fighting between Red and White Guards continued, but as Japanese forces were withdrawn from the Maritime Province, the fall of the Vladivostok Government before the oncoming Reds was expected.

Bolshevik troops closed in on Vladivostok on October 19, 1922. The Japanese gave an opportunity to General Dieterichs, the Russian officer who had been an associate of the Czechs, to Merkulov's successor, to his troops, and to fifteen thousand civilians, to leave the city and then handed over to the Red command what remained of those military stores which years earlier the Allies, among other reasons, had intervened to protect.

Japanese transports, carrying the last soldiers of the Sunrise Kingdom, left Vladivostok on October 20, 1922. A Japanese garrison remained, however, in North Sakhalin.

An observer of Japan's policy in the Russian Far East must not be too condemnatory of either the Tokyo Government or her representatives in the field. The Japanese command suffered many provocations to reprisals in the disappearance of individuals, squads, and even whole platoons which were wiped out at isolated points. Conditions among White, Red, and middle elements of the population, where ferocity mingled with weakness, were aggravating factors throughout. The impotence of the Russians to achieve a stable government was in itself an invitation to the strong military faction of Japan to seize power.

Tokyo had been in a state of confusion and fear. During the Great War and after its close, intrigues were prevalent among different groups in Japan. The military were seeking to aggrandize themselves, though in the end they failed to do so. They did, however, receive temporary support for their policies in attempting to seize territory. In addition they induced many Japanese to invest, especially in buildings and improved property, in Eastern Siberian cities.

The Japanese were intensely afraid of Bolshevism, a fear which explains many of the acts of both the government and of the military command. Japan did not expect to occupy any large part of Eastern Siberia. All she could possibly hope to accomplish was to hold Vladivostok, with a small zone surrounding the city. The severity of the Siberian climate did not appeal to Japanese immigrants who would not willingly occupy some of their own northern islands. Territorial gains in this area were considered not so much in relation to future settlements as for protection against Red Russia.

Tokyo would have welcomed a buffer state in Eastern Siberia if one could have been organized under auspices which would have guaranteed its permanence. It is probable that, if the United States had favored such a government, Japan would have coöperated. The complaints of disappointed investors and the hope that the United States might at least change its policy and coöperate with them in setting up a buffer state, could explain in a good light Japan's delay in withdrawing from the country. The actions of her military in the field cast no glory upon her arms. Intervention in Siberia was very unpopular among many groups in Japan, as well as among numbers of her officers and soldiers.

Japanese intervention was particularly distasteful to Russian patriotism, not only because of the memories of 1904-1905, but also because Japanese troops at times behaved with exceptional cruelty. Patriotic Russians were compelled to ask themselves what power could rid them of their professed friends.

That the Far Eastern Republic was sooner or later to be engulfed by the triumphant Red Power was a foregone conclusion. As a buffer state, it was in an impossible position. Too small to have its own policy, it could not help becoming either a satellite or a province of some more powerful neighbor. Although Communism as preached from Moscow in 1922 was repugnant to many in Eastern Siberia, the restoration of any government capable of being set up by such White leaders as they had experienced was unthinkable.

Many Russians were reluctant to acknowledge that their destiny lay with Trotsky's ragged legions, but such was the case. They had experienced the inhumanity of the Whites— they were now to know the harsh rule of the Reds.

The last step toward Red Russia was taken by the Far Eastern Republic on November 17, 1922, when its National Assembly voted to amalgamate with the Russian Socialist Federated Soviet Republic. Kalinin, President of the All-Russian Central Executive Committee, issued a formal proclamation on November 19th that the republic had been annexed.

Thus the last foot of Russian soil, exclusive of the old Baltic provinces, Poland, Finland, and Bessarabia, which had been carved out of the territories of the former empire at Brest-Litovsk, came under the Red banner of the Soviets. At the close of the bloodiest civil war in history, men whose names had been known only upon the files of the Secret Police now controlled the destiny of half a hundred tribes and tongues scattered over a vast domain conquered and annexed by a score of Czars in the long years of Russian history.

Chapter XVIII

VÆ VICTIS—THE ÉMIGRÉS

At no point in the Civil War had followers of White leaders been able to change the social, economic, and political judgment day which had rushed upon the country in 1917.

Lacking consistent moral and military aid from without, devoid of the advantage of a unique command which their adversaries possessed, suspected by the governments of new nations carved out of Old Russia, inheriting the animosities of large sections of the population to whom they seemed advocates of reaction, frustrated by unstable civil organizations in their rear and worn out by unequal battles, one by one the commanders of White armies, with blunted sabers and bitter hearts, were compelled to flee the scene of action. Red and White alike were forced on by a *Zeitgeist* to triumphs and defeats for which they were less than half responsible. History was against the anti-Bolshevik armies, while the stars in their courses were fighting for the Reds.

Executions and reprisals on both sides exceeded the brutal limits of ordinary warfare in acts that paled the sieges of the Middle Ages. Asiatic ferocity had been abroad in the land. Within the focus of three years the Russian people were reaping the whirlwind whose beginnings had been sown by all the Romanovs and their incompetent courts and bureaucrats for centuries. As was the sowing so was the reaping—*Væ Victis!*

Exile, death, or suppression was the lot of the defeated. All through the period of Civil War, noncombatants who were out of sympathy with the Soviet régime had been fleeing Russia. But these were the happy ones who had money, jewels, or furs and could buy or bribe their way to foreign soil. Tens of thousands whose political opinions were known could not move and remained in subordinate positions beneath the suspicion and quite often the persecution of their new masters. Loyal White troops, particularly the officers, and their families had only one course open when the fortunes of war turned against them—expatriation!

Where are the White leaders of yesteryear? Kaledin, Ataman of the Don Cossacks, dead by his own hand, rests in the soil his wild ancestors had held for many Czars against the yellow tribes of the Middle East. General Kornilov, son of the people, mingles his bones with the dust of the Cossack steppe. General Alexeyev, distinguished strategist and servant of the Czar, dead from overwork, is buried on the Don.

Krasnov, elected Ataman of the Don Cossacks in 1918, joined Yudenich's forces when he was superseded by General Bogayevsky. After the defeat of the Northwestern Army, Krasnov traveled to Germany and later to France. There he began the publication of volumes on the Russian cataclysm. His first book, *From Double Eagle to Red Flag,* met a wide response in many countries, and his *The Unforgiven,* a tale of the intellectual proletarians under Red rule, also enjoyed a favorable reception.

General Petlura, the Ukrainian Nationalist and patriot, accused by the Jews of massacring their people, was slain in Paris on May 25, 1925, by Schwarzbart, a Ukrainian Jew, to avenge the blood of his people. Vladimir Vinnichenko lives in Paris. Professor Michael Hrushevsky, after being in exile in mid-Europe for several years, was granted an amnesty by Moscow and returned to Kiev, where he is a member of the Academy of Science. Hetman Skoropadsky fled when his Teutonic support collapsed, and lives in Germany. Grigoryev, the Ukrainian Czarist officer who turned bandit, was murdered by the followers of his brother brigand, Makhno. When the Reds threatened to make short work of Nestor Makhno he fled to Poland in 1922 with a beautiful Jewish girl whom he had taken prisoner in one of his raids. Having killed her family, he fell in love with the young woman, baptized and married her. It is alleged that she had a good influence on him, saving many of her people from further pogroms.

General Romanovsky, Denikin's chief-of-staff, was murdered in Constantinople. General Lukomsky and General Denikin are in Paris. Both Lukomsky and Denikin have published their memoirs. Admiral Kolchak, Ataman Kalmykov, General Rozanov, and Baron Ungern-Sternberg are dead in Siberia. Ataman Semyonov is an exile in Japan. During the Sino-Japanese conflict in 1932 he turned up in Mongolia, fomenting unrest in the interest of Japan.

Baron Wrangel, after heroic efforts to better the lives of his followers, died in Belgium in 1928, having published his account of the great Russian tragedy. His body was brought to Belgrade to be buried in the Russian Church. The funeral cortège constituted the last parade of the old Russian armies. Delegations were sent from many military and naval formations throughout the world. Six men came from far-off South America. The marshal of ceremonies was General Kutepov. The guard of honor was composed of thirty Kuban Cossack noncommissioned officers, all of whom wore the Cross of St. George for valor under fire. The training of these men astounded foreign official representatives. Three hundred wreaths were borne, from different cultural, military, and naval societies.

Later General Kutepov journeyed to Paris. While in residence there he was kidnapped. The general opinion was that he was chloroformed in the process and died. At any rate, he has never been heard of again.

General Miller, commander of the White Russian forces at Archangel, lives in Paris. Those of the troops who escaped when the Bolsheviks occupied North Russia either went over to the Reds, escaped into Finland, or journeyed by slow stages to the countries of the West.

After Admiral Kolchak's death his defeated armies sought refuge in Mongolia, Manchuria, China, and Japan. The men found what employment was available in foreign trading

Cossack lancers

Russian machine gun in action

Misery   Journey's end

establishments, restaurants, and as soldiers. Women turned to needlework, cooking, and teaching. Not a few fell into prostitution to earn bread and shelter. White Russians may be found in all the great cities of the Orient.

General Syrový returned to Prague a military hero in the eyes of his people, to become commander-in-chief of the Czechoslovak Army. Gajda, after his unsuccessful coup at Vladivostok in November of 1919, betook himself to Czechoslovakia where, with others, he organized the Prague Bank of Czechoslovak Legionnaires. For a time he studied at the French Staff College. At one period Gajda was chief-of-staff of the Czechoslovak Army, but in 1926 he was tried on the charge of having participated in the preparation of a Fascist *coup d'état* and deprived of his rank. In 1924, influenced by the flood of autobiographies from the pen of figures in the World War, he published his memoirs, *Moje pameti*, in Prague. He was recently implicated in a reactionary plot and imprisoned, but secured his release. Many others of the Legionnaires have occupied high positions in professions, politics, and business.

General Dutov, Ataman of the Orenburg Cossacks, was killed by one of his men in China in 1922. General Bogayevsky, of the Don Cossacks, lives in Paris. Many of the best of the Cossack officers and men lie dead on a hundred different battlefields from the Caspian and the Astrakhan steppes to Kharkov and Odessa in the west.

General Yudenich, General Bulak-Balakhovich, and General Alexander Pavlovich Rodzianko after their disaster on the Baltic made their way to various European countries. General Rodzianko has written his memoirs. Many of Yudenich's officers and men escaped into Finland, while large numbers took up their abode in Esthonia or migrated to Germany and Western Europe.

Of the Red leaders, Lenin and Dzherzhinsky are dead. Trotsky is in exile in Turkey. Many of his chiefs are dead. Some have risen to high office, others have been exiled or forced into inferior positions. Stalin, the opponent of Trotsky, controls the Red State. Krasnoshchekov, the organizer of the Far Eastern Republic, became President of the Commercial and Industrial Bank of Moscow, and held many important posts, but in 1924 he was removed from office and sentenced to six years in prison for irregularities in connection with the management of the bank. Simon Mikhailovich Budenny is a general in the Soviet Army, a member of the Revolutionary Military Council, and Inspector of Red Cavalry.

The last evacuation of a large contingent took place when General Wrangel ordered his battalions aboard ship for the dolorous journey to Constantinople. When the flotilla arrived in the Bosphorus on November 19, 1920, the last remnant of those who had come by ones and twos to the Don when Kaledin had raised his lance against the Bolsheviks, found themselves unwelcome guests in a hungry city under Inter-Allied occupation.

General Lukomsky remarked of this period:

In those days of November when the streets of Constantinople were filled with thousands of Russian soldiers and officers, when Russian flags waved above the numerous ships crowding the strait, when one heard the soldiers' hearty greetings at sight of their superior officers making the round of the ships, and when the evening prayer, sung by thousands of Russian voices, sounded in the stillness of the Bosphorus, one might have thought that the ancient Russian dream had come true, and that Tzargrad had become a Russian city. That dream, which would have become a reality had Russia not gone through a revolution and retired from the field of European battle, was belied by the stern realities which drove to the shores of the Bosphorus the wreckage of the Russian State, not as conquerors and masters, but as hapless emigrants from their mother country, seeking a temporary shelter on foreign soil.

The Black Sea Navy found itself in a different category than ships carrying civilians. Each naval craft flew the French flag on the forward mast and, aft, the St. Andrew's flag of the Russian Navy. The ships with civilians entered the Bosphorus without any trouble. Most of the naval vessels, including a dreadnaught, a cruiser, some destroyers, a transport, and four submarines—in all, a total of some thirty flags—were compelled to remain outside in the Black Sea. The radio was busily employed by General Wrangel in attempting to arrange a transfer of the Russian naval vessels and their crews to the service of Alexander, then Regent of Yugoslavia. Yugoslavia at the time was in desperate need of some type of coast defense from Trieste to Durazzo. It had been generally supposed that Yugoslavia was to receive a large section of the old Austrian fleet, but the Italians succeeded in blowing up two of the best vessels and blocked the remainder in Trieste. So favorably were the negotiations proceeding that men on the Russian vessels lying off the Bosphorus were ordered to prepare Yugoslav flags. Italy raised objections, however, and France, under whose protection the vessels rested, was compelled to prevent the transfer.

England objected to the Russian submarines entering the Bosphorus, as no country could be held responsible for their actions. For three days the undersea craft floated in rough water on the edge of the Black Sea. During this period they were bombarded by offers from various armies and governments. The Reds radioed to them that all was forgiven, that if they would enter the Soviet service they would be paid well. Those who did not wish to stay in Red Russia would be sent to Constantinople. Their own commander, Admiral Kedrov, ordered them to stand fast, that arrangements were being made to transfer them to the Yugoslavian service. Mustapha Kemal Pasha, who was then mustering his forces against the Greeks, offered the sailors sixty gold lire per month, high salaries to all officers, guarantees of protection, and the promise of any Greek boats which they might capture.

Meanwhile, Lieutenant Offenburg, on one of the submarines, called his crew and officers together for a council of war. They had on board fuel for 2,000 miles, 200 shells for every gun, 12 Whitehead torpedoes, an abundance of machine-gun and rifle ammunition, and food for 20 days. No one wanted to go back to Soviet Russia and no one trusted

Kemal. They decided to wait three days for permission to enter the Bosphorus and if no such permit were forthcoming, then frankly turn pirate! After they should capture a few vessels they would either make for the Rumanian coast or Trebizond, sink the submarine, and run for it. The condition of the crews was desperate. For months they had gone without sufficient food and numbers had the scurvy. On the night of the third day they received a radio to proceed to Tschili Light at the entrance to the Bosphorus, where they were picked up by a British destroyer and escorted into the Bosphorus to the French naval base at Serkidzi. Commandant Ravenner of the French Navy came aboard the submarines and promised that no French sailors would be allowed aboard the Russian ships. He insisted, however, that as the Russians had come from a country contaminated by typhus and cholera they should go ashore to a delousing train for a thorough clean-up.

When the men were in the train, soaping themselves and enjoying a bath, a company of Senegalese soldiers surrounded the lot of them. The crews were taken and put on board a French transport with only a skeleton force of four men, including the captain, first mate, and two sailors whom the captain should choose for each submarine. Meanwhile, many of the men and officers, taking matters into their own hands, left their ships and mingled with the population.

When his ships were anchored, General Wrangel and his higher officers gave themselves to the complex problem of feeding and housing their army and noncombatants and caring for the wounded. They immediately planned for the preservation of the army as a center around which all loyal elements of the Russian *diaspora* could unite.

Several foreign relief agencies such as the American Red Cross and the Near East Relief gave aid to the homeless multitude. Admiral Mark Bristol of the American Navy and individuals of many nations befriended hundreds as they sought passports, or work, or lost members of their families. Miss Nan Mitchell, an American lady, through privately raised funds, befriended hundreds of families. She secured visas, furnished clothing, medical assistance, housing and food, and founded relief centers—an extraordinary labor of human kindness.

The entire city took on a Russian cast. Naval and military uniforms of the Imperial and the White armies were everywhere in the streets and shops. The bazaars were loaded with Russian arms, field glasses, furs, and jewelry.

The human horde on the ships lying at anchor in the Bosphorus were scattered into various camps, 25,000 at Gallipoli, under General Kutepov, 1,500 on Lemnos, 15,000 at Tchatldja, near Constantinople, under General Abramov; over 30,000 were placed in Serbia, Rumania, Bulgaria, and Greece. Russian and Allied hospital ships received the sick and wounded.

The Russian fleet of thirty vessels, with crews of six thousand men in all, were sent to the French naval station at Biserta in Northern Africa, where the officers and men gradually found work ashore or emigrated to France. One young lieutenant who had formerly been in Archangel where he had formed a guerrilla fleet of armed motor boats, made his way to the United States and later to a Latin American country. During a revolution he was commissioned to arm motor boats, and with their help the revolutionists won the war. The government thereupon offered him a position as admiral of the navy and Minister of Marine! He later secured a position as chief engineer of their wharves and docks and hired some half dozen of his old friends of the Naval Academy at Petrograd as assistants.

The plight and spirit of these unfortunate people in the camps about Constantinople and upon the Ægean Islands amazed the world. The disaster which had overtaken them was for many a sobering and liberating influence. The past was gone, a new life was before them. In Constantinople they painted, blacked boots, and cleaned streets; generals with zigzag gold epaulets upon their shoulders sold papers on the pavements. Princesses and wives of generals served as waitresses in bars and restaurants or did needlework for barely enough piastres to keep from starving. Workshops, mutual aid societies, and labor groups were formed. Russian dancers and artists were seen in the Petits Champs, Stella's, and in all the show places and cabarets in Pera. The insignia of every rank and arm of the Russian Army and Navy gleamed among the soberer costumes of Armenians, Turks, Greeks, Bulgarians, Albanians, Serbians, Rumanians, Egyptians, every tribe and tongue and color of the Levant. In the cafés those with money in their pockets ate and drank with American, French, Italian, Greek, Bulgar, British, Indian, and Japanese soldiers and sailors. Some fell into the underworld of vice and crime. Many were grievously exploited by hard taskmasters.

The White movement did not come to an end with the evacuation of the Crimea. General Wrangel took energetic measures for the relief of intolerable conditions. He stated his aims to be: to succor the sick and wounded; to train all men capable of military service; to enter into negotiations with friendly Slavic countries and with Hungary, in order to transfer the army where it could exist independently and at the same time not be a burden to the nations which received it; to prepare for the day when White forces could again take the field against the Bolsheviks; to unite the Russian military scattered over Europe; to make the army a basis for Russian social and cultural life; and to secure help for the anti-Bolshevik cause.

The soldiers at first refused to disarm, clinging to the fiction that they were still an army. General Wrangel considered himself head of all Russian diplomatic and consular institutions outside of Russia and claimed control of government funds on deposit in foreign banks. The French, on the contrary, argued that the Russians were now refugees and not a military organization. Under the irresistible pressure of cold fact, the illusion that they were still an army could not persist. A warning came from France in December, 1920, that Paris could not continue to provision the refugees after the first of the year, whereupon the military organizations began to melt.

Soon Allied assistance decreased. Constituencies were demanding of French deputies and English members of Parliament why they should be supporting an Imperialist Russian Army which had been driven out of Russia by their own countrymen. England led, followed by Italy and finally France. M. Lygues, President of the French Senate, remarked: "So far as the Government of General Wrangel is concerned, the defeat of his Army being admitted, France regards herself as relieved of all obligations to him, and will only assist his soldiers on humanitarian grounds."

General Charpy, French representative at Constantinople, put pressure upon the Russian soldiers to return to their country and warned the camps that supplies would soon cease. In February of 1921, some fifteen hundred were repatriated to Novorosiisk, where some were shot by the Bolsheviks. A proposal was made that the military migrate to the State of Saõ Paulo in Brazil. Those who went to Brazil found they were not considered as colonists but as peons. General Brousseau, commanding the camp at Lemnos, had even used violence in compelling the embarkation of Russian soldiers.

Friction increased between the French and the high-spirited and haughty Wrangel, who had, in addition to handing over Russian ships, placed securities amounting to some 100,000,000 francs in the hands of the French as a pledge for supplies. His contention with the French grew so heated that finally he was ordered not to visit the camps.

Wrangel had organized the semblance of a government in connection with the army, in March of 1921. The French retorted by declaring that they would soon stop all credits for the maintenance of the refugees, that Wrangel's troops and civilian followers had the choice of returning to Russia, emigrating to Brazil, or taking care of themselves. Wrangel suggested that his men be armed and equipped and landed on the Black Sea littoral. This, General Pellé, who had recently arrived as French High Commissioner in Constantinople, said was opposed to French policy of noninterference in Russian affairs. On April 4th, General de Bon asked Wrangel to resign as commander-in-chief and received the reply: "Remove me by force."

The situation was made easier in April, 1921, when General Pellé removed General Brousseau and continued the rations to the camps. Amid pitiable conditions the soldiers did what they could to keep their integrity. Classes, orchestras, schools, and troops of actors were organized. Among the personnel were many artists and craftsmen who utilized the scanty materials at hand to make attractive their crude dwellings.

Following its declared policy, France on April 17, 1921, issued a strong statement to the effect that France had already spent two hundred million francs on the refugees, that the existence of the Russian Army on Turkish soil contradicted international law, that the hope of continuing the struggle against Bolshevism was "an illusion," that Wrangel's army no longer existed, and that its members were free to do as they pleased, and in future France could only help them to take care of themselves.

The evacuation of the refugees from Gallipoli and the other camps began in full force. Some returned to Russia, others were shipped to the Balkans and to Batum. Several military units were transferred intact to various Balkan nations in August of 1921. Yugoslavia received some eighteen thousand regular cavalry and Kuban Cossack units as road builders and frontier guards. Bulgaria located seventeen thousand soldiers within its borders. One thousand Don Cossacks found work on the farms of Czechoslovakia, while over three thousand Don and Kuban Cossacks set up a new life in Greece. A smaller number found their way to Budapesth and other localities in Hungary.

Efforts were made to preserve these units unbroken for future patriotic action. Bulletins and pamphlets were widely circulated to keep up the spirit of the exiles and to inform them of the international situation and of events in Russia. Slowly soldiers laid aside sword and rifle and lost themselves in the populations of nations where they found a livelihood. Their organization was maintained for several years by regimental funds for the sick and needy. In ones and twos and threes, hundreds sought new homes in France, Germany, Switzerland, England, America, and a score of other nations.

A General Union of Old Officers of Russia was formed, transcending political lines, with voluntary discipline, legally organized under the laws of the countries where branches are located, preserving a sense of unity and comradeship among the expatriated men who had fought against the Germans and the Bolsheviks.

For the first year the men sent to Balkan states who needed aid were supported by the Russian staff, but in the summer of 1922 Wrangel announced that such funds were exhausted and it would be necessary for the men to become self-supporting. This they did, retaining, however, their organization. Reserve funds were accumulated to help the unemployed or those who were unable to work.

Military academies, as well as schools for girls, the daughters of Russian army and navy men, were opened and supported by the Yugoslav Government. The French Government established a naval school at Bizerta. Two gymnasia for Russian orphans, whose expenses were met by the Russian Army, were founded in Bulgaria. Russian students in rags made their way to every university in mid-Europe, over fifteen hundred settling in Prague, many without passports, having walked the long road from Byzantium, crossing frontiers at night, and working where they could, begging bread from peasants and townspeople along the way.

Due to the hospitality of the governments of the Slavic nations, some thousands of Russian youth have been enabled to complete their higher training. Czechoslovakia gave scholarships to many Russian university men and to not a few women, while Yugoslavia, Bulgaria, and Czechoslovakia have placed Russian professors in university chairs. Profes-

sors have also found employment in universities in Western
Europe and in America. Several universities have been organized for Russian students by professors of the old Imperial institutions of higher learning. There are Russian
schools of law in Prague and Harbin and an Agricultural
Coöperative Institute in Prague. By the spring of 1923 the
last camp, at Gallipoli, had been evacuated.

The survivors of Zemstvo and Town Committees in the
diaspora, employing funds in the former Russian embassies
abroad, have established schools and gymnasia for refugee
children. Vernadsky reports that in 1926-27 the Zemstvo and
Town Committees maintained eighty such schools in Europe
with an enrollment of four thousand and twenty-three
students.

A work of great value for the education of Russian youth
in exile was carried on for many years by Mr. Thomas
Whittemore, with the assistance of Mme. Nadine Somov and
Mme. Adelaide Jecouline. Not only kindergartens and
schools of the lower grades, but a number of gymnasia, libraries, foreign language, and agricultural courses were made
possible through the work of this group. Over four hundred
students were assisted to enter the universities of Central
and Western Europe and America to complete their higher
and professional studies. Not a few hundred organizations to
relieve the destitution of the *émigrés* have sprung up throughout the world which also aid in their education and the training of their children.

The Russian Theological Institute of St. Sergius was established in Paris, the only school of higher studies under the
Russian Church which now trains men for spiritual leadership among their people throughout the world. A faculty of
unusual caliber has been gathered, including Professor Bulgakov, the head, and Professors Bezabrazov, Zamkovsky,
and Glubokovsky. The graduates are scattered throughout
Metropolitan Eulogious' diocese in fourteen different
nations. Some have been sent to minister under other Metro-
politans, others to the Autonomous Russian Orthodox

Church of Poland, and still others to Podkarpatsky Russ or Ruthenia in Eastern Czechoslovakia. Students attend the Institute from the Baltic States, Finland, Poland, Bulgaria, and America. The publications and influence of this spiritual center have followed groups of Russians in their search for peace and bread throughout the earth. The faculty have associated themselves constructively with the major movements in church life internationally and the students with various Christian Student Movements among college and university men. The significance of the Institute is beyond that of an ordinary seminary because of its unique place, the widely scattered emigration, and the opportunity it possesses to correlate and enrich the Russian Church with whatever it may find of value in the religious life of the West. Special attention is being given to the religious and moral instruction of the young.

Russian political tension has wrought havoc in many of the Russian Church establishments throughout the world. The Russian Church Hierarchy in the United States consists of several rival factions. The largest group supports Metropolitan Platon as ruling Archbishop of the Russian Orthodox Church in America, appointed by the late Patriarch Tikhon when that venerable leader was in prison in Moscow. The triumph of the Reds and the foundation under their auspices of a radical "Reform" Church in Russia and the persistent anti-religious movement left the Russian Orthodox community in exile without leadership from their home country. Metropolitan Platon was given general recognition in the United States. However, under the leadership of Metropolitan Antony, of Kiev, a group of Orthodox bishops accepted the hospitality of the Serbian Church and settled in Karlovitz. There they constituted themselves as the central canonical authority for their Church. This claim, although acknowledged by the Serbian Orthodox Church, has been denied by the Ecumenical Patriarch at Constantinople. Despite the lack of general recognition, the Karlovitz group established a hierarchy in America under the leadership of

Archbishop Apollinary. A third group was established in 1923 by the Bolshevik elements in the Russian Church in America, under John Kedrovsky. Through legal action he secured the Russian Orthodox Cathedral in New York City, but a supplementary decree of the Supreme Court in New York transferred a number of Orthodox properties to a new corporation called the Russian Orthodox Diocesan Trustees. Upon the board of these trustees both Platon and Kedrovsky are represented.

Another movement was initiated by the Orthodox Carpatho-Russians in America which resulted in the consecration of Adam Philipovsky to be their bishop. For a time Philipovsky was under Apollinary, but recently cordial relations have been established with Platon. At the present time there is practically no antagonism between the Platon, the Apollinary, and the Philipovsky groups. Platon has the largest number of followers, Philipovsky comes second. Apollinary has very few followers and Kedrovsky even less. Through the friendly offices of the Episcopal and other churches, Russian Orthodox people are being drawn into closer unity and into vigorous church life without reference to hierarchical claims.

The *émigrés* continue to maintain a shadowy army organization. A magazine, *Chasovoi* (*The Sentinel*) is published by them in Paris. In celebration of the bicentenary of the birth of Suvorov, who suppressed the Polish Insurrection of 1794, a volume, *Armiya i flot* (*Army and Navy*), a directory of the military in exile, was published in 1930. In the introduction are these words: "The Russian army abroad has preserved its personnel, and is preparing its successors from among the nationalistically-minded young *émigrés*. It has carried its banners into a strange land, and when the times are ripe it will return with them to the liberated Fatherland." The *Almanach of Russian Emigration*, 1920-30, published in Belgrade in 1931, recounts that:

During these ten years (1920-30) much occurred that is of historic importance, and at this moment we are perhaps nearer than ever to a triumphant return to Russia. And if it should happen, and if we, the *émigrés*, all the many thousands of us, are destined to return to our native land, we can say with pride that we, too, have had a share in the salvation of Russia.

And, indeed, does not exiled Russia, scattered as it is over all the continents of the globe, deserve universal recognition and admiration because of its adaptability, its spirit of organization, its firm will to fight for Russia? No matter how we may be divided by party, professional, and ideological differences, we all have one thing in common—the desire to see our country delivered from the Bolsheviks, prosperous, strong, and great. Every one of us by the very fact of his residence abroad is an active fighter for Russia's better future.

One of the greatest disabilities of the Russian emigrant has been the matter of his legal status. Dr. Nansen in 1921, as High Commissioner of the League of Nations, took up the matter of Russian refugees and the League furnishes them with passports. The International Labor Office at Geneva has also taken measures to alleviate this condition. In 1928 a conference was held in Geneva to determine the legal status of both the Armenian and the Russian refugees, as a result of which, since February, 1921, a commissariat has been arranged by the League of Nations in France whereby a High Commissioner acts for them in the same capacity as a national consulate.

Large numbers of the Russian refugees are incapable of hard work because of age, disease, or wounds and for them the problem of bread and shelter is very acute. The intellectuals, thrown out of their orbits into an alien civilization, most of them being unable to pursue their previous professional or other callings, turn with their humbler fellows to manual labor in factories, mines, and farms. The average wage of Russians in France is thirty dollars per month.

This mass of humanity shifted from country to country. In 1923 over a half million *émigrés* were living in Germany, and only a few thousand in France. At present over 400,000 are in France, 150,000 in Germany, 90,000 in Poland, 80,000 in China, 35,000 in Yugoslavia, 30,000 in Czechoslovakia,

25,000 in Bulgaria. The late Dr. Nansen estimated the number of Russian refugees at a little less than 1,000,000. Other estimates are from 1,500,000 to 2,000,000. Several thousand have located in the United States and in colonies in South America. Over 3,000 Russian army and naval officers and their families settled in and around New York.

In many corners of the world Russian colonies work out a precarious existence, tragic eddies from the Russian maelstrom. In 1932 two colonies of refugees from Harbin were settled in new homes in South America. Three hundred and seventy Mennonites, after long negotiations by the Central Bureau for Relief of the Evangelical Churches of Europe and the League of Nations, were conveyed to Shanghai, whence, in the midst of the Japanese attack, they sailed via France to the Gran Chaco in Paraguay, landing at the time of the Paraguayan-Bolivian War of 1932. A larger group of Lutherans were sent from Harbin by the same means via Shanghai and Marseilles to Brazil, which was in revolution.

Some of the members of the Romanov family live in Denmark, some in England, France, and Germany. One royal princess paints, another runs a fashion establishment in Paris, several princes and princesses have married into wealthy American and European families. One Romanov has written mystic treatises and has lectured in the United States. Many of the nobility live with more prosperous relatives in Europe.

The largest group among the *émigrés* are the former combatants, many of whom are from the old intellectual classes. The Russian Military Union, with headquarters in Paris and branches in European countries, the Far East, and America, is a nonpartisan but anti-Bolshevik mutual aid society, with a membership largely composed of officers. Within the Union are various smaller organizations. Admiral Rusin, head of the Union of Naval Officers, works as a bank clerk in Paris.

Many Russian soldiers found shelter in the French Foreign Legion, others fought with the Riffs in the recent war with Spain and France. The majority of the Riff general staff was composed of Russian Moslem officers.

Among the *émigrés* are some tens of thousands of Cossacks. A Union of Cossacks, with headquarters in Paris, has been organized, headed by Ataman Bogayevsky. They have preserved their native terminology upon alien soil, their branches being called *stanitzas,* each one electing an ataman responsible to the General Assembly, or *Krug*. This group forms a closed fraternity. Serge Jaroff's Don Cossack Male Chorus has toured the world. Their concerts have met with marked success in hundreds of musical centers in Europe, the Far East, Australia, and America. Hundreds of Cossacks have gone to South America, many entering military service in Peru.

Russian refugees have turned their hands to every sort of endeavor. Parisian and provincial factories employ thousands of Russian ex-soldiers. Russian men and women have found employment in hundreds of shops and restaurants. Balalaika orchestras, men's and women's choirs, have made their appearance in every city of Western Europe and of America. All liberal professions are represented in the emigration and their members have their own professional associations. Half the cab drivers of Paris are former soldiers of some White Army. *The Russian Chauffeur,* their official organ, appears once a year. Manual laborers, mostly from former military units, are in the majority among Russian refugees. Many Cossacks have settled upon the land; 1,435 settled as farmers in France in 1927 and 1928. One enterprising officer, Jaques M. Lissovoy, a colonel of the Russian general staff of the old army, chief-of-staff of the Don Army under General Kaledin, and Chief of the Political Division of the Volunteer Army under Alexeyev and Kornilov, directed a Museum of Contemporary Events in Russia which he exhibited in many countries of Europe and in America. The collection contained posters, art exhibits, autographs, paintings, and memorabilia of the War and Revolution.

All the heterogeneous elements of the *diaspora* had at least one thing in common—hostility to the Red régime which they had left behind. Yet they disagreed violently among themselves with regard to political and social views. The endless discussions which they had carried on in bivouacs on the steppe, aboard transports, and in hovels of Constantinople have been continued on the streets and in the salons of a dozen European cities.

A Brotherhood of Russian Truth has sections in practically every country, including the United States, which issues a thin sheet called *Russian Truth,* printed apparently in Belgrade (no place of publication is given). There is also a fortnightly Bulletin of the American section. A recent issue of *Russian Truth* bears this slogan:

"Russians, you have four weapons in your hands:
1. Armed uprisings throughout the land.
2. Anti-Red Terror carried out by the common people.
3. Sabotage against the Red government apparatus.
4. Russian fraternal propaganda."

Funds are collected for the Brotherhood through "The Russian Emancipation Treasury."

The Liberals—that is, the Constitutional Democrats, or Cadets—had early recognized the futility of military resistance to Bolshevism. In May, 1919, the Paris section of the Cadets had issued a memorandum regarding the White movement:

The attempt to solve the agrarian problem in the interests of the land-owning class, which alienated the peasantry; the return to power of the old military and civil bureaucracy and old abuses which alienated other elements of the population, particularly the intellectuals; the pursuit of a narrowly nationalistic tradition in the handling of the nationality problem, which alienated the non-Russian minorities; the prevalence of military and, to a certain extent, private interests, which interfered with the restoration of economic life.

On December 21, 1920, they issued a Declaration which affirmed the three principles of Republic, Federation, and Radical Solution of the agrarian problem. At the same time, the Cadets proposed to create a National Committee for the defense of Russia's international interests, which would function as an organ of public opinion rather than as an institution with official pretensions.

The Socialist-Revolutionaries abroad were sympathetic and a conference took place in Paris in January, 1921, which elected a committee of nine from among members of the abortive Constituent Assembly. The purpose of the committee was to defend the interests of Russian citizens abroad and was to make preparations for the creation of the National Committee advocated by the Cadets. However, the decision to work with the Socialist-Revolutionaries brought about a split among the Constitutional-Democrats. The more liberal faction, which wished to go hand in hand with the Socialist-Revolutionaries, seceded and in July, 1921, formed the so-called Republican-Democratic wing of the Constitutional-Democratic Party. A National Committee was set up, but it has failed to play any significant part in the life of the *diaspora*.

If the Republican elements in the emigration sought to organize themselves, the Monarchists, too, came out into the open. A conference of avowed Monarchists, which took place at Reichenhalle, a small Bavarian town, in June, 1921, elected the "Supreme Monarchist Council" as the organ of the General Monarchist Alliance. This group envisaged the salvation of Russia in "the restoration of the monarchy, headed by the lawful sovereign of the Romanov house, in accordance with the fundamental laws of the Russian Empire." These relics of the empire had for a while the support of the German and Hungarian royalists, who formed what the liberal press termed a "Black Internationale for the division of Europe."

Several shades of opinion existed among the Monarchists, but the extreme reactionaries prevailed in the end. In July, 1922, Grand Duke Cyril Vladimirovich issued a proclamation in which he proclaimed himself Guardian of the Russian Throne, after referring to the unquestionable decease of the Emperor of all the Russias and to his right to the crown. Another faction, however, worked to leave open the question of succession. A squabble followed, many Monarchists pinning their faith to Grand Duke Nikolai Nikolayevich. Propaganda in his favor as head of a new national movement was very energetic. The Monarchists were influential in Bulgaria, and particularly so in Yugoslavia.

Due to a rumor that Nikolai Nikolayevich would lead his followers into an attack against the Bolsheviks, Cyril proclaimed himself Emperor at Coburg on August 31, 1924. The Dowager Empress Maria Fedorovna declared this step "premature," and Grand Duke Nikolai Nikolayevich did not acknowledge Cyril's authority. The Pretender is now residing in France. On his estate at Saint-Brience is an imperial chancery, which confers ranks, degrees, and decorations, both civil and military.

The rumor of an impending foreign intervention, intimating the possibility that remnants of the White armies might be used in the armed forces of Poland and Rumania, was circulated by the Monarchists in 1926. A conference was called in April of that year for the purpose of creating an organ headed by Grand Duke Nikolai Nikolayevich, which would rule the Russian *diaspora* in the spirit of the old régime, but democratic elements were absent and the meeting failed of its purpose.

Since the death of Grand Duke Nikolai Nikolayevich in 1929 Cyril Vladimirovich is the sole hope of the Monarchists. The Right Wing is the weakest among the *émigrés*. Miliukov offers the following graphic "political spectrum" of the various shades of opinion prevailing among the Russians abroad.

LEFT	CENTER	RIGHT
	Republicans	
Socialists	Non-Socialist Democrats	
Social Democrats and Social Revolutionists	Non-Partisan	Republican Democrats Democrats
Internationalists	Center Right	

Thus ends the chronicle of the Russian Counter-Revolutionary Armies, defendants of an order which had expanded the empire until it was the largest nation in the world, with its own peculiar religious and cultural genius, halfway between Europe and Asia, but which had, since the Russo-Japanese War, developed ominous symptoms of mortal disease.

The old way of life in the Russian world has gone forever. White battalions played their part in a gigantic dance of death in which armies moved to disaster as if directed by an evil spirit bent on bloodshed and destruction. Both Whites and Bolsheviks—men, hundreds of thousands of men, and with them their wives and children—seized in one of the crises of history, paid penalty in mind and body for the sins of their forbears.

The road before the *émigrés* is as hard as the March of Ice, whose decoration bore a crown of thorns pierced by a dagger. Hundreds have taken their own lives. Some will go long distances in professions, in science, letters, art, finance, and invention, thousands will continue to earn their bread in accidental callings, not a few discouraged by barriers of language and differences in culture will exist in poverty and degradation.

With the defeat of Denikin, Kolchak, Yudenich, and Wrangel, the curtain fell on a vast drama of forces that had been contending in Russia for centuries. The shout, "All power to the Soviets," meant not only the death of an ancient state but also a possible parting of the ways for Western civilization. The fathers had eaten sour grapes and the children's teeth were set on edge.

BIBLIOGRAPHY

WORKS IN RUSSIAN

Alexandrov, Y. *Belyye dni*. (White Days.) Berlin, 1922.

Almanakh Russkaya Emigratziya, 1920-1930. (Russian Emigration: 1920-1930.) Belgrade, 1931.

Anishev, A. *Ocherki po istorii grazhdanskoĭ voĭny*. (History of the Civil War.) Leningrad, 1925.

Antanta i Vrangel (The Entente and Wrangel.) Vol. 1. Moscow, 1923.

Antonov-Ovseyenko, V. and B. Shaposknikov, *Boyevaya rabota Krasnoi armii i flota*, 1918-1923. (Military Activities of the Red Army and Navy.) Moscow, 1923.

Antonov-Ovseyenko, V. *Zapiski o grazhdanskoĭ voĭne* (Memoirs of the Civil War.) Vols. 1-2. Moscow, 1924-1928.

Anulov, F. *Proryv*. (The Line Is Pierced.) Leningrad, 1929.

Arkhiv grazhdanskoĭ voĭny (Archives of the Civil War.) Vols. 1-2. Berlin, 1922.

Arkhiv russkoĭ revolutzii (Archives of the Russian Revolution.) Vols. 1-20. Berlin, 1921-1930.

Arshinov, P. *Istoriya makhnovskovo dvizheniya*. (A History of the Makhno Movement.) (Same in German, same date, same place: *Geschichte der Machno Bewegung*.) Berlin, 1923.

Boldyrev, V. G. *Direktoriya, Kolchak, interventy*. (The Directory, Kolchak, Intervention.) Novonikolayevsk, 1925.

Borba za Petrograd. (The Struggle for Petrograd.) Moscow, 1923.

Borisov, B. *Dalnii Vostok*. (Far East.) Vienna, 1921.

Budberg, Aleksey. *Dnevnik belogvardeĭtza*. (The Journal of a White Guard.) Leningrad, 1929.

Buĭski, H. *Borba za Krym i razgrom Vrangelya*. (The Struggle for the Crimea and the Defeat of Wrangel.) Moscow, 1928.

437

Byeloye dyelo (The White Cause.) Vols. 1-6. Berlin, 1926-1928.

Byelyĭ arkhiv (White Archives.) Vols. 1-3. Paris, 1926-1928.

Bystryanski, V. *Iz istorii grazhdanskoĭ voĭny v Rossii.* (A Contribution to the History of the Civil War in Russia.) Petrograd, 1921.

Davatz, V. *Gody: ocherki pyatiletnei borby.* (Years: Sketches of Five Years' Struggle.) Belgrade, 1926.

Davatz, V. *Russkaya armiya na chuzhbine.* (The Russian Army Abroad.) Belgrade, 1923.

Davatz, V. *Na Moskvu.* (To Moscow!) Paris, 1921.

Delert, D. *Don v ogne.* (The Don on Fire.) Rostov, 1927.

Denikin, A. *Ocherki russkoi smuty* (Sketches of Russia's Troubled Times.) Vols. 1-5. Paris, 1921-1926.

Denisov, S. *Zapiski* (Memoirs.) Constantinople, 1921.

Derevenski. *Bandity.* (Bandits.) Byloye, Vol. 24. Leningrad, 1924.

Doblestnaya zashchita Petrograda. (The Heroic Defense of Petrograd.) Moscow, 1921.

Dobrynin, V. *Borba s bolshevizmom na yuge Rossii.* (The Struggle Against Bolshevism in the South of Russia.) Prague, 1921.

Dorokhov, P. *Kolchakovshchina.* (The Kolchak Movement.) Moscow, 1924.

Drabkina, Y. *Gruzinskaya kontr-revolutziya.* (The Georgian Counter-Revolution.) Leningrad, 1928.

Dreyer, V. *Krestnyĭ put vo imya rodiny.* (The Way of the Cross in the Name of One's Country.) Berlin, 1921.

Drozdovski, M. *Dnevnik.* (Diary.) Berlin, 1923.

Gimmer, N. *Zapiski o revolutzii* (Memoirs of the Revolution.) Vols. 1-7. Berlin, 1922-23.

Gins, G. *Sibir, soyuzniki i Kolchak.* (Siberia, the Allies, and Kolchak.) Pekin, 1921.

Gorn, V. *Grazhdanskaya voĭna na Severo-zapade Rossii.* (The Civil War in the Northwest of Russia.) Berlin, 1923.

Goryachev, N. *V koltze ognya.* (In the Ring of Fire.) Moscow, 1927.

Grazhdanskaya voĭna: boyevyye deistviya. (The Civil War: Military Activities.) Vols. 2-3. Leningrad, 1925-1926.

Grazhdanskaya voĭna: Materialy. (The Civil War: Materials.) Vols. 1-3. Moscow, 1923-1924.

Grazhdanskaya voĭna. Materialy po istorii krasnoi armii. (The Civil War. Materials for the History of the Red Army.) Moscow, 1923.

Gul, R. *Belyye po chernomu.* (The Whites on the Black Sea.) Moscow, 1928.

Gul, R. *Ledyanoĭ pokhod.* (The Ice Campaign.) Berlin, 1921.

Gurvich, V. *Realnaya politika v revolutzii.* (Realpolitik in the Revolution.) Prague, 1923.

Gurovich. *Zapiski emigranta.* (The Memoirs of an Émigré.) Petrograd, 1923.

Gusev, S. *Grazhdanskaya voĭna i krasnaya armiya.* (The Civil War and the Red Army.) Moscow, 1925.

Hackebusch, M. *Na rekakh vavilonskikh.* (By the Rivers of Babylon.) n. p., 1921.

Ignatyev, V. *Nekotoryye fakty i itogi 4 let gr. voĭny* (Some Facts and Results of Four Years of Civil War.) Vol. 1. Moscow, 1922.

Ivanov, V. *V grazhdanskoĭ voĭne.* (In the Civil War.) Harbin, 1901.

Kakurin, N. *Kak srazhalas revolutziya.* (How the Revolution Fought.) Moscow, 1925.

Kakurin, N. *Strategicheski ocherk grazhdanskoĭ voĭny.* (A Strategic Sketch of the Civil War.) Moscow, 1926.

Kalinin, I. *Pod znamenem Vrangelya.* (Under Wrangel's Flag.) Leningrad, 1925.

Kalinin, I. *Russkaya Vandeya.* (Russian Vendée.) Moscow, 1926.

Kamski. *Sibirskoye deĭstvo.* (The Siberian Drama.) St. Petersburg, 1922.

Kapustyanski, M. *Pohid ukrayinskikh armii* (The Campaign of the Ukrainian Armies.) Vols. 1-3. Lwow, 1921-22.

Karabchevski, N. *Chto glaza moi videli.* (What My Eyes Have Seen.) Berlin, 1921.

Karmashev, V. *Posledniye dni sovetskoĭ vlasti v Zapadnoĭ Sibiri.* (The Last Days of Soviet Power in Western Siberia.) Moscow, 1921.

Kedrov, M. *Za Sovetski Sever.* (For the Soviet North.) Leningrad, 1927.

Kerenski, H. *Izdaleka.* (From Afar.) Paris, 1922.

Kin, D. *Denikinshohina.* (The Denikin Movement.) Leningrad, 1927.

Kirdetzov, G. *U vorot Petrograda.* (At the Gates of Petrograd.) Berlin, 1921.

Kluyev, L. *Borba za Tzaritzyn.* (The Struggle for Tsaritsyn.) Moscow, 1928.

Kolosov, Y. *Krestyanskoe dvizhenie pri Kolchake.* (The Peasant Movement Under Kolchak.) Byloye, v. 23. Petrograd, 1920.

Konstantinov, M. *Posledniye dni kolchakovshchiny.* (The Last Days of the Kolchak Movement.) Moscow, 1926.

Krasnyi arkhiv. (Red Archives.) Moscow, 1922 to date (current).

Krasnov, P. *Na vnutrennem fronte.* (At the Inner Front.) Leningrad, 1927.

Krol, L. *Za tri goda.* (Three Years.) Vladivostok, 1921.

Kutyakov, I. S. *S Chapayevym po uralskim stepyam.* (With Chapayev through the Ural Steppes.) Moscow, 1928.

Kuzmin-Karavayev, V. *Obrazovaniye Severo-zapadnovo pravitelstva.* (The Formation of the North-Western Government.) Helsingfors, 1919.

Lebedev, V. *Borba russkoĭ demokratii protiv bolshevikov.* (The Struggle of the Russian Democracy Against the Bolsheviks.) New York, 1919.

Lelevich, G. *V dni samaarskoĭ uchredilki.* (In the Days of the Samara Constituent Assembly.) Moscow, 1921.

Lukomski, A. *Vosvominaniya.* (Reminiscences.) 2 vols. Berlin, 1922.

Maiski, I. *Demokraticheskaya kontr-revolutziya.* (The Democratic Counter-Revolution.) Moscow, 1923.

Makarov, P. V. *Adjutant Gen. Mai-Mayevskovo.* (The Adjutant of Gen. Mai-Mayevski.) Leningrad, 1928.

Maksakov, V. *Partizanskoye dvizheniye v Sibiri.* (The Partisan Movement in Siberia.) Moscow, 1926.

Maksakov, V. *Khronika grazhdanskoĭ voĭny v Sibiri.* (The Chronicle of the Civil War in Siberia.) Moscow, 1926.

Margulies, M. *God interventzii.* (A Year of Intervention.) Berlin, 1923.

Marushevski, V. *Belyye v Arkhangelske.* (The Whites at Archangel.) Leningrad, 1930.

Melgunov, S. P. *Chaĭkovski v gody grazhdanskoĭ voĭny.* (Chaikovski in the Years of the Civil War.) Paris, 1929.

Melgunov. *Tragediya Adm. Kolchaka* (The Tragedy of Admiral Kolchak.) 3 vols. Belgrade, 1929-1931.

Milyukov, P. *Rossiya na perelome.* (Russia in Crisis.) Paris, 1927. (Same in German: *Russland's Zusammenbruch.*)

Milyukov. *Istoriya vtoroy russkoi revolutzii.* (A History of the Second Russian Revolution.) Sofia, 1921-24.

Milyukov. *Tri popytki.* (Three Attempts.) Paris, 1921.

Na ideologicheskom fronte bordy s kontr-revolutziey. (At the Ideological Front of the Struggle Against the Counter-Revolution.) Moscow, 1923.

Nadezhny, J. *Na podstupach K Petrogradu.* (The Approaches of Petrograd.) Moscow, 1928.

Nazhivin, I. *Zapiski o revolutzii.* (Memoirs of the Revolution.) Vienna, 1921.

Nemirovich-Denchenko, G. *V Krymu pri Vrangele.* (In the Crimea Under Wrangel.) Berlin, 1922.

Nikulikhin, Y. *Na frente grazhdanskoi voiny.* (At the Front of the Civil War.) Petrograd, 1923.

Obolenski, V. *Krym pri Vrangele.* (The Crimea Under Wrangel.) Moscow, 1928.

Parfenov, P. *Grazhdanskaya voina v Sibiri.* (The Civil War in Siberia.) Moscow, 1925.

Parfenov, P. *Borba za Dalni Volstok.* (The Struggle for the Far East.) Leningrad, 1928.

Podshivalov, I. *Desantnaya ekspeditziya Kovtyukha.* (Kovtyukh's Expedition.) Moscow, 1927.

Pokrovski, G. *Denikinshchina.* (The Denikin Movement.) Berlin, 1923.

Polovtzev, L. *Rytzari ternovovo ventza.* (The Knights of the Crown of Thorns.) Prague, 1921.

Popov, A. *Bibliografiya interventzii i grazhdanskoi voiny na Severe.* (A Bibliography of Intervention and Civil War in the North.) Archangel, 1928.

Popov, K. *Dopros Kolchaka.* (The Trial of Kolchak.) Leningrad, 1925.

Popov. *Vosvominaniya Kavkazskovo grenadera.* (Reminiscences of a Caucasian Grenadier.) Belgrade, 1925.

Posledniye dni Kryma. (The Last Days of the Crimea.) Constantinople, 1920.

Proletarskaya revolutziya. (Proletarian Revolution.) Moscow, 1921-31.

Pushkarev, G. *Sibirskaya nov.* (The Virgin Soil of Siberia.) Novosibirsk, 1927.

Putilov, V. *Khronolog. tablitzy po istorii Rossii i U. S. S. R.* (Chronological Tables for the History of Russia and U. S. S. R.) Leningrad, 1929.

Rakovski, G. *V stane belykh.* (In the Camp of the Whites.) Constantinople, 1920.

Rakovski, G. *Koretz belykh.* (The End of the Whites.) Prague, 1921.

Revolutsiya i grazhdanskaya voĭna v opisaniyakh belogvrdeĭtzev, (Revolution and Civil War in the Descriptions of the White Guards.) 6 vols. Moscow, 1926-27.

Revolutziya na Dalnem vostoke. (Revolution in the Far East.) Moscow, 1923.

Rodzianko, A. *Vospominaniya o severo-zapadnoi armii.* (Reminiscences of the North-Western Army.) Berlin, 1920.

Sakharov, K. V. *Belaya Sibir.* (White Siberia.) Munich, 1923.

Savinkov, B. *Borba s bolshevikami.* (The Struggle Against the Bolsheviks.) Warsaw, 1920.

Savinkov, B. *Nakanune novoĭ russkoĭ revolutzii.* (On the Eve of a New Russian Revolution.) Warsaw, 1921.

Savinkov, B. *K delu Kornilova.* (The Trial of Kornilov.) Paris, 1919.

Shafir, Y. *Grazhdanskaya voĭna v Rossii i menshevistskaya Gruziya.* (The Civil War in Russia and Menshevik Georgia.) Moscow, 1921.

Shchegolev, P. *Yudenich pod Petrogradom.* (Yudenich at the Gates of Petrograd.) Leningrad, 1927.

Shulgin, V. *1920 god.* (The Year 1920.) Sofia, 1921.

Smirnov, I. *Borba za Ural i Sibir.* (The Struggle for the Ural and Siberia.) Moscow, 1926.

Smolenski, S. *Krymskaya katastrofa.* (The Crimean Catastrophe.) Sofia, 1920.

Sobolev, A. *Krasnyi flot v grazhd. voine.* (The Red Navy in the Civil War.) Leningrad, 1926.

Sokolov, K. *Pravleniye Gen. Denikina.* (The Régime of Gen. Denikin.) Sofia, 1921.

Solodovnikov, B. *Sibirskiya avantury i Gen. Gajda.* (The Siberian Adventures and Gen. Gajda.) Prague, 191(?).

Stankevich, V. *Vospominaniya.* (Reminiscences.) Berlin, 1920.

Stankevich, V. *Sudby narodov Rossii.* (The Destinies of the Peoples of Russia.) Berlin, 1921.

Struve, P. *Razmyshleniya o russkoĭ revolutzii.* (Reflections on the Russian Revolution.) Sofia, 1921.

Subbotovski, I. *Soyuzniki, russkiye reaktzionery i interventziya.* (The Allies, Russian Reactionaries and Intervention.) Leningrad, 1926.

Torne, A. *V tzarstve Lenina.* (In Lenin's Kingdom.) Berlin, 1922.

Trotzki, L. *Kak vooruzhalas revolutziya.* (How the Revolution Armed Itself.) 3 vols. Moscow, 1923-25.

Turunov, A. and Vegman. *Revol. i grashd. voina v Sibiri.* (Revolution and Civil War in Siberia.) Novosibirsk, 1928.

Ustinov, S. *Zapiski nachalnika kontr-razvedki.* (Memoirs of the Head of the Secret Service.) Belgrade, 1923.

Valentinov, A. *87 dnei v poyezde Gen. Vrangelya.* (87 Days in Gen. Wrangel's Train.) Berlin, 1922.

Vasilevski, I. *Belye memuary.* (White Memoirs.) Petrograd, 1923.

Vetoshkin, M. *Revolutziya i grazhdanskaya voĭna na Severe.* (Revolution and Civil War in the North.) Vologda, 1927.

Vladimirov, I. *Molodezh v grazhdanskoĭ voĭne.* (Youth in the Civil War.) Moscow, 1926.

Vladimirova, V. *God sluzhby sotzialistov kapitalistam.* (The Socialists in the Service of Capitalists.) Moscow, 1927.

Volin, V. *Don i dobrovocheskaya armiya.* (The Don and the Volunteer Army.) Novocherkassk, 1919.

Voronich, N. *Zelionaya Kniga.* (Green Book.) Prague, 1921.

Voronich, N. *Sbornik materialov i dokumentov.* (Collection of Materials and Documents.) Prague, 1921.

Winawer, M. *Nashe pravitelstvo.* (Our Government.) Paris, 1928.

Yakovenko, V. *Zapiski partizana.* (Memoirs of a Partisan.) Moscow, 1925.

Yakushev, K., editor. *Materialy dlya sibirskoĭ bibliografii: grazhdanskaya voina i interventziya v Sibiri.* (Materials for Siberian Bibliography: the Civil War and Intervention in Siberia: 1917-1920.) Prague, 1930.

Yakushkin, E. *Kolchakovshchina i interventziya v Sibiri.* (The Kolchak Movement and Intervention in Siberia.) Moscow, 1928.

Yakushkin, Y. and S. Polunin. *Angliiskaya interventziya.* (English Intervention.) Moscow, 1928.

Yanchevski, N. *Grazhdanskaya borba na Severnom Kavkaze.* (Civil War in Northern Caucasus.) Vol. 1. Rostov, 1927.

Zelenov, N. *Tragediya Severnoi oblasti.* (The Tragedy of the Northern Region.) Paris, 1922.

Zenzinov, V. *Gosud. perevorot adm. Kolchaka v Omske.* (Admiral Kolchak's Coup d'État at Omsk.) Paris, 1919.

WORKS IN LANGUAGES OTHER THAN RUSSIAN

Ackerman, Carl W. *Trailing the Bolsheviki.* New York, 1919.

Albertson, Ralph. *Fighting Without a War.* New York, 1920.

Alexinsky, G. *Les Russes hors de la Russie.* (*Grande Revue*, Paris, 1930, v. 131, p. 601-32).

American Intervention in Russia. *Current History.* April, 1930.

Anjou, Durassow. *Constantinopoli e la responsabilità inglese.* Roma, 1922.

Archangel: the American War with Russia: by a Chronicler (Cudahy, John.) New York, 1924.

Baerlin, Henry, *The March of the Seventy Thousand.* London, 1926.

Bechhofer, C. E. *In Denikin's Russia.* London, 1921.

Bowman, Isiah. *The New World.* New York, 1921.

Brandstrom, Elsa. *Unter Kriegsgefangenen in Russland.* Berlin, 1922.

Buchan, John. *The Baltic and Caucasian States.* London, 1926.

Bullitt, Wm. C. *The Bullitt Mission to Russia.* New York, 1919.

Cambridge Magazine, Cambridge. England, 1917-1922.

Červinka, J. *Cestou našeho odboje.* (Through the Road of Our Revolution.) Praha, 1920.

Chessin, Serge. *L'apocalypse russe.* Paris, 1921.

Chicherin, Geo. *Two Years of Foreign Policy.* New York, 1920.

Congressional Record (United States Government), 1917-1922.

Current History (*New York Times*), Oct., 1917-Sept., 1922.

Davatz, V. *Fünf Sturmjahre mit Gen. Wrangel.* Berlin, 1927.

Delage, J. *La Russie en exil.* Paris, 1930.

Denikin, Anton I. *The Russian Turmoil.* London, 1922.

Denis, E. *V boji.* Praha, 1923.

Doty, Madeleine Z. *Behind the Battle-Line.* New York, 1918.

Dubarbier, Georges. *En Sibérie après l'armistice.* Paris, 1924.

Dukes, Paul. *Red Dusk and the Morrow*. London, 1922.

Esthonian Review, The. July-August, 1919. London, 1919.

Far Eastern Republic. Japanese Intervention. Published by the Special Delegation of the Far East. Rep. to the U. S. A. Washington, 1922.

Gajda, R. *Moje paměti*. (My Memories.) Praha, 1920.

Far Eastern Republic. A short outline. Washington, 1922.

Florinsky, M. T. *The End of The Russian Empire*. New Haven, 1931.

Francis, David R. *Russia from the American Embassy*. New York, 1921.

Gaillard, Gaston. *L'Allemagne et le Baltikum*. Paris, 1919.

Goleman, Frederick A. *Japan Moves North*. London, 1918.

Golovine, N. N. *The Russian Army in The World War*. New Haven, 1932.

Goltz, Rüdiger von der. *Meine Sendung in Finnland und im Baltikum*. Leipzig, 1920.

Graves, William S. *America's Siberian Adventure*. New York, 1931.

Great Britain Foreign Office Handbooks. Courland, Livonia, and Esthonia. London, 1920.

Great Britain Foreign Office Handbooks. Finland. London, 1920.

Great Britain Parliamentary Debates (Hansard), 1917-1922.

Great Britain Parliamentary Papers, 1919, vol. 53, Cmd. Paper S. London, 1919.

Great Britain Parliamentary Papers, 1920, vol. 51. Cmd. Paper 587. London, 1920.

Great Britain Parliamentary Papers, 1920, vol. 28. Cmd. Paper 818. London, 1920.

Great Britain Parliamentary Papers, 1921, vol. 43. Cmd. Paper 1240. London, 1921.

Great Britain Parliamentary Papers, 1920, vol. 28. Cmd. Paper 772. London, 1920.

Great Britain War Office. The Evacuation of North Russia. London, 1920.

Grondijs, Ludovic H. *La guerre en Russie*. Paris, 1922.

Grondijs, Ludovic H. *Episoden uit den Russischen revolutie-oorlog*. Haarlem, 1925.

Gusev, S. *Die Lehren des Bürgerkrieges*. Hamburg, 1923.

Janin, Maurice. *Moje učast na československem boji za svabodu.* (My Participation in the Czechoslovak Struggle for Freedom.) Praha, 1928.

Janin, Maurice. *Fragments de mon journal sibérien.* (*Monde slave,* Paris, 1924-5.)

Karžansky, N. *Rusko a československé legie.* (Russia and the Czechosloval Legions.) Praha, 1919.

Kerenski, Aleksandr. *The Catastrophe.* New York, 1927.

Kerenski, Aleks. *My Last Stand.* Concord, N. H., 1923.

Kerenski, Alex. *The Prelude to Bolshevism.* London, 1919.

Kirieleison, Domenico. *La partecipazione militare italiana.* Privately printed (n. d.).

Knox, Alfred W. F. *With the Russian Army.* London, 1921.

Krejčí, F. V. *Návrat sibiřských legii.* (The Return of the Siberian Legions.) Praha, 1920.

Kudela, J. *Rok 1917 v dějinách odboje* (The Year 1917 in the History of the Revolution.) 2 vols. Brno, 1927.

Kudela, J. *Rok 1918 v dějinách odboje* (The Year 1918 in the History of the Revolution.) 2 vols. Brno, 1928.

Kudela, J. *S našim vojskem na Rusi* (With our Army in Russia.) 2 vols. Praha, 1922-26.

La Chesnais, P. G. *La guerre civile en Finlande.* Paris, 1919.

Langer, F., ed. *Pamětní kníha I střeleckého pluku.* (Memorial Book of the First Regiment.) Praha, 1923.

Langer, F., ed. *Železný vlk.* (The Iron Wolf.) Praha, 1927.

Lanseger, E., ed. *Pod slavnýimi prapory starodružiniků. Historické vzpomínky.* (Under the Glorious Flags of the Old Company. Historical Reminiscences.) 4 vols. Praha, 1927-29.

Ledré, C. *Les émigrés russes en France.* Paris, 1930.

Levine, Isaac Don. *Stalin.* New York, 1931.

Lippmann, Walter and Charles Merz. *A Test of the News.* An examination of the news reporter in the *New York Times* on aspects of the Russian Revolution, March, 1917-March, 1920. A Supplement to *The New Republic* of Aug. 4, 1920, New York, 1920.

London Gazette, 1920.

Loris-Melikov, Ivan. *La révolution russe. Paris,* 1920.

Lukomsky, A. *Memoirs of the Russian Revolution.* London, 1922.

McCullagh, Francis. *A Prisoner of the Reds.* London, 1921.

Mašin, Emil, *Česká Družina* (The Czech Company.) Prague, 1922.

Maynard, C., Sir. *The Murmansk Venture. London,* 1928.

Medek, Rudolf. *Veliký pochod Čechoslováků* (The Great Campaign of the Czechoslovaks.) Prague, 1929.

Merz, Charles, see Lippmann, above.

Mirsky, D. S. *Lenin.* New York, 1931.

Montandon, Geo. *Deux ans chez Koltchak.* Paris, 1923.

Moore, J. R., Mead, H. H., Jahns, L. E. *The History of the American Expedition Fighting the Bolsheviks.* Detroit, 1920.

Nabokoff, Konstantin. *The Ordeal of a Diplomat.* London, 1921.

Nachbur, Albert, *La Vérité sur Koltchak.* Pekin, 1920.

Norton, Henry K. *The Far Eastern Republic of Siberia.* London, 1923.

Oldenburg, S., editor. *Le coup d'état bolchéviste.* Paris, 1929.

Palmieri, Aurelio. *La politica asiatica dei Bolscevichi.* Bologna, 1924.

Pares, Bernard, Sir. *My Russian Memoirs.* London, 1931.

Pasvolsky, Leo. *Russia in the Far East.* New York, 1922.

Patejdl, J. *Sibiřska anabase.* (Siberian Anabasis.) Praha, 1923.

Pernot, Maurice. *L'épreuve de la Pologne.* Paris, 1921.

Pichon. *Le coup d'état de l'amiral Koltchak.* Monde slave, Paris, 1925.

Pítra, R. *Z Penzy do Ufy.* (From Penza to Ufa.)

Pollock, John. *The Baltic States and the Bolsheviks.* (Nineteenth Century, v. 87, 1920).

Price, Morgan Phillips. *War and Revolution.* London, 1918.

Rimscha, H. *Der russische Bürgerkrieg und die russische Emigration,* 1917-1921. Jena, 1924.

Rimscha, H. *Russland jenseits der Grenzen,* 1921-1926. Jena, 1927.

Roberts, C. E. B. *In Denikin's Russia.* London, 1921.

Rosen, R. *Forty Years of Diplomacy.* London, 1922.

Ross, Edw. A. *The Russian Soviet Republic.* New York, 1923.

Rougerol. *La Guerre de rouges et de blancs.* Paris, 1929.

Ruhl, Arthur B. *New Masters of the Baltic.* New York, 1921.

Russian Information Bureau in the United States Bulletin, 1-44, New York, 1920-1921.

Savchenko, E. *Les insurgés du Kouban.* Paris, 1929.

Savinkov, Boris. *Memoirs of a Terrorist.* New York, 1931.

Sakharov, Konstantin. *Das weisse Sibirien*. Munich, 1925.

Schuman. *American Policy Toward Russia*. New York, 1929.

Scott, A. MacCallum. *Beyond the Baltic*. New York, 1926.

Seidlová, Božena. *Přes bolševické fronty*. (Over the Bolshevik Fronts.) Praha, 1920.

Skácel, J. *S gen. Syrovym v Sibiri*. (With General Syrový in Siberia.) Praha, 1923.

Skrznski, A. *Land and Peace*. London, 1923.

Slavonic and East European Review, London, June, 1922-1932.

Söderhjelm, Henning. *The Red Insurrection*. London, 1918.

Soviet Russia. New York, 1919-1922.

Spaeth, B. *Als Kosak und Matrose unter Koltschaks Fahne*. Konstanz, 1925.

Steed, Henry W. *Through Thirty Years*. London, 1924.

Steidler, František, V. *Československé hnuti na Rusi*. (The Czechoslovak Movement in Russia.) Praha, 1922.

Struggling Russia. Published by Russian Information Bureau. Vols. 1-2. New York, 1919-20.

Texts of the Finland Peace. United States State Department. Washington, 1918.

Times, The. London, 1917-1921.

Toynbee, A. J. *The World After the Peace Conference*. London, 1925.

Trotsky, Leon. *My Life*. New York, 1930.

Trotsky, Leon. *History of Russian Revolution*. 3 vols. New York, 1932-33.

U. S. Department of State. Papers relating to Foreign Relations of the United States; 1918, Russia. Vol. I, Wash., D. C., 1931. Vol. II, Wash., D. C., 1932.

U. S. Senate. Hearings before the Com. on Educ. and Labor, 67th Congress, 2d Sess., Pt. I. Washington, 1922.

Verhalten der Tschechen im Weltkrieg, Das. Vienna, 1918.

Vernadsky, George. *A History of Russia*. New Haven, 1929.

Vernadsky, George. *Lenin, Red Dictator*. New Haven, 1931.

Vernadsky, George. *The Russian Revolution: 1917-1931*. New York, 1932.

Volkonsky, M. *The Volunteer Army*. Russ. Liberation Com. pub. no. 7, 1918.

Vondráček, F. *Husité dvacateho století*. (The Hussites of the Twentieth Century.) Praha, 1922.

Ward, John. *With the "Die-Hards" in Siberia.* New York, 1920.

Wasilewski, Leon. *La paix avec l'Ukraine.* Geneva, 1918.

Wrangel, P. *Memoirs.* London, 1929.

Wrangel, W. *Der Vormarsch af St. Petersburg.* Baltische Monatschr., 59 (11), 1928.

Yarmolinsky, A. *The Jews and Other Minor Nationalities Under the Soviets.* New York, 1928.

Zmrhal, K. *O samoprávu a democracii v sibiřské armádě.* (For Self-rule and Democracy in the Siberian Army.) Praha, 1923.

INDEX

216, 236; near Yamburg, 226; propaganda, 237-238, 263, 351, 366, 379; capture Ufa, 255; in desperate straits beginning of 1919, 257-258; take Ekaterinburg and Chelyabinsk, 284; follow White retreat with victories, 295; Krasnoyarsk turns Red, 301; triumph on Ob front, 303; Allied blockade terminated, 314; execute Kolchak and Pepelayev, 317; get imperial gold reserve, 317; occupy Irkutsk, 317; and Vladivostok, 331, 411; take Kharkov and Odessa, 339; outbreak of war with Poland, 365; advance on Crimea, 374; peace with Poland, 374; and Far Eastern Republic, 379, 392, 399, 413; attempt to secure a footing in Mongolia, 402; reverse policy to support China, 403; shoot Ungern-Sternberg, 404
Bolshie Ozerki, 191-192, 201, 206, 273
Bon, Gen. de, 424
Borovsky, Gen., 162
Borzia, 269, 287, 393
Bosphorus, 418-421
Botha, Gen., 177
Botkin, Eugène Sergevich, 115
Borok, 200
Brazil, 423, 430
Bredov, Gen., 343
Breskovskaya, Katherine, 104
Brest-Litovsk, 43-46, 49-50, 54, 56, 65, 73-74, 82-83, 86, 92, 102, 105, 127, 152, 155, 157, 210-211, 220, 274, 326, 328, 329, 350, 413
Bristol, Mark, 420
Britain and British, 28, 49, 54, 73-75, 79, 82-83, 85-86, 88-89, 94, 109, 113-115, 118-119, 133, 136, 138, 140, 146, 153-158, 160, 162-164, 166-167, 170, 172, 174, 184, 186, 191, 194-195, 197-200, 202-203, 206, 214, 220, 223-224, 226-229, 235-237, 239-240, 242-244, 246, 248, 250-251, 253, 256-258, 264-266, 270, 273, 276-277, 279, 285-286, 293, 297, 300, 307, 314, 319, 321, 331-332, 334-335, 346, 348, 350, 353, 356-358, 360, 363-364, 367, 369-370, 407, 419-420, 422-423, 425, 430
Brotherhood of Russian Truth, 432

Brousseau, Gen., 423-424
Brusilov, 8, 12, 30, 121, 241, 365
Budapesth, 46, 424
Budberg, Aleksey, 242, 297
Budenny, Gen., 67, 182, 336, 346, 366-367, 372, 374, 418
Bugulma, 273
Buguruslan, 111, 117, 273, 277
Bukovina, 46, 78, 177
Bukretov, Gen., 363, 367
Bulak-Balakhovich, 211-212, 217, 222, 232, 417
Bulata, 232
Bulgakov, Prof., 426
Bulgaria and Bulgarians, 49, 78, 421-422, 425, 427, 430, 434
Bullitt, Wm. G., 165
Buriats, 130, 142, 314, 398
Burlin, Gen., 288
Buzuluk, 111, 117, 272-273
Bykhov, 16, 26-27, 40
Byzantium, 425

Cadets. See Constitutional Democrat
Canada and Canadians, 118, 136, 163, 266, 332
Capitaine Saken, 346
Carpathians, 30, 98
Caspian, 31, 75, 103, 158, 160-161, 166
Castri, de, 406
Catherine the Great, 25, 70
Caucasia and Caucasians. See Caucasus
Caucasus, 6, 28, 39, 45, 65, 68, 70, 73-74, 96-97, 157-162, 170, 174-176, 182-184, 224, 274, 336-337, 342, 349, 363, 379
Čeček, Gen., 104, 109, 121
Central Powers, 13, 43, 47, 49-50, 75, 77, 80-81, 100, 102, 127, 206
Československý Deník, 120
Chadim, 330
Chaikovsky, Nikolai Vasilyevich, 92-93, 149, 194, 343
Chang-Chun, 244, 410
Chang Tso Lin, 403
Chaplin, 93
Charjui, 159
Charpy, Gen., 423
Chaska Chai, 259
Chasovoi, 428
Chekuyevo, 94, 187, 191
Chelomir, 179

Bolshevik bases on Dvina, 200; recognize Kolchak as head of All-Russian Government, 205, 243; Reval turns to, 214; victories in Latvia, 216; and Esthonian grievances, 219-220, 226-228, 233-236; retake Yamburg, Pskov, 232; sink Red torpedo boats, 236; Boldyrev hostile to Kolchak, 244; exile of political leaders to China, 244; Gajda commands Northern Army, 246; capture Perm, 254; prepare to attack Moscow, 263; British support Kolchak, 270; forcible enlistment, 271; Kolchak's successes, 272-273; Kolchak recognizes Finland, 274; Semyonov submits to Kolchak, 274; Kolchak never within four hundred miles of Moscow, 279-280; U. S. assists Kolchak, 283; reformed into three new armies, 284; Rozanov's hostages, 293; uprising against Kolchak, 297; lose Omsk, 299; Kolchak's government at Irkutsk attempts more liberal régime, 302; Kolchak and imperial treasure, 304, 307-308; armistice at Irkutsk, 307; Kolchak surrenders his person to Czechs, 307-308; Semyonov declares himself temporary ruler of Siberia, 308; Siroboyarsky's letter to Gen. Janin, 308-311; reasons for failure, 320-322, 348-355; start retreat toward Rostov, 341; Denikin sails from Constantinople to England, 348; Wrangel decides to continue war, 360; Wrangel's army leaves Russia, 376; and Far Eastern Republic victories, 407; reinforced by Japanese, 408; will return to Fatherland, 428-429; parties of, 434

White Sea, 81, 83, 86, 91, 163, 202
White Siberia, 319
Whittemore, Thomas, 426
Windau, 214, 216
Winter Palace, 2, 18
Wilson, Henry, 198, 205, 207, 220
Wilson, Woodrow, 114, 133, 135, 143, 163-165, 256, 283, 292, 314, 332-333
World War. See Great War
Wrangel, Gen., 30, 52, 68-70, 159-160, 166, 169, 174-176, 180-182, 184, 321-322, 336-340, 342-345, 347, 355-364, 367-376, 400-401, 408, 416, 418-420, 422-425, 435

Yakuts, 130, 142
Yalta, 361, 369, 375
Yamburg, 217-218, 221-222, 225-226, 230, 232-233
Yamschiks, 129
Yarensk, 196
Yaroslavl, 57-58, 115, 144
Yenesei, 381, 392
Yershov, 272-273
Yevsievskaya, 191
Yoshie, Gen., 269
Yudenich, Nicholas, 152, 183, 205, 209, 222, 225-226, 228-230, 232-237, 274, 276, 281, 285, 300, 353, 417, 435
Yugoslavia and Yugoslavs, 419, 424-425, 429, 434
Yurin, 407
Yurovsky, 115
Yuzefovitch, Gen., 159-161, 176

Zaborov, Battle of, 104
Zaichnevsky, 22
Zák, Col., 111, 115, 121
Zakatalsk, 74
Zakataly, 158
Zamkovsky, Prof., 426
Zaporojtzy, 27
Zaproghian Sitch, 70
Zbruch, 178, 180-181
Zeitlin, 407
Zelenyi, 178
Zemstvos. See Whites, etc.
Zeya, 380
Zhoba, 371
Zhuravskaya, 42
Zilovo, 288
Zimmerwald, 23
Zinoirev, 17
Ziska, 330
Zlatoust, 103, 106, 111

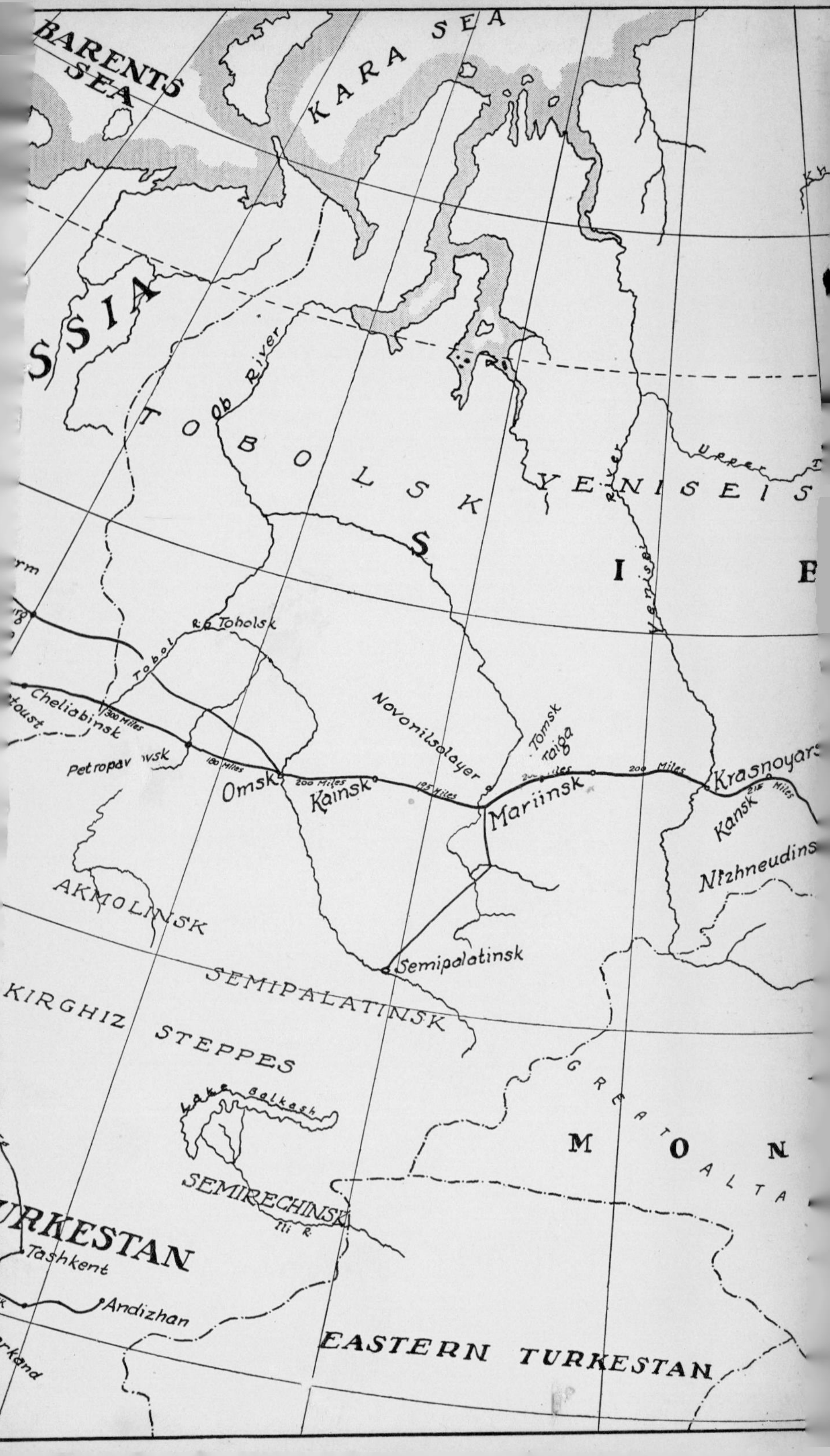
BARENTS SEA
KARA SEA
SSIA
TOBOLSK
Ob River
YENISEIS
S
I
E
Upper
Yenisei River
Toholsk
Tobol R.
Cheliabinsk
300 Miles
Petropavlovsk
180 Miles
Omsk
200 Miles
Kainsk
Novonilsolayer
195 Miles
Tomsk
Taiga
Mariinsk
200 Miles
Krasnoyars
Kansk
215 Miles
Nizhneudins
AKMOLINSK
Semipalatinsk
SEMIPALATINSK
KIRGHIZ STEPPES
Lake Balkash
SEMIRECHINSK
Ili R.
URKESTAN
Tashkent
Andizhan
GREAT ALTA
M O N
EASTERN TURKESTAN